ROGERS MEMORIAL LIBRARY

T4-ACT-887

# Aliens in Popular Culture

# Aliens in Popular Culture

Michael M. Levy and
Farah Mendlesohn, Editors

GREENWOOD™

An Imprint of ABC-CLIO, LLC
Santa Barbara, California • Denver, Colorado

Copyright © 2019 by ABC-CLIO, LLC

All rights reserved. No part of this publication may be reproduced, stored in a retrieval system, or transmitted, in any form or by any means, electronic, mechanical, photocopying, recording, or otherwise, except for the inclusion of brief quotations in a review, without prior permission in writing from the publisher.

**Library of Congress Cataloging-in-Publication Data**

Names: Levy, Michael M., editor. | Mendlesohn, Farah, editor.
Title: Aliens in popular culture
  Michael M. Levy and Farah Mendlesohn, editors.
Description: Santa Barbara, CA : Greenwood, [2019] | Includes bibliographical
  references and index.
Identifiers: LCCN 2018047458 | ISBN 9781440838323 (hardcopy : alk. paper) |
  ISBN 9781440838330 (ebook)
Subjects: LCSH: Extraterrestrial beings in popular culture. |
  Extraterrestrial beings in literature.
Classification: LCC CB156 .A45 2019 | DDC 001.942—dc23
LC record available at https://lccn.loc.gov/2018047458

ISBN: 978-1-4408-3832-3 (print)
      978-1-4408-3833-0 (ebook)

23  22  21  20  19     1  2  3  4  5

This book is also available as an eBook.

Greenwood
An Imprint of ABC-CLIO, LLC

ABC-CLIO, LLC
147 Castilian Drive
Santa Barbara, California 93117
www.abc-clio.com

This book is printed on acid-free paper ∞
Manufactured in the United States of America

# Contents

Preface  xi
 *Farah Mendlesohn*

Introduction  xiii
 *Gregory Benford*

**Essays  1**

Inventing the Alien in Early Science Fiction  3
*Sean Guynes-Vishniac*

Alien Invaders or Aliens Invaded  9
*Joan Gordon*

The Alien Child  13
*Emily Midkiff*

Aliens in Video Games  18
*Michael M. Levy*

**Entries: A–Z  25**

*The Abyss*  27
*Alien* (Series)  29
*Alien Autopsy (Fact or Fiction?)*  32
*Alien Nation*  33
Alien Spaceship Design  36
Aliens Did Not Build the Pyramids  38
*Aliens Love Underpants*  40
Almond, David  42
*Animorphs*  44
Arnason, Eleanor  46
*Arrival*  48

*Avatar* 51
*Babylon 5* 54
Banks, Iain M. 56
*The Body Snatchers* 58
Bowie, David 60
Brin, David 62
*The Brother from Another Planet* 64
Burroughs, Edgar Rice 66
Butler, Octavia E. 69
Card, Orson Scott 72
Cavendish, Margaret 74
Cherryh, C. J. 76
*The Clangers* 78
Clarke, Arthur C. 80
Clement, Hal 82
*Close Encounters of the Third Kind* 84
*Cloverfield* 86
The Condon Report 88
*Contact* 90
*Cowboys and Aliens* 93
*Critters* 94
*The Dark Crystal* 97
*Dead Space* 99
Dick, Philip K. 101
*District 9* 103
*Doctor Who* 104
Donaldson, Stephen R. 107
Dr. Xargle 109
Ellison, Harlan 112
*Enemy Mine* 114
*E.T. the Extra-Terrestrial* 116
*Farscape* 119
*Firefly/Serenity* 121
Flammarion, Camille 123
Fort and Forteanism 125
*FTL: Faster Than Light* 127
*Futurama* 129

*Galaxy Quest*   133
Grays   135
Green Lantern   137
Gwyneth Jones's Aleutians   139
*Half-Life 2*   141
*Halo: Combat Evolved*   143
Heaven's Gate   144
Heinlein, Robert A.   147
*The Hidden*   149
*The Hitchhiker's Guide to the Galaxy*   151
*Invasion of the Body Snatchers*   155
Le Guin, Ursula K.   158
Lem, Stanislaw   160
*Lesbian Spider Queens of Mars*   162
*Lilo and Stitch*   164
Liu, Cixin   166
Lovecraft, H. P.   168
*The Man Who Fell to Earth*   171
Martian Manhunter   173
*Mass Effect* (Trilogy)   175
*Masters of the Universe*   177
The Mekon   179
*Men in Black*   181
*Metroid*   183
Miéville, China   185
Mœbius   188
Moore, C. L.   190
*Mork & Mindy*   192
*Nemesis the Warlock*   195
Niven, Larry   196
*Oddworld*   199
Okorafor, Nnedi   201
*Pacific Rim*   203
Polar Aliens   205
*Prometheus*   207
*Quatermass* (Series)   210
*Repo Man*   213

Reynolds, Alastair 214
Roswell (Place) 216
*Roswell* (TV) 219
Russell, Mary Doria 221
*Saga* 224
Sawyer, Robert J. 226
Simak, Clifford D. 228
Smash Martians 229
Smith, E. E. "Doc" 232
*Solaris* 234
*Space Invaders* 236
Stapledon, Olaf 238
*Star Trek* 240
*Star Wars* 243
*StarCraft* 245
Sterling, Bruce 247
*Steven Universe* 249
Strugatsky, Arkady and Boris 251
Sun Ra 253
Superman 255
*Teletubbies* 258
*Tenchi Muyo!* 260
Tepper, Sheri S. 262
*They Live* 264
*The Thing* 266
*Third Rock from the Sun* 269
Thompson, Tade 271
Tiptree Jr., James 273
*Torchwood* 275
*Transformers* 277
*2000 AD* 280
*V* 282
Vinge, Vernor 284
*The War of the Worlds* 287
*Warhammer 40,000: Dawn of War III* 289
Watts, Peter 291
*The Way of Thorn and Thunder: The Kynship Chronicles* by Daniel Heath Justice 293

Weinbaum, Stanley G. 295

The Wess'Har Series by Karen Traviss 297

White, James 299

Whitlatch, Terryl 301

"Who Goes There?" 303

Wilson, Robert Charles 305

*X-COM, XCOM* 308

*The X-Files* 310

About the Editors and Contributors 313

Index 325

# Preface

Farah Mendlesohn

The idea of the alien comes relatively late to science fiction. Although Margaret Cavendish introduced us to aliens in her novel *The Description of a New World, Called the Blazing-World* in 1666, and we meet moon dwellers in *The Adventures of Baron Munchausen* in 1785, these aliens are fanciful direct descendants of the residents of folk tales and faery. It isn't until H. G. Wells's *The War of the Worlds* (1897) that the alien as something distinctly different from us, with different physical needs, different ways of thinking, and different desires, enters into the picture. Furthermore, it is only with Wells that we begin to see aliens as, like other human cultures, in competition with ours: a competition we may not win.

This may be what is at the heart of the "modern" fascination with aliens. Most science fiction has been written in the colonialist West, and it is not difficult to see, as Joan Gordon details in her essay "Alien Invasion, Aliens Invaded," that there is a good deal of fear, in the writing of "the alien," that what our cultures once did to others will one day be done to us. One reaction to this has been the utilitarian deployment of the alien as something so other that it can be shot at, or laughed at—sometimes both—without emotional or intellectual consequence.

There is also a more critical approach, one that reverses the position and argues for a different kind of alien encounter that might help us critique and challenge the colonialist presumptions of our own cultures. Both these positions inherently position the alien as a metaphor. Other approaches have tried to consider what a nonhuman culture might truly look like: what its premises are, how it might build, how it might think, and what the consequences for cultural encounter might be. Some creators have used this to critique humans from the outside, as in one classic and unexpected hit: Smash instant mashed potato advertisements. A relatively small number of creators have dispensed with the human completely and tried to enter entire into a constructed other, to try to imagine what it would feel like.

This collection brings together a set of essays on the portrayal of the alien across a broad range of platforms, from conventional written text to movies, television, advertisements, and computer gaming. Texts (and all of these things are considered to be "texts") have been selected not wholly on the grounds of their quality but because they have specific and unique things to say and questions to ask about "the alien" and our interaction with it. There has been a conscious attempt to consider science fiction as a single field in which fans are rarely confined to one medium and in which quality exploration of "the alien" exists for all age groups, so that there is consideration of picture books, cartoons, long-running series (TV and novel), and intensely complex and philosophical writings. Because some authors have gathered a reputation specifically for the aliens they have created, there is a lengthy series of author entries. For (almost) every entry there is a short list of further reading to aid expansion.

The collection begins with five introductory essays. The first, by the award-winning science-fiction author Gregory Benford, provides an overview of the conversation that science fiction has been having about the alien for over one hundred years. The second, by Sean Guynes-Vishniac, considers the invention of the idea of the alien in early science fiction. The third, by Joan Gordon, considers one of the worst aspects of the "alien" story, the role it has played in the propensity of humans to commit genocide. This is followed by an essay by Emily Midkiff on "the alien child" that explores the ways in which the alienness of our own past as children has come under scrutiny and become material for the construction of the alien. The final essay, by Michael Levy, focuses on video games, a platform that is only now being taken seriously as material for critical and political analysis.

**EDITOR'S NOTE**

This book was originally commissioned from Michael M. Levy. He died in 2017, of a fast-moving cancer, before it could be completed. The proposal was his, and many of the articles began with his drafts. Many of the essays in this volume have been written by Mike's friends and colleagues to honor his legacy.

Thank you to the editorial team who supported me through this project: Edward James, Maureen Kincaid Speller, Susan A. George, and Rich Erlich.

# Introduction

Gregory Benford

There is probably no theme in science fiction more fundamental than the alien. The genre reeks of the desire to embrace the strange, exotic, and unfathomable nature of the future. Often, the science in SF represents knowledge—exploring and controlling and semisafe. Aliens balance this desire for certainty with the irreducible unknown.

A lot of the tension in SF arises between such hard certainties and the enduring, atmospheric mysteries. And while science is quite odd and different to many, it is usually used simply as a reassuring conveyor belt that hauls the alien on stage.

By alien I don't merely mean the familiar ground of alienation that modern literature has made its theme song. Once the province of intellectuals, alienation is now supermarket stuff. Even MTV knows how commonly we're distanced and estranged from the modern state, or from our relatives, or from the welter of cultural crosscurrents of our times.

Alienation has a spectrum. It can verge into the fantastic simply by being overdrawn, as in Kafka's *The Metamorphosis*, which describes a man who wakes up one morning as an enormous insect. Only one step beyond is Rachel Ingalls's *Mrs. Caliban*, in which a frog-man simply steps into a kitchen, with minimal differences from ordinary humans. He is a puppet representing the "good male" and can be read as a figment of the protagonist's imagination. The novella isn't about aliens; it's a parable of female angst. We don't describe our neighbors as alien just because they drive a Chevy and we have a Renault. What SF does intentionally, abandoning lesser uses to the mainstream, is to take us to the extremes of alienness. That, I think, is what makes it interesting.

I deplore the *Star Trek* view, in which aliens turn out to be benign if you simply talk to them kindly; this fits into a larger program of some SF, in which "friendly alien" isn't seen for the inherent contradiction it is. Friendliness is a human category. Describing aliens that way robs them of their true nature, domesticates the strange.

Yet much early SF was permeated with the assumption that aliens had to be like us. In *Aelita, or The Decline of Mars* by Alexei Tolstoi (1922), the intrepid Soviet explorers decide even before landing that Martians must necessarily be manlike, for "everywhere life appears, and over life everywhere man-like forms are supreme: it would be impossible to create an animal more perfect than man—the image and similitude of the Master of the Universe." Plus the Martians are Marxists!

It's a long way from such boring certitudes to hard SF's meticulously constructed worlds for fantastic creatures. Aliens have been used as stand-in symbols for bad humans or as trusty native guides, as foils for expansionist empires, and so on.

For me, the most interesting problem set by the alien is in rendering the alienness of it. How do you set the ineffable in a frame of scientific concreteness? This is a central problem for SF, yet very seldom has it been attempted in full, using the whole artistic and scientific arsenal.

We all know that one cannot depict the totally alien. This is less a deep insight than a definition. Stanislaw Lem's *Solaris* asserts that true contact and understanding is impossible. As genre criticism, it seems ponderously obvious. Its targets—anthropomorphism, the claustrophobic quality of intellectual castles, and cultural relativism—have become rather cold meat. Indeed, everybody now assumes without discussion that, in writing about the very strange, we must always gesture toward something known, in order to make analogies or provide signs. So we're careful, because unless we keep reminding the reader that this creature is to be taken literally, it readily becomes a metaphor.

In the mainstream, walk-on aliens come with metaphors and labels worn on the sleeve. How could they not? In "realistic" fiction, aliens can't be real. Science fiction insists that they are—and that important issues turn upon admitting alien ways of knowing. Even in SF, though, I must inveigh against the notion that we make statements about the alien in the form of a work of art.

While this reductionist view is useful for inquiring into epistemology, or diagnosing contemporary culture, or other worthy purposes, it has little to do with what happens when we confront the alien in fiction. Naturally, there are always people who want to put art to use for some purpose—political, social, or philosophical. But it is so easy to forget, once we're done using art, that it is not only about something, but that it *is* something.

The alien in SF is an experience, not a statement or an answer to a question. An artistic—that is, fulfilling, multifaceted, resonant—rendering of the alien is a thing in the world itself, not merely a text or a commentary on the world.

All the deductions we can make from a story about the truly alien give us conceptual knowledge. So does science. But the story should—must—also give us an excitation, captivating and enthralling us. When SF works, it gives us an experience of the style of knowing something (or sometimes, not knowing).

This means that a prime virtue in depicting the truly *alien* alien is expressiveness, rather than "content"—a buzzword that provokes the style/substance illusion in criticism. We don't read *The War of the Worlds* for its views on Martian biology or psychology, but for the sensations of encounter.

This may well be the most original thing that SF does with the concept of irreducible strangeness. It's worthwhile to inquire into the underlying ideas and approaches scholars and writers take in its pursuit.

Scientists often say that communication with aliens could proceed because we both inhabit the same physical universe. We should agree on the basic laws—gravitation, electromagnetism, stellar evolution, and so on. This is the gospel of the universal language. I'm not so sure. After all, we must frame our ideas in theory, or else they're just collections of data. Language can't simply refer to an agreed-upon real world, because we don't know if the alien agrees about reality.

There's an old anthropologists' joke. In the outback, one anthropologist is trying to learn a native's language by just pointing at objects until the native says what the object is in their language. He wanders around pointing and gradually getting more excited. He tells a colleague that these people have built into their language the concept that nature is all one essence, because whatever he points to, the native says the same word.

It is a great discovery. Only much later do they discover that the word the native used is the one for "finger."

So we can't rely on raw data. We must somehow convey concepts—which mean theory. And in science, theory inevitably leads to mathematics.

Indeed, the standard scenario for communicating by radio with distant civilizations relies on sending interesting dit-dah-dit patterns, which the receiving creatures dutifully decompose into pictures. Those sketches show us, our planetary system, some physical constants (like the ratio of the proton mass to the electron mass), and so, most confidently, on and on.

Let's play with some notions that go against this grain. Suppose the aliens don't even recognize the importance of dit-dah-dit. Their arithmetic could be nonnumerical—that is, purely comparative rather than quantitative. They would think solely in terms of whether A was bigger than B, without bothering to break A and B into countable fragments.

How could this arise? Suppose their surroundings have few solid objects or stable structures—say, they are jelly creatures awash in a soupy sea. Indeed, if they were large creatures requiring a lot of ocean to support their grazing on lesser beasts, they might seldom meet even each other. Seeing smaller fish as mere uncountable swarms—but knowing intuitively which knot of delicious stuff is bigger than the others—they might never evolve the notion of large numbers at all.

For these beings, geometry would be largely topological, reflecting their concern with overall sensed structure rather than with size, shape, or measurement, à la Euclid. Such sea beasts would lack combustion and crystallography but would begin their science with a deep intuition of fluid mechanics. Bernoulli's Law, which describes simple fluid flows, would be as obvious as gravitation is to us.

These creatures might never build a radio to listen for us. But even land-based folk might not share our assumptions about what's obvious. Remember, our concepts are unsuited to scales far removed from those of our everyday experience. Ask what Aristotle would have thought of issues in quantum electrodynamics and you soon realize that he would have held no views, because the subject lies beyond his conceptual grasp. His natural world didn't have quanta or atoms or light waves in it. In a very limited sense, Aristotle was alien.

Perhaps only in the cool corridors of mathematics could there be genuinely translatable ideas. Marvin Minsky takes this view. He believes that any evolved creature—maybe even intelligent whorls of magnetic field, or plasma beings doing their crimson mad dances in the hearts of stars—would have to dream up certain ideas or else make no progress in surviving, or mathematics, or anything else. He labels these ideas Objects, Causes, and Goals.

Are these fundamental notions any alien must confront and use? We've cast a pale shadow of doubt over Objects, and I wonder about Causes. Causality isn't a crystal-clear notion even in our own science. There are puzzles about quantum cats and, as I elaborated in my novel *Timescape*, fundamental worries about the sequence of time, too.

Why should Objects, Causes, and Goals emerge in some otherworldly biosphere? Minsky holds that the ideas of arithmetic and of causal reasoning will emerge eventually, because every biosphere is limited. Basically, it's economics—eventually, some inevitable scarcity will crop up. The smart bunny will turn into a fast-track achiever since he'll get more out of his efforts. Such selection will affect all his later biases. Math is central to the whole issue of communication because it allows us to describe "things" accurately and even beautifully without even knowing what they are. Richard Feynman once said, to the horror of some, that "the glory of mathematics is that we do *not* have to say what we are talking about" (emphasis his).

This is quite a threat to the humanists, who often wish that scientists would become more fluent in communicating. Feynman means that the "stuff" that communicates fields, for example, will work whether we call it wave or particle or thingamabob. We don't have to have cozy pictures, as long as we write down the right equations.

I'm reasonably comfortable with this idea. As David Politzer of Caltech once remarked, "English is just what we use to fill in between the equations." Maybe scientists will themselves make useful models for aliens.

Delving into the artistic pursuit of alienness always brings up the problem of talking. As I've sketched here, there are sound reasons to believe that some aliens are genuinely unreachable. We must share a lot to even recognize aliens as worth talking to—note how long it's taken us to get around to thinking about whales and dolphins.

But suppose we finesse the communication card for a moment. How does a writer assume that some chat can occur and then create the sensation of strangeness?

One of my favorite SF stories is Terry Carr's "The Dance of the Changer and the Three," in which a human visiting a world remarks that he "was ambassador to a planetful of things that would tell me with a straight face that two and two are orange."

This reminds me of surrealism in its deliberate rejection of logic. Notice, though, that even while it is commenting on the fundamental strangeness of the aliens, this sentence tries to impose a human perspective—why should the natives have a "straight face" at all? Or any face?

For contrast, consider one of the most famous stories about alien encounter, Fredric Brown's "Arena" (1944). A man is trapped inside a desert-floored dome and told he must fight it out with an implacable alien foe for mastery of the galaxy. In their struggle, the alien "roller" reaches the man telepathically (avoiding the whole language problem).

But if the roller were utterly alien, it would be incomprehensible. As the critic John Huntington has pointed out, it is *understandable* alienness that so horrifies the human. In fact, it is horrible because it stimulates difficult, inexpressible feelings in the man. He understands the alien by reading his own feelings. He can't deal with them, so he attacks their origin.

"Arena" is usually read as a paean to hard-boiled, Campbellian rationality. I think you can read it as covertly pushing unconscious emotionality. This program is completely different—intellectually and emotionally—from Carr's.

Oscar Wilde remarked that in matters of supreme moment, style is always more important than substance. So, too, here. We cannot know the true deep substance of the totally alien, but we can use conscious and conspicuous style to suggest it. Some of the best SF takes this approach using styles and approaches first developed in the dawning decades of the twentieth century, in what the critics term modernism. Breaking with the whole nineteenth-century vision, modernism evolved methods to undermine consensual reality and achieve a more personal, dislocated view. In the Joycean stream of consciousness, in the Faulknerian wrenchings of *The Sound and the Fury*, literary devices dynamite cozy assumptions.

When science fiction uses such methods, they have different content. This is, I think, one of the most important contributions the genre has made to literature as a whole. Run-on sentences don't merely mean internal hysteria, flooding of the sensorium, runaway ennui, and so on. Instead, the method suggests genuinely different ways of perceiving the world, emerging not from psychology and sociology but from evolution, genetics, even physics.

Unnoticed, SF has taken "mainstream" methods of breaking down traditional narrative and turned them to uniquely science-fictional ends. (I'd almost term it using modernism to achieve a kind of SF postrealism.) Nor has this ground been fully explored. One of the most interesting uses of these methods in SF is to render the scientifically unknowable—or, at least, that which is unfathomable by humans. The blizzard-of-strangeness motif is persistent even among hard-science types.

Time and again in SF, encounters with the alien swamp mere humans. Thus, one underlying message in SF is that the truly alien doesn't just disturb and educate, it breaks down reality, often fatally, for us. Here SF departs quite profoundly from the humanist tradition in the arts. Science fiction nowhere more firmly rejects—indeed, explodes—humanism than in treating the alien. Humanist dogma holds that man is the measure of all things, as Shakespeare put it. Science fiction makes a larger rejection of this than did modernism or surrealism, because it discards even the scientists' universal language and the mathematicians' faith in Platonic "natural" ideas. Science fiction even says that the universe may be unknowable, and its "moral" structure might forever lie beyond humanity's ken.

This makes Camus and Sartre and nihilism seem like pretty small potatoes. If you're shopping for literary alienation, SF offers the industrial-strength, economy-size stuff. Yet it also contains the symbols of certainty, through science.

I suspect that the longstanding antagonism between the literary world and the SF community isn't merely the old story of the stylish effetes versus the nerd engineers. Instinctively, without much overt discussion, the two groups dispute the fundamental ideals behind humanism. Science-fiction writers take different views of the universe and can't be reconciled by a few favorable notices in the *New York Times Review of Books*.

Rendering the alien, making the reader experience it, is the crucial contribution of SF. Such tales can argue over communication, spring trapdoors, and inundate the reader with stylistic riverruns—all to achieve the end of a fresh experience. That's what the alien is really about.

# Essays

# Inventing the Alien in Early Science Fiction

Sean Guynes-Vishniac

Many of the world's literary traditions record tales of voyages beyond or off Earth to populated worlds inhabited either by physiologically similar humans, humanoids, or nonhumanoid aliens. What follows offers a brief glimpse of the ways in which science fiction shaped the figure of the alien, from the early sources of the Western literary tradition to the beginning of the "Golden Age" of science fiction in 1939.

Perhaps the most famous premodern example of aliens in literature is Lucian of Samosata's second-century AD parodic *True History*, detailing Lucian's imagined travels into the Atlantic Ocean, whereupon his ship is shot by a waterspout to the moon. Once there, Lucian and his companions witness a war between the peoples of the moon and sun over rights to colonize Venus, satirizing contemporary imperial contests over land in the Mediterranean and North Africa. Lucian's aliens include mushroom people and dog-faced people who ride flying acorns, exotic beings drafted into the armies of the rulers of the moon and sun. Lucian's *True History* projected humorous folk and mythological understandings of the possibilities of nonhuman existence beyond the pale of the "civilized" world, long discussed in relation to the geographical expanses beyond the known world of Europe, Africa, and Asia, to the stellar bodies known to the Greek astronomers. In the ever-continuing debate over the "first" work of science fiction, Lucian's *True History* is often pointed to as a forerunner. It certainly marks the earliest extant entry of the alien into the Western imagination and presents the alien in ways familiar still: as entertainment, as allegory, as extrapolative possibility.

In the centuries that followed, the existence—or not—of aliens in Western fiction and thought rested on key epistemic, metaphysical, and theological debates over the nature of the universe, existence, and divinity. Perhaps the single greatest influence on understandings of what inhabited other planets was the development in Islamic and later Christian humanist thought of cosmic pluralism, building on earlier writing by ancient Greek philosophers and natural historians like

Anaximander, Plato, Aristotle, and Epicurus. For some Islamic and Christian scholars, cosmic pluralism explained that God created many worlds like Earth—and therefore many kinds of human and animal for each world. Developing notions of cosmic pluralism were employed in satiric and utopian fiction by British writers such as Francis Godwin, John Wilkins, Margaret Cavendish, and Jonathan Swift in the 17th and 18th centuries. Cavendish's *The Blazing World* (1666), to take one example, justified the central authority of monarchy through the story of a woman's journey to a world in another part of the universe, where the night sky is composed of stars differing from Earth's and which is populated by anthropomorphic animals (bee-men, wolf-men, bird-men) over whom the traveler becomes empress. Godwin, an Anglican bishop and great-uncle of Swift, writing 30 years before Cavendish, utilized the emerging trope of alien beings living on other worlds to detail a voyage to the moon by Diego Gonsales, who discovers giants living in a sin-free utopia. These writers, most often working in the adventure template of the Robinsonade, are representative of attempts to grapple with growing knowledge, in the era of the scientific revolution, that life on other worlds might not only exist but be radically different in some ways from humanity—even if, after a satiric fashion, many of these alien societies recapitulated the political, social, and economic woes of Earth or, following a utopian impulse, argued for better lives lived under one of many competing value systems in the intellectual furor of the Enlightenment.

As more and more, throughout the 19th century, the natural sciences explored the stars, as advancements in telescoping equipment allowed astronomers to view

Lithograph of the "ruby amphitheater" from one of six articles published in New York City's *The Sun* newspaper in 1935 about the purported discovery of life on the Moon, and falsely attributed to the famous astronomer Sir John Herschel. (Library of Congress)

celestial bodies, and as biologists began their efforts to catalog organic life in the wake of the Darwinian revolution, so too did fiction and scientific theory respond to greater awareness of the potential for extraterrestrial life-forms, particularly on the nearby moon and Mars. That the average Euro-American was willing to believe in the existence of aliens in the 19th century is evidenced, starting in the 1830s, by the popularity of hoaxes attempting to provide evidence for extraterrestrial life. Edgar Allan Poe attempted to convince readers of the *Southern Literary Messenger* in June 1835 of a voyage to the moon by balloon with "The Unparalleled Adventure of One Hans Pfaall" but was trumped by a journalist in New York City who published the so-called Great Moon Hoax in August 1835, in a series of six articles that ran in the politically conservative broadsheet *The Sun*. The articles described the alleged discovery by the well-known British natural philosopher Sir John Herschel of a thriving ecosystem on the moon, complete with anthropomorphic beaver-men and bat-men. Moreover, the hoax satirized popular Scottish minister and astronomer Thomas Dick, who calculated in his 1823 book *The Christian Philosopher* that the universe had 21 trillion inhabitants and gave approximate populations for various planets and moons. Not surprisingly, by the end of the 19th century the alien was a familiar cultural figure.

The *fin de siècle* alien sparked fictional and scientific debate over the nature of life and patterns of evolution, the limits of consciousness in relation to organic and inorganic matter, and the organization of society. The alien came to be seen as no longer just a hoax or an allegorical blank space but rather a figure for extrapolating the real possibilities for nonhuman difference from the basis of contemporary knowledge of biology, astronomy, and human society. At the same time, the alien retained its allegorical power as a figuration for the other, especially the non-Western non-male non-heterosexual other. From the 1860s to the 1890s, French astronomer and writer Camille Flammarion wrote compellingly in science and fiction of aliens evolving on other worlds in ways wildly dissimilar from humans and humanoids; J.-H. Rosny, though not speaking explicitly of aliens, followed suit with *Les Xipéhuz* (1887), a novel about intelligent crystals; and, perhaps most influential, in 1897 H. G. Wells published *The War of the Worlds* and "The Star," both featuring sentient Martians. Though the aliens of the latter lack any significant description, Wells's tentacled imperialist Martians in the former made a lasting impact on the alien imaginary in the next century. *The War of the Worlds* not only embodied Victorian British anxieties about the revolt of the colonies through an attack by the alien other on England herself but also made of the invading alien a monstrous, uncommunicating, destructive force, seemingly untethered to human conceptions of morality. Wells's aliens were horrifying monsters, setting a precedent that established the nonhumanoid alien as signaling a biological alterity so great that the peaceful coexistence of differences between alien and human became impossible.

It is with Wells that the alien emerged, or at least became recognizable, as a powerful generic trope for mediating questions of alterity, difference, and the other in science fiction. Of course, by the 1890s there already existed numerous figurative, fantastical, and fictional metaphors for the other in Western fiction, such as those expressed in both the emergent fantasy and re-emergent Gothic genres, or more realistically (if often Orientalized) in the form of the colonial adventure story. The alien, while an important figure for mediating metaphors of otherness, was nothing new. What was new, however, was that the alien wed popular allegories of alterity with the real scientific potential for a confrontation or communion with (nonhuman) difference. Aliens, moreover, as opposed to vampires, Mr. Hydes, mummies, jungle children, lost African nations, and rediscovered living fossils, extrapolated the possibility for life beyond Earth from contemporaneous scientific knowledge to create a scientized figure for otherness.

Just over a decade after Wells established the trope of the alien as an explicitly nonhuman, nonhumanoid, even monstrous and likely violent other, Edgar Rice Burroughs popularized the nearly human alien of the interplanetary romance in *A Princess of Mars*, serialized in 1912 and published as a novel in 1917. Burroughs's Barsoom stories of John Carter on Mars brought the Western to space, complete with its red men, desert setting, fight against the decay of civilization, and themes of renewing individual liberty and cultural life in the violence of the frontier. Burroughs's aliens were nearly human: the green ones had four arms, big tusks, and a tightly knit socialist society; the red ones were, for all intents and purposes, attractive Native Americans with a sophisticated urban culture; the black ones were superstitious but supremely powerful stand-ins for African Americans or Africans; and the holy Therns were akin to white people, standing above the rest as a technologically advanced race of immortals. Throughout his career, Burroughs created other, more nuanced aliens for his planets, but his first novels established that life on other worlds would not look so different or be beset by radically different political and social problems. Burroughs thus marked one end, and Wells the other, of a spectrum of the alien imaginary in early science fiction. The two positions were differentiated largely by their presentation of the biological and physical differences (or similarities) between aliens and humans, but regardless of the superficial differences between tripod-tentacle-jellyfish or four-armed-and-green-humanoid Martians, the figure of the alien remained alive to the social, political, economic, and other concerns of science fiction's Euro-American readers.

As science fiction boomed in the pulp magazines, thanks to Hugo Gernsback's founding of *Amazing Stories* and his imitators' successes in creating a science-fiction market, stories of aliens became the genre's common fare, alongside super-science tales, what-if yarns, space operas, and robot stories. The alien continued to appear either as another cohabitor of the largely humanoid galaxy, with minor differences in appearance and biological function, or as a biological monstrosity. Aliens were particularly popular in space opera, which exploded in the 1920s not only in prose fiction (for example, in stories by Homer Eon Flint, E. E. "Doc" Smith, and Edmond Hamilton) but also in comic strips and early film serials (for example the early transmedia property Buck Rogers). When not used to meditate on the ways that evolution might turn, say, a fish-like or bug-like genus into a sentient humanoid, aliens often took on the role of sociological subject, allowing authors to extrapolate minor and major variations on human social organization, or to explore how language might evolve given different communication apparatuses. While most space opera featured humanoid aliens coexisting peacefully or fighting with humans in various galactic conflicts, some, like Nictzin Dyallhis's

"When the Green Star Waned" (1925), published in *Weird Tales*, distilled an attempt to think about utter alien biological difference into a tale of otherwise typical intergalactic struggle, in this case pitting amoeba-aliens from the moon against brave defenders of Earth.

The 1930s marked a significant period in the history of science fiction's dalliance with the alien, an experimental period leading to the widely recognized Golden Age of the 1940s. Writers like Olaf Stapledon, Stanley G. Weinbaum, John W. Campbell, and A. E. Van Vogt popularized what Paul A. Carter in his 1977 history of the science fiction pulps, *The Creation of Tomorrow*, calls "alienism"—imaginative exercises in extrapolating the wildest, most bizarre possibilities for nonhuman(oid) alien difference in an effort to upset the epistemological and metaphysical grounds on which our understanding of consciousness and the uniqueness of human existence rest. Indeed, in the mid-1930s Stapledon wrote of sentient stars and Weinbaum about Martians who were distinct in every way from humans, birdlike if compared to anything terrestrial, yet sentient and emotionally compelling subjects of his two stories about the "Tweel." In 1938, Campbell published the moody horror/science-fiction novella "Who Goes There?," a nihilistic, posthumanist tale about an encounter with a shapeshifting alien upsetting any easy identification of the boundary between species—alien, human, or otherwise—and suggesting, ultimately, that aliens might be too different from humans for their encounters to have much intelligible meaning. Rounding out the decade's experimentations in presenting the incommensurably *alien* alien, Van Vogt's "Black Destroyer," published in the July 1939 issue of Campbell's *Astounding*, presented the panther-like Coeurl, a being who survives on phosphorus, possesses psionic capabilities, and whose tale is told not from the perspective of the intrepid human explorers but from Coeurl's own as he seeks to kill the humans and drain them, one by one, of their phosphorous.

The 1930s saw a revolution in the alien imaginary. As cultural attitudes toward difference and the possibilities of diplomatic resolutions to potentially violent conflicts in the wake of World War I and the early years of World War II shifted toward a prevailing vision of cosmic pessimism, so too did the understanding of the alien become something grimmer in the work of key science-fiction writers of the mid-to-late 1930s. It is not wholly surprising that Van Vogt's "Black Destroyer" is often claimed as the moment when the Golden Age began, so lofty were his intentions to present the internal, emotional life of a being so different from humans. Visions of the alien continued in the following decades to reflect basic allegorical models of encounters with the other, with the nonwhite or more often the non-Allied other, but they also shifted alongside the generic emphasis on marginal extrapolative realism to match rapidly advancing knowledge about the possibility of life on other planets inside the Kuiper Belt, which by the 1970s had been discovered to be virtually nonexistent (at least above the microbial level).

The alien imaginary of early science fiction underwent significant changes as a result of theological, cultural, and scientific understandings of the possibility of life on other worlds, conceding ultimately that alien life must be possible but never agreeing what forms life would take. Science fiction in its early years offered a means to think through both scientific extrapolations of what those life-forms might be, while also using the alien as a figure for mediating cultural and social conflicts operating in the world of science fiction's creators and consumers.

**FURTHER READING**

Ashley, Mike. *The Time Machines: The Story of the Science-Fiction Pulp Magazines from the Beginning to 1950.* Liverpool University Press, 2000.
Carter, Paul Allen. *The Creation of Tomorrow: Fifty Years of Magazine Science Fiction.* Columbia University Press, 1977.
Cheng, John. *Astounding Wonder: Imagining Science and Fiction in Interwar America.* University of Pennsylvania Press, 2012.
Lavender, Isiah, III. *Race in American Science Fiction.* Indiana University Press, 2011.
Rieder, John. *Colonialism and the Emergence of Science Fiction.* Wesleyan University Press, 2008.

# Alien Invaders or Aliens Invaded

Joan Gordon

Tellingly, and depressingly, the science-fiction works that most often explore questions of genocide are those of alien contact and invasion, whether homo sapiens are the invaded or the invaders. This pattern began with H. G. Wells's *War of the Worlds* (1898) and continues into the present. Here I use Michael Ignatieff's definition of genocide: "any systematic attempt to exterminate a people or its culture and way of life" (123). This definition acknowledges that extermination can take many forms, from the lethal roundup of Tasmanian Aboriginals referred to by Wells to the cultural destruction of Native American and First Nations languages at reservation schools. The word "genocide" came into use only after the mass murder of Jews and other targeted groups by Nazi Germany in World War II, but the practice has a long and ugly history as a tool of empire. Here I will look at how alien-invasion narratives have explored genocide in SF.

Wells's foundational alien-invasion story suggests two of the ways in which genocide is perpetrated in SF and in the real world it metaphorizes. The Martians who systematically destroy all human beings in their path when they land are directly compared to the British murderers of the Tasmanian Aboriginals. The Martians are finally defeated not by superior firepower but by the common cold, an accidental infection that may remind Native Americans of the purposeful infection of their populations using the blankets of smallpox victims. Both are examples of the "systematic attempt to exterminate a people" practiced in colonial invasion.

John W. Campbell's chilling novella "Who Goes There?" (1938) provides a metaphorical example of cultural genocide, the destruction of a people's way of life. In the story, scientists at an Antarctic base discover an alien spaceship. When warmth revives the alien being inside, it takes over the shapes and minds of the people (and animals) on the base until no one can tell who is human and who is alien: Campbell thus literalizes the fear of one's "race" being absorbed by the alien other, something pre–World War II Americans might have worried about. By the 1950s, when Jack Finney wrote *The Body Snatchers* (1956), the Cold War inspired xenophobia about a Communist takeover. All of this strikes us now, perhaps, as ironic, since American colonization of indigenous people, like that of the British, French, and other examples, was so zealous in erasing the cultural legacies of the people colonized.

William Tenn's "The Liberation of Earth" (1953), another Cold War story, sees beyond American cultural and political fears to condemn all forms of imperial overreach while also acknowledging the assured mutual destruction threatened by the atom bomb. This bitter satire is written from the point of view of a defeated human being who sees his cultural debasement, and the destruction of most of the human race, as the triumphant will of his alien oppressors. In an act of extreme cultural cringe, Tenn equates liberation with humanity's cultural and physical genocide.

All of the examples above reflect a hegemonic panic leading to stories of reciprocal genocide: those in power fear that their own genocidal actions might lead to similar actions by the colonized, the oppressed, the others, the aliens. In later works, often by women, this fear of the other and impulse toward genocide are examined in more nuanced ways, critiquing the damage of colonization in erasing indigenous populations (as Paul Park does in *Celestis* [1995]); or of well-meaning conversion (*The Sparrow* [1996], *Children of God* [1998] by Mary Doria Russell); or curing (Octavia Butler's Xenogenesis series [1987–1989]) of the invaded people, human, or alien. Alternatively, they may look at ways to move past the genocide through atonement, as in Orson Scott Card's *Ender's Game* (1985) and *Speaker for the Dead* (1986); compromise, as in *The Mount* (2002) by Carol Emshwiller; or diplomacy, as in Eleanor Arnason's *Ring of Swords* (1993).

Paul Park's *Celestis* is a damning story of the invasion of a planet by human colonizers that directly refers to the colonization of India by the British. Human invaders are confronted by two alien "races": small, cooperative "Aborigines" and taller, vulpine "Demons." They treat the former as servants and the latter as savages to be killed off. Here are the two methods of genocidal extermination outlined in Ignatieff's definition: the Aborigines have their culture, language, and even their appearance erased, while the Demons, who refuse to assimilate or make contact in any way, are hunted down and killed. Park's novel also shows two ways in which colonized peoples have responded to invasion or been forced to respond: by assimilation or by separation. The novel does not sympathize with the human invaders, and it concludes with the native people returning to their own physical and cultural being as they rebel against their human invaders. Park does not tell us, however, whether the rebellion is successful, whether the invaders or the invaded are destroyed, or whether some other solution is reached.

The invaders of Mary Doria Russell's novel sequence demonstrate the dangers of more benign invasion. The human characters, Jesuit priests and sympathetic laypeople, make their journey to an alien world in order to find the source of "heavenly" music, seeing the hand of God in its inspiration. Instead, they find two sentient races about whom they make complacent assumptions. One race, the Runa, are peaceful rural vegetarians, while the other, the Jana'ata, are more aggressive urban traders. The well-meaning invaders offer the Runa help with agriculture, leading to a population explosion. When they see the Jana'ata deal with the imbalance by eating the Runa, they are horrified. Eventually, the humans teach the Jana'ata self-loathing, while the Runa set out on a war to utterly annihilate the Jana'ata. Thus, the ecology of the planet is upturned, mass violence ensues, and the invaders cause destruction as surely as if their intents had been malignant. What the humans saw as a cruel hegemony had actually been an ecological balance in which both races could benefit. Humans did not recognize their own cultural blinders, any more than European-missionary expeditions to North America and Asia did, leading to both cultural and physical genocide.

Octavia Butler's Xenogenesis series imagines an alien invasion the reverse of Russell's: the alien Oankali invade Earth with equally benign intent. The Oankali come to rescue a human race devastated by the aftermath of war, introducing life-saving hybridizing measures that will cure them not only of their diseases but of their tendency to violence. Nevertheless, as Gerry Canavan outlines in his book on Butler, "one finds that the Oankali are guilty of every variety" of the UN's definition of genocide (106). Canavan sees their behavior as "a sort of gaslighting" in which the invading Oankali "exacerbate a neocolonial situation in which humans are radically and permanently disempowered, and then step in to provide 'assistance'" (106). While the human beings might need rescuing, their own physical and cultural identity will be destroyed in the process, until they will be as "liberated" as the poor creatures of William Tenn's story.

To invade is to assume that one's own identity and well-being are of higher value than those of the invaded. In the line of invasion stories about hostile insect-like aliens, from Heinlein's *Starship Troopers* (1959) through Joe W. Haldeman's *The Forever War* (1974) to Orson Scott Card's *Ender's Game* and *Speaker for the Dead*, the invasions of and by alien species begin with assumptions of the innate worthlessness of the enemy's lives and the innate value of the invaders'. In *Starship Troopers*, there is no communication between the invading ant-like "Bugs" and human beings and no hint of motive, while in *The Forever War*, the interstellar war between humans and "Taurans" is caused by miscommunication, later resolved. Only in Card's working out of the invasion story is genocide directly invoked. The main character, "Ender" Wiggin, destroys an entire planet's inhabitants, known as "buggers," while deploying what he mistakenly thinks is a war simulation. Upon learning that he has committed genocide against sentient beings, Ender attempts to atone for his actions by "speaking for" the value of these aliens and protecting the survivors from further violence. Of course, there is no actual atonement possible for murder, much less for the mass murder that is genocide, but his actions at least forestall further violence.

Far better to find ways in which to prevent genocide in the first place. If first contact is inevitable, and if that contact is an invasion, then a way through will be difficult, since violence breeds violence. The examples cited thus far come close to equating colonization with genocide: to colonize is to take over another civilization and substitute it with that of the invader. In the struggle for hegemony, genocide is often the result. Decolonization, too, can be a bloody struggle, as is apparent in *Celestis*, for example, and later in Carol Emshwiller's *The Mount*.

Emshwiller describes Earth invaded and colonized by alien beings who, after decimating the human population, use the remainder as chattels: riding them like horses, infantilizing them as inferior intellects, discouraging them from speech. The story is told from the viewpoint of a young boy who has internalized his enslavers' idea of his worth: no more than a pet and a tool of his colonizers. Escaped human beings, including his father, have preserved their culture in secret, and when they attempt rebellion, the "pet" boy and the alien child "owner" are taken into the human enclave, while the rest of the alien community is slaughtered. Like the Aboriginal people of Australia referenced in *War of the Worlds*, the human beings have preserved a cryptoculture hidden from the alien overlords, surviving, as James Tiptree Jr., famously said, "in the chinks of [the] world machine" (140). Their decolonization is, however, a brutal process, in danger of becoming as bloody as their colonization. The novel resolves conflict by having the two species, through mediation by the boy and his alien companion, draw up a compromise in which both parties can thrive without debasing one another.

Ideally, of course, there would be no bloodbath to abate, no genocide to call off, and the whole notion of invasion and colonization would be averted in contact between cultures, alien or otherwise. That would require diplomacy, the tactic of Eleanor Arnason's *Ring of Swords*. In the clash between two intelligent species, the humans and the alien hwarhath, each side first considers genocide of the other, until, through cautious and complex diplomacy, both determine that they have commonalities that acknowledge the value of all their lives. It takes a powerful writer such as Arnason to make such a sensible, nonviolent solution dramatically effective, but the lesson is necessary.

Invasion narratives emphasize difference between the invaders and the invaded in order to justify violence by one side or another. When that difference makes it possible to dismiss the value of the other's life, the justification can extend to genocide. It would be wise to question such totalizing narratives, in which one side is absolutely justified and the other is absolutely negligible, in favor of a different imagining of contact between cultures or species. That is what the philosopher Kwame Anthony Appiah suggests when he asks us to see the world (or the universe) "as a network of points of affinity" (viii). The arc of development I have traced in SF invasion narratives reflects the possibility of movement from difference to affinity.

## FURTHER READING

Appiah, Kwame Anthony. *In My Father's House: Africa in the Philosophy of Culture.* Oxford University Press, 1993.

Canavan, Gerry. *Octavia Butler.* University of Illinois Press, 2016. Modern Masters of Science Fiction.

Ignatieff, Michael. "The Scene of the Crime." *Granta*, vol. 63, Autumn 1998, pp. 121–28.

Tiptree Jr., James. "The Women Men Don't See." *Her Smoke Rose Up Forever*, edited by James Tiptree Jr., Arkham House, 1990, pp. 121–48.

# The Alien Child

Emily Midkiff

From the star-child of *2001: A Space Odyssey* to the yellow alien toddler in the picture book *Beegu*, the concept of childhood offers a unique approach to thinking about aliens and, in turn, reconsidering assumptions about human children. Unlike the call to "save the children" by killing aliens, as demonstrated by Newt in *Aliens* (1986), the use of individual alien/child characters offers a critical perspective of childhood and alienness.

The term "alien child" can literally refer to young aliens, but the same stories also often depict human children as figuratively alien. This results in two categories: the "alien as child" and the "child as alien." The alien-as-child category describes young aliens like Tony and Tia in Alexander Key's *Escape to Witch Mountain* (1968) and the eponymous alien of Nick Butterworth's *Q Pootle 5* book/TV/movie series (2000–). The child-as-alien category features human children who feel alien or become alienlike by association, such as Elliot in *E.T. the Extra-Terrestrial* (1982) and the Triacus children in *Star Trek: The Original Series* ("And the Children Shall Lead," 1968). These alien-child categories offer a poignant intersecting commentary on colonial othering, since the cultural associations with aliens and children both have a long history with this theme.

In stories intended for children, the alien child questions othering and innocence, but with significantly less horror than in stories intended for adults. The titular alien in Alexis Deacon's *Beegu* (2003) toddles through a simple picture book that questions adult and child capacities for empathy based on difference. *Lilo and Stitch* (2002) contrasts a child and childlike alien to demonstrate the Victorian legacy of believing children to be simultaneously wild and innocent, while questioning those terms in both the alien and the child. However, an unfortunate number of books for the very young rely on the dull premise of alien children in familiar settings like school or bedtime, with just a few shallow differences to make them "alien" and funny without much if any speculation. Entirely too many stories, like the *Blast Off Boy and Blorp* series (2000–2002) by Dan Yaccarino, narrate an intergalactic school exchange, playing on the "innocence" (read: foreignness) and slapstick mistakes of both the alien and the human child for laughs. Stories for older children often better utilize the alien child. In Craig Thompson's *Space Dumplins* (2015), the alien-as-child category is used to question the efficacy and proclivities of both human and alien youth. The child-as-alien category is essential to the *Animorphs* series (1996–2001), wherein the young protagonists wield alien power in battle, ultimately obliterating their innocence and interrogating the ethics of children in war. The alien J.Lo in *The True Meaning of Smekday* (2007) is childish enough to make the initial alien invasion less scary, but his later naïve arguments with the human child, Tip, highlight the insidious justifications of othering through references to the United States' history of mistreating Native Americans. Even the alien school exchange story can be successfully utilized to speculate about othering and prejudice, such as in *Earthling!* (2012) by Mark Fearing.

Crossover stories that appeal to audiences young and old can address the perception of childhood from both perspectives simultaneously. Marvel's *Moon Girl and Devil Dinosaur* series follows Lunella, or Moon Girl, as she faces off against peers and adults who directly or indirectly claim that children are inherently helpless. Even the Hulk, a clear Marvel hero, condescends to her as a child in issue #3 (2015). The narrative does not take his side, challenging adult readers to consider childhood agency and encouraging child readers to discover it. It is no coincidence that each issue of this comic book opens with a quotation from science icons like Marie Curie and Neil deGrasse Tyson that talk explicitly about the place of children/childishness in scientific progress, a field where children are excluded categorically. Lunella's infection by alien gene-altering chemicals further complicates these questions about her age (not to mention her race and gender) by making her an exemplar of intersectional othering.

The alien as child encourages sympathy with aliens through associations with childhood innocence and vulnerability. The "bugger" aliens of Orson Scott Card's *Ender's Game* (1985) are portrayed as terrifying, but the newborn queen's cocoon at the end evokes a sense of vulnerability and need that the insectoid creatures could not achieve throughout. Through association with the helpless child, Ender's cocoon, and other alien-as-child examples, we can speculate if aliens are other enough to deserve different or inhumane treatment. In turn, the alien as child in comedy regularly lambasts this concept of helplessness, as in the cartoon *Invader Zim* (2001–2006) where both the alien child and the human child are world-wise and brutal. Some aliens are depicted as childlike rather than literally young, for similar effect to the alien as child. In *E.T. the Extra-Terrestrial* (1982), E.T.'s childlike stature, language learning, and choice of young companions initially disguises his advanced and incomprehensible knowledge, questioning associations between youth, helplessness, and a lack of understanding. The alien-as-child category refers to extraterrestrial youth but ultimately reflects human definitions and expectations of childhood. While some alien children in popular culture evoke animal rather than human life cycles, such as the amphibian childhood of Kif's species in *Futurama* ("Kif Gets Knocked Up a Notch" 2003), even these tend to criticize human age categories and parenting styles through comedy.

The "star-child" from *2001: A Space Odyssey* (1968), directed by Stanley Kubrick. (MGM/Photofest)

When human children display unexpected depths of knowledge, they become figuratively alien. Child-as-alien stories depict children as unfamiliar and sometimes frightening beings through imbuing them with power, intelligence, or prescience that contradicts their supposed innocence or lack of experience. Kubrick's transcendental star-child in *2001: A Space Odyssey* (1968) gains much of its sublime awe through conflating the most inexperienced concept of a child, a fetus, with comprehensive understanding of the universe. When juxtaposed with literal aliens, the child as alien repurposes the question of whether aliens are different to speculate about what makes children different from adults and whether those differences are actually more desirable when it comes to alien/other encounters. Children like Barry in *Close Encounters of the Third Kind* (1977) and Hogarth in *The Iron Giant* (1999) exemplify the benefits of a child's unique connection to extraterrestrials through openness and a lack of learned fear. In a chilling twist, however, the children in Ray Bradbury's "Zero Hour" (1947) use this same fearless connection with aliens to betray the adults.

Since the child as alien is both familiar and unfamiliar, it often evokes the uncanny. Children become creepy if they know too much and therefore undermine adult othering and definitions of childhood, as demonstrated by the eeriness of Alia's transgenerational knowledge in *Dune* (1965) by Frank Herbert. When combined with aliens, this youthful knowledge becomes a powerful question of what adults value in children. In Arthur C. Clarke's *Childhood's End* (1953), children begin to manifest powers beyond those of the adults and evoke the Freudian fear of being replaced by one's double. Similarly, an especially creepy variant of the alien as child occurs when an alien mimics a child, such as in "Cold Fire" (1995) from *Star Trek: Voyager* or "The Empty Child" (2005) from *Doctor Who*. The mimicking alien child intensifies the uncanny of the child as alien to interrogate the appearance of innocence. *Men in Black* (1997) pokes fun at this same supposed innocence when James explains why he (correctly) shot the cutout of a little girl rather than the cutouts of blatantly frightening aliens.

Lewis Padgett's "Mimsy Were the Borogoves" (1943) and its loose film adaptation *The Last Mimzy* (2007) play with this fear of the child as alien. In both versions, the children develop different abilities due to future humanity's educational technology, but the adults blame it on aliens. In contrast, the parents in John Wyndham's *Chocky* (1968) are keen to blame mental disorders rather than admit to the possibility that an alien has possessed their son with advanced knowledge. The adults move fluidly between the benign othering of childhood and the hostile othering of aliens, depending upon what better suits their fears. These stories demonstrate an adult drive to alienate children who appear different or not sufficiently childlike through conflating mental difference and/or aliens. This tendency gains a sinister sheen in the context of popular folk stories about aliens and children, like the 12th-century legend of the sickly green children of Woolpit or the contemporary conspiracy societies that try to use alien abduction to explain childhood attention-deficit disorders and autism. Similar to legends of changelings, the popular narrative of aliens can become an othering framework against physically different or neuro-diverse real children. Stories that critically undermine the othering of children and aliens are all the more important in this context.

Finally, some narratives address both the alien-as-child and child-as-alien categories simultaneously through a human-alien hybrid child, like the haunting children in John Wyndham's *The Midwich Cuckoos* (1957). More recently, Emily Sim in *The X-Files* and Naomi Wildman in *Star Trek: Voyager* exemplify this hybrid use of the alien child in popular culture, albeit in very different ways. *The X-Files* uses Emily for an uncanny effect, in keeping with the "spooky" tone of the show. She is on screen only for two episodes ("A Christmas Carol" and "Emily," both in 1997), but in doing so extends the body horror of Dana Scully's abduction and the theft and misuse of her ovum. The show portrays three-year-old Emily as innocent of the federal/corporate machinations that produced her, as seen in Scully's repeated attempts to adopt her despite the trauma of her origins. At the same time, Emily's existence threatens a future of malicious hybrid alien/human eugenics; even her hybrid blood is toxic to humans. As a alien-child hybrid, Emily brings up questions about the place of children in adult human vs. alien disputes, positioning her innocence in opposition to her dangerous alienness. On the other hand, Naomi's childhood is regularly presented in the ever-hopeful atmosphere of *Star Trek: Voyager*, beginning with "Fury" in 2000. Set among the mixed, alien, and adult crew members, her differences from being half-alien and a child are both framed as possibly beneficial. Additionally, her presence invites comparison with the treatment and behavior of the Vaadwaur and Borg children. Naomi opens the door to questions of children's innocence, cruelty, intelligence, and the idea of childhood potential—whether human, alien, or even alien cyborg.

When used well, the alien child in popular culture questions perceptions of aliens and children through the contradictory binary between the dangerous and innocent other. Children and alien characters each tend toward one side of the binary, which causes the combination to dovetail neatly. Alien stories often represent the unknown, dangerous other as something to be feared, such as in the case of science fiction/horror classics like *The Thing* (1982) and *Invasion of the Body Snatchers* (1956). In alien-invasion narratives since H. G. Wells's *The War of the Worlds* (1897), the alien has been used as an aggressive outsider who ultimately helps unite and define humanity by contrast. Meanwhile, children evoke the naïve, innocent aspect of the other that calls to be guided into civilization, as demonstrated in children's classics like Maurice Sendak's *Where the Wild Things Are* (1963) and Rudyard Kipling's *The Jungle Book* (1894). Scholars like Perry Nodelman have theorized that children are othered in society by adults who define them as inherently different, silence children by doing all the speaking for and about them, and study children for the benefit of adults. The alien child in popular culture sits at the crux of these aspects of othering, combining them to either benefit from or challenge the concept of alienating other intelligent beings or age groups.

## FURTHER READING

Malmgren, Carl D. "Self and Other in SF: Alien Encounters." *Science Fiction Studies*, vol. 20, no. 1, 1993, pp. 15–33.

Nodelman, Perry. "The Other: Orientalism, Colonialism, and Children's Literature." *Children's Literature Association Quarterly*, vol. 17, no. 1, 1992, pp. 29–35.

Sobchack, Vivian. "Child/Alien/Father: Patriarchal Crisis and Generic Exchange." *Camera Obscura*, vol. 5, no. 315, 1986, pp. 7–35.

# Aliens in Video Games

Michael M. Levy

Video games combine artistic expression with the highly technical art of computer programming, resulting in interactive and engaging user-driven experiences. The form a video game takes, however, is influenced by several other factors. For example, technological limitations can have a significant impact on how a video game looks and behaves, while a game's development budget can create tension between fulfilling a vision and creating a timely, functional, and profitable product. These factors, along with an awareness of a changing sociological climate, require a multifaceted approach to analyzing video games.

Aliens and their UFOs have been a favorite subject of video games since the beginning of the medium's commercialization in the early 1970s. Historically, video game aliens have most frequently appeared as aggressive invaders out to destroy the human race. *Computer Space* (Syzygy Engineering, 1972) was the first coin-operated video game to feature battles against the iconic saucer-type UFOs. Players maneuvered a spaceship across a star field in a shoot-or-be-shot duel against the aliens. Although *Computer Space* was very simple and received a lukewarm reception from the public, it established the beginnings of shooting aliens in commercial video games. More importantly, it was the first video arcade game created by Nolan Bushnell, who, with Ted Dabney, founded Atari shortly after the game's release.

Unlike *Computer Space*, Tomohiro Nishikado's *Space Invaders* (Taito, 1978) had an immediate impact on its audience and later games. In the classic arcade game, a block of aliens gradually descended from the top of the screen to the planet's surface, while UFOs cruised above. The player, as a lone laser turret, hid behind a set of shields that eroded under a withering hail of alien projectiles. The more aliens the player shot, the faster the remaining horde moved. The game's design gradually increased tension and eventually induced panic in the player as the last alien darted across and down the screen at an alarming speed. The player who succeeded in destroying the alien invasion was, however, given only a brief moment to savor the victory before a new block of aliens appeared at the top of the screen. The invasion was ongoing and infinite. There was no way to truly "win." *Space Invaders* became an international phenomenon that helped reinvigorate the stalling arcade industry of the late 1970s. It also marked the beginning of the arcade's Golden Age, a highly successful period in the history of arcade games that lasted through the mid-1980s.

Following *Space Invaders*, aliens appeared in a slew of shooting-based arcade games as well as games for home computers and cartridge-based consoles. Game developers, both large and small, created clones or outright bootlegged versions of *Space Invaders* in an attempt to replicate the game's success, while others modified the basic *Space Invaders* formula to create new gameplay experiences. In *Galaxian* (1979), *Galaga* (1981), and *Xevious* (1982), for instance, Namco progressively moved away from *Space Invaders*' monolithic block of invaders by adding dynamic movements for the aliens and providing the player with more ways of shooting them. In Williams Electronics' *Defender* (1981), the concept centered on rescuing abducted astronauts by shooting down UFOs in a side-scrolling world. Other games of the period, such as Atari's *Asteroids* (1979) and *Battlezone* (1980), featured UFOs as bonus targets that tempted players away from the game's main goals.

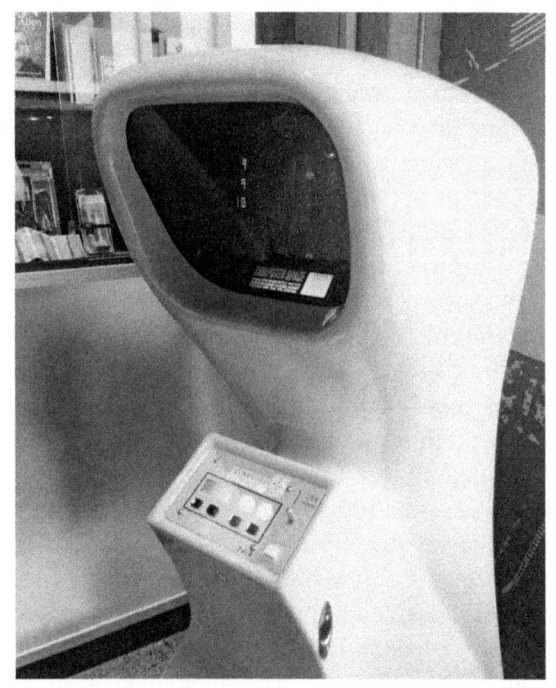

*Computer Space*, developed in 1971, was the first arcade video game, and the first video game that was commercially available. (Emily743/Dreamstime.com)

Although many games clearly derived inspiration from these sources, arcade games of the late 1970s to the mid-1980s were also heavily conditioned by technological and economic factors unique to video games. Programmers of the time strained to make games fit within the relatively limited (and expensive) memory of arcade machines. Black backgrounds were common in the period, as they were a more efficient use of the memory. The blackness of outer space thus proved to be an ideal setting. Additionally, arcade games of all genres were designed to make money, which influenced the design of gameplay: shorter play sessions generated more money. The narrative of the unwinnable struggle against a never-ending invasion of aliens proved a perfect fit with gameplay that was designed to be intense and brief.

The popularity of the unwinnable alien-invasion scenario waned quickly after the arcade's Golden Age, as arcade games increasingly incorporated narrative structures with definitive endings. These narratives often centered on aliens as an infestation that needed to be cleansed. The arcade game *Area 51* (Mesa Logic,

Inc., 1995), for example, took place after aliens infiltrated and took control of the eponymous facility. Players used light gun controllers to shoot aliens and zombie-like human soldiers who jumped out from various locations in the game's computer-generated 3D backgrounds. The game's ultimate goal was to eradicate the invasion by detonating the base's nuclear self-destruct system. The arcade game *Alien vs. Predator* (Capcom, 1994), based on the respective graphic novel stories, pitted a team of human and predator players against a xenomorph invasion of California in 2D side-scrolling, beat-'em-up gameplay. Incorporating familiar adversaries such as Weyland Industries and the iconic alien queen, the conclusion of *Alien vs. Predator* involved using a nuclear detonation to eradicate the aliens. Although the games were difficult, any player who was willing to insert enough coins could achieve the end goals of both games.

In addition to arcades, video games on home consoles and home computers significantly grew in popularity after the mid-1980s, as they provided a wider array of game types designed for longer play sessions and could better accommodate narrative elements. Nintendo's action-shooter *Metroid* (1986) illustrated the growing differences between games for arcades and games for the home. In it, the player navigated a sprawling underground base on an alien planet in an attempt to destroy a parasitic life-form called "Metroid," before space pirates forced it to multiply and used it as a biological weapon. After defeating the game's final "boss" character, the player used a large bomb to destroy the facility and prevent any risk of a Metroid infestation.

Although far from the featureless black backgrounds of outer space, alien invasion/infestation-themed, first-person shooters contained the essential shooting-based gameplay of earlier Golden Age arcade games. Games such as *Blake Stone: Aliens of Gold* (JAM Productions, 1993), *Duke Nukem 3D* (3D Realms, 1996), *Quake* (id Software, 1996), *Unreal* (Epic Games, 1998), *Half-Life* (Valve Corporation, 1998), *Halo: Combat Evolved* (Bungie, 2001), and *Crysis* (Crytek, 2007) all focused on familiar invasion themes and the threat that aliens posed to humanity. Nearly all culminated in an epic sequence in which the player either battled a final boss character, as seen in *Half-Life*, or played through a sequence of intense events, such as escaping an exploding spaceship in *Halo: Combat Evolved*. In either case, the story always led to a grand victory for the players and defeat for the aliens.

Alien invaders in video games were commonly members of larger organized bodies. *Halo*'s Covenant, the Reapers of *Mass Effect* (BioWare, 2007), the xenomorphs of the Alien vs. Predator games, and even the adversaries of *Space Invaders* all consisted of multispecies collectives. Although frequently tremendous in variety, video games tend to present members of a particular species as all behaving the same, thus eliminating any sense of individuality. This casts the aliens as anonymous "others" (literally alien) singularly dedicated to human eradication—a quality that further enhances their menacing nature and makes them easier for the player to kill. While prominent antagonists, such as boss characters, receive a greater degree of individuality, their personalities often recall well-known villain archetypes.

Although it is often the intent of a game's developer to present antagonists as negatively as possible, anonymous, multispecies alien collectives are also a product of the game-design process itself. As discussed above, games commonly struggle against limitations like processor power, computer memory, and budgetary restrictions that result in the need to be as efficient as possible. One method of saving development time while still bringing life to the gameworld is to create a handful of representative aliens and replicate them over and over in the game. Multispecies adversaries also offer an effective way to communicate different types of behaviors to the player. The presence, absence, or number of each species can dramatically affect how a player strategizes and plays. For example, the *Alien vs. Predator* arcade game mentioned above featured nine types of fully grown alien xenomorphs distinguished by a range of color schemes and attack patterns, while enemies of *Metroid* frequently appeared in two color palettes that effectively doubled the total number of enemy types.

Aliens cast as a game's main protagonist, in contrast to invaders, frequently function as a way to highlight the "alien" characteristics of humanity. In effect, they become "non-alien aliens." In *E.T. The Extra-Terrestrial* (Atari, 1982), designed for the Atari 2600 home console, the player adopts E.T.'s quest to "phone home" by gathering components scattered through a range of environments. The game presented Earth as hostile to nonhuman beings: E.T. steadily lost life during his search, FBI agents took away gathered phone components, and scientists forcibly detained E.T. for scientific study. By contrast, the boy, Elliot, could chase away the other humans and bring E.T. the phone components he needed. Although these themes and scenarios were explored in the film on which the game was based, the limited capabilities of the Atari 2600, coupled with an extremely short development time, made the theme of humanity's xenophobic reactions to the unknown, the central core of the game.

The "stranger in a strange land" theme of E.T. was employed to a greater extent in the Sega Genesis game *ToeJam & Earl* (Johnson Coorsanger Productions, 1991), in which two aliens accidentally crash-land on Earth and search for pieces to repair their spacecraft. The game was unique, as it employed a contemporary hip-hop and funk-inspired aesthetic, rather than the prevalent techno-futurism of other alien-related titles. The red, multi-legged ToeJam wore gold chains, high-tops, and a backward baseball cap, while Earl, large, orange, and shirtless, sported high-tops and thick sunglasses. Both "highly funky aliens" originated from the planet Funkotron, whose multispecies inhabitants used slang phrases like "Yo, wassup?" These elements were juxtaposed with a set of grotesquely humorous human characters such as a man in a carrot suit, a female opera singer dressed as a Valkyrie, dentists, herds of nerds, Santa Claus, and a cigar-smoking, rotund, middle-aged man pushing a lawnmower. The game's sequel, *ToeJam and Earl: Panic on Funkotron* (Johnson Coorsanger Productions, 1993) further subverted conventions associated with aliens, as humans stowed aboard ToeJam and Earl's spaceship on its return to Funkotron and infested the planet. ToeJam and Earl, thus, have to gather the invading humans and send them back to Earth. As in its predecessor, the human characters were represented in unflattering ways: gawking tourists with cameras, misbehaving children, and singing nudists wearing cardboard boxes.

Both games presented elements of the period's youth culture as "alien," while conventional mass culture was viewed through a funhouse mirror. Music played an important role in both games, as the soundtrack consisted of various funk-inspired riffs. The first game featured a "Jam Out!" mode in which players could create a freestyle rhythm of beats and sound effects, while ToeJam and Earl danced on brightly colored backgrounds. The overall tone of both games fit into Sega's larger marketing strategy of the early 1990s as it sought to brand its Genesis console as teen oriented, edgy, and hip relative to its main competitor, Nintendo. By the time of the much later third game, *ToeJam & Earl III: Mission to Earth* (ToeJam & Earl Productions, 2002), teen-oriented themes were normal in video games, causing the third ToeJam & Earl game to lose much of its subversive nature.

*Halo, ToeJam & Earl III: Mission to Earth*, and several other games of the 2000s represented something of a revival of aliens and the invader theme in video games after a relative period of decline. This resurgence followed familiar patterns in popular culture, as genres tend to move toward deconstruction, parody, and eventually revival. With each direction, video-game aliens evolved in new and creative ways.

In some games, aliens were used as a way to address or critique social issues. BioWare's 2007 action role-playing game *Mass Effect* and its sequels, for example, included the common narrative of humanity resisting eradication by a group of aliens. Although the main gameplay was action oriented, the game series also featured optional subplots revolving around hetero- and homosexual relationships, some of which occurred between human and alien characters. These relationship options stemmed from developer BioWare's desire to present players with a view of love and romance as it might exist in the future, a time in which politically charged social issues such as sexual preference would be entirely irrelevant.

Other games, such as the social-media management simulation *Redshirt* (The Tiniest Shark, 2013) presented a mixed view of the future and relationships between alien species. As a "redshirt" in a thinly veiled *Star Trek* universe, the player attempted to achieve career goals while managing relationships through their online "Spacebook" profile. As in *Mass Effect*, the concepts of gender and sexuality were more fluid, as players were able to set their gender through a slider and specify romantic interest in male, female, or both. Far from a utopian future, however, coworkers, supervisors, and even romantic interests in *Redshirt* could display a significant degree of bigotry. Playing as a member of the universally objectified, green-skinned, all-female Asrion species, for example, led to a higher number of unwanted advances from other Spacebook users, who would flood the player's page with suggestive messages. This put the player in an awkward position, as nearly all interactions, regardless of how benign they were, would be seen as flirtatious, a scenario that could alternately hinder or help in the player's career advancement. The game, thus, provided a satiric but sober view of issues related to workplace and online sexual harassment through its deconstruction of alien tropes.

Other developers treated the classic alien-invasion concept with a heavy degree of irreverence and parody. The "B movie"–themed *Destroy All Humans!* (Pandemic Studios, 2005) and its later sequels, for example, allowed players to play as invading aliens and wreak havoc on Earth by using their psychic powers to levitate, vaporizing humans using ray guns and knocking down buildings with UFOs. The Serious Sam first-person shooter games such as *Serious Sam: The First Encounter* (Croteam, 2001), with their ironically hyper-masculine hero, featured over-the-top battles against outrageous numbers of alien monsters. Most recently, aliens took the crime-themed Saints Row franchise from quirky to outright batty in *Saints Row IV* (Volition, 2013), as the president of the United States tries to save humanity after invaders destroy Earth and enslave its people in a simulation that grants its users superpowers.

Alien invaders have also functioned as nostalgic throwbacks to an earlier time in game history as part of a larger "retro revival" in the 2010s. The highly praised *XCOM: Enemy Unknown* (Firaxis Games, 2012), for example, is a contemporary remake of the earlier game *XCOM: UFO Defense* (Mythos Games/MicroProse Software, 1994), in which the player commanded a squad of special soldiers in turn-based skirmishes with alien invaders. Other games such as first-person shooters *Duke Nukem 3D*, *Aliens Versus Predator*, and *Halo* were all revised for play on modern systems and commercially rereleased. Even *Space Invaders* itself reappeared a number of times, first as a series of reissued arcade game cabinets and later as a small "retro arcade" joystick that plugged directly into the television and allowed players to relive the endless invasion. Nostalgia and irony frequently came together for certain independent game developers who investigated and reworked the long-since-abandoned 2D pixel art and gameplay of arcade games. Alien-invasion themes like those of *Alien Hominid* (The Behemoth, 2004), *Axiom Verge* (Thomas Happ Games, 2015), and *Alien Shooter 2* (Sigma Team, 2007) fit well with games based on fast-paced, arcade-like gameplay.

Changes in the representation of aliens in video games mirror the growing sophistication of the medium since their ascendancy in video games from the early 1970s onward. Through technological, economic, cultural, and artistic influences, aliens in video games have grown from simple pixelated outer-space invaders to frightened visitors, exotic objects of affection, vehicles for pointed social commentary, and back to invaders. Aliens thus provide captivating snapshots of video games and societal fluctuations and help in understanding the direction of change in a medium that evolves rapidly. All of these issues are explored further in game-specific articles in this book.

# Entries: A–Z

# A

## *The Abyss*

Director James Cameron's monumentally ambitious third feature film, *The Abyss* (1989), was released in August 1989, following one of the toughest and most infamous film shoots in cinema history. The film cost a then-unprecedented $70 million and necessitated the building of a huge underwater set within the 7.5 million gallon reactor vessel of an abandoned nuclear power station; further, the cast and crew were required to become certified divers. The film became a significant milestone for the development of CGI and, fittingly, won the Academy Award for best visual effects and was nominated for best art direction, best sound, and best cinematography. Despite this, the film underperformed financially and was heavily criticized for its abrupt and sentimental ending. However, a much-anticipated 171-minute extended cut negated many criticisms and led to the film's rerelease in 1993. This version garnered considerably stronger acclaim.

Starting out as a short story Cameron wrote during his teenage years, *The Abyss* concerns the crew of a submersible oil rig based on the ocean floor—*Deepcore*—who are pressed into facilitating the military's urgent search for a crippled U.S. nuclear submarine. Because it is suspected to have been downed by a Soviet submarine, World War III becomes a terrifying likelihood. When a hurricane severs Deepcore's communication with the surface and an otherworldly presence is discovered in a nearby abyssal trench, tensions escalate between the rig's crew—led by "Bud" Brigman (Ed Harris) and his estranged engineer wife, Lindsey (Mary Elizabeth Mastrantonio)—and the increasingly unstable and dangerous Navy SEAL commander, Lieutenant Coffey (a superbly unhinged Michael Biehn).

Affectionately named "NTIs" (nonterrestrial intelligences) by *Deepcore*'s crew, the subaquatic extraterrestrials in *The Abyss* are among the most optimistic—and beautiful—portrayals of alien life in all of science fiction; they are like bioluminescent butterflies that live in the ocean's depths. Ultimately, it is revealed that the creatures' paramount concern is to protect life on Earth by averting humanity's imminent self-destruction via nuclear conflict. For at least the first half of the film, however, the NTIs' status as friend or foe is deliberately kept ambiguous. The mysterious sinking of the U.S. submarine is caused by an encounter with the aliens, and later, while *Deepcore*'s crew searches the sunken sub for survivors, crew member Jammer (John Bedford Lloyd) is approached by an NTI that disrupts his oxygen intake, rendering him comatose. The navy wrongly assume the extraterrestrials to be some form of Soviet weapon and summarily salvage a nuclear warhead from the submarine to use against them. Initially, only Lindsay does not believe they pose a threat. The rest of *Deepcore*'s personnel choose to trust the NTIs only after witnessing their attempts at communication: mimicking human facial expressions with an animated water tentacle (known as the "pseudopod").

Though it follows in the footsteps of earlier works that imagine other worlds lurking beneath our oceans—Disney's *20,000 Leagues under the Sea* (1954), Irwin Allen's *Voyage to the Bottom of the Sea* (1961), and Michael Crichton's novel *Sphere* (1987), later adapted for the big screen by Barry Levinson in 1998—*The Abyss* is thematically aligned with alien narratives that take place above sea level. It possesses the same sense of awestruck wonder as Steven Spielberg's *Close Encounters of the Third Kind* (1977) and shares overt antiwar sentiments with Robert Wise's *The Day the Earth Stood Still* (1951), Wolfgang Petersen's *Enemy Mine* (1985), and Denis Villeneuve's *Arrival* (2016), among others. Though slightly more optimistic than Wise's seminal Cold War narrative, *The Abyss*—itself a late Cold War allegory—bears great similarity to *The Day the Earth Stood Still* in its denouement: in both films, humanity is threatened by extraterrestrials that demand it halt its pursuit of nuclear war, warning that much greater destructive powers are present in the universe. But while the extraterrestrial visitor in *The Day the Earth Stood Still* issues only a verbal warning, in the extended version of *The Abyss* the NTIs use their ability to harness water in order to summon colossal tsunamis that threaten the world's coastlines, demonstrating their capability to eradicate humankind should we continue to frivolously pursue destruction.

But upon witnessing Bud's self-sacrificial descent into the abyss to retrieve a nuclear warhead launched by Coffey to destroy the NTIs, the megatsunamis miraculously subside, and Bud's life is saved. As M. Keith Booker observes, "*The Abyss* opts for the far more sentimental argument that humanity is worth saving because of the human capacity for love and self-sacrifice" (231). The NTIs then serve as tolerant arbiters, a higher power that forces humanity to consider the consequences of its actions. Indeed, this theme of reconciliation connects with other elements in the narrative, particularly Bud and Lindsey's ultimate reunion and the implication that the Cold War will finally cease following the NTIs' tidal display. *The Abyss* would prove somewhat prescient, as the Berlin Wall—an ideological symbol of the Cold War—was ordered to be destroyed mere months after the film's 1989 release.

So while Cameron's ultimately tender message at the center of *The Abyss* may seem jarring and marginally at odds with contemporaneous political tides, it is worth remembering that—from visions of America being ravaged by a technological apocalypse in *The Terminator* (1984) to a military force being toppled by a native alien race in *Avatar* (2009), via *Aliens*' (1986) unmistakable Vietnam War inflections—Cameron's films are largely dominated by antiwar subtexts. Though *The Abyss* quickly developed a cult following and increased critical stature, the logistical nightmare of its production and its lackluster box office performance ensured the unlikelihood of a follow-up. Furthermore, studios in the 1990s would display a clear contrast to Cameron's optimism by opting to fund mega-budgeted extravaganzas in which extraterrestrials are most definitely foes—for example, *Mars Attacks!* (1996), *Independence Day* (1996), and *Starship Troopers* (1997).

*Liam Hathaway*

*See also*: *Arrival*; *Avatar*; *Close Encounters of the Third Kind*; *Enemy Mine*.

## FURTHER READING

Abbott, Joe. "They Came from Beyond the Center: Ideology and Political Textuality in the Radical Science Fiction Films of James Cameron." *Literature/Film Quarterly*, vol. 22, no. 1, 1994, pp. 21–27.
Booker, M. Keith. *Alternate Americas: Science Fiction Film*. Praeger, 2006.
Clarke, James. *The Cinema of James Cameron*. Wallflower Press, 2014.

## *Alien* (Series)

After *Star Wars* and *Star Trek*, the *Alien* series is probably the most famous work of cinematic science fiction of the 20th century. From *Alien* (1979) it has grown to include six films as well as several computer games, novels and novelizations, comic books, and other tie-in products. This article will focus on the first three films in the series. Directors in this franchise include Ridley Scott, James Cameron, David Fincher, and Jean-Pierre Jeunet. Films were released in 1979, 1986, 1992, 1997, 2012, and 2017.

In *Alien,* a commercial cargo spaceship, the *Nostromo,* lands on the unexplored world of LV-426 to investigate an apparent distress signal. Aboard a crashed spaceship, one of the *Nostromo*'s crew becomes forcibly impregnated with an alien embryo, which bursts from his chest, killing him. The crew attempt to hunt down the alien aboard *Nostromo*; the only survivor, Ripley, eventually destroys *Nostromo* and kills the alien, which has followed her onto its lifeboat. In the sequel *Aliens* (1986), set 57 years later, Ripley returns to LV-426 with a military expedition after a new colony on the planet falls silent; they encounter a large number of the aliens, and Ripley, one surviving soldier, and a colonist child escape. *Alien3* (1990) sees the survivors crash-land on a prison world. Ripley gradually realizes that an alien has arrived on the planet with her, and she leads the prisoners in a successful attempt to kill it. The series continued with *Alien: Resurrection, Prometheus,* and *Alien: Covenant*; further films are planned.

It is worth making a few points about what the *Alien* films are and are not about. *Alien* is not a film about first contact. Other nonhumans exist in the *Alien* universe; the pilot of the crashed ship, nicknamed the Space Jockey (itself also apparently a victim of alien impregnation), is a humanoid giant with a trunked face. Living nonhumans also exist; the marines in *Aliens* reminisce about previous "bug hunt" operations, mock Ripley's supposed expertise, and even seem to have a running joke about sex with "Arcturians." And the crew of *Nostromo* show no surprise on encountering a crashed nonhuman spaceship, though they do admit that the type is unfamiliar. Nor does the series fall into the category of cosmic horror (though, according to *Alien* scriptwriter Dan O'Bannon, it was heavily influenced by his fondness for Lovecraft). Essential to that genre is the idea that humanity is both vulnerable and irrelevant; we are the ants crushed by the footfalls of disinterested creatures far older and more powerful than ourselves with motives we cannot possibly comprehend. The message of *Alien* is exactly the opposite. No relationship in nature, except possibly that of a mother and her child, is as intimate as that between parasite and host. The aliens care very deeply about humans, and their motives are extremely obvious.

*Alien* (1979), directed by Ridley Scott and starring Sigourney Weaver. The film was unique for the horror genre, in that it had a strong female lead, but the key to its success was the striking visual elements, including the alien's design by Swiss artist H. R. Giger. (AF archive/Alamy Stock Photo)

However, the *Alien* films unquestionably form a horror story, and one whose success as film and as horror depends on the aliens themselves. The human cast of the *Alien* films comprised competent character actors rather than A-list stars, though Sigourney Weaver, playing Ripley, arguably became a star as a result of her role. The unique merit of the series comes from the alien's design, by the Swiss artist H. R. Giger, and its memorable reproductive strategy.

The British archaeologist Steven Mithen, in *The Prehistory of the Mind* (1999), speculates that the modern human mind is the result of a merger between specialized mental modules. Early humans had a partitioned mind, with modules for dealing with physical objects, living creatures, and social interaction; merging these allowed mental leaps such as domestication of animals (animals regarded as social beings) and innovative tools (animal parts like bone, sinew, and fur regarded as physical objects) and abstract advances like humor, supernatural beliefs, and religion.

It is not stretching Mithen's theory too far to suggest that the origin of the horror story dates from about the same time. The same inventive incongruity that produces jokes (talking animals) and animism (intelligences associated with natural objects) is also at the root of horror. Zombies are dead people who are alive; those possessed by spirits are human-shaped but not human; a cannibal is a human acting like a predatory animal.

Giger used the term "biomechanical art" to describe his work, including the painting *Necronom IV*, on which he based the design for the alien. It is clear to see why: Giger's art is disturbing and at times horrifying because it transgresses

Mithen's boundaries between human and animal and between human and machine. It is difficult to tell where the machine ends and the living tissue begins—an effect produced in the films not only in the alien's biomechanical body plan and the Jockey's control chair but also in several scenes in which aliens and inert matter (shuttle machinery, piping, hive walls) are briefly confused by characters, and also, of course, by the audience.

The alien's reproductive method was invented by O'Bannon's cowriter Ronald Shusett to solve a plot problem: how would the alien sneak back onto the *Nostromo*? His answer, "it *impregnates* one of them," was aimed at "all of our buttons, all our unresolved feelings about sexuality" in a portrayal of interspecies rape, male pregnancy, and the catastrophic "birth" of an alien child, three transgressions of boundaries.

The aliens have attracted a good deal of critical interpretation and analysis over the years—and it is interesting to note that this analysis begins within the films themselves. In each of the three films, other characters see them as superior to humanity. The villainous android Ash in *Alien* envies them as "perfect organisms ... unclouded by conscience, remorse, or delusions of morality." The Company man Burke in *Aliens* sees them as perfect soldiers for the "bioweapons division" (and Ripley contrasts their loyalty favorably with human treachery). The religious maniac Golic in *Alien3* regards the alien as quasi-divine, apparently worshipping it and calling it the Dragon (a term taken from the Revelation of Saint John).

Ripley's own relationship with the aliens centers around motherhood. The aliens' behavior is driven by reproduction and birth, at which they are catastrophically successful. The computer aboard *Nostromo*, Ash's quiet ally in his attempt to bring an alien on board, is called Mother; Ripley screams her name as she tries to reverse the ship's self-destruction. Ripley's first realization after awakening in *Aliens* is that she has failed as a mother to her own daughter, Amanda, who has aged and died during her long sleep (in an earlier treatment, Ripley meets Amanda as an old woman, bitter at her perceived abandonment). Ripley acquires a surrogate daughter, the colonist child Newt, only to lose her to the aggressively maternal and fertile Alien Queen; in the climactic sequence she rescues Newt and escapes by threatening the queen's eggs, her own biological children. In *Alien3* Newt is dead—Ripley has failed again as a mother—and she discovers, in a moment of real irony, that she is carrying an alien larva; she is, 60 years after the birth of her daughter, about to become a mother again. A conventional action film would have finished with the adult alien's death; *Alien3* finishes with Ripley's suicide.

*Alexander Campbell*

See also: *Cowboys and Aliens*; *Critters*; *Prometheus*.

## FURTHER READING

Graham, Elizabeth, editor. *Meanings of Ripley: The Alien Quadrilogy and Gender.* Cambridge Scholars, 2010.
Kuhn, Annette. *Alien Zone.* Verso, 1990.
Thomson, David. *The Alien Quartet.* Bloomsbury, 1998.

## Alien Autopsy (Fact or Fiction?)

In the mid-1990s, television docu-series about UFOs and unexplained phenomena proliferated. Brenda Denzler called them "tabloid-style" shows that blurred the lines between fact, fiction, faith, and belief. Viewers flocked to scripted dramas such as Fox's *The X-Files,* a paranormal procedural series. The growing popularity and accessibility of the Internet gave conspiracy theorists and skeptics alike a platform to debate the possibility of UFOs, aliens, and the requisite conspiracies to conceal the truth from the public. On August 28, 1995, Fox (United States), Channel Four (United Kingdom), and dozens of other networks around the world broadcast *Alien Autopsy (Fact or Fiction?)* (1995), a heavily hyped prime-time special that promised shocking footage of the secret 1947 medical examination of an extraterrestrial being.

It was an overnight sensation, rebroadcast repeatedly and then repackaged for home-video distribution. The show launched the career of Fox executive Mike Darnell, turning him into what the *New York Times* called "a latter-day P. T. Barnum." British music and film promoters Ray Santilli and Gary Shoefield claimed to have purchased 17 minutes of black-and-white footage from a retired military cameraman, who claimed he shot the film at a secret base in Fort Worth, Texas. Producer Robert Kiviak used that footage as the topic of a program that purported to objectively analyze the footage. Hosted by Jonathan Frakes, an actor well known for his role on the popular science-fiction series *Star Trek: The Next Generation*, the show opened with a screen advisory: "The following program deals with controversial subjects. The theories, opinions and beliefs expressed are not the only possible interpretation. Viewers are invited to make a judgment based on all available information." *Time* said Fox "stimulated the liveliest debate of any home video since the Zapruder film."

Two figures in crude white safety suits examine a humanoid figure on a table while a third individual in a surgical mask watches from behind an observation window. Over the course of the hour, a variety of witnesses and experts are interviewed on camera about the validity of the footage, including individuals who grew up in Roswell and remember the rumors of the crash, experts from Eastman Kodak, medical experts, and Hollywood visual effects specialists. The show ended with Frakes intoning, "We don't claim to have the answer. . . . we've given you the opportunity to hear from all sides. . . . Until we know more, you'll have to decide." Stan Winston later told *Time* that his comments were edited to suggest that he was unconvinced and that he stated plainly on camera his certainty that the footage was a hoax. *The X-Files* aggressively satirized *Alien Autopsy (Fact or Fiction?)* in the 1996 episode "Jose Chung's From Outer Space," in which Agents Mulder and Scully debunk an absurd show titled *Dead Alien! Truth or Humbug?*

In 1998, Darnell and Fox hyped a new prime-time special, *The World's Greatest Hoaxes and Secrets Revealed!*, which debunked *Alien Autopsy (Fact or Fiction?)*, as though other medida had not satisfactorily done the debunking already. In 2006, Santilli made new headlines when he admitted to journalist Eamonn Holmes that the footage in *Alien Autopsy (Fact or Fiction?)* was faked. However, he claimed it was not faked to deceive anyone but was instead a necessary staged reconstruction because the original footage was too degraded to view. Special effects creator John Humphreys, who built the alien body in 1995, also confessed on camera. *Eamonn Investigates: Alien Autopsy* aired on Sky TV in the United Kingdom on April 4, 2006. Three days later, a feature film titled *Alien Autopsy*, directed by Jonny Campbell, opened in theaters. The mockumentary-style biopic depicts Santilli and Shoeford as young men who happen upon this miraculous footage, which disintegrates before they can share it with the world. They rally friends and family to recreate it, sell the rights around the world, and evade shadowy forces in the U.S. government who conspire to discredit them and their film. Humphreys, now an established visual effects artist, recreated his original alien body for the new film. Santilli and Shoefield were executive producers of *Alien Autopsy*.

The cultural relevance of *Alien Autopsy (Fact or Fiction?)* lies not in the debate it purported to open or the shocking secrets it claimed to reveal. In short order, it was debunked by all but the most ardent believers, as evidenced by the selection of articles and interviews republished as a collection by Kendrick Frazier et al., while Toby Smith traced the idea of little green men through decades of popular culture. Santilli and Shoeford launched their footage into the world at a cultural moment poised to accept ideas about both visitors from another world and nefarious government conspiracies.

*Rebecca Stone Gordon*

*See also*: Aliens Did Not Build the Pyramids; Condon Report, The; Grays; Roswell (Place); *X-Files, The*.

**FURTHER READING**

Denzler, Brenda. *The Lure of the Edge: Scientific Passions, Religious Beliefs, and the Pursuit of UFOs*. University of California Press, 2003.
Hesemann, Michael and Philip Mantle. *Beyond Roswell: The Alien Autopsy Film, Area 51, and the U.S. Government Coverup of UFOs*. Marlowe, 1997.
Smith, Toby. *Little Green Men: Roswell and the Rise of Popular Culture*. University of New Mexico Press, 2000.

## Alien Nation

Following on from the 1988 film of the same name (dir: Graham Baker), *Alien Nation* (September 8, 1989–May 7, 1990) is a science-fiction police procedural created by Kenneth Johnson that follows the partnership of human detective Matt Sikes (Gary Graham) and alien detective George Francisco (Eric Pierpoint). The series is set following the 1990 arrival of 250,000 Tenctonese, known as the Newcomers, who crashed into the Mojave Desert while escaping from enslavement at the hands of the Overseers. Unlike the arguably more realistic *District 9* (2009) and *Star-Crossed* (2014), the Newcomers of *Alien Nation* are enthusiastically embraced as immigrants rather than as refugees and are integrated into American society rather than shunted into slums. While the film can be easily classified as a noir piece, the television series focused on the buddy-cop dynamic, integrating it into the science-fiction setting to create an extended tension between Francisco

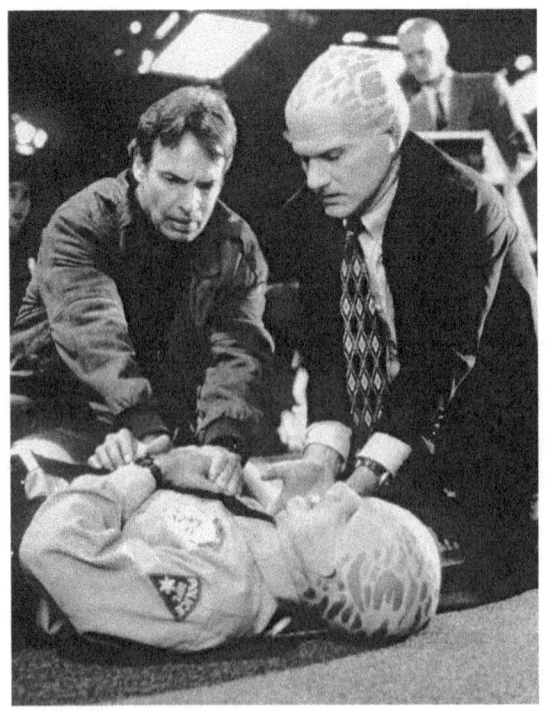

*Alien Nation: The Udara Legacy* (1997), one of five television movies that followed the popular series prematurely canceled by FOX due to the network's financial difficulties. Shown (from left) are Gary Graham as Detective Matthew Sikes, Sean Six as Buck Francisco, and Eric Pierpoint as Detective George Francisco. (Fox Broadcasting Co./Photofest)

and Sikes that never truly resolves itself. Despite this tension, over the course of the series Sikes and Francisco begin to reach across their cultural divide to trust each other as partners as they encounter racism and the ever-present threat of the Overseers. Interwoven into this is the duality of alien otherness and human familiarity, creating a consistent thread of defamiliarization to mirror the plot tensions. Due to financial problems at Fox in 1990, the series originally ended on a cliffhanger, though this was resolved by a graphic novel and a series of novels. The series was so popular that it was brought back for five television movies between 1994 and 1997. The translation from film to television brought significant changes, most notably in the overall tone of the series.

The Newcomers/Tenctonese are a humanoid alien race bred and genetically engineered for intelligence and strength in order to perform hard labor in any environment. Newcomers have larger skulls than humans, no external ears, and markings instead of hair. The markings continue down the spine and function both as erogenous zones and as a means of identifying individuals and their family. Perhaps the most significant difference between humans and Newcomers is that three genders are required to reproduce, with the rare catalyzing gender referred to as the Binnaum. Newcomer pregnancies are also shared between genders, as females initially carry the fetus, but males carry it to term and give birth. While the Tenctonese were enslaved, hallucinogenic gases were used to control them, with children removed from their parents at the age of ten. Overseers were Tenctonese themselves, trained to control their own people, though it is not clear whether the ultimate rulers were Tenctonese or another alien race. Due to their genetic engineering, Newcomers are stronger and smarter than humans, with an average life span of 140 years.

Newcomers are represented as an immigrant culture attempting to integrate into American society. Alongside traditional Newcomer religions, the most common being Celinism (practiced by the Francisco family), Newcomers engage in human behaviors, such as the juvenile rebellion of the oldest Francisco child, Buck

(Sean Six). With the exception of the Binnaum's monk-like clothing, Newcomers generally wear human clothes and take on human professions, such as Francisco's own position as detective and Sikes's Newcomer neighbor who works as a biochemist. However, the naming of Newcomers has a significant othering effect in the series, as many of the human names they were assigned—notably, by human INS agents—were jokes or puns; George Francisco's name was originally Sam Francisco, and other Newcomer names include Albert Einstein (Jeffrey Marcus), Lance Lott (John Meese), and Paul Revere (David Opatoshu). While intended to be whimsical, these names instead set the Newcomers apart from the American culture they are intended to integrate with. Newcomers are seen as a threat not just by the human Purist movement, but also by Francisco's partner, Sikes, who regularly feels threatened by Francisco's greater strength, superior intelligence, and longer life span.

The racist terms "slag," "spongehead," and "rubberhead," and the abusive nickname "Slagtown" for the area of Los Angeles known as "Little Tencton," indicate the speed at which racism and xenophobia take hold. The Newcomer response to this treatment is nuanced; Susan Francisco (Michele Scarabelli) and Buck Francisco's campaign for Tenctonese suffrage in "The Spirit of '95" and the Newcomer insults for humans, "tert" and "Slo'ka," indicate that the Newcomers are not content to simply accept abuse, with their responses ranging from peaceful activism to insults and even physical violence.

Although racism is explored in the series, it is ultimately an optimistic contribution to the American melting-pot mythos, though not unrealistic. The Francisco family are dedicated to their integration while preserving their own culture, and it appears that both Newcomer and human leadership are eager for this to take place on a wider scale. In "Real Men," Francisco's pregnancy demonstrates the fundamental cultural and physiological differences between humans and Newcomers. Sikes, who begins the series as a bigot, not only learns to accept Francisco's family but also begins a relationship with his Newcomer neighbor Cathy Frankel. However, in the final episode, "Green Eyes," Sikes is angry when Francisco is promoted instead of him. Furthermore, Newcomer integration is not seamless, as seen with the 16-year-old Newcomer prostitute in "Little Lost Lamb" and the transformation of the Overseers into a mafia-style criminal organization.

Unfortunately, *Alien Nation*'s cancellation meant that the potential of its first season was never fully realized. There are many possibilities: the tensions between humans and Newcomers would have needed to come to a head; to suggest a few scenarios, successive governments could have changed their policy on integration, or the arrival of another ship, still under the control of the Overseers, could have changed everything. Even without such a significant event, the everyday life of the Newcomers and the humans living alongside them would have provided a multiplicity of viewpoints for understanding a culture so completely different from our own. Ultimately, the nature of the series can be understood through its dual title: the alienation of an alien nation stranded on another world.

*Jennifer Harwood-Smith*

See also: *District 9*; Gwyneth Jones's Aleutians; *V.*

**FURTHER READING**

Fisher, Bob. "Alien Nation: Unbelievable Becomes Everyday." *American Cinematographer*, vol. 71, no. 10, October 1990, pp. 89–98.
Gross, Edward. *Alien Nation: The Unofficial Companion*. Renaissance Books, 1998.
Shapiro, Marc. "Newcomer Cop." *Starlog*, no. 160, November 1990, pp. 29–33.

## Alien Spaceship Design

Representing the alien for audiences creates an artistic tension between the other and the familiar. Depictions that are too strange tend to produce a distancing effect, as audiences struggle to connect with them. This problem is often resolved by hybridizing and/or altering forms, species, or objects that are familiar when constructing alien species, ecology, technology, or spaceships. The silhouettes of rocket ships, the shapes recounted by observers of "real" UFO sightings, and design elements from more mundane methods of air travel are often incorporated into the design of alien spacecraft, signaling how we are supposed to interact with their creators.

However, there is also a tendency to use shapes that are resolutely *not* aerodynamic or designed for thrust and are thus resolutely inexplicable by modern science: thus, simple geometrical shapes like cigars, spheres, crescents, and saucers characterize reported sightings of what observers believe to be alien vessels, and this design aesthetic has influenced depictions of many iconic alien ships. The massive mother-ships that loom over entire cities in Roland Emmerich's *Independence Day* (1996) are saucer shaped, and the small fighters they carry share a similar silhouette, though with more tapered architecture that gives them the appearance of barbs. Similarly, the Cylon Basestars from Glen A. Larson's *Battlestar Galactica* (1978–1979) television series consist of two saucer segments, each shaped like a closed pair of cymbals, joined together with a short central pillar section. These vessels, like the Borg cubes and spheres from the *Star Trek* franchise, dwarf other vessels they encounter and convey a sense of their creators' power and drive for domination.

However, this is not the case with the alien craft in Steven Spieberg's *E.T. the Extra-Terrestrial* (1982). When his fellow creatures come to collect E.T. after the small, leathery alien successfully "phones home," the whimsical vessel they arrive in resembles a squat, bubble-shaped rocket ship with a ring of spherical thrusters and round lights throughout the body of the ship. Its appearance is anything but threatening. The brightly lit saucer from Spielberg's *Close Encounters of the Third Kind* (1997) alters the classic saucer by incorporating structures that resemble a city skyline, and, combined with the multicolored lights and sounds used to communicate with the vessel, instills a sense of wonder in audiences. The "city in space" design also occurs in Alex Proyas's *Dark City* (1998), where what appears to be a 1940s–1950s noir-style city for much of the film is revealed to be a space habitat surrounded by a force field, whose buildings and human inhabitants are endlessly redesigned and reprogrammed by the alien Strangers. When the sinister

Strangers are overthrown, the city is turned toward the sun and sees daylight and hope for the first time.

Many films that blend science fiction and horror depend on the feeling of dread that is central to the latter genre, and this is reflected in the design of their alien vessels. The dim blue lights of the black ship carrying the vampiric aliens from Tobe Hooper's *Lifeforce* (1985) serve to enhance the darkness of the vessel rather than illuminate it. All the elements of its design—from the claw-tipped "umbrella" that resembles a partially closed fist to the long, sinuous body that looks like warped and tangled vines to the twisted tendrils trailing off at the opposite end—create a feeling of danger and unease. Similarly, the Engineers' crescent-shaped juggernaut featured in Ridley Scott's *Alien* (1979) and subsequent films in the franchise employs curves and textured inner walls that conjure the feeling of bone and blood vessels, giving the sense of moving through a fossilized carcass, not a ship, a feeling difficult to dismiss after discovering the xenomorph eggs in the belly of the vessel.

The blurring of the boundary between the biological and mechanical, the programmed and the sentient also factors into the design of some alien ships. The ships of the Shadows and Vorlons in J. Michael Straczynski's *Babylon 5* (1994–1998) television series both exhibit this fusion of opposing systems. The Vorlon ships make use of curves and tendrils, and their silhouette resembles a jellyfish with an elongated body; luminescent, petal-shaped sails; and a mottled hull that looks more like skin than metal. The Vorlon vessels are sentient, and when the pilot of one vessel dies in the show, the grieving ship flies into a sun to join him in death. The Shadow vessels are as dark and unsettling as the Vorlon ships are beautiful and bright. They possess an oily, inky skin, and while the overall shape of the ship resembles a butterfly, spider-like spikes—rather than the solid wings of a butterfly—fan out from its core. Shadow ships use a sentient creature as the ship's central processor, which makes the vessels dangerously responsive but leaves them vulnerable to telepathic attack. The Shadow vessel is not a companion; it is a slave.

The servitude and freedom can also be seen in the living leviathan ships of Rockne O'Bannon's *Farscape* (1999–2003). The gentle leviathans, whose silhouette resembles an elegant horseshoe crab, are bio-organic ships that have their own personalities and collective culture. They are capable of giving birth to other leviathan vessels, and each unique vessel shapes itself to the needs of its crew. The leviathan Moya was enslaved by the militaristic Peacekeepers, but she and the captives she is transporting gain their freedom and become companions and allies.

The design of alien vessels can also provide a subtler commentary on the cultures that produce them, as the alien ships of *Babylon 5* demonstrate. The vessels of the warrior Narn are heavily armed and resemble arrowheads with vivid red and black markings. They look sharp and dangerous. The sleek silver-white ships of the philosophical Mimbari have an ethereal art-deco influence and incorporate structures that echo the bone ridges the species also possesses, while the decadent Centauri vessels proudly display the purple and gold colors of royalty and employ fan-like silhouettes not unlike the high collars of a rococo noble's coat or the hair crests of Centauri men. In this manner, the vessels inform us about the cultures that produced them and what our likely relationship to the aliens who travel in them might be before they even exit their ships.

*Barbara Lucas*

See also: *Alien* (Series); *Babylon 5*; *Farscape*.

**FURTHER READING**

The Babylon Project. babylon5.wikia.com/wiki/Main_Page.
The Farscape Encyclopedia Project. farscape.wikia.com/wiki/Leviathan.
Guffey, Ensley and Dean Koontz. *A Dream Given Form: The Unofficial Guide to the Universe of* Babylon 5. ECW Press, 2017.
Moran, Michael. "What Should a Sci-Fi Spaceship REALLY Look Like?" *The Register*, November 24, 2011. www.theregister.co.uk/2011/11/24/spaceship_design./

## Aliens Did Not Build the Pyramids

The theory that alien astronauts visited Earth and created or influenced ancient civilizations captivated the public in the late 1960s. In France, Louis Pauwels and Jacques Bergier's *The Magic of the Magicians* (1960) and Robert Charroux's *One Hundred Thousand Years of Man's Unknown History* (1963) laid the groundwork, but it was Swiss writer Erich von Däniken's *Chariots of the Gods?* (1968) that turned this vein of speculative nonfiction into a global phenomenon. Proponents claimed that aliens visited Earth, manipulated human evolution, and bestowed advanced technologies on early humans. This extraterrestrial knowledge enabled otherwise primitive people to build megalithic structures such as pyramids in Egypt and Mesoamerica, the Easter Island Moai, and Stonehenge. *Chariots of the Gods?* was published in Germany in 1968, serialized in the American tabloid *National Enquirer* in 1970, and published in the United States as a book in 1970.

German Director Harald Reinl's film adaptation received an Academy Award nomination in the documentary feature category in 1971, lending additional credibility to von Däniken's claims. In 1973, NBC broadcast a reedited version of Reinl's film, retitled *In Search of Ancient Astronauts*. It was the pilot episode of what would become the popular *In Search of . . .* series, with Leonard Nimoy replacing Rod Serling as the show's regular host. Von Däniken published prolifically and influenced scores of writers. Television series such as the History Channel's *Ancient Aliens* (2010–) continue to propose alternate theories about ancient artifacts, earthworks, and structures, with ancient Egyptian culture as a popular recurring topic. When a field is as complex and multidisciplinary as Egyptology, which includes archaeologists, paleopathologists, historians, linguists, art, and architectural historians, the claims of pseudoarchaeologists pose special challenges (Fritze 2016).

A form of pseudoscience, pseudoarchaeology eschews academic consensus and methodological rigor, cherry-picking historical and scientific evidence to support the conclusion that certain prehistoric cultures could not survive or develop without alien intervention. Pseudoarchaeology can be used for self-promotion and monetary gain, of course, but archaeologists are most concerned about the ways that science can support nationalism, racism, and religious oppression. Ancient-alien proponents flatten or distort the historical record, taking advantage of the collapsed temporality tourists and museum visitors experience when they visit a site or exhibit in which artifacts or structures of vastly different ages sit side by side. Von Däniken writes, "If we meekly accept the neat package of knowledge that the Egyptologists serve up to us, ancient Egypt appears suddenly and without transition with a fantastic ready-made civilization" (von Däniken 1970). The immense amount of specialized data and analysis is anything but neat, but the ancient-aliens theory capitalizes on the static picture of what is actually millennia of Egyptian history and culture to reinforce the idea that a grand civilization inexplicably arose out of whole cloth.

Interest in ancient Egyptian history and culture overflows academia, and, as scholars such as Ronald Fritze have observed, Egyptomania regularly sweeps through Western culture. Egyptomania has taken benign forms—influencing cemetery designs, fashion, or furniture trends. It can also, as scholars such as Scott Trafton have shown, support more sinister projects, such as the creation and perpetuation of racism, as it did in the 19th century. Ancient-alien theories gained traction at a time in the late 20th century when debate over the ethnicity of ancient Egyptians and their relationship to other African cultures was overturning traditional colonial interpretations. Ascribing the skills, tool making, and intelligence necessary for complex activities such as pyramid building to aliens propagates negative attitudes toward non-Western cultures and inhibits public understanding of the diversity and vitality of cultures around the world and across time.

Over a period of thousands of years, ancient Egyptians constructed many pyramids. Egyptologists have documented over 100 remaining or partially preserved pyramids within the borders of modern-day Egypt. Because of the long span of time over which the pyramids were built, scholars have observed that changes in building technique and design took place over time. While there is not a definitive theory for how any of these different styles were constructed, researchers agree that ancient people had the tools, skills, and intelligence to design and build pyramids. Although there are many unanswered questions, there is also abundant information about the mortuary function pyramids served. In some locations, Egyptologists have reconstructed some of the aspects of daily life for the artisans and workers, further humanizing individuals whose individual stories are lost to time. Mark Lehner was part of a team who conducted scientific analysis of materials used to build, as well as the construction debris these ancient workers left behind. He writes, "Such close encounters with pyramids reveal not the 'footprints of the gods,' but rather the 'fingerprints of the people': straw and reed, wood, fragments of rope and stone tools, flecks of copper and sherds of pottery" (Lehner, 6).

*Rebecca Stone Gordon*

*See also*: Fort and Forteanism; Roswell (Place); *X-Files, The*.

**FURTHER READING**

Anderson, David S. and Jeb Card, editors. *Lost City, Found Pyramid: Understanding Alternative Archaeologies and Pseudoscientific Practices.* University of Alabama Press, 2016.

Brier, Bob and Jean-Pierre Houdin. *The Secret of the Great Pyramid: How One Man's Obsession Led to the Solution of Ancient Egypt's Greatest Mystery.* Harper Collins Publishers, 2008.

Fagan, Garrett, editor. *Archaeological Fantasies: How Pseudoarchaeology Misrepresents the Past and Misleads the Public.* Routledge, 2006.


## *Aliens Love Underpants*

*Aliens Love Underpants* (2007) is the first in a series of best-selling picture books written by Claire Freedman and illustrated by Ben Cort. In each formulaic volume in the U.K. series, aliens, monsters, pirates, or dinosaurs conspire to obtain their most coveted desire—underpants—from their hapless (usually human) owners. Since the publication of *Aliens Love Underpants*, the series has become immensely popular, spawning a sticker coloring book, a sound book, plush toys, and even a lively children's stage production, produced by Adam Brampton Smith, in addition to its many sequels. Four of the books in the series, including *Aliens Love Underpants* (2007), *Aliens in Underpants Save the World* (2009), *Aliens Love Panta Claus* (2010), and *Aliens Love Dinopants* (2015), center on the exploits of round, cheerful aliens who are far more interested in gathering up and playing with underpants than they are in meeting Earthlings. Although the books appear to be intended to inspire a love of underpants among young children of toilet-training age rather than curiosity concerning the wonders of the cosmos, children's television producers seem keen to use the books in an effort to spark an early interest in science; the BBC CBeebies *Bed Time Story* presentation of *Aliens Love Underpants* was read by British-Nigerian space scientist Maggie Aderin-Pocock, and Canadian astronaut Julie Payette read the book to Bookaboo, the rock star puppy, on his namesake show. Yet, read as science fiction, the aliens' zany antics seem less like a delightful romp than an effort at teaching children that colonial resource exploitation isn't so bad.

Although in almost all circumstances, strangers (aliens) arriving and making off with intimate garments without consent is creepy, Freedman and Cort's aliens are painted to be anything but threatening. In many ways, their features echo common tropes of aliens in science fiction—some have eyes on stalks, or fins protruding from their backs, or more than the usual number of arms—but they're also squat and round, with stubby legs and big feet, and it is difficult not to laugh at their contagious grins and cartoonish movements. Those aliens who have acquired underpants wear them pulled up high around their middles, which makes them look disarmingly goofy. The aliens also behave like humans in several ways, so that they appear friendly rather than intimidating: one of the first spreads in *Aliens Love Underpants* shows aliens pushing alien babies in strollers, aliens walking alien pets on leashes, and aliens reading alien books and magazines. The aliens also affix bumper stickers to their flying saucers and build monuments to objects and events of significance to their culture—namely underpants and the brave aliens who, in *Aliens in Underpants Save the World*, protected the source of their most precious resource from annihilation.

The aliens' alien understanding of the function of underpants also makes their relationship to humans appear less exploitative than it actually is. Although the aliens sometimes wear underpants the way humans do, they also experiment and play with them, using "grandpa's woolly long johns" as "a super-whizzy slide," wearing underpants on their heads, or seeing how many aliens they can cram into a pair before it falls off the line. This allows young children reading the story to feel a sense of expertise and mastery; they know more about how underpants work and what they're meant for than the foolish aliens. Unlike older humans, the aliens do not appear to be concerned about whether or not they are naked, which liberates them to use underpants in unusual, hilarious, and at times even heroic ways— as in *Aliens in Underpants Save the World*, when the aliens sew thousands of pairs of pants together to make giant underpants and repel a meteor that is set to knock the Earth from its orbit.

Yet, in spite of the book's efforts to portray the aliens as a benign source of laughter—both within the narrative itself and in its paratext, which suggests that "You'll laugh your pants off!"—*Aliens Love Underpants* is a story of invasion that ultimately functions as an argument for and defense of the theft of resources from the invaded group. In casting pants pinching as a hilarious romp, the story subtly makes contemporary decolonizing movements, and perhaps also opposition to sexual harassment, seem a little silly and anti-fun. The narrative, which addresses its reader in the second person and represents that reader as a white (almost always) male child in the closing spread of each book, sets that reader up to sympathize with aliens and to keep their secret. At the same time, it also informs them that what the aliens are doing is theft, and the aliens are portrayed as having no regard for either Mum's labor in picking up the underpants that the aliens have dropped or the cost of underpants, which lower-income families might not be able to afford to replace so easily. If the aliens' representation as hapless tourists, consulting brochures about underpants and taking photographs and videos of their adventures on Earth, is meant to make them seem a little silly, it also draws attention to the fact that the tourist gaze objectifies and commodifies those upon whom it falls and that the aliens are treating the humans in ways that are dehumanizing. *Aliens in Underpants Save the World* concludes with an argument that the aliens' actions are ultimately in the humans' best interests: "So should your pants go missing / There's no need to make a fuss, / Let the aliens have their fun / They've done so much for us!" This echoes and supports the patronizing and paternalistic historic and contemporary treatment of indigenous peoples by colonial powers around the world. If *Aliens Love Underpants* is meant to get children excited about science and space exploration (in addition to underpants), it does so cynically, in a way that supports a status quo that excludes and exploits rather than opens up possibilities.

*Meredith Snyder*

See also: *Clangers, The*; Dr. Xargle; *Steven Universe*; *Teletubbies*.

**FURTHER READING**

Mendlesohn, Farah. *The Inter-Galactic Playground: A Critical Study of Children's and Teens' Science Fiction.* McFarland, 2009.
Nikolajeva, Maria and Carol Scott. *How Picturebooks Work.* Routledge, 2006.
Nodelman, Perry. *Words about Pictures: The Narrative Art of Children's Picture Books.* University of Georgia Press, 1988.

# Almond, David

The presence of the miraculous in everyday life is a persistent theme in the work of British author David Almond (1951–), whose influences range from William Blake to García Márquez. The liminal landscapes of Almond's novels place wildness and industrial decay side by side, providing space at the boundaries for the unknown. As Almond's child protagonists enter these borderlands, they discover marvelous beings: a winged man in a trash heap, a creature made from muck and clay, a mysterious girl retrieved from the mud. Strange and unfamiliar, Almond's outsiders are nonetheless in plain sight, discoverable to those who embrace the world with imagination and wonder. Both spiritual and mundane, these alien figures help to catalyze the children's fall from innocence into a world of experience. In *Skellig* (1998), *Heaven Eyes* (2000), and *Clay* (2005), Almond's eponymous strangers facilitate a transformation of the self, while illuminating a world of transcendent beauty.

In *Skellig*, Almond's most famous novel, a boy named Michael befriends a winged creature he finds deteriorating in a junk-filled garage. It's impossible to say whether the decrepit birdman is a fallen angel, an owl-like product of evolution, or something else entirely. Provoking a sense of wonder, Skellig is nonetheless utterly real, as Michael and his friend Mina realize when they find the crushed wings and bent feathers hidden beneath the birdman's filthy clothes. Skellig is neither an obvious ally nor an obvious threat, as his motives are inscrutable and his history is unknown. His body and mind ossified by disuse, the birdman is fragile and broken. Supplementing his diet of spiders and mice with Michael's donated aspirin and leftover food, Skellig eventually gains the strength to return to the world of flight, but not before offering a reciprocal act of healing to Michael's younger sister. As Skellig embraces the ailing baby, the child's mother briefly glimpses ethereal wings sprouting from the infant's shoulder blades. "We [are] surrounded by angels and spirits," the children learn, echoing William Blake. "We must just open our eyes a little wider, look a little harder" (ch. 34). An unlikely spiritual figure found in a trash heap, Skellig is a purely alien creature, fostering growth and healing in those who are willing to look a little harder.

In Almond's *Heaven Eyes*, a lyrical novel with echoes of *The Tempest*, muck and spirit once again find incarnation in the body of an outsider, while children who enter a wasteland and embrace the unknown are profoundly altered by their experience. "No need to go far," the narrator Erin Law observes. "The most miraculous of things could be found a few yards away, a river's-width away" (part 3, ch. 2). When Erin and her friend January flee their orphanage by taking a raft downriver, they founder in the mud and are assisted by a girl named Heaven Eyes. A pale child with webbed fingers and toes, Heaven Eyes is simultaneously an ordinary orphaned girl and a "froggy thing" dragged up from the primordial mud. This visionary stranger can "see through all the darkness in the world to the joy that lies beneath" (part 1, ch. 1). Cared for by the anxious and forgetful Grampa, she is a guide to the liminal environment at the river's edge, dredging up treasures from the garbage-strewn mud. When Grampa dies and the children uncover the mummified body of a "saint," the saint's luminous spirit escorts Grampa's ghost across the Styx-like river to the world beyond. Heaven Eyes then joins the other children in the everyday world, transformed into an ordinary girl as the other children undergo sea changes of their own.

Almond's novel *Clay* features another inscrutable being, this one a humanoid figure drawn from the earth itself. Directly referencing Mary Shelley's *Frankenstein* and the mysteries of Almond's Catholic childhood, *Clay* engages with the godlike power of the artist's imagination. Set in 1960s Felling, an English town located beside an abandoned quarry, *Clay* is narrated by Davie, an imaginative boy who desires something more than an ordinary life. Davie falls under the hypnotic and destructive influence of Stephen, a disturbed loner whose powers extend from hypnosis to animating clay figurines. Using bread and wine stolen from Mass, Davie helps Stephen create a golem-like creature from the quarry's clay. If "we are muck *and* we are spirit," as Davie's art teacher suggests, then the creature Clay is no different, being both a monster formed from dust and a triumph of the artistic imagination (part 2, ch. 16). Alienated and adrift, Davie realizes that he too has become Stephen's creature, molded like clay and disconnected from his true self. When Stephen boasts that he has compelled Clay to assist him in murdering a bully, Davie experiences a spiritual crisis. Breaking with Stephen, Davie regains his mystical connection to the world of nature, but only by destroying his own creation. As he sends Clay back to the muck and dirt from which he came, Davie is transformed by his experience, losing his childlike faith but finding joy in the beauty of a postlapsarian world.

Hopeful and compassionate, *Heaven Eyes* is ultimately revealed to be a human child, an outsider whose humanity is confirmed by her interactions with Erin and her friends. In contrast, *Clay* and *Skellig* are beyond conventional understanding: they are inhuman, though not necessarily inhumane. David Almond's novels are set on the edges of civilization, and his child protagonists, characterized by imagination and wonder, make journeys into the unknown, where alien beings emerge from rubble, dust, and mud. Both supernatural and earthly, Almond's aliens foster growth and maturation in the children they encounter, transforming these young characters as they move from innocence to experience. For Almond, the strangers in our midst reveal that the world is truly a magical place, and "[the] most astounding things can lie waiting as each day dawns, as each page turns" (*Heaven Eyes*, part 3, ch. 10).

*Jonna Gjevre*

See also: *Animorphs*; *E.T. the Extra-Terrestrial*; Simak, Clifford D.

**FURTHER READING**

Levy, Michael M. "Children and Salvation in David Almond's *Skellig*." *Foundation*, no. 88, Summer 2003, pp. 19–25.

Levy, Michael M. "Images of Masculinity in the Recent Fiction of David Almond." *Foundation*, no. 102, Spring 2006, pp. 49–59.

Levy, Michael M. "They Thought We Were Dead, and They Were Wrong: Children and Salvation in *Kit's Wilderness* and *Heaven Eyes* by David Almond." *Foundation*, no. 88, Summer 2003, pp. 26–32.

## *Animorphs*

K. A. Applegate (1956–) has written three major science-fiction or fantasy series for young adults—*Animorphs*, *Everworld*, and *Remnants*—but *Animorphs* (1996–2001) was the most successful, selling around 35 million copies. It comprised 64 books about a team of teenagers able to transform into animals, a power they use to launch a secret campaign against an alien invasion. Written for monthly consumption, with support from a team of ghostwriters for later installments, the books never won awards, but they became a popular sensation, manifesting in trading card, video game tie-ins, and even a short-lived television series. Applegate closely links her work to the popular culture of the day and makes use of stock characters to facilitate her production speed. However, she distinguishes herself by addressing mature themes, including war, fractured families, mortality, and PTSD. Her aliens, numerous in type and form, inject the series with an ongoing meditation on cultural collisions between forces of imperialism, totalitarianism, and ecology.

The *Animorphs* story line opens when a group of five teenagers make contact with an Andelite alien named Elfangor, who is severely injured in a battle intended to protect an unaware Earth from alien invasion. Knowing his army has been eradicated by the invading Yeerks and unwilling to leave the planet unprotected, Elfangor gives the children his advanced technology, allowing them to absorb the DNA of any living animal they touch and then morph into that creature. The series recounts the titular team's ongoing struggle to protect Earth until Andelite reinforcements arrive. Such a framework, and the 1990s climate that birthed the series, echoes the political dynamics of the Cold War and the way superpowers fought each other on the soil of third-party nations.

The initial aggressors in the war, Yeerks seem unassuming: Applegate describes them merely as large slugs. However, they possess the horrifying ability to crawl into a body through the ear and wrap themselves around the mind of the victim, giving them uncontested control over a person's actions and full access to their memories and thoughts. In their most basic function, Yeerks represent totalitarian and imperialistic regimes from history, the ultimate violation of free will, agency, and identity.

Andelites, in contrast, appear as noble guardians who promote progress through scientific achievement, but measuredly. One science-fiction trope argues that science and technology come at the expense of the natural world, but Andelites signal a more ecologically responsible approach. Firstly, Andelites seem more animal than humanoid, appearing as blue-furred centaurs with four eyes (two atop flexible stalks) and long tails that end in a curved blade; they do not have mouths, instead absorbing nourishment from plants and water through their hooves. Consequently, Andelite ships contain large tracts of grassy terrain to imitate their homeworld, feed their crews, and keep them connected to their home and people. Such an eco-mindful approach to life, despite their advanced technology, seems to keep Andelite technology from overwhelming the species.

Applegate estranges humans and human readers with the introduction of sentient beings who inhabited the Earth millions of years before humans. The Mercora are recognizably alien: they travel in flying saucers and plant crop circles. Nevertheless, the Mercora not only predate humans on Earth but also make contributions to its ecosystem (e.g., genetically engineering broccoli), suggesting that their claim to "own" planet Earth is at least as strong as that of humans. The discovery that the Mercora considered Earth "home" millennia before humans did, along with the protagonists' decision to annihilate the Mercora, sets up humans as alien invaders on planet Earth. Humans exist only because they have performed a hostile takeover of a planet that other sentient species claimed as their own.

The humans' current dominance of the planet is further questioned when the Animorphs travel to the bottom of the ocean and encounter the Nartec, who are "vaguely human in shape," though "they definitely weren't human" (*The Mutation*, 51–72). Inside an underwater cave, the Animorphs discover the Nartec's massive ship graveyard: "these people . . . had stuffed and preserved Vikings and Roman warriors, pirates . . ." (*The Mutation*, 75). Once the Animorphs learn that the Nartec plan to attack the "Surface-Dwellers" (humans), they conclude "We can't let them [get] to the surface," making a clear division between the humans ("we") and the Nartec ("them") (*The Mutation*, 78). The Animorphs kill dozens of Nartec to prevent an invasion, even though the Nartec arguably have as much claim to Earth as humans do. The Animorphs cast the Nartec as villains: "[the Nartec] could go one-on-one with the Yeerks in the Evilpalooza" (*The Mutation*, 139). The Nartec, however, have more in common with humans than with Yeerks: they share humans' physicality and home planet. The Animorphs continuously claim the moral high ground in their war because, as one Animorph tells the Yeerks, "it's you invading my planet, not the other way around" (*The Departure*, 43). The Nartec disrupt the human/alien dichotomy, placing the Animorphs in a nebulous space where they are both defending Earth against alien invaders and are themselves aliens invading Earth.

Science fiction frequently portrays humans' relationship to Earth as their greatest strength against invaders, often showing the planet itself rejecting aliens: H. G. Wells's Martians die from the common cold, Jack Finney's Body Snatchers cannot tolerate human emotion, and Applegate's Yeerks are allergic to oatmeal (*The Underground*). However, Applegate suggests that this close connection between humans and their environment is temporary and illusory, the product of both momentary luck and deliberate human action to kill other species who might also claim the planet. Applegate questions whether humans have the implicit right to defend Earth from the Yeerk invaders or whether they are simply fending off the latest threat to their current tenuous position as the dominant species on the planet.

Written in a decade emerging from the Cold War, Applegate's aliens represent the central concern of cultural collision: disruption of a species' natural development by interaction with more advanced superpowers. The Yeerks had not yet achieved any post-Neolithic technology and so lacked any context for their place in the universe. They lacked an ethical basis to mitigate their actions, making a bid for intergalactic conquest natural. Humans, comfortable as Earth's dominant species, similarly find themselves suddenly wrenched from a worldview to an interstellar-view where that superiority is completely upended. Early in the series, one Andelite suggests that in a future day humans, galvanized by Andelite technology, might prove a threat to galactic peace. Applegate's ethics rest with the Andelites, who achieved scientific excellence on their own, re-forming their ethics with each new development.

*Catharine Kane, Kelly Kane, and Paul Williams*

See also: Almond, David; Okorafor, Nnedi; *War of the Worlds, The*.

## FURTHER READING

Anon. "K. A. Applegate." *Authors & Artists for Young Adults*, vol. 37, Gale Group, 2001, pp. 1–6.

Mendlesohn, Farah. *The Inter-Galactic Playground: A Critical Study of Children's and Teens' Science Fiction*. McFarland, 2009.

## Arnason, Eleanor

In the 1970s Eleanor Arnason (1942–) published a handful of well-respected stories, mainly in *Orbit* anthologies edited by Damon Knight. In 1978 Pamela Sargent included one of Eleanor Arnason's stories in *New Women of Wonder* (1978), along with others from such writers as James Tiptree Jr., Joanna Russ, and Joan Vinge, often described in critical discussions as "second wave" feminists. Aliens were not a primary focus of these early stories, acting mostly as window dressing or in an unusual role in "The House by the Sea," where they serve as sympathetic diversion from the arrogance of the protagonist and underline her repellent if comic assumptions of noblesse oblige.

Arnason's first novel, *The Sword Smith*, appeared in 1978, a picaresque narrative of the attempt by the title character to escape his titular role in pursuit of nonviolence, making plowshares out of swords. In a vaguely early European fantasy landscape, he encounters dragons, which play a similar role to that of aliens in many stories. (Arnason described them in an interview as "sentient therapod dinosaurs"). These lizard-like nonhumans have a logical and technical culture that is mostly contrasted favorably to the low-tech superstitious society of humankind. Nargri, a saddlebag-sized juvenile dragon who accompanies Limper, the hero, in his anti-quest, is one of Arnason's most sympathetic characters. Nargri functions almost as a conscience or alter ego/psychotherapist in Limper's discussions with himself, though sometimes biting or threatening to bite antagonists—belying attempts to "read" her as a purely psychological construct of a lonely Limper.

Arnason's second novel, *To the Resurrection Station* (1986), was another episodic but more satirical narrative, sending up the gothic romance novel and a good many SF tropes as the heroine rejects marriage to an alien prince—who is himself a misfit and reject from his own culture. Not much attention is devoted to portraying this alien people; instead, the novel focuses more on robots, artificial intelligence, and evolved animals on earth. The third novel, an ironic fantasy novel set partly on Earth and partly in a fantasy otherworld, *Daughter of the Bear King*, features some monsters that might be compared to aliens, but again they were not much developed either as characters or as a coherent society.

*A Woman of the Iron People* (1991), Arnason's more substantial fourth novel, received much attention and praise, as well as two genre awards. In this first-contact narrative, a human woman, Lixia from Earth, meets the humanoid alien woman of the title in the course of an anthropological visit to the planet. Sexual differences between males and females are greater among the aliens of this planet than among humans. Males leave society after puberty and live solitary lives in the wilderness, and females seek them out, annually, when they go through an estrus cycle. The alien cultures that Lixia and Nia visit, eventually accompanied by both human and alien males, might easily have been based upon readings in anthropology and animal studies, but Arnason keeps her characters individual and believable with humor and sometimes unexpected incidents. The alien stories and mythologies prove no less efficacious and reliable than the Marxism and other political and anthropological mythologies and cultural beliefs professed by the visitors from Earth.

Most of Arnason's subsequent work has been devoted to two series, those unfolding around Lydia Duluth, an interstellar adventurer, and a number of stories about the "Hwarhath," a humanoid alien race of outer-space explorers encountered by the expanding human empire. Hwarhath culture is organized along a gender dichotomy featuring normative homosexual relationships. Both of these series featured stories nominated for Hugo or Nebula Awards, as well as one short Lydia Duluth novel and one longer Hwarhath novel. In addition, Arnason has produced a number of other stand-alone projects, such as her *Mammoths of the Great Plains* and *Hidden Folk*. Most of these do not feature aliens in the science-fictional sense, though perhaps their otherworldly gods and fairies and ghosts may offer some interesting comparisons.

The Duluth stories featured interesting aliens, particularly in the short novel, *Tomb of the Fathers*, which includes a militant female army that has to be confined to their home planet and other aliens in the visiting party of explorers accompanying Lydia Duluth, such as Vagina ("Gina") Dentata, whose name promises more than Arnason delivers. These stories feature clever and loony ideas but not a lot of development of well-rounded alien characters.

Arnason's major achievement is in the thoughtful and extended developments of the Hwarhath stories, particularly in the novel *Ring of Swords*. In a valedictory essay, Brian Attebery argues that the book is a masterpiece of SF. His focus is not on the Hwarhath, particularly, but on the development and literary aspects of Arnason's novel. Nonetheless, the aliens and their logical inversion of human heterosexual society, undergirded by their slightly different biology (females are a little bigger than the males on average, for example), and clearly informed by readings in primatology and other animal behavior and biology, provide a setting in which characters like Ettin Gwahar or Tsai Alma Ul emerge as sympathetic and yet alien characters. In subsequent stories (mostly collected in *Hwarhath Stories* [2016]), Arnason fills in details of the development of the alien society and history on their home planet and explores the implications of their alien biology and culture. In *Ring*, another alien species also plays an important function. The question of its intelligence overshadows the whole novel in a way that many readers have perhaps missed, but not Ursula Le Guin. She says, "The shadowy presence of a third species runs through it both unifying its ideas and always putting all assumptions back in question—a beautiful symbolic device. A beautiful book."

David Lenander

*See also*: Cherryh, C. J.; Le Guin, Ursula K.; Tepper, Sheri S.

## FURTHER READING

"An Eleanor Arnason Page." rivendellergroup.com/authors/eleanor-arnason/.
Gordon, Joan. "Implications of the Other in Eleanor Arnason's Science Fiction." *Future Females, The Next Generation: New Voices and Velocities in Feminist Science Fiction Criticism*, edited by Marleen S. Barr, Rowman & Littlefield, 2000, pp. 247–28.
Pearson, Wendy. "The Queer as Traitor, the Traitor as Queer: Denaturalizing Concepts of Nationhood, Species, and Sexuality." *Flashes of the Fantastic: Selected Essays from The War of the Worlds Centennial, Nineteenth International Conference on the Fantastic in the Arts*, edited by David Ketterer, Praeger, 2004, pp. 77–92.

## *Arrival*

In *Arrival* (2016), based on Ted Chiang's "Story of Your Life" (1998) and directed by Denis Villeneuve, 12 alien spaceships appear in the skies, distributed with little regard for terrestrial geopolitics or iconic architectural signifiers, above China, Greenland, Japan, Pakistan, Russia, Sierra Leone, Sudan, the United Kingdom, the United States (in Montana), Venezuela, and the Indian Ocean west of Australia. Aboard each is a pair of seven-limbed "heptapods." In the United States, linguistics professor Louise Banks (Amy Adams) is recruited to interpret their language, while astrophysicist Ian Donnelly (Jeremy Renner) heads the science team. Deep in the ship, Banks sheds her hazmat suit, showing her face and her mistrust of the heptapods to maintain the habitable environment they have created. She makes a breakthrough by investigating written as well as spoken heptapod, painstakingly building a written vocabulary with Donnelly's aid. The alien language is not glossographic but semasiographic; their "words" or logograms do not approximate the sound of their language but express meaning directly. Their complex and beautiful orthography is temporally nonlinear, as if a human were to write a sentence with both hands simultaneously working toward each other from both ends of it.

When finally asked "What is your purpose?" the heptapods respond, "Offer weapon," a message better translated as "visitors friends heptapods offer give donate award technology apparatus method humanity man woman host person." Nonetheless, the Chinese General Shang orders the aliens to leave his country's airspace or face all-out attack; other countries follow suit, and communication between the national scientific teams is shut down. One of the aliens helps Banks to unlock the "gift" that comes with learning heptapod and downloads an unprecedented amount of information, sacrificing itself to save her and Donnelly from a bomb planted by nervous soldiers.

Throughout the film, Banks has had flashbacks to her estrangement from her husband and her young daughter's slow death from a rare disease. However, learning heptapod has altered her perception of time—heptapods experience time simultaneously rather than sequentially—and these flashbacks were actually flash-forwards. She will choose to have a daughter with Donnelly and will eventually admit her foreknowledge of the palindromically named Hannah's illness, the cause of their estrangement. Banks also has a flash-forward to a banquet celebrating global unification, where she meets General Shang, who thanks her for phoning him with the message that brought the world back from the brink of destruction; he then gives her the information necessary for her to have done so, and she then does so. With international collaboration guaranteed—each scientific team is given one-twelfth of heptapod knowledge, all of which parts are necessary to read any of it—the aliens depart, knowing that because of their intervention, humans will have survived to come to their aid when needed in 3,000 years.

Chiang's story prefers exposition—of linguistics, physics, and compatibilist philosophy—to the film's geopolitical shenanigans and unambiguous conclusion. Its heptapods remain hidden in orbit, communicating through "looking glasses"—112 screens dotted around the world, nine of them in the United States. The film's spaceships initially look like pebbles, or elongated eggs, with one end resting on the ground; they are actually poised dozens of feet in the air and shaped like mushroom caps. Chiang's heptapods, their gray skin ridged like corduroy, look like barrels "suspended at the intersection of seven limbs" terminating in four digits. With seven eyes positioned around the "barrel," they have no front or back, left or right. Banks calls them Flapper and Raspberry. In the film, Donnelly dubs them Abbott and Costello, gendering them male but also implying the oddly asexual homosociality of a traditional male comedy double act (this happens just after Banks *sans* hazmat suit steps forward with a hand raised in greeting, role-reversing the image on the *Pioneer* plaque and making even Donnelly aware that he is not the protagonist). These heptapods look like trees standing up on thick roots or like cephalopods; Costello's movements are especially aquatic when fleeing the bomb. Although they have no apparent eyes, they do have orientation. Their mottled bodies ripple, swell, and inflate. Their flexible limbs are at times jointed like those of the facehugger xenomorph, a crustacean, or an arachnid (Villeneuve's *Enemy* [2013] ends with a vision of a giant spider stalking the Toronto skyline). Each limb terminates in seven digits, resembling a starfish, and these "hands" excrete the jets of "ink" that "write" hetapod orthography in the air. Each logogram takes the form of a ring with a complex, shifting structure, some sections dense with fractal detail. Their spoken language evokes whale song, Predator chittering, Triffid rattling—and didgeridoos.

This last is significant, given the film's risibly U.S.-centric worldview. It depicts China, Russia, Pakistan, Sierra Leone, Sudan, and Venezuela as inherently violent, lacking America's commitment to peace, cooperation, rationality, and reasonableness. When Agent Halpern (Michael Stuhlbarg) argues that the heptapods want nations to fight each other until there is only one dominant one left to deal with, he can cite only precedents from other countries' imperialism. When Banks wins an argument by telling a story about Captain Cook's encounter with Australian Aboriginals, Colonel Weber (Forest Whitaker) retorts, "Remember what happened to the Aboriginals." This is a shockingly phlegmatic response to genocide, especially as it comes from an African American character in a first-contact narrative reworking the colonial encounter and championing communication over conflict.

Weber selects Banks because she argues that the Sanskrit word for "war" does not mean, as the other contender insists, "argument" but "the desire for more cows," demonstrating her talent for context, nuance, and motivation as well as a tendency not to presume confrontation. Later, she is troubled that the Chinese are somehow using mah-jongg to communicate with the heptapods, since a competitive game is framed in terms of opposition, conflict, and winners and losers. An early scene contrasts the spatial/hierarchical opposition between teacher and students in a lecture theater with the (supposedly) more democractic, lateral connectivity of social media that alerts Banks's students to the aliens' arrival; they are then all subject to hierarchy as they together become an audience for television news coverage. Images of screens proliferate: televisions, computer monitors, the giant window overlooking the lake behind Banks's house, and even the entrance into the heptapod vessel. As she and Donnelly rise up into the belly of the ship, above and—when the heptapods flip gravity through 90°—in front of them, there is a small white rectangle, like a cinema screen at the end of an extended auditorium. In the chamber, the heptapods appear behind a transparent wall, the surface of which becomes particularly active and communicative when Banks and Abbott touch "hands" through it. Military and political hierarchies, obsessed with screening-as-concealment, sequester and embargo information, but, from Banks's whiteboard to Abbott's massive download in the seconds before his foreknown death, the human and alien linguists use screens to communicate.

*Mark Bould*

See also: *Abyss, The*; *Contact*; Miéville, China.

## FURTHER READING

Chiang, Ted. *Stories of Your Life and Others*. Small Beer Press, 2010.
Greenblatt, Susannah. "Three Translators Respond to 'Arrival'." *Words Without Borders*, April 3, 2017, www.wordswithoutborders.org/dispatches/article/three-translators-respond-to-arrival-susannah-greenblatt.
Mayer, Sophie. "Girl Power: Back to the Future of Feminist Science Fiction with *Into the Forest* and *Arrival*." *Film Quarterly*, vol. 70, no. 3, Spring 2017, pp. 32–42.

## Avatar

*Avatar* (2009), directed by James Cameron, owes much of its commercial success to the richly imagined world of the lush forest moon Pandora and its hauntingly beautiful bioluminescent alien ecosystem and indigenous people, the blue-skinned Na'vi.

In the year 2154, Earth faces ecological and energy crises arising from the depletion of the planet's natural resources. The Resources Development Administration (RDA) sends an expedition to Pandora to mine a valuable mineral called unobtanium. Because Pandora's atmosphere is toxic to humans not wearing breathing equipment, the RDA constructs avatars, genetically engineered and artificially grown Na'vi bodies that contain both human and Na'vi cellular material. This hybrid biology allows the human whose DNA is incorporated into the avatar to have his/her consciousness transferred into the Na'vi body and inhabit it as if it were his own, while his own body lies in stasis.

When his identical twin brother Tom is murdered, paraplegic ex-marine Jake Sully (Sam Worthington) is given the chance to take his brother's place on the expedition to Pandora, bond with his brother's avatar, and act as a bodyguard to the scientific team, led by Dr. Grace Augustine (Sigourney Weaver), who use avatars to interact with and study the Na'vi. Colonel Miles Quaritch (Stephen Lang), chief of security at the Hell's Gate human colony and main antagonist in the film, secretly tasks Sully with spying on the Na'vi and members of the scientific team. Quaritch needs intelligence he can use against the Na'vi, whose community in the massive living Hometree lies over a rich deposit of unobtanium.

In return for Sully's assistance, the RDA will pay for the expensive spinal surgery required to heal his paralysis. However, the more Sully inhabits his avatar, explores Pandora, and learns about the Na'vi, while falling in love with their princess Neytiri (Zoe Saldana), the more he identifies with them and their way of life and the more he finds the RDA's actions immoral and unjust. When the RDA destroys the Hometree of Neytiri's people, who can't repel the heavy firepower of the RDA security forces, Sully rallies the Na'vi clans and leads them into battle to drive off the human invaders and reclaim their planet.

The Na'vi ("The People") have large amber eyes, pointed ears, and long tails. They are taller than humans, standing 10 feet tall, and have longer limbs and torsos, smaller heads (in proportion to their body), and more slender physiques. All Na'vi have an external nerve cord, the queue, on the backs of their heads, which they protect by insulating it inside a braid of hair. This cord allows the Na'vi to psychically bond with those Pandoran plants and animals who have similar cords, as well as with each other. This connection, called tsaheylu ("the bond"), allows for sharing memories and information. It also makes the spiritual connection a tangible, physical act. At the Tree of Voices, a luminescent willow-like tree, tsaheylu can be used to commune with the spirits of the ancestors.

Na'vi society may be primitive in terms of technology, arrows, and spears being its main weapons, but it has a rich culture of music, dance, and storytelling, celebrating Na'vi connectedness to each other, all life on Pandora, and their deity, Eywa, an intelligence who permeates the world and its creatures and peoples. Eywa also maintains and protects the balance of life. The Tree of Souls, similar in

*Avatar* (2009), directed by James Cameron and starring (from left) Sam Worthington and Zoe Saldana. (20th Century Fox/Photofest)

appearance to the Tree of Voices, provides the strongest connection to Eywa and is a sacred spot for all Na'vi. When the humans drive Neytiri's people from their home, they retreat to the Tree of Souls, where they make their final stand, and it is at the tree where Sully's human body dies as his consciousness is transferred fully to his avatar.

The classic alien-invasion trope, found in films like *Independence Day* (1996) and *War of the Worlds* (2005), pits humans against technologically advanced aliens who want to conquer or destroy Earth. In the face of subjugation or destruction, humans are forced to put aside their differences and band together to repel the invaders and save humanity and the planet. While *Avatar* makes use of the alien-invasion narrative, it inverts the trope by casting humans as the high-tech invaders intent on destroying the Na'vi and their world. For their part, the Na'vi must not only come together as a people, but they must also unite with those humans who oppose the RDA's actions on Pandora.

Cameron has cited *Dances with Wolves* (1990) as an inspiration for *Avatar*, and this influence can be seen in two problematic tropes shared by both films. The first is that of the noble savage who lives a simple, primitive, idealized life, uncorrupted by civilization and technology. While lacking sophistication and culture, the noble savage possesses a deep wisdom, moral strength, and strong connection with nature. Indigenous people of color often fall victim to this representation. The romanticized and uncorrupted state of noble savages in science fiction often provides a contrast with the degenerate culture of more technologically advanced peoples.

Both films also employ the "white savior" motif, whereby a white male from an oppressive society finds himself in close contact with a marginalized community of color. He is able to integrate himself into the society and rise in prominence among its people. Eventually, he turns his back on the corruption of his own society and leads his chosen community in a rebellion against them. Working in tandem, these two tropes undermine the inversion of the alien-invasion motif, as the character responsible for overcoming the colonizing forces of the RDA is, himself, one of those self-same oppressors. While Sully's goals are more noble than those of Quaritch, the film ends with Sully, not a heroic Na'vi warrior, earning a position of power, respect, and prestige over the indigenous people of Pandora.

*Barbara Lucas*

*See also*: *Abyss, The*; *Way of Thorn and Thunder, The*.

## FURTHER READING

Baxter, Stephen. *The Science of* Avatar. Orbit, 2012.
Fitzpatrick, Lisa. *The Art of* Avatar: *James Cameron's Epic Adventure*. Abrams, 2009.
*Pandorapedia—The Official Field Guide*. www.pandorapedia.com/pandora_url/dictionary.html.

# B

## *Babylon 5*

The five seasons of *Babylon 5* (1994–1998) were aired on U.S. television between January 1994 and November 1998. The show was the creation of J. Michael Straczynski, who wrote 92 of the 110 episodes. Babylon 5 is the fifth of the Babylon stations to be created and the last to survive: it was intended as a kind of Galactic United Nations, designed to allow ambassadors of the various spacefaring species to come together and to keep the peace. "Humans and aliens, wrapped in 2,500,000 tons of spinning metal . . . all alone in the night," as the first-season introduction put it.

Straczynski started with the good intention of portraying the range of possible alien species. We are told that there are over 20 alien races, 14 of which live inside the "alien sector" in quarters that have atmospheres tailored to each species. Only 19 were portrayed, including the sinister Shadows, who do not take part in the Babylon project. There are certainly around nine species who live in the same atmosphere as the humans. The Vorlon ambassador is the only alien from the "alien sector" whom we see frequently. Budgetary restraints meant that the insectoid alien called N'Grath, also living in the "alien sector," was written out early on in season 1.

Kosh, the Vorlon ambassador, appears once simply as a bright light, behind a screen. In only one episode, in order to save Commander Sinclair, does Ambassador Kosh voluntarily leaves his encounter suit; each witness to that event sees him as a divine being from his or her own mythology. It is not until season 4, when a Vorlon encounter suit of Kosh's replacement shatters, that we discover that Vorlons resemble cephalopods. Vorlons like creating mystery, which Kosh enhanced by speaking almost entirely in enigmatic phrases. Only in the third season do we discover that they were among the oldest and most powerful galactic species, instrumental in eliminating the threat from the Shadows in previous eras.

The Shadows are shown only fleetingly. When they come on the space station, to accompany their human liaison Morden, they are generally invisible. When we are allowed to see them, they appear as mantis-like beings (the only aliens to be consistently computer generated). Their ships, like many-legged arachnoids, fit the image, and indeed there are hints that the ships are themselves somehow alive.

All the aliens who are seen frequently in the show are humanoid in appearance, even the Narn, who clearly have reptilian ancestry. The Centauri look and dress like 18th-century nobility, save that instead of a white wig, they have shaved foreheads and a crest of black hair on the crown of their heads. (The information that Centauri males all have six prehensile penises is something alluded to in only two or three episodes and briefly seen in only one; allegedly, Straczynski drew back from his original idea of showing a naked Centauri female.)

*Babylon 5* (1994–1998), created by writer and producer J. Michael Straczynski. Shown (from left) are Andreas Katsulas as Ambassador G'Kar, Mira Furlan as Ambassador Delenn, and Bill Mumy as Lennier. (Warner Bros. Television/Photofest)

Practicality also solved the problem of communication almost as simply as in *Star Trek*. Translation gadgets are mentioned but rarely seen, although the Vorlon ambassador always uses one. Most of the aliens whom we see the most speak excellent English, although some have Eastern European accents (the actress who played Ambassador Delenn is Croatian).

The humanoid aliens whom we see most frequently, in most episodes, are representatives of the Minbari, the Narn, and the Centauri; the action occasionally shifts to their worlds. Our ideas about these three alien races shift and deepen as the series progresses. At first the reptilian Narn seem aggressive and warlike; the Centauri rather jolly, if pompous; and the Minbari rather monastic, and even cowardly, since we learn early on that the last space battle in the Earth-Minbari War ended with their abject surrender. But one lesson of *Babylon 5* seems to be that it takes time to understand aliens; the second is that one can't judge an alien race by a single individual.

At the beginning of season 1, the Narn make an apparently unprovoked attack on a Centauri colony planet. It is a skirmish that heralds an all-out war, culminating in the destruction of the Narn homeworld and the enslavement of most surviving Narn. The Centauri victory was in part due to an alliance with the Shadows, negotiated by Ambassador Mollari himself, although this remained secret for a long time. The Shadows were generally seen as a threat to all civilizations in the Galaxy (which did not stop the Earth government apparently negotiating with them as well). In consequence, our sympathies transfer to the Narn, particularly since we learn how ruthless a power seeker Londo Mollari is. But Mollari is not necessarily a typical Centauri: his deputy on *Babylon 5* is Vir Cotto, perhaps the most sympathetic character in the whole series, thanks in large part to the acting of Stephen Furst.

The Minbari are also discovered to be much more complex than initially seen. Like Mollari, Ambassador Delenn is far from typical. She is of the religious caste, and we later meet the much less sympathetic warrior caste. We learn that the reason the Minbari surrendered to Earth had nothing to do with cowardice: they had come to believe that Minbari souls were reborn as Earth humans and that therefore there were profound links between humans and Minbari. At the end of season 1, Delenn puts the theory to the test by transforming herself into a new being, half-human and half-Minbari. She increasingly reveals herself to be an able leader and politician, and by the end of the fifth season she is president of the Interstellar Alliance, ready to lead aliens and humans together into peace and friendship. The story would have been continued in the planned five seasons of the spin-off, *Crusade*, but the show was canceled even before the first season was shown, in 1999.

*Edward James*

See also: *Farscape*; *Firefly/Serenity*; *Star Trek*.

## FURTHER READING

James, Edward and Farah Mendlesohn, editors. *The Parliament of Dreams: Conferring on* Babylon 5. Science Fiction Foundation, 1998.
Lancaster, Kurt. *Interacting with* Babylon 5. University of Texas Press, 2001.
Lane, Andy. *The Babylon File: The Definitive Unauthorised Guide to J. Michael Straczynski's TV Series* Babylon 5. Virgin, 1997 and 1999, 2 volumes.

## Banks, Iain M.

Iain Menzies Banks (1954–2013) wrote (often very experimental) mainstream fiction under the name Iain Banks and (often very traditional) science fiction under the name Iain M. Banks. From the publication of his first novel, *The Wasp Factory*, in 1984, his fiction was highly successful if sometimes controversial. All but three of the works published under the name Iain M. Banks (in total, nine novels, one novella, and a few short stories) were set in the universe of the Culture. This series, depicting a highly advanced spacefaring, left-leaning, utopian civilization, was the work that most fully engaged with the notion of the alien.

With the exception of some figures in the background of the novella, *The State of the Art*, every character in the Culture series is an alien. The seven or eight species that make up the group civilization that is the Culture are all humanoid, but none originate on Earth. The galaxy presented in these stories is teeming with intelligent life. As Banks describes it in "A Few Notes on the Culture," there are "a few dozen major spacefaring civilizations, hundreds of minor ones, tens of thousands of species who might develop space travel," not to mention those who have, for whatever reason, sublimed, retreated from space, or disappeared from the scene completely. Some of these are humanoid, as is the Culture, but most are not, yet the appearance and physical attributes of the different species plays no part in how the various civilizations interact. In *Excession*, more space is devoted to describing the raucous, militaristic culture of the Affront than is spent on their appearance. In a subplot of *Look to Windward*, we are introduced to the behemothaurs, vast, mysterious creatures that spend their lives circling the edges of the galaxy. However, they are mysterious not because of their immense size or their strange biology but because their life span, which can extend for tens of millions of years, makes them culturally unknowable to other beings.

Central to all of the Culture novels is the contention that "the nature of space itself determines the type of civilizations which will thrive there" (Notes). In other words, simply being a space-going civilization necessitates recognizing other such civilizations as equals; differences are a matter of culture, not race or appearance or taste or anything else. Therefore, an emotional response to the alien—hatred, disgust, fear, superiority, or inferiority, a response analogous to feelings between the races on Earth—has no place in Banks's universe.

Citizens of the Culture are long-lived. One character in *The Hydrogen Sonata* is some 10,000 years old. This is exceptional, but most people routinely live for several hundred years. When they die, their personalities can be translated into a cloned or an artificially created body, or they can be digitally stored until such time as they choose to be resurrected. In *Surface Detail* one character is killed and wakes aboard a Culture vessel, reborn in a new body, identical to her former body but without the tattoos that marked her as a slave. The body itself, whatever shape it might take, is not the person. We are specifically told that most Culture citizens change sex at least once during their lifetime, an experience that (in the utopian mode of these novels) simultaneously improves sexual experience and eliminates gender discrimination. The ability to change appearance more or less at will can be taken to even greater extremes. In *Matter*, one Culture agent has chosen to take the form of "a small, rootless, spherical bush made from tubes and wires" (81). In the first published Culture novel, *Consider Phlebas*, the protagonist is a shapeshifter who is an enemy of the Culture, but as the series goes on we see that all Culture citizens have the ability to shape-shift in any way they choose at any time they choose. And when form and appearance are so fluid, the only thing that matters in any relationship with the other, whether a fellow citizen or an alien race, is individual personality and culture.

There is also another way in which the novels engage with an alien other: Culture ships, orbitals, and many other facilities are under the control of Minds, powerful, independent artificial intelligences. But these Minds are not under the control of humans; they are autonomous beings, each an unquestioned and fully equal citizen of the Culture. Whether machine intelligence or biological intelligence, what matters in these books is the word "intelligence."

The universe explored within the Culture novels comes across as a utopia, though it is an ambiguous utopia at best. There are certainly actions pursued by the Culture that are at the very least questionable, and some in which the Culture clearly and intentionally ignores its own fairly loose moral strictures. Nevertheless, one of the ways in which the society is consistently utopian is in its disdain for any form of discrimination. On those occasions, in *The Player of Games*, for instance, or *Look to Windward*, when the Culture does come into contact with a society that practices any form of discrimination, whether based on class, caste, or any other metric, this not only justifies Culture enmity but is seen as a reason why the society in question is not yet fit to become one of the major spacefaring civilizations. Without ever needing to spell it out in so many words, the Culture novels make it plain that there is a practical as well as a moral issue at stake: all races, whatever form they might take, must be considered equal partners in the quest to survive in the hostile environment of space.

Thus, although in one sense the Culture novels are teeming with aliens, in another, more important sense, there are no aliens here. There are simply characters who may take one side or another in any war, who may behave nobly or with ill intent. But in the end they are all characters, it's just that some may be machine intelligences and some may be reptilian, or many-legged, or bushes, or possibly even human.

*Paul Kincaid*

*See also*: Liu, Cixin; Reynolds, Alastair; Vinge, Vernor.

**FURTHER READING**

Caroti, Simone. *The Culture Series of Iain M. Banks: A Critical Introduction*. McFarland, 2015.
Colebrook, Martyn and Katherine Cox, editors. *The Transgressive Iain Banks: Essays on a Writer Beyond Borders*. McFarland, 2013.
Kincaid, Paul. *Iain M. Banks*. University of Illinois Press, 2017. Modern Masters of Science Fiction.

## *The Body Snatchers*

Jack Finney's 1954 novel *The Body Snatchers*, first serialized in *Collier's*, imagines an extraterrestrial species of highly adaptable mimics. These alien beings travel the universe as spores in search of new planets to colonize, overrun, and wholly deplete before moving on to the next. In Finney's original narrative, these life-forms prove able to transform themselves into exact replicas of any body or object containing organic matter, although later adaptations tend to depict only the threat that these invaders pose to humans. Finney's aliens propagate themselves by means of uncanny pods of vegetable appearance: a large seedpod located near a person's body will begin to grow a duplicate body as the host sleeps. When the process has completed, the original body collapses into dust, and the duplicate body will emotionlessly pursue the agenda of the aliens while also retaining the memories of the original human that has been replaced. The uncanny effect that this disaffected duplicate has on loved ones mirrors a genuine psychiatric disorder called the Capgras delusion, in which an individual suspects another of having been replaced by an identical imposter. Finney's narrative, although far from original in its depiction of alien life-forms infiltrating human society through mimicry or "conversion" of host bodies—compare the parallel and sometimes convergent traditions inspired by Campbell's "Who Goes There?" (1938) and Heinlein's *The Puppet Masters* (1951)—has shown extraordinary staying power across media and in the broader cultural imagination. For example, the phrase "pod people," while itself rarely appearing in more direct adaptations of the story, has nevertheless entered *The Oxford English Dictionary*, which defines a "pod person" as someone "considered to be conformist, unoriginal, or emotionless; one who lacks personality or individuality."

The numerous film adaptations of Finney's novel are products of very different cultural moments, and each encodes somewhat different anxieties attendant on the specter of an invasion of body-snatching extraterrestrials. Finney himself consistently denied any particular allegorical or political intention, but this disclaimer has not prevented readings of the image of the subverted pod person as reflective of a number of possible Cold War anxieties: some scholars have interpreted the pervasive paranoia of the text as anticommunist, and others as anti-McCarthyite. Don Siegel's fairly close adaptation in his 1956 film *Invasion of the Body Snatchers* has provoked a comparable range of critical comment, and its success has inspired three other major Hollywood adaptations: Philip Kaufman's 1978 remake of the same title; Abel Ferrara's *Body Snatchers* (1993); and Oliver Hirschbiegel's *The Invasion* (2007). Kaufman's remake exchanges the small-town claustrophobia of the original for urban disaffection, exploring the San Francisco cultural scene in the age of conspiracy mania and cult pseudoscience. While the settings of these four films differ dramatically, their plots converge, developing into chase narratives against overwhelming odds, featuring, for example, attempts to hide among the pod people by restraining displays of emotion. Among these adaptations, the nature of the alien invaders may vary in certain respects, but all four share an anxiety about the coercive absorption of a person's individuality into an emotionless collective.

*Body Snatchers*, for instance, shifts the setting to a military base: the protagonist is a young woman upset about a stepparent having "replaced" her deceased mother, and her father is an EPA inspector visiting the base to assess the possible contamination of the surrounding area due to chemical and biological agents stored on the base. Themes of conformity in military hierarchies and familial dysfunction mesh well with and expand on the concerns of the original narrative. Similarly, *The Invasion* reconfigures the same premise in order to explore concepts of infection, contamination, and vulnerability in a thoroughly networked post–9/11 world: the pods have vanished entirely, but "pod people" are created through a viral infection. The invaders promise—and begin to deliver on—world peace, yet we also hear about plans to vaccinate entire populations of third-world countries with a free AIDS vaccine, presumably in order to spread the alien lifeform further, in a mirror image of colonial-imperialist domination. The protagonists succeed in finding a cure, and, because the original host bodies are not destroyed as in most versions, the process can be inoculated against and even reversed. The bleakness of the film's ending therefore lies not in the impending destruction of humanity, but its restoration—and the concomitant resumption of global violence.

Whatever the details of plot or the particular mechanism of reproduction, this generalized conception of imitative "pod people" has proved widely influential over the past half century or so. In addition to the adaptations detailed above, *The Body Snatchers* has inspired a bumper crop of indirect and direct retellings and parodies, including, for example, a Bugs Bunny short titled *Invasion of the Bunny Snatchers* (1992), in which extraterrestrial carrots terrorize the cartoon landscape, replacing familiar nemeses with flat, crudely drawn imitations. Several other unrelated films also appear to have drawn on the popularity of the concept—or at least the association of "pods" with insidious alien life—as in the case of Mickey Keating's science-fiction/horror film *Pod* (2015), and also *Los nuevos extraterrestres* [*The New Extraterrestrials*], a 1983 film directed by Juan Piquer Simón and marketed under the English-language title *Pod People*. This latter film is perhaps best known for airing in 1991 as the third episode of the third season of the "riffing" comedy series *Mystery Science Theater 3000*, in which the introducer of the film quips with reasonable accuracy about its tenuous relationship to Finney's pod-bearing aliens: "It has nothing to do with pods. It has nothing to do with people." If the "body snatchers" or "pod people" register the anxieties of their respective times, so too have they sometimes become vessels for levity.

*T. S. Miller*

See also: *Invasion of the Body Snatchers*; *V*; "Who Goes There?"

## FURTHER READING

Breen, Jon L. "The Fiction of Jack Finney." *They're Here...Invasion of the Body Snatchers: A Tribute*, edited by Kevin McCarthy and Edward Gorman, Berkley, 1999, pp. 23–36.

Seed, David. "Alien Invasions by Body Snatchers and Related Creatures." *Modern Gothic: A Reader*, edited by Victor Sage and Allen L. Smith, Manchester University Press, 1996, pp. 152–70.

Sloan, De Villo. "Self and Self-less in Campbell's 'Who Goes There?' and Finney's *Invasion of the Body Snatchers*." *Extrapolation*, vol. 29, no. 2, Summer 1988, pp. 179–88.

## Bowie, David

David Bowie (1947–2016) was the consummate rock star of the alien. His first musical expression of the alien theme was the 1969 single "Space Oddity," a response to Stanley Kubrick's *2001: A Space Odyssey*. The iconic ballad tells the story of Major Tom, the first man to explore space. Like *2001*'s Dave Bowman, Major Tom becomes lost in the greater cosmos, and the song ambiguously suggests an alien encounter. Bowie revisits the Major Tom character in the 1980 single "Ashes to Ashes," in which the alien encounter is made more explicit in the accompanying music video—one of the most iconic in the genre—where Major Tom appears to be held in alien captivity, and in the later songs "Hallo Spaceboy" (1996) and "Blackstar" (2016).

Bowie's most sustained performance of the alien began in 1972 with the release of his fifth album, *The Rise and Fall of Ziggy Stardust and the Spiders from Mars*. The songs formed a loose narrative morphing between the alien and a critique and embodiment of rock-star ascension and downfall. The songs "Moonage Daydream," "Starman," "Lady Stardust," and "Ziggy Stardust" create a tapestry of alien imagery and a desire for first contact, not only with the extraterrestrial, but with alterity within the broader compass of the human. Bowie embodied this alterity while performing as Ziggy Stardust, through elaborate costuming and stage shows, as the band toured throughout 1972 and 1973. The Ziggy character was an androgynous spaceman celebrating discovery, exuding sexuality, and embracing otherness. The character's sexual ambiguity was complemented by the ambiguity of Ziggy's origin: was the character meant to be a space alien or merely a rock star pretending to be an alien? Bowie's exploration of a fluid identity using the alien imagery of science fiction was a significant cultural moment and opened up the possibility of identity fluidity for later generations.

Bowie pushed the boundaries of the Ziggy character and alien identity further in the 1973 follow-up album *Aladdin Sane*, which Bowie referred to as "Ziggy Goes to America." Most of the album was written as the band toured the United States in late 1972. Although the songs primarily reflect Bowie's experiences in America and seldom delve directly into the alien theme, they are, nonetheless, songs of *alienation*. They are also songs written not by David Bowie, but by David Bowie *in the character of* Ziggy Stardust. In this sense, the *Aladdin Sane* album is just as alien-oriented as its predecessor. Three months after the release of *Aladdin Sane*, Bowie announced the dissolution of the Spiders and the end of the Ziggy persona at a London concert captured in the documentary film *Ziggy Stardust and the Spiders from Mars* (released 1983). The film shows the theatricality Bowie brought to the Ziggy character and the impact it had on the young fans of the era. Bowie's Ziggy look did not entirely disappear, however; the *Nineteen-Eighty-Four*–inspired *Diamond Dogs* (1974) continued to convey the alien alterity of Ziggy, especially in the cover art portraying a wereBowie (half dog, half androgyne) in front of a sign reading "The Strangest Living Curiosities."

Bowie's next foray into the alien was as the star of Nicholas Roeg's 1976 film *The Man who Fell to Earth*, based on the novel by Walter Tevis. Bowie portrays an alien who has come to Earth seeking water for his dying planet. After building an enormous financial empire by introducing transformative alien technologies into the economy, Bowie's alien, who goes by the name Thomas Jerome Newton, attempts to return to his homeworld after forging a relationship with a young hotel employee named Mary-Lou, who introduces Newton to the cultural practices and indulgences of late-20th-century America. Newton's alien identity is exposed by Dr. Nathan Bryce, a chemist hired to develop rocket fuel for Newton's spaceship (the interior of the ship appears on the album cover of Bowie's *Station to Station* [1976]), and in a memorable scene Newton reveals his alien self to Mary-Lou: removing hair, eyebrows, ears, contact lenses that hide his alien eyes, nipples, and genitalia. Newton fails to return home, first succumbing to the peculiar human addictions of alcohol and television and then falling victim to human avarice: a takeover of his financial holdings, followed by incarceration, leaves him trapped on Earth. Newton remains in captivity for years, finally escaping the facility in which he's been held when the door is left unlocked; it appears his captors have lost interest and forgotten him. As the film concludes, an alcoholic and broken Newton records alien rock songs to play on the airwaves, in hope that these messages will reach his home planet. Bowie offers a consummate performance of the alien other, alienation, and the addict in his portrayal of Newton. The cover art for *Low*, Bowie's next album, the first of the introspective "Berlin Trilogy," shows a somber Bowie as Newton, in sharp juxtaposition to the former Ziggy persona. The aforementioned "Ashes to Ashes," from the 1980 album *Scary Monsters*, serves as a capstone to this period of self-reflection after a decade exploring the alien in various forms.

The alien theme continued to be a part of Bowie's music as his career progressed, although increasingly through the lens of maturity and sober reflection. The 1997 album *Earthling* is, in part, a reflection on Ziggy Stardust 25 years later, evidenced particularly by the single "Little Wonder" and its music video. On the album cover, with his back to us, Bowie stands looking out upon an idyllic terrestrial landscape, costumed in an outfit that at once recalls and deflects Ziggy Stardust. The title itself conveys a linkage and an opposition to Bowie's past alien persona.

Bowie's final album, *Blackstar* (2016), recorded while he was terminally ill, brought Bowie full circle in his exploration of *human* experience through the lens of the alien theme. The album's inner jacket shows a starscape: the greater cosmos in which Major Tom lost himself, and in which David Bowie found much of his musical and lyrical inspiration.

*Michael R. Page*

See also: *Man Who Fell to Earth, The*; Sun Ra

**FURTHER READING**

Doggett, Peter. *The Man Who Sold the World: David Bowie and the 1970s*. Bodley Head, 2011.

Keen, Tony. "Gotta Make Way for the Homo Superior: Finding Philip K. Dick in David Bowie's 'Oh! You Pretty Things'." *Vector*, no. 286, Autumn 2017, pp. 20–21.

King, Maureen. "Future Legends: David Bowie and Science Fiction." *Trajectories of the Fantastic: Selected Essays from the Fourteenth International Conference on the Fantastic in the Arts*, edited by Michael A. Morrison, Greenwood, 1997, pp. 129–38.

## Brin, David

David Brin (1950–) is the author of more than a dozen novels and dozens more short stories. However, the work he did in creating the Uplift universe may be his most memorable legacy. Covering six novels and a few short pieces, it is an infinitely storyable universe full of Galactic-wise aliens and the Humans and other Terrans making their way among them.

The fundamental dynamic underpinning this universe is that of Uplift: the idea that while species evolve wherever they are, it takes intervention from a more senior race to Uplift a species from animal awareness to true conscious intelligence (sapience). Except for the long-departed and perhaps mythical Progenitors, every intelligent species in this universe can trace a particular lineage—Species A was uplifted by Species B, which was uplifted by Species E, who also uplifted Species C and D . . . etc. An uplifted (or client) species owes a debt of servitude for some (very long) period of time to their patrons, until they are "mature" enough to become patrons themselves. Aliens arrange themselves into clans based on these debts of servitude and obligation, and of course form alliances, enmities, and the other political and religious dynamics of space opera.

Humanity bursts on the scene some few hundred years into our future. They have, without knowing the universal context, uplifted chimpanzees and dolphins into intelligent tool users that are perfectly intelligent on their own and can converse in several languages. Humans believed that they have evolved on their own—in this Galactic society, a feat not achieved since the fabled Progenitors. The Galactics largely dismiss the Humans as wolflings, wrongly and rudely abandoned by some irresponsible and unidentified patron, unguided in the ways of Galactic society and politics. However, Humanity has uplifted two client species, and this grants them their own sort of status in this situation. The whole Terran clan goes about trying to survive in a universe mostly indifferent and sometimes hostile to their existence.

This universe is explicitly colonial, and, especially in the novels *Sundiver* (1980) and *Startide Rising* (1983), we are given some alien perspectives to show how well, but mostly how poorly, advanced alien patrons treat their clients. Genetic engineering is the most common technique of uplift, and many patrons are not above tinkering with client species to make them particularly servile, or even insane if the insanity serves military ends. Some species are more violent, others more diplomatic, but all have more experience of Galactic society than the poor bootstrapped Humans. Humans, in contrast, treat their two clients as well as they can, given their limitations. The starship *Streaker* of *Startide Rising* is captained by a brilliant dolphin and crewed by over 100 dolphins, with only seven humans and a chimpanzee aboard. In *The Uplift War* (1987), the focus turns to a world more favorable to chimpanzees.

This parallels a reading of world history that is popular in America, where (white, Christian) Americans are the scrappy upstarts overturning the tables of (stodgy, bureaucratic) European society, lifting themselves up without substantial help from the European powers and making themselves a new creative and energetic force in global affairs, rejecting colonial bureaucracy in favor of entrepreneurial dynamism that brings wealth and technological improvement to all, or at least to more than the old colonial system. This reading of American history insists that America has never been a colonial power, since it has never held formal colonies (Puerto Rico is an unincorporated territory, not a colony. It also has the unfortunate effect of representing colonialism as "uplift") and tends to elide the way that the foundation of American wealth and power was built on the backs of the American Indians from whom resources were forcibly taken and the African slaves whose labor and lives were stolen. However, this interpretation of world history may also function as a direct challenge to colonialist practices, depending on the reading.

Brin treats his aliens with respect and creativity. Aliens are treated as individuals with their own motives, not as monolithic representatives of their race. We get their first-person POVs on the action of the stories as well as those of the Terrans, as Brin tends to favor short chapters from dozens of different character perspectives to tell his stories. And especially in the *Uplift Storm* trilogy (1995–1998, starting with *Brightness Reef*), we are able to see humans and aliens coexisting in more collaborative and less combative ways. That branch of the story starts on a world declared as fallow, although fugitive ships of at least seven different species have all landed to start small, illegal colonies. (Life-bearing worlds are theoretically leased for millions of years at a time to different species, who are then required to vacate the planets and let them lie fallow for millions more, to allow biodiversity to spring up once more.) The members of these species all have their reasons for hiding, in some cases because they differ dramatically from their more Galactically powerful brethren. This is especially true for the Traeki, a species with a consensus consciousness made up of multiple semi-independent rings that are a pacifist offshoot from the dreadful Jophur we met in the previous novels, which were depicted as focused and remorseless killers.

While the Uplift universe may privilege Terrans in imagining even poor wolflings to be cleverer and more creative than the average Galactic (recordings of whale and dolphin music make a particular splash in Galactic pop culture, and even on the fallow world it is the late-coming Humans who first think to name the constellations), it places Humanity on an equal footing with a wildly diverse Galactic culture filled with aliens who might be violent and abusive but who can also be kind, humorous, inventive, and even humane in their turn.

*Karen Burnham*

See also: *Enemy Mine*; Niven, Larry; White, James.

**FURTHER READING**

Bogstad, Janice M. "*Startide Rising* by David Brin (1983)." *The Greenwood Encyclopedia of Science Fiction and Fantasy: Themes, Works, and Wonders*, edited by Gary Westfahl, Greenwood, 2005, pp. 1276–278.
Brin, David. "The Profession of Science Fiction, 35: A Shaman's View." *Foundation*, no. 39, Spring 1987, pp. 21–26.
Brin, David and Kevin Lenagh. *Contacting Aliens: An Illustrated Guide to David Brin's Uplift Universe*. Bantam, 2002.

## *The Brother from Another Planet*

Equal parts science fiction, religious parable, and racial satire, *The Brother from Another Planet* (1984) tells the story of a fugitive slave on the run from intergalactic bounty hunters. Crash-landing in the waters off New York City's Ellis Island, the mute, black-skinned humanoid finds himself a stranger in a strange land. Written in a week, shot in a month, and produced for a meager $350,000, according to Andrew Kopkind in *The Nation*, (October 6, 1984), *The Brother from Another*

*Planet* demonstrates the progressive possibilities of the space alien trope when it meets B-movie budgets and sensibilities.

In contrast to cosmic blockbusters of the era—George Lucas's *Star Wars* (1977) and Steven Spielberg's *Close Encounters of the Third Kind* (1977) and *E.T. the Extraterrestrial* (1982)—Director John Sayles, the avatar of American independent cinema, makes productive use of the alien-encounter narrative in a sly investigation of race, difference, and community.

There are three prominent tropes in Hollywood portrayals of extraterrestrial beings at work in the film: first, the *sublime encounter* with the otherworldly; second, the alien as *messianic figure*; and third, what I'm calling *alien mixers*—shorthand for social integration between humans and extraterrestrials. Hollywood consistently renders the moment of "first contact" between humans and extraterrestrials as being transcendent and frequently ecstatic. Such depictions tap a rich vein in American culture: the sublime. Following cultural historian David Nye (*American Technological Sublime*, 1994, xvi), we can detect in these dramatic moments "repeated experiences of awe and wonder, often tinged with an element of terror." Few filmmakers are as closely associated with this trope as Steven Spielberg, whose bravura renderings of first contact yield equally awestruck responses from audiences. Spielberg characteristically depicts this moment—an uncanny fusion of fear and fascination—from a Terran perspective. Consider the awe and wonder Spielberg infuses in such moments in *Close Encounters of the Third Kind*. Likewise, *E.T.* focuses primarily on the young boy Elliott's curiosity and astonishment about his otherworldly visitor. Only rarely do we see this cosmic encounter from an extraterrestrial point of view.

*The Brother from Another Planet* offers just this perspective. Sayles establishes the alien point of view in the film's opening minutes. Badly injured, the Brother—Joe Morton, in a masterful and moving performance—finds himself inside the historic immigration center, where he can hear the voices of millions of immigrants who have preceded him. The following morning, his torn-off leg regenerated, the Brother makes his way from lower Manhattan to Harlem, where his dark skin and mild manner allow him to blend into the neighborhood with relative ease. Sayles generates sympathy for the newcomer as he struggles to meet basic necessities: food, shelter, and, most urgently, shoes to conceal his horned, three-toed feet.

Frightened but enthralled with his new surroundings, the Brother appears a little lost to local residents, who razz him about his curious wardrobe but otherwise accept him as one of their own. Long before the term was popularized, the Brother's *intersectionality* elicits audience empathy: black, poor, mute, and recently arrived on these shores, the Brother is a quintessential fish out of water. Nonetheless, Sayles avoids romanticizing (or depoliticizing) the alien-encounter narrative by punctuating his script with ironic wit. Following a close encounter of the erotic kind, a glamorous singer (Dee Dee Bridgewater) tells the smitten Brother: "You were great in bed last night. But you're going to have to do something about those toenails." First contact has never been quite so sublime, nor as droll.

Eluding the police for unwittingly shoplifting from a Korean market, the Brother happens upon a religious supply store. He stands spellbound before a depiction of the crucifixion of Jesus Christ. Just then, a white cop pushes a black teenager against a parked car. The young brother is spread-eagled as the policeman pats him down. The Brother immediately recognizes this racial animus for what it is: state-sanctioned persecution of people of color. And just as Roman authorities persecuted Christ, alien bounty hunters (John Sayles and David Strathairn)—the original men in black—doggedly pursue the Brother. Moreover, like E.T, another alien as Christ figure, the Brother has miraculous healing powers that can bind wounds—and repair electronics—with the laying-on of hands. Finally, like an omniscient deity watching over his beloved community, the Brother removes his eye to surveil unsuspecting drug dealers and bring them to justice. In short, *The Brother from Another Planet* follows in a long line of movie aliens, most notably, perhaps, Klaatu, the messianic figure of Robert Wise's classic *The Day the Earth Stood Still* (1951).

Two of the most successful science-fiction media franchises—Gene Roddenberry's *Star Trek* and George Lucas's *Star Wars*—habitually depict social integration between humans and extraterrestrials as routine and unexceptional. From the bridge of the USS *Enterprise*, where Captain Kirk and Mr. Spock forge an enduring friendship, to the Mos Eisley cantina, where Luke Skywalker first meets Han Solo, starships and spaceports are depicted as spaces of diversity and inclusion. Typically, these alien mixers are set in the distant future or some far-off galaxy. By contrast, the Brother finds such a space in contemporary Harlem, at Odell's, a neighborhood watering hole where the barflies engage in some good-natured trash talk. The regulars at Odell's offer the Brother camaraderie and a shared sense of community. But, in a cunning take on the alien-mixer trope, at the film's conclusion it is fellow fugitives from the Brother's home planet who ultimately deliver him from the bounty hunters. Like the Brother, they have integrated into human society, where they have found liberty and freedom in the new world.

*Kevin Howley*

See also: *District 9*; *E.T. the Extra-Terrestrial*; *Man Who Fell to Earth, The*;

**FURTHER READING**

Boyd, Melba. "But Not the Blackness of Space: *The Brother from Another Planet* as Icon from the Underground." *Journal of the Fantastic in the Arts*, vol. 2, no. 2 (6), 1989, pp. 95–107.

Subramanian, Janani. "Alienating Identification: Black Identity in *The Brother from Another Planet* and *I Am Legend*." *Science Fiction Film & Television*, vol. 3, no. 1, 2010, pp. 37–56.

## Burroughs, Edgar Rice

Edgar Rice Burroughs (1875–1950) is perhaps best remembered for Tarzan, but in his day Burroughs was almost as well known for his many tales set on other planets. Chief among them is the 11-volume Mars series, beginning with "Under the Moons of Mars," first published as a six-part serial in the magazine *The All-Story* in 1912; it was then revised for book publication as *A Princess of Mars* (1917). The Mars novels were wildly successful in the fantastic pulp magazines and, along with the Tarzan books, made Burroughs the highest paid author of fantastic fiction in America throughout the first half of the 20th century. In addition to his Mars books, Burroughs published a five-volume series set on Venus, beginning with *Pirates of Venus* (1934), and a three-volume moon series, beginning with *The Moon Maid* (1926). *Beyond the Farthest Star*, a pair of novellas set on a planet far outside our galaxy, was published posthumously in 1964.

Author Edgar Rice Burroughs in 1929. Burroughs, best known as the author of the Tarzan series, wrote more than 70 books during the first half of the 20th century, including many novels of science fiction. (Library of Congress)

The first and most influential of Burroughs's planetary adventures is set on Mars, or Barsoom as it is called by its inhabitants. Burroughs's Mars is a desert-like, dying world kept alive only by the advanced science of the humanoid Red Martians. When John Carter, a former Confederate Army officer, reaches Mars through means far more mystical than scientific, he becomes something of a superman because of the planet's lesser gravity. After a series of adventures that are both violent and romantic, he rises to the top of the political hierarchy of the Red Martian city of Helium and marries their princess, the incomparable Dejah Thoris.

Although set on different worlds, Burroughs's other space adventures feature many of the same elements as his Mars books. A hero finds himself transported to another world—the oceans of Venus, the hollow interior of the moon, or the distant planet of Poloda—where native warriors of varying degrees of cultural sophistication give him a chance to prove his combat prowess while winning the heart of a beautiful native princess. The aliens the various heroes encounter also follow similar patterns. Each series features noble humanoid races with whom the hero quickly allies himself and more "savage" races that are often the hero's primary antagonist. The civilized Red Martians of Barsoom face off against the barbarian hordes of Green Martians; Venus's noble Vepaja must contend with the ape-like, cannibalistic Nobargans; the cultured U-gas fight against the brutish Kalkars of the moon's hollow interior; and Poloda, where the nations of Unis and Kapar are locked in an endless war.

The alien races are generally humanoid, with the more humanoid often being the most civilized, while the less humanoid, "savage" races often lack a recognizable culture. Perhaps the best example of this is the Red Martian civilization of the Barsoom novels, which reads like a cross between the age of chivalry and early-20th-century America. Notably, each of the series is also linked to a distinctly unchivalrous earthly conflict. John Carter was a solider in the American Civil War, the bloodiest single conflict in American history. The novels set on Venus, the moon, and Poloda all explore the evils of fascism. The second novel in the moon series was written in response to the Bolshevik Revolution of 1917. Collectively, the novels were written against the backdrop of two world wars, so it is perhaps not surprising that they seem tailor-made as wish fulfillment for the type of noble combat no longer possible in a world of machine guns, nerve gas, and atomic bombs.

The civilizations of the "noble" aliens are often defined by idealized characteristics. The Red Martian civilization, for example, is built on the principles of honorable combat. The best fighters are often the best people, while individuals who attempt to triumph through deceit and trickery are painted as villains who are eventually defeated. The Venusian city of Havatoo is founded on principles of scientific rationality. By privileging intellectual merit, the people of Havatoo have created a technologically advanced civilization and virtually eradicated crime. The U-gas of the moon, meanwhile, represent a cultured refinement and nobility that is imperiled by the Kalkars, clear analogs of Bolshevik and Communist revolutionaries.

Yet all of these civilizations could easily be dystopias. The combat-oriented Red Martians must always be ready for battle, and as the Barsoom novels often note, few Martians live long enough to die of old age. On Venus, Havatoo's focus on scientific rationality makes its society tyrannical. Individuals' employment, ability to have children, and even their very lives are determined by a council whose rulings are absolute. The moon's U-gas are a hereditary ruling class, and while their own history is left vague, it is difficult to forget that their earthly analogs often built their wealth on the backs of enslaved and indentured peoples.

That the various noble civilizations in Burroughs's extraplanetary stories are portrayed as ideals rather than as cautionary tales points to the novels' deep connections with chivalric values. Although the stories' connection to chivalric honor may have contributed to their popularity, it also ignores the costs associated with white, male, WASP cultural supremacy—which contributed to the global conflicts Burroughs's works attempt to distance themselves from. Yet Burroughs's tales of heroic adventures are part of science fiction's DNA and have significantly influenced generations of science-fiction fans. Ray Bradbury's *The Martian Chronicles* (1950) are directly influenced by Burroughs's depiction of Mars, and George Lucas has admitted that the similarities between the Mars novels and *Star Wars* are far from coincidental. James Cameron's *Avatar* (2009) has many of the elements of a Burroughs space adventure, and Cameron credits the Mars books as an inspiration for the film. But there is danger in buying into Burroughs's heroic fantasies without thinking critically about their imperialist underpinnings. Modern-day fans of the genre must be careful that, in looking to Burroughs for inspiration, they do not ignore the negative effects of such beliefs, both within science fiction and in the physical world of everyday life.

*Jennifer Kavetsky*

See also: *Avatar*; *Star Wars*; Weinbaum, Stanley G.

**FURTHER READING**

DeGraw, Sharon. "Burroughs." *The Subject of Race in American Science Fiction*, edited by Sharon DeGraw, Routledge, 2007, pp. 1–52.
Lupoff, Richard. *Barsoom: Edgar Rice Burroughs and the Martian Vision*. Mirage, 1976.
Porges, Irwin. *Edgar Rice Burroughs: The Man Who Created Tarzan*. Brigham Young University Press, 1975; New York: Ballantine, 1976.

## Butler, Octavia E.

In addition to winning multiple Hugo and Nebula Awards and a PEN American Centre lifetime achievement award, Octavia Butler (1947–2006) was the first science-fiction writer to receive a MacArthur Foundation "Genius" Grant. Issues of gender, race, and otherness feature prominently in much of her work. The focus of her extraterrestrial fiction is not merely the entanglement of these complex elements but the ways in which they interrelate when the very nature, and future, of humanity is questioned. By exploring the interplay of essentialism, interdependency, and alien-human hybridity, Butler adds philosophical depth and complex realism to many of her most notable alien representations: the Tlic in her short story "Bloodchild" (1984), the Oankali in her Xenogenesis series, and the Stranger-Communities in her short story "Amnesty" (2003).

In "Bloodchild" (1984), humans have taken refuge on an alien planet where they are confined to a preserve, and the indigenous Tlic use them as hosts for the birth of their ravenous, wormlike young. Butler could have presented the Tlic as a monolithic, monstrous "other," but instead she describes them as intelligent and cultured—seemingly attempting to reforge a naturally parasitic relationship into a symbiotic one. While some humans are willing hosts, eager to accept the interdependency of their situation, others maintain a more essentialist view, detesting the Tlic for their practice of reproductive surrogacy. In the end, the main character, a young man named Gan, agrees to be a host and becomes a hybrid figure, both in terms of his physiology and his ideology. The story is often read as an allegory of slavery, but Butler always denied that this was her intent. Issues of power and psychological manipulation cannot simply be ignored, but the story introduces a multifaceted view of morality and identity, which is further developed in many of Butler's later works.

In *Dawn* (1987), the first installment in Butler's Xenogenesis trilogy, Lilith awakens aboard an alien ship, having been rescued from the ruins of Earth. She is irrationally revolted by the tentacled form of the deeply alien, three-sexed Oankali, establishing a clear link between difference and distrust. The Oankali (somewhat reminiscent of the Tlic) have an unusual breeding imperative. Each extremely long-lived generation of this nomadic, starfaring race must interbreed with an alien species, sharing their DNA and creating a new generation of Oankali distinctly different from their predecessors. Afflicted with sterility, humankind will be able to reproduce only if they bear hybrid offspring. Emotionally, Lilith desires to defend the essence of her human identity, but, as she learns more about the Oankali and is augmented—given enhanced strength, speed, healing ability, and memory—she begins to question the perceived sanctity of her species. Eventually, Lilith is forced to serve as intermediary between the Oankali and her fellow humans, a role for which she is rejected by the humans she seeks to help. She is neither alien enough to truly understand the Oankali nor human enough for her own people, who, despite her new physical capabilities, consider her to be philosophically subhuman, an animal without independent will or worth used simply for breeding.

*Adulthood Rites* (1988) and *Imago* (1989), the other two novels in Butler's Xenogenisis trilogy, are set on a newly regenerated Earth after the results of human-Oankali interbreeding become evident. Instead of being monstrous, as Lilith had feared, the construct children are presented as rational, intelligent, and respectful of life. Human and Oankali alike are portrayed as information systems in keeping with a posthumanistic reading—cells, organs, bodies, collectives, world ships. Instead of achieving a biological "consensus," humanity attempts to override physical desire intellectually and is thus unable to embrace the aliens' holistic perspective.

"Amnesty" (2003), like "Bloodchild" and the novels of Xenogenesis, deals with power dynamics, humanity's perhaps innate distrust of difference, and matters of mutually beneficial—but often unequal and disquieting—relationships. Noah, another aptly named protagonist, is an alien abductee. Having been returned to Earth, she chooses to work as a translator for the alien Stranger-Communities, functioning as an intermediary between them and humanity. Much like Lilith, Noah suffers greatly at the hands of her own people as a result of their distrust. Gender is perhaps less a factor in this short story than it is in the other works discussed herein, but species, physical boundaries, and the necessity of practical compromise at the expense of idealistic independence all recur throughout.

Despite the regularity with which extraterrestrials are used as stand-ins for minorities, artificially homogenized others, and persons a writer might prefer to leave unnamed, that is not Butler's approach in these works. The Tlic and Stranger-Communities complicate and challenge what it means to be human and exist to prompt difficult questions. Furthermore, instead of simply representing objective, external observers, the Tlic, Stranger-Communities, and especially the Oankali are far from detached figures of implied contrast. Butler's work as a whole resists being collapsed to fit within a singular analytical framework—presenting behaviors, situations, and emotional responses without imposing binary conclusions such as right and wrong. No one is ever free of external influence. There is no isolated, autonomous self, and this message has continued relevance to an increasingly posthuman society. Fundamentally, through Butler's depictions of extraterrestrials, humanity's strengths and faults are explored, as is the inevitability of compromise among interdependent individuals and species. Identity is ultimately portrayed as more constructivist than essentialist, and hybridity can be viewed as a natural state, even if the emotional appeal of essentialism remains a torment to many of Butler's characters, if not readers.

*Lauren Maguire*

*See also*: Gwyneth Jones's Aleutians; Le Guin, Ursula K.; Tepper, Sheri S.

## FURTHER READING

Butler, Octavia E. *Bloodchild and Other Stories*. Seven Stories, 1996.

Canavan, Gerry. *Octavia E. Butler*. University of Illinois Press, 2016. Modern Masters of Science Fiction.

Dowdall, Lisa. "Treasured Strangers: Race, Biopolitics, and the Human in Octavia E. Butler's Xenogenesis Series." *Science Fiction Studies*, vol. 44, no. 3, November 2017, pp. 486–503.

# C

## Card, Orson Scott

Orson Scott Card (1951–) is an American author who has written in many genres but who is best known for his science-fiction novels. Perhaps the most famous of these is the Nebula- and Hugo Award–winning *Ender's Game* (1985), which was turned into a film and is the opening novel of the saga of Andrew "Ender" Wiggin. While not the best example with which to discuss aliens in Card's work, it is an important work in the canon, as it introduces the alien race the "Buggers"—later referred to in *Ender's Shadow* (1999) as the "Formics"—one of the prominent alien races in the Ender universe.

Card's Ender Saga is alien-encounter science fiction, and the first three novels are chiefly concerned with the philosophy behind first contact with aliens. In *Ender's Game*, this first contact has already happened. Humankind has been through two devastating wars with the Buggers and is preparing for a third. Gifted children are taken into a battle school to train for fighting the Buggers. It is not until the end of the novel that the Buggers are encountered once again.

However, the Buggers are always in the collective thoughts of humankind. Described as insectoid creatures, with a hive mind structure of less sentient workers or soldiers controlled by a queen, they are completely alien to humankind. They are a constant threat to humankind because of their otherness, which Ender and his commanders cannot bring themselves to understand. There is no way to communicate with them, nor is there any way that the two cultures can live together. To the humans, the Buggers must simply be destroyed before they can destroy what is left of humankind. It is perhaps their lack of active presence in the novel that provides the sense of tension, the threat.

The twist is that the games that Ender was playing in the battle school were not games; he was in fact in control of the human fleet sent to eradicate the Buggers' homeworld. Without knowing it, Ender has committed the genocide of an entire race. After he leaves the battle school, he encounters the last remaining egg of a Bugger queen that tells him, in an ironic twist, that the Buggers had no idea that the humans were sentient until it was too late. Through fear it was so easy for humankind to kill something alien to them, but is it really the otherness that they fear? This concept gives Card the ethical dilemma and discussion that are central to the entire Ender Saga: what is it to be human and alien? Card's skill as a writer lies in the moral messages of his writing, of which the Ender Saga is a primary example.

However, Card wrote *Ender's Game* to provide the backstory for *Speaker for the Dead* (1986), which was drafted first but published as a sequel, and which also won the Nebula and Hugo awards. While *Ender's Game* was perhaps a commentary on the military machine, it is through *Speaker for the Dead*, set 3,000 years later, that Card uses the prominence of aliens to really ask moral questions. On a planet that the humans dub Lusitania, a second alien race has been found. They are called "Pequeninos," which is Portuguese for "little ones": Piggies for short. *Speaker for the Dead* could be described as a commentary on the Catholic conquest of South America, and on colonialism in general. With the genocide of the Buggers still within human memory, the colonists are conscious of protecting the Piggies' culture. They are protected by a wall, which the piggies see as keeping them away from the rest of the universe. For the humans it is a protective method, but for the aliens it is restrictive.

The Piggies are less threatening than the Buggers, being smaller than humans and having porcine features. They climb trees, much like apes, and it is easy for the humans to look down on them, both literally and figuratively. Here Card seems to use similarity rather than the otherness of the Buggers to further the philosophical discussion. The fence that protects them has resonances of a zoo, and the Piggies have been relegated to something to be observed by humans rather than interacted with. Their strange culture and rituals, which include the brutal murders of two human characters, are difficult to understand; one character even refers to them as "savages." Their actions make more sense as the alien biology of the planet is understood: the Piggies reproduce through a dangerous virus, the Descolada, that breaks down genetic material and allows it to bond with others. This is problematic, as the Piggies' genders are described as Male and Female and their social status as Wives, Husbands, and Brothers, but the very nature of Piggie biology is more complex than this.

An interesting concept that is introduced by Card and that furthers the philosophy of alien encounters is the hierarchy of foreignness, which is a five-point scale from "dju," nonsentient and unable to understand, to "utlänning," a stranger recognized as human. This discussion of the morality of humankind continues into the third novel, *Xenocide* (1992), where once again humanity has ordered the destruction of an alien race, this time to wipe out the Descolada virus and punish the colonists of Lusitania for helping the Piggies to advance their culture. These moral discussions continue throughout the rest of the Ender novels, so far eight, beginning with *Children of the Mind* (1996); and the Formic Wars novels, set during the first wars with the Buggers, which to date include four novels, beginning with *Earth Unaware* (2012). A number of these novels revisit the same discursive ground as Card's earlier novels.

*Michael J. Hollows*

*See also*: Brin, David; Heinlein, Robert A.; Sterling, Bruce.

## FURTHER READING

Bowman, Cole. "Bugger All!: The Clash of Cultures in *Ender's Game*." *Ender's Game and Philosophy: the Logic Gate Is Down*, edited by Kevin S. Decker, Wiley, 2013, pp. 101–111.

Campbell, James. "Kill the Bugger: *Ender's Game* and the Question of Heteronormality." *Science Fiction Studies*, vol. 36, no. 3, 2009, pp. 490–507.

Collings, Michael R. *In the Image of God: Theme, Characterization, and Landscape in the Fiction of Orson Scott Card*. Greenwood, 1990.

## Cavendish, Margaret

Margaret Cavendish (née Lucas) (1623–1673) was the youngest child of a prominent Royalist family. With the outbreak of the English Civil war, she traveled to France with Queen Henrietta Maria. There she met the Duke (then Marquess) of Newcastle, recently widowed and one of Charles I's generals. The Duke of Newcastle is best known for his sponsorship of dressage and the management of horses, but he was also a scientist interested in ballistics. He encouraged his young wife in both her scientific and literary interests, and in the Restoration she emerged as an energetic voice in the new science. She was the first woman to attend a Royal Society Meeting in 1667 and was a correspondent of Thomas Hobbes, René Descartes, and Robert Boyle.

Margaret Cavendish published extensively under her own name at a time when most women published under a pseudonym or anonymously for fear of social censure. A polymath, Cavendish's writings touched on a vast swathe of topics, including philosophy, politics, gender roles, and numerous scientific disciplines; she also published in a wide variety of genres, including plays, essays, memoirs, and prose romances.

One of these romances, *The Description of a New World, Called the Blazing-World*, is often hailed as an early example of science fiction because of its depiction of travel between multiple worlds and the strange inhabitants of one of these planets, the titular Blazing-World. The story principally concerns a noblewoman (whom we later discover comes from a planet other than Earth and is therefore herself an alien) abducted from her homeland and the sole survivor of a trip to the North Pole, where lies the only bridge between two different worlds. She is brought to the emperor of the new world, who immediately falls in love with her and makes her empress, giving her leave to reorganize society on this world. Cavendish even inserts herself into the narrative as a character whose soul befriends that of the empress and teaches her to imagine worlds (authorship, essentially), becoming "Platonick Lovers, although they were both Femals" (part I), a situation with strong homoerotic undertones despite the impossibility of a physical relationship, as their two planets are not coterminous.

Initially published in 1666 as a companion to Cavendish's scientific tract, *Observations upon Experimental Philosophy*, much of the text is dedicated to explanatory dialogue in several scientific fields, including astronomy, geology, meteorology, optics, chemistry, and biology. Taken with discussions on politics, religion, and spirituality, the alien setting and creatures of *The Blazing-World* exist in order to outline the form of a utopian society; whereas medieval and early modern writers set utopias in distant countries and undiscovered islands, Cavendish uses an alien world in order to outline her notion of the ideal society.

The aliens in Cavendish's work can be so described because they are the inhabitants of other worlds, though their forms and society are familiar. The empress and her native people appear basically human in form and culture—indeed, it is only when Cavendish inserts herself into the narrative that we discover that the empress's original world was not Earth but a world similar to our own. The Blazing-World, for its part, is inhabited by a large variety of anthropomorphized animal species who "went upright as men" (part I) but have the shape of bears, foxes, worms, ants, spiders, lice, and birds (including parrots, magpies, jackdaws, etc.), among others. Some of the other species draw on a classical mythological register, including sirens and satyrs (which are also anthropomorphized animals) and giants. Finally, several of the species on this world appear human but have a variety of unusual skin tones like green, purple, and orange, as foreign to the empress as they would be to Cavendish's own audience.

The wide variety of sentient species on this world derives from Cavendish's stated belief in "Infinite Nature" (part I). This is particularly manifest when the Empress and her mystical advisors discuss the vast array of possible worlds represented by the stars—and when the character Cavendish wonders whether she could conquer such a world and install herself as empress, we are informed that all worlds are inhabited by intelligent species with similar methods of governance and standing armies as our own world. That so many of the Blazing-World's species are animals imbued with human form and intelligence reflects Cavendish's advocacy on behalf of animals (for instance, in her opposition to animal testing). Likewise, the empress's assignation of a specific scientific discipline to become the field of study and expertise for each of the various species (e.g., "The Bear-men were to be her Experimental Philosophers, the Bird-men her Astronomers," and so on [part I]) shows animals as sentient beings fully capable of participating in human-like society and science. The peaceful coexistence of the various species of animals, mythical creatures, and rainbow array of human skin tones is a strong statement is favor of diversity but also comes with an important caveat: Cavendish believes such unity is made possible only by the presence of a strong ruler and common religion that forestalls the divisions and strife that would otherwise occur—an argument that suggests that, after the strife of the English Civil War, it was possible for Britons of varying backgrounds and ethnicities to be united, so long as they adhered to a shared political and religious ideology.

The text itself is rather uneven in tone and genre, alternating between adventure, utopianism, and allegorical debate. It eventually ends with an early example of the alien-invasion narrative when the empress returns to her original planet at the head of a powerful navy. This armada includes the scientific advances that the Blazing-World's aliens have developed at the empress's prompting, including early submarines. In contrast to later alien-invasion narratives, however, neither she nor her alien subjects remain on this world to rule; they intervened only to ensure that the empress's original nation now dominates this world. Despite the uneven tone and massive amounts of exposition, *The Blazing-World* is a groundbreaking text, both because it articulates a deliberately female perspective on early science fiction and because it represents an early example of tropes popular in later science fiction, such as the idea of multiple worlds, the use of alien worlds for utopian purposes, and the alien-invasion narrative.

Readers interested in other early aliens and the use of other worlds for satirical or utopian purposes are directed to Cyrano de Bergerac's *Comical History of the States and Empires of the Moon* (1657) and *The States and Empires of the Sun* (1662).

*Steve Asselin*

*See also*: Flammarion, Camille.

## FURTHER READING

Hanlon, Aaron. "Margaret Cavendish's Anthropocene Worlds." *New Literary History*, vol. 47, no. 1, 2016, pp. 49–66.
Roberts, Adam. "Seventeenth-Century Science Fiction." *The History of Science Fiction*, edited by Adam Roberts, Palgrave Macmillan, 2006, pp. 36–63.
Whitaker, Katie. *Mad Madge: Margaret Cavendish, Duchess of Newcastle, Royalist, Writer and Romantic.* Chatto & Windus, 2003.

## Cherryh, C. J.

Most of the science-fiction novels by Carolyn Janice Cherry (1942–), who writes as C. J. Cherryh, are set in the future history timeline of the Union/Alliance Universe. The timeline includes human exploration and expansion into space and the future histories of a number of sentient, alien species. Within the Union/Alliance timeline, "Compact Space" refers to stories concerning seven alien races: four oxygen-breathing species and three methane-breathing species. Although Cherryh's fiction cannot be reduced to a single trope or strategy, her fiction does consistently—insistently—represent and confront the other.

Cherryh makes the encounter with otherness central to her work. On her website, Cherryh discusses some of her considerations when developing an alien species and its culture: the physical environment from which the species emerges; the kinds of dwelling they inhabit, their diet, and their means of food production/apprehension; their eating habits and rituals; their knowledge-production and -dissemination systems; their beliefs, customs, and rituals regarding death and the afterlife; and their notions of self and of the universe/reality.

One of Cherryh's common strategies is to place a single human among an alien race. This has been the inspiration behind her ongoing "Foreigner" series (19 volumes by 2018), but it was a common theme in earlier fiction too. For example, in *Brothers of Earth* (1976), Cherryh places a human among the nemet, whose society resembles ancient Rome. While Kurt Morgan initially chafes at the values and strictures of nemet society, he begins to identify with them more and more. In *The Faded Sun: Kesrith* (1978), Cherryh places a single human, Sten Duncan, among the mri, a tall, slender race of warriors with dark complexions and bronze or golden manes. In the same novel, she places George Stavros among the regul, a short, squat species that contracts out its physical labor (and wars). Both Duncan and Stavros learn the ways of the aliens but for very different reasons. In *The Pride of Chanur* (1982), Cherryh introduces a lone human, Tully, among the han, a species that in many ways resembles an upright lion. Tully struggles mightily to fit in among the han and to earn his place among them. In *Cuckoo's Egg* (1985), Cherryh introduces a human infant, Haras (aka Thorn), into shounin society in an effort to make him a "native informant." While Haras has little to compare his life experiences with, his upbringing tests the bounds of his mental and physical capabilities. Finally, in her long-running Foreigner series (19 volumes to date), she has a lone ambassador, Bren, living among the atevi and struggling to learn their complex mores. Each of these examples allows the human reader to occupy the marginalized subject position, to identify (in some way) as the othered. That shared subject position can be fraught with shortcomings, however; although the narrative device invites "us" to engage with otherness, just who are "we"? The narrative experience of othering reads differently for those readers who already occupy a marginalized position.

A significant variation of Cherryh's strategy is to represent radical otherness. Cherryh offers a number of aliens with whom neither common ground nor understanding can be attained. For example, in *Hunter of Worlds* (1977), Cherryh features the iduve, a humanoid species with indigo skin, dark hair, and amethyst eyes, who make no distinctions regarding sex or gender. However, they are ruthless hunters who take what they want without regard for any other species. They believe in their own superiority, and they will not compromise. And yet, Cherryh does not fall into the trap of representing otherness as purely or simply evil. *Serpent's Reach* (1980) features the majat, a nonhumanoid life-form that resembles insects in its appearance, social structure, and hive mind. Further, the hive mind offers the majat an effective immortality. When the human Raen a Sul hant Methmaren enters the hive, she finds it difficult to understand the motivations of the majat. In the Chanur series (1982–1992), Cherryh creates three methane-breathing species, the tc'a, the chi, and the knnnn. The tc'a feature a "multipartite brain" that enables/necessitates multipart speech (12). Tc'a speech is represented as a "matrix," listing all the simultaneous elements in a grid, while the knnnn's speech and motivations remain utterly alien. Finally, the alien in *Voyager in Night* (1984) is the corrupted computer memory of an unknown and unnamed alien species. The "personalities" of the computer program are signified by symbols (<>, ((())), and =====), and they show neither understanding of nor mercy toward the three humans aboard their vessel.

In Cherryh's xenological SF, some of the alien species have human analogs. For example, nemet society clearly draws from Roman society, and both the ahnit (*Wave without a Shore*, 1981) and the People (*Hestia*, 1979) parallel indigenous Earth populations that were destroyed by colonizers. Others have nonhuman analogs, such as the han (lions) and the majat (hive insects), while the calibans and ariels from *Forty Thousand in Gehenna* (1983) resemble lizards. So, while absolute otherness cannot be represented, Cherryh presents otherness from a variety of human and nonhuman perspectives. She represents other modes of being, and frequently (except in *Hestia* and *Wave without a Shore*) she represents humans as marginal and powerless while the alien is powerful.

The human among the aliens assumes a familiar ideology and mind-set, while the aliens represent another. At the same time, the narrative places the human in the role of the other, placing many readers into what may be an unfamiliar position. This strategy simultaneously assumes that the "human" ideology and mind-set resemble a particular Western subject and that the reader does not already inhabit a marginalized subjectivity. The epigraph of *Wave without a Shore* reads: "Man is the measure of all things." In the case of C. J. Cherryh, perhaps we could amend Protagoras to read: "The alien is the measure of man."

*Ritch Calvin*

*See also*: Brin, David; Card, Orson Scott; Heinlein, Robert A.

**FURTHER READING**

Heidkamp, Bernie. "Responses to the Alien Mother in Post-Maternal Cultures: C. J. Cherryh and Orson Scott Card." *Science Fiction Studies*, vol. 23, no. 3, 1996, pp. 339–54.

Monk, Patricia. "Gulf of Other Minds: Alien Contact in the Science Fiction of C. J. Cherryh." *Foundation*, no. 37, Autumn 1986, pp. 5–21.

Stinson, J. G. "The Human as Other in C. J. Cherryh." *The Cherryh Odyssey*, edited by Edward Carmien, Wildside/Borgo, 2004, pp. 133–48.

## *The Clangers*

*The Clangers* (1969–1972, 1974, 2015–) is a stop-motion animation for children made by Smallfilms in the United Kingdom. The original company consisted of Oliver Postgate (writer, narrator, and animator) and Peter Firmin (puppet maker and designer), their children, and Firmin's wife and had already made a number of animations for children, such as *Noggin the Nog* (1959–1965, 1979), *Ivor the Engine* (1959, 1975–1977), *Pingwings* (1961–1965), and *Pogles' Wood* (1965–1968). In one of the *Noggin the Nog* books, *Noggin and the Moonmouse* (1967), an alien crashed into a horse trough and it is this design that inspired Postgate and Firmin when commissioned by the BBC to make a new animation in color. Postgate wanted to tap into the popularity of the Apollo moon missions. Smallfilms made two series of 13 episodes, each 15 minutes long, and initially broadcast during children's afternoon television, often just before the news. A final episode, "Vote for Froglet," was shown on the day of the second general election in 1974. When the series was revived in 2015, it was written by Dan Postgate, Dave Ingham, Myles McLeod, Lisa Akhurst, Chris Parke, and others. It was directed by Chris Tichborne and Mole Hill, with music by John Du Prez.

The Clangers are a largely friendly group of aliens, very distinct from the threatening invaders usually depicted in *Doctor Who* and clearly designed to be positive role models. They interact with the Soup Dragon—who provides them with Green Soup—the Iron Chicken, the three Froglets, and the Sky Moos, and they live in literal harmony with musical trees, a lonely musical cloud, and the planet of the Hoots. Their encounters with humans are less successful—a salvaged television set is too noisy, a view through a telescope of New York leads them to abandon a space mission, and having offered blue string pudding to an astronaut, they scare him off.

Each episode begins either with a shot of the Earth from space or of empty space, with a voiceover either describing Earth as busy, noisy, and industrial or as cozy, green, and full of life before the camera pans to the Clangers' unnamed planet, which is somewhere within the solar system (although the script sometimes does not distinguish between stars and planets).

We meet only the family of Clangers—Major Clanger (suggesting an unseen military system), Mother, Small, Tiny, and Granny, as well as three that remain unnamed. Their planet is described as cozy, especially in the caves that riddle its interior, with a suggestion that they spend little time on the surface. There appears to be an atmosphere—although the Clangers can survive brief expeditions into orbit. Musical trees, whose fruit-like notes can provide levitation for a boat, flourish outdoors. The Clangers can build rockets, although they are not entirely in control of the equipment. Their technology and engineering skills are advanced—they rebuild the Iron Chicken from its individual parts—but they are fearful of industrialization. When they find a machine that mass-produces plastic goods, it is rejected and disposed of.

Rather like the Earth-based Wombles—in books written by Elisabeth Beresford (1968–1976) and animated for BBC television by FilmFair (1973–1975)—the narratives were often built around the characters finding and dealing with rubbish and debris and making use of it. Tiny Clanger is frequently depicted in space with a magnet or net collecting these items. Portrayed as brave, inquisitive, and (usually) moral, she offers a strong female role model who in the second series is more prominent than the male Small Clanger. At the same time, both the Soup Dragon and Iron Chicken become mothers in the course of the series—albeit with no obvious male partners.

Central to the series is food, with repeated visits to the Soup Dragon or attempts to deliver Green Soup to the dining room. Sharing food is fine—the dragon provides it, although he dislikes being taken for granted, and visitors are discouraged from helping themselves. Supposedly everyone likes blue string pudding, but this is not true of the Astronaut, the Iron Chick (who prefers nuts and bolts, like his mother), or the Froglets. When Tiny finds what she takes to be gold coins, she hoards them, briefly seduced by capitalism in a society based on gift and exchange, but these are shared when it turns out they are actually chocolate money. Food is central to children's fiction from at least *Alice's Adventures in Wonderland* (1865) to *His Dark Materials* (1995–2000), with mealtimes idealized as a place for community and sanctuary. The program's broadcast at a time when families had just eaten or were about to eat makes it even more appropriate.

Community is also explored through shared music and performance, through woodwind and brass instruments, with the Clangers communicating with each other with sounds like swanee whistles. While the Soup Dragon enjoys psychedelic rock, the others are scared by it. Music allows interaction with a cloud, the Hoots and the Hoot planet, and other quasi-sentient objects. The music for the series was provided by Smallfilms' regular composer, Vernon Elliott, a bassoonist, composer, and conductor.

During an episode of "The Sea Devils" (1972) in *Doctor Who*, the Master is seen watching the episode "The Intruder" and takes it to be a documentary about aliens. In 2001, a soundtrack album of music and sound effects was released by Jonny Trunk, with the first act of *The Clangers Opera* with a libretto by Postgate.

In 2015, Postgate's son Dan Postgate agreed to make a new series. After two specials, a series of 52 episodes was produced, with Dan writing some of the scripts and Michael Palin doing the narration. A further series followed in 2017. While some computer animation was used, this augmented the stop-motion technique rather than replacing it. It was more obviously repetitive in its use of specific sequences and more educational, such as in the exploration of the Solfège scale and colors in "I am the Eggbot." The original series has enchanted several generations of viewers and still holds young children captivated.

*Andrew M. Butler*

See also: *Aliens Love Underpants*; Dr. Xargle; *Teletubbies*.

**FURTHER READING**

Postgate, Oliver. *Seeing Things: An Autobiography*, illustrated by Peter Firmin. Sidgwick & Jackson, 2000.

Trunk, Jonny, editor. *The Art of Smallfilms: The Work of Oliver Postgate & Peter Firmin*. Four Corners, 2014.


## Clarke, Arthur C.

Arthur C. Clarke (1917–2008) was the most influential British science-fiction (SF) writer of the postwar period and one of the most influential SF writers of the 20th century. Born in Somerset in 1917, Clarke began his professional writing career in earnest in the mid-1940s when he started publishing stories in American SF magazines and continued until the early 21st century, by which time his output mainly consisted of collaborations with other authors.

Clarke's liminal position between two distinct SF traditions—the British and the American—is reflected in his early reading tastes. Clarke was influenced by British writers such as H. G. Wells, Lord Dunsany, and particularly Olaf Stapledon, and by U.S. writers John W. Campbell, E. E. "Doc" Smith, and Jack Williamson.

In his earliest stories, Clarke reflects the humanist bias common to alien-encounter stories from the "Golden Age" of American SF: according to Isaac Asimov, John W. Campbell, editor of *Astounding Science Fiction*, refused to publish any story that implied human inferiority to an alien species. The Martian civilization in "Loophole" (1946), for instance, fearful of humanity's growing technological capacities, issues a directive warning humanity not to attempt space travel—in response, humanity use matter teleportation to transport atomic bombs to the red planet and thereby wipe out Martian civilization. In another early story, "Rescue Party" (1946), an alien expedition, following radio signals beamed out from a ruined Earth, encounters a massive fleet of human spaceships in search of a new homeworld and comments approvingly on humanity's technological ambition. The aliens in these early stories matter less than the humanity with which they are contrasted: in both cases, the alien merely provides an outsider viewpoint from which Clarke may extol the resourcefulness and tenacity of the human race.

Beginning in the late 1940s, however, Clarke's attitude toward the alien undergoes a change. "History Lesson" (1949), for example, can be read as a corrective to "Rescue Party," insofar as the relative significance of the human and the alien is reversed. Adopting a similar structure (an alien race, this time from Venus, arrives to survey to a lifeless Earth), "History Lesson" takes greater care to paint a convincing picture of an alien world. The Venusians are an amphibious reptilian race, technologically advanced yet peaceable, while Venus itself is presented as a "warm, rich world" covered in oceans. Clarke made some noble attempts throughout his career to depict such genuinely nonhuman races: the intelligent, kangaroo-like "Atheleni" of "Second Dawn" (1951), the vast, jellyfish-like natives of Jupiter in "A Meeting with Medusa" (1971), and the aquatic "sea scorpions" depicted in *The Songs of Distant Earth* (1986) are good examples here.

More significantly, in "History Lesson," humanity appears in a humbler role than in previous stories, perhaps reflecting a diminished faith in notions of human progress brought about by the tremendous violence of the 1940s. The human "creatures" of the story, extinct by the time the Venusians reach Earth, are characterized as intelligent but irrational warmongers, their legacy reduced to a sole cultural artifact—a Walt Disney cartoon—rescued from the dead planet by the Venusians. In a much later work, *Rendezvous with Rama* (1973), Clarke reverses this narrative structure. Here, humanity encounters an apparently lifeless generational spaceship, *Rama*, as it passes through the solar system and attempts, without much success, to learn something of its alien architects. Even here, however, the awesome scale of the *Rama* spaceship serves as a sobering reminder of humanity's own technological limitations.

British science-fiction novelist, futurist, and inventor Arthur C. Clarke poses in front of a radio telescope, ca. 1981. (David Farrell/Getty Images)

This sense of human humility in the face of powerful alien forces soon became the dominant characteristic of Clarke's portrayal of human-alien interaction. *Childhood's End* (1953), for example, depicts the arrival to Earth of a powerful race of aliens called the Overlords, who resemble biblical demons, complete with "leathery wings," "little horns," and "barbed tail[s]" (ch. 5). These alien beings defy their fiendish appearance, working to transform earthly civilization into a utopia. Their ultimate objective, however, concerns not the whole of humanity but only its children: it is revealed that the Overlords have been sent by an even more powerful and mysterious alien entity, the Overmind, to guide humanity's children toward the next stage of human evolution. The children of Earth, having formed a kind of hive mind, eventually merge with the Overmind, transcending the material world and destroying Earth—and the rest of humanity—in the process. Similarly, in *2001: A Space Odyssey* (1968), astronaut David Bowman, after arriving to Iapetus (a moon of Saturn) to investigate strange transmissions coming from the region, is inexplicably transported to another stellar system by an advanced yet unseen alien race who transform him into a powerful uplifted being called the Star Child.

The view of the alien that emerges from these two works suggests a paradoxical sense of inferiority to *and* equivalence with the alien. Although humanity is generally portrayed as inferior to the alien entities, there is also a recurrent emphasis on the possibility for harmonious union with these beings, evident in the depictions of human-alien interface in *Childhood's End* and *2001*. Humanity, it is suggested, by embracing the radical possibilities for mutual communion offered by more advanced alien entities, such as the Overmind, the Star Child, or the Great Ones of *The City and the Stars* (1956), may itself achieve evolutionary transcendence, thereby ensuring its own survival. The presence of the alien thus hints at a vision of radical harmony between disparate kinds of beings—a powerful concept in the Cold War era, with its ever-present threat of nuclear holocaust between opposing peoples—as well as the transcendence of humanity's own technological and ontological limitations.

From its initial deployment as a hubristic narrative device to reflect human achievement, then, the alien in Clarke's work eventually comes to represent a utopian means for surmounting human limitations. In this way, notwithstanding his few depictions of genuinely alien Others, Clarke's aliens most often reflect very human preoccupations—but "human" understood in an expanded metaphysical, rather than narrowly chauvinistic, sense.

*Thomas Connolly*

*See also*: Clement, Hal; Heinlein, Robert A.; Stapledon, Olaf.

## FURTHER READING

Hollow, John. *Against the Night, the Stars: The Science Fiction of Arthur C. Clarke*. Ohio University Press, 1987.
Olander, Joseph D. and Martin Harry Greenberg, editors. *Arthur C. Clarke*. Taplinger, 1977.
Reid, Robin Anne. *Arthur C. Clarke: A Critical Companion*. Greenwood, 1997.

## Clement, Hal

Hal Clement (1922–2003), whose real name was Harry Clement Stubbs, was one of the writers most closely connected to the idea of hard science fiction: science fiction that attempts to avoid the violation of known scientific laws. An experienced bomber pilot during World War II, he held degrees in astronomy, education, and chemistry and spent most of his working life teaching astronomy and chemistry at Milton Academy in Massachusetts, one of the top preparatory schools in the United States.

Clement is best remembered for his first three novels: *Needle* (1949), which was followed by a much later sequel, *Iceworld* (1951), and most importantly *Mission of Gravity* (1953), which engendered two sequels. The three original books all saw their first appearances as serials in *Astounding Science Fiction*, then edited by John W. Campbell Jr. Clement also wrote several other novels and many short stories, all in a similar vein. His aliens were among the least humanlike ever created, and the worlds that he built for them were exceptionally well-realized.

For *Needle* he created an intelligent, jellyfish-like alien that lived symbiotically inside other life-forms. The novel is thought to have been the inspiration for the classic schlock 1950s sci-fi film *The Brain from Planet Arous*; the Trill symbionts of the *Star Trek* universe might also trace their origins to Clement's novel. As the novel opens, one such being, a police officer of sorts known as the Hunter, pursues a dastardly criminal of the same species to Earth, where their spaceships crash in the Pacific Ocean, killing their hosts. The Hunter immediately chooses a new host, a teenager named Robert Kinnaird, only to discover that the boy is leaving the Pacific island where he picked up the alien, and where the Hunter's quarry remains, in order to return to school on the other side of North America. The Hunter must then identify himself to his host, explain the situation, and convince Robert to return home so that he can capture or execute his prey, who has by this time also taken over a human host of its own, Robert's father. The Hunter and the teen must work together to trick the criminal into leaving Mr. Kinnaird's body and then kill it.

*Iceworld* has a somewhat similar plot, concerning an alien police officer (the viewpoint character) who must team up with human beings on Earth, an incredibly cold place from the police officer's point of view, in order to stop a drug ring that is attempting to smuggle tobacco to a planet circling the star Sirius, where the natives find it both addictive and deadly. What is unique about *Iceworld* is the alien point of view, which makes Earth seem the alien planet.

*Mission of Gravity* is Clement's masterpiece and the first novel he set on an alien world. The planet Mesklin is a significantly flattened sphere with a mass 16 times Jupiter's and a surface gravity that varies from 665 g at the poles to a mere 3 g at the equator. The protagonist, Barlennan, a methane-breathing, centipede-like creature designed by evolution to function successfully across the planet's varying environment, is a ship's captain by trade. Barlennan and crew are near the equator on their ship the *Bree* when they encounter Charles Lackland, a human being and, from Barlennan's point of view, a truly bizarre alien, who enlists them to recover a probe that crashed near the pole. Aided by human technology, the *Bree* sails to the pole, having adventures with a variety of well-realized alien life-forms as it goes, and Barlennan eventually recovers the probe. He refuses to return it to the Earth man, however, until he has brokered a deal that will lead to the gradual release of human technology and knowledge to his civilization. As preface to the closing installment in *Astounding*, Clement wrote the article "Whirligig World," which detailed the physical characteristics of Mesklin and how it works. The article is a classic example of world building.

Barlennan and his crew return in *Star Light* (1970), where they are sent to the planet Dhrawn by their human colleagues. Dhrawn is a high-gravity planet the size of Jupiter, which also poses a challenge to its Mesklinite explorers in having no high-pressure hydrogen in its atmosphere. *Star Light* ties the Mesklinites to an earlier novel, *Close to Critical*, which had appeared in *Astounding* in 1958, through the character of Elsie "Easy" Hoffman, a linguist and diplomatic liaison well versed in Mesklinite language and culture. In *Close to Critical*, Easy, then aged 12, is trapped in a bathyscaphe with a younger alien boy, a Drommian, an otter-like species that measures 10 feet in length in adulthood, during a planetary exploration narratively similar to that in *Mission of Gravity*. The young Easy Hoffman is among Clement's most endearing characters. A later novella, *Under* (2000), returns Barlennan and crew to Mesklin for another adventure.

Another novel from the 1950s, which went straight to book publication, was *Cycle of Fire* (1957), which depicts another instance of human/alien cooperation. Here, a human space traveler named Nils Kruger crashes on the planet Abyormen, a planet that fluctuates between periods of extreme heat and cold. Kruger makes contact with a resident alien named Dar Lang Ahn, a squat and beclawed humanoid, who has also crashed his glider far from home, and the two trek across the planetary geography to the haven of Dar's home before the hot cycle begins, becoming good friends along the way and calling to mind the classic meeting of Jarvis and Tweel in Stanley Weinbaum's "A Martian Odyssey."

Clement remains a writer to whom experts invariably refer when they want to discuss science fiction's ability to create believable alien worlds inhabited by believable alien beings, though in recent years his aliens have occasionally been criticized as too human in their thought patterns and emotions, something Clement, a physical scientist, may simply have been less interested in attempting.

*Michael M. Levy and Michael R. Page*

*See also*: Brin, David; Clarke, Arthur C.; Heinlein, Robert A.

### FURTHER READING

Drake, H. L. "An Interview with Hal Clement." *Extrapolation*, vol. 40, no. 2, 1999, pp. 129–45.
Hassler, Donald M. *Hal Clement*. Starmont, 1982.
Trunick, Perry A. "Hal Clement's Alien: Bridging the Gap." *Foundation*, no. 36, Summer 1986, pp. 10–21.

## *Close Encounters of the Third Kind*

The aliens of *Close Encounters of the Third Kind* (1977) form a distinct contrast with those that were represented in 1950s science-fiction films in an era of UFO sightings begun by George Adamski's 1946 close encounter. SF films of the 1950s provided a series of Cold War parables, either offering terrifying warnings about the possibility of invasion by Russian or Chinese communist forces—within recent memory of Pearl Harbor and World War II—or else satirizing such worries. The invasion would typically begin in a small town, witnessed early on by an everyman figure whom no one would believe. Some invasions are stopped within city limits, others get as far as the familiar landmarks of New York or Washington, D.C. *Close Encounters* has its spaceships observed in out-of-the-way places, but in the end they offer escape from the humdrum world of wage slavery and family life for a chosen individual. The narrative is not about facing the potential end of the world and trying to prevent it but—in the immediate aftermath of American involvement in Vietnam—escaping from a crisis to another world. It may be worth noting that production was under way during the American Bicentennial.

Director Steven Spielberg had been working on the project since the start of the 1970s, when Erich von Däniken's *Chariots of the Gods?* (1967) became a bestseller and as various stories about the so-called Bermuda Triangle appeared, culminating with Charles Berlitz's *The Bermuda Triangle* (1974). For his title, Spielberg drew on J. Allen Hynek's typology: a sighting of a UFO within 500 feet; a sighting with a physical effect; and first contact. The much-rewritten script was put to one side while Spielberg made the hit *Jaws* (1975), which gave him a lot of creative control over the film. Delays in special effects and editing pushed back its release, meaning that it was not in direct competition with the other blockbuster of 1977, *Star Wars* (dir. George Lucas).

The film begins with the discovery by scientists, in the Sonoran Desert, of the planes of Flight 19 that have been missing for 30 years—a staple of UFO lore. Meanwhile, in Indiana, Jillian Guiler and her son, Barry, witness a UFO; in a second encounter, the child is taken. Elsewhere in the state, electrician Roy Neary has an encounter with a UFO that causes burning to his face, and he becomes obsessed with the encounter, causing his wife to leave him. Neary and Guile both see a news story about a disaster near Devils Tower, realize that the monolith is connected to the aliens, and make their way there. Scientists are already at Devils Tower, intending to use music to communicate with arriving UFOs. The Flight 19 crews are released from the mothership, and Neary is escorted to join the aliens before the spaceship departs.

The "mothership" from *Close Encounters of the Third Kind* (1977), directed by Steven Spielberg. (Columbia Pictures/Photofest)

Robin Wood describes the aliens as "frail, little, asexual, childlike" (177), and for most of the film they remain offscreen. Various spaceships are seen through the film, most notably a red glow, often behind the others, that is a kind of homage to Tinkerbell and *Peter Pan*, bringing with it an intertext of Neverland and the Lost Boys. While Spielberg was to return to J. M. Barrie's play most problematically with *Hook* (1991), he has tended to favor a man-child protagonist who has never quite grown up. Wood suggests that Neary is "[d]ivested of the encumbrances of wife and family" (177) and has regressed to an earlier level of maturity, sculpting a Devils Tower from mashed potato in the manner of a toddler playing with food. In Spielberg's next representation of alien encounters, *E.T. the Extra-Terrestrial* (1982), he brings its titular alien child into close contact with 10-year-old Elliott and his friends and locates adults as potential enemies. Elliott, child of a broken family, does not get to escape; as Wood suggests, Spielberg can only reassert "the 'essential' goodness of family life in the face of all the evidence he himself provides" (176). Post *Star Wars*, many Hollywood science-fiction films worked to recoup a sense of American privilege, heroism, and paternalism, segueing seamlessly into Reaganism. Nearly 30 later, Spielberg offers a more adult vision of aliens with the Martians in *War of the Worlds* (2005), with Tom Cruise playing a protagonist who seems keener to reconstruct his family after a more destructive meeting with aliens. The importance of patriarchy in the face of the other remains.

The aliens of *Close Encounters* clearly have technology superior to humanity's. Hugh Ruppersburg argues that "The aliens are exalted by their own technological sophistication. They behave as exalted beings. . . . Technology has redeemed them from original sin, made them godlike, sent to us with the best of intentions. . . . And as if to underscore their mission, they choose to carry up into space a man who has lost his family and job struggling to prove that he actually saw them" (162). In the process, they seem unaware of the impact that they have on their witnesses or the families of the humans that they have kidnapped. Neary's family suffer neglect thanks to his growing obsession, and at the end of the film they are abandoned. Neary, meanwhile, is one of 12 encounterers to make it to Devils Tower—where the alien mothership lands—and is selected to be one of 12 astronauts at the rendezvous. His shift from disciple to messiah is perhaps undercut by the sense that—unlike the alien-uplifted Dave Bowman in *2001: A Space Odyssey* (1968)—he does not return to Earth with the ability to bring salvation but rather stays in an unseen heaven.

A bit more footage of the aliens on the mothership was added to the Special Edition of the film released in 1980, with other scenes trimmed. Spielberg evidently thought better of this, as in 1998 he removed this new scene for the LaserDisc version, which has since been marketed as the Collector's Edition. We are left with a sense of the sublime driven by special effects.

*Andrew M. Butler*

See also: Condon Report, The; *E.T. the Extra-Terrestrial*; Grays; Roswell (Place).

**FURTHER READING**

Gordon, Andrew. "Close Encounters: The Gospel According to Steven Spielberg." *Literature Film Quarterly*, vol. 8, no. 3, 1980, pp. 156–64.
Ruppersburg, Hugh. "The Alien Messiah in Recent Science Fiction Films." *Journal of Popular Film & Television*, vol. 14, no. 4, 1987, pp. 158–66.
Wood, Robin. *Hollywood from Vietnam to Reagan*. Columbia University Press, 1986.

## *Cloverfield*

*Cloverfield* (2008), directed by Matt Reeves and produced by J. J. Abrams and Bryan Burk, is a highly successful science-fiction horror blockbuster. Rooted in conspiracy theories about aliens, the film is presented as found footage from a personal camcorder recovered by the United States Department of Defense that was presumably leaked and made available to the spectator. The plot follows six young New Yorkers who witness a catastrophic attack on the city while videotaping a friend's farewell party and end up fleeing from the otherworldly perpetrator of mayhem: a giant, reptilian monster.

*Cloverfield*'s immersive aesthetic is based on the thematic concept of the entire film being found footage. With the city in flames and loved ones dying all around, one of the characters operates a handheld camcorder, doing his best to document the cataclysmic event. The subjective camera is designed to give us a sense that we are part of the diegetic world. The visual effects encompass the cinéma vérité, single point of view, handheld camera style of the film while seamlessly integrating the CG character—the alien monster central to the narrative. As the camera swoops and jiggles in the style of a nonprofessional videographer, we catch glimpses of the monster stomping and crashing through the streets of New York City. *Cloverfield* incorporates the aesthetic of 9/11 footage, and references to the events of that day are made throughout the film.

The alien monster in *Cloverfield* was originally conceived by producer J. J. Abrams, designed by artist Neville Page, and developed by visual effects supervisor Kevin Blank and the Tippett Studio. Affectionately named "Clover" by the production staff, the creature is a colossal, lizard-like monstrosity with long, thin limbs and white skin, as if it has had very little exposure to sunlight. Following the *Jaws* rule, for most of the film the monster is not presented clearly but is shrouded in destruction and chaos within the limited frame of a handheld camera, out of full frame. But the more the creature is revealed, the more the audience is able to see of its body, muscles, and face, and even the veins and pulsating clots just beneath the surface of its translucent skin become visible. Smaller "parasite" creatures fall off its body to attack the humans. Clover's minions are dog-sized beasts with a "rabid, bounding nature" and the ability to climb walls. When bitten by one of the parasites, the human victim becomes ill and bleeds profusely, mainly from the eyes, and shortly after, the torso expands and explodes.

The concept of a giant creature wrecking a major metropolis is not new. *King Kong* (Merian C. Cooper, Ernest B. Schoedsack, 1933) was directly responsible for the making of *The Beast from 20,000 Fathoms* (Eugène Lorié, 1953), which, in turn, helped to inspire Ishirô Honda's highly influential *Gojira* (1954). *Cloverfield* was inspired by this groundbreaking film, whose immediate success triggered the rise of *Kaiju* (a Japanese film genre that features giant monsters) and caught the eye of American filmmakers. In that same decade, Hollywood established the cycle of the giant creature film and cemented the conventions of the genre with *Them!* (Gordon Douglas, 1954), *It Came from Beneath the Sea* (Robert Gordon, 1954), and *Tarantula* (Jack Arnold, 1955), among others. In 1956, an American version of *Gojira* came out, entitled *Godzilla, King of the Monsters!* (Ishirô Honda, Terry Morse, 1956) and made specifically to suit the American public.

Released in a period of renewed interest in the genre—after the *Jurassic Park* trilogy (Steven Spielberg, 1993, 1997, 2001), the remake of *Godzilla* (Roland Emmerich, 1998), and the remake of *King Kong* (Peter Jackson, 2005)—*Cloverfield* follows the pattern of the giant monster flick, although it functions as a contemporary reimagining of the low-budget sci-fi B films of the 1950s. Just like its cinematic relatives, the Clover monster is seemingly resistant to military force and wreaks havoc in an urban landscape. However, Clover is not the conventional radioactive mutant creature of the Cold War narratives, but an alien abomination in the mold of H. P. Lovecraft's Great Old Ones—alien gods from outer space who once ruled the Earth and who are meant to return in an age of chaos and violence to reclaim their dominion and wipe out humanity. Not by chance, the emergence of Clover remains a mystery and culminates in deadly encounters between the monster and the hapless humans who cross its path. *Cloverfield* breaks previous conventions of the genre, such as providing a happy ending, as it does not provide a possibility for resolution. The film ends in tragedy for the main characters, and the situation is unresolved for them and the audience.

The *Cloverfield* monster was first referred to in the viral marketing campaign for the film, including a recording of its roar, foreign news clips about a monster attack, and sonar images. A similar creature appears in the manga series *Cloverfield/Kishin* (2008) by Yoshiki Togawa, which serves as a spin-off to the film. While a proper sequel to *Cloverfield* has not yet been produced, the film did serve as the first installment in a cross-media franchise set in a common universe. In recent years, giant monsters from outer space (or from the depths of Earth) have returned as a recurring trope in sci-fi productions like *Pacific Rim* (Guillermo del Toro, 2013) and *HELP* (Justin Lin, 2015). The latter, whose narrative bears strong similarities to *Cloverfield*, is Google Spotlight Stories' first immersive film, a 360-degree live-action in which a meteor falls in Los Angeles, spawning a gigantic alien monster. The second installment of the *Cloverfield* franchise was released in 2016 and, unsurprisingly, totally abandoned the concept of *kaiju*. Directed by Dan Trachtenberg, produced by J. J. Abrams and Lindsey Weber, and written by Josh Campbell, *10 Cloverfield Lane* does not build upon the story line established by its predecessor, although it features the same elements, the frightening atmosphere, and the theme of the alien invasion of Earth.

*Lúcio Reis-Filho*

*See also*: Lovecraft, H. P.; *Pacific Rim*.

**FURTHER READING**

Arp, Robert and Patricia Brace. "*Cloverfield*, Super 8, and the Morality of Terrorism." *The Philosophy of J. J. Abrams*, edited by Patricia Brace and Robert Arp, University Press of Kentucky, 2014, pp. 293–314.

Hantke, Steffen. "The Return of the Giant Creature: *Cloverfield* and Political Opposition to the War on Terror." *Extrapolation*, vol. 51, no. 2, 2010, pp. 235–57.

Wilson, Scott. "When Does the Hurting Stop? *Cloverfield* and the (Re)Enabling of Fantasy in the Post-9/11 City." *Terror and the Cinematic Sublime: Essays on Violence and the Unpresentable in Post-9/11 Films*, edited by Todd A. Comer and Lloyd I. Vayo, McFarland, 2012, pp. 29–41.

## The Condon Report

The Condon Report (1968–1969) is the informal name for the document officially titled *Scientific Study of Unidentified Flying Objects*. The study was commissioned by the U.S. Air Force and conducted at the University of Colorado in the late 1960s as the University of Colorado UFO Project. The report, delivered to the Air Force in late 1968 and released publicly in 1969, was assembled by a committee of scientists headed by physicist Edward Condon, after whom both the committee and the report are named, and stated that the study of UFOs would not add to scientific knowledge. It has been controversial among UFO conspiracy theorists since its inception due to its denial of UFOs as a significant scientific phenomenon.

The purpose of the project, according to the original Air Force request, was to analyze reports of UFO or alien sightings and to determine if there was scientific value in continuing to study these reports. As their source material they took the records from Project Blue Book—the Air Force's own collection and study of UFO-related material from 1952 on—and from NICAP (National Investigations Committee on Aerial Phenomena) and APRO (Aerial Phenomena Research Organization), two civilian groups concerned with the UFO phenomenon. The Condon Committee also analyzed sightings reported during the tenure of their investigation, which lasted from 1966 to 1968. Previous to the Condon project, a less formal study had been made of the Project Blue Book records. This report, the O'Brien Report, suggested a larger investigation and led directly to the formation of the Condon Committee.

The report consists of the data and analysis conducted by the team, as well as a brief section at the beginning called "Conclusions and Recommendations," written by Condon himself. This section, which serves as an introduction, summarizes the project by stating that "Our general conclusion is that nothing has come from the study of UFOs in the past 21 years that has added to scientific knowledge. Careful consideration of the record as it is available to us leads us to conclude that further extensive study of UFOs probably cannot be justified in the expectation that science will be advanced thereby" (1).

As a result of the Condon Report, the government ceased study of UFO phenomena, and Project Blue Book was closed down. The report was considered the final—and negative—word on the existence of UFOs

American physicist Edward U. Condon, author of the 1968 report titled *Scientific Study of Unidentified Flying Objects,* discusses UFOs at the University of Colorado at Boulder in Boulder, Colorado, January 1969. (Carl Iwasaki/ The LIFE Images Collection/Getty Images)

by the general community, but UFO enthusiasts have been skeptical of the report from the very start. In fact, one of the original members of the committee, David Saunders, a psychology professor who was let go from the project partway through because of "incompetence," wrote a book, *UFOs? Yes! Where the Condon Committee Went Wrong*, that was published almost concurrently with the Condon Report, detailing his experience on the committee. In the book, Saunders claims that the committee deliberately covered up or ignored actual evidence of UFOs and that he was fired from the project for releasing a memo showing that those in charge of the project were intending to have a negative result from the beginning. Condon, on the other hand, claims never to have received a copy of that memo and disputes many of Saunders's other claims. Major Donald Keyhoe, an author of several books on UFOs, claimed the Condon Report was a whitewash for the Air Force. In 1972, astronomer J. Allen Hynek published a book about UFOs, *The UFO Experience: A Scientific Inquiry*, in which he stated that the Condon Report was biased and that Condon's introduction tried to hide that there actually was evidence for UFOs hidden within the case studies. Almost 20 years after the publication of the report, in 1987, physicist Peter Sturrock published "An Analysis of the Condon Report on the Colorado UFO Project," which scrutinized the Condon Report and critiqued its method; since then, UFOlogists have continued to criticize the Condon Report as anything from an out-and-out cover-up to a good-faith effort that was methodically flawed.

*Elizabeth Miller*

*See also*: Aliens Did Not Build the Pyramids; Grays; Roswell (Place).

## FURTHER READING

Condon, Edward U., editor. *Scientific Study of Unidentified Flying Objects*. Bantam, 1969.
Saunders, David R. *UFOs? Yes! Where the Condon Committee Went Wrong*. World Publications, 1969.
Sturrock, Peter A. *The UFO Enigma. A New Review of the Physical Evidence*. Warner, 1999.

## Contact

*Contact: A Novel* (1985), astronomer and Pulitzer Prize–winning science writer Carl Sagan's only published work of fiction, and the Robert Zemeckis film (1987) based on it explore the planetary, societal, and personal realizations and revelations that result when an alien radio transmission emanating from the vicinity of the star Vega is intercepted by an earthbound radio telescope facility in New Mexico. The story's central character, Dr. Eleanor "Ellie" Arroway, whom we meet as a precocious, rebellious, and awe-filled child in both novel and film, is a SETI (Search for Extraterrestrial Intelligence) scientist who is part of—or, in the book, leads—the team of radio astronomers, astrophysicists, and engineers that first detects this "Message," as it comes to be called. Buried beneath the alien signal's surface layer of prime numbers, Ellie's team and a worldwide coalition of other

*Contact* (1997), directed by Robert Zemeckis, and starring Jodie Foster as Eleanor "Ellie" Arroway. (Warner Bros./Photofest)

radio observatories eventually detect and decode three more layers of information: an alarming return-transmission of Hitler's nationalistic 1936 Olympic Opening Ceremony speech (the first television signal strong enough to leave Earth's atmosphere); a series of detailed blueprints for what is likely a vehicle intended for human interstellar travel; and the primer needed to decipher the schematics.

The Machine is built on the eve of the Millennium, after years of political wrangling, transnational suspicion and cooperation, sabotage and death, and questions about the differences between religious faith and scientific seeking lie at the core of the story. In the novel, Ellie and four international colleagues—and in the movie, Ellie alone—climb aboard the vehicle, fall through the spinning bezels of the Machine, and are whisked through a series of wormholes to the center of the galaxy and, at last, an affecting rendezvous with the aliens. Rather than the "little green men" Ellie is accused of having wasted her life searching for, the aliens manifest for each of the human travelers as someone dearly loved by them. For Ellie, this is her father, Theodore Arroway, who passed away when she was a child, and, in the film version, encouraged the curiosity that led her to become a scientist but took away with him, when he died, her sense of connectedness and her ability to love without reserve.

The meeting with the aliens is brief. In fact, despite the story's title, the moment of contact itself covers fewer than 30 pages of a 434-page book and takes up only a small fragment of the film's running time. Although it is true that the aliens as physical beings remain peripheral for much of the narrative, their presence in the form of their message—both capital "M" and small "m"—is what drives the plot and is consequential for humanity on every scale, from the global to the personal. In reaction to the aliens' existence, institutions and individuals alike find themselves suddenly forced to recontextualize their accomplishments and concerns within a vastly expanded universal framework. Predictably, and in an echo of the typical alien-invasion story arc, some can only conceive of the extraterrestrials as a physical or existential threat: for the Soviets (who still existed when the novel was written), the Machine is seen as a possible "Trojan horse" that will open a gateway for an alien army; for many others, who fear the collapse of their worldview and a concomitant loss of meaning, the way to neutralize this terrifying sense of diminishment is by strengthening ties to existing religions or forming new ones that variously deny, demonize, or embrace the alien presence.

Because Sagan was an optimist, however, his aliens have as much power to inspire hope and cooperation as they do fear and withdrawal. For the first time in history, the deciphering of the Message and the building of the Machine present all of Earth's cultures and governments with a common problem to solve and a common goal to accomplish. The worldwide pooling of financial and intellectual resources and the focusing of energies in this one area result in an unprecedented moment of global stability and a previously unknown level of intergovernmental collaboration. But governments will be governments, and distrust and one-upmanship are unavoidable in their interactions with one another; the purest form of cooperation in *Contact* occurs among the scientists whose task it is to bring the plan to fruition so that the aliens, who seem neutral and scientific themselves, may at last be known and understood.

The question of what the aliens might reveal about the origin of the universe and its sentient beings, and whether this will justify a scientific or religious doctrine, is truly the central tension of the story. Ellie experiences a challenger to her perspective in the form of Palmer Joss, an unorthodox religious figure who is both her foil and her philosophical complement—and who in the film is a one-time and perhaps future love interest. Although in the novel the relationship begins with a verbal standoff, soon Ellie and Joss find commonality and respect for the other's faith in their own worldview. And this commonality is echoed and strengthened for Ellie in her encounter with the alien who appears in her father's form. From him, she learns that his species perhaps sees no difference between a scientific not-knowing and the religious version. For them, these are one and the same: ancient as they themselves are (he mentions billions of years), they know there was another, older species that created the transit system that brought Ellie to this rendezvous point—but that civilization disappeared and left behind only hints of its existence that his people continuously seek to discover and understand. In this, Ellie finds a parallel to the common human belief in a creator and learns two things that the film perfectly articulates: that at their core, religion and science both seek to discover answers, and that connectedness is the one thing that makes existence tolerable.

*Susana Brower*

*See also*: *Abyss, The*; *Arrival*; *E.T. the Extra-Terrestrial*.

## FURTHER READING

Gulyas, Aaron J. *Extraterrestrials and the American Zeitgeist: Alien Contact Tales Since the 1950s*. McFarland, 2013.
Newman, Marc T. "The Land of Faery as Cosmic Cheat: A Lewisian Analysis of Robert Zemeckis' *Contact*." *Journal of Religion & Popular Culture*, vol. 22, no. 1, 2010, Special Section, pp. 1–23.
Sagan, Carl. "Science Fiction: A Personal View." *Broca's Brain*, edited by Carl Sagan, Random House, 1979, pp. 37–146.

## *Cowboys and Aliens*

*Cowboys and Aliens* (2011) is a movie from Industrial Light and Magic, directed by Jon Favreau and based on a graphic novel of the same name by Scott Mitchell Rosenberg (2006). In New Mexico Territory, 1873, the town of Absolution is attacked by "demons," and people are abducted, forcing outlaw Daniel Craig, cattle baron Harrison Ford, and lone traveler Olivia Wilde to band together with residents to rescue them and exact revenge. As the power of the demons becomes apparent, the townsfolk also join with Chiracahua Apache and bandit groups to combat their mutual enemy. Gradual rapprochement between the groups is a major narrative theme, with the Apache joining the alliance despite blaming white people for the arrival of the "monsters."

Three meters tall and humanoid, the alien "demons" are bipedal but incorporate many insectoid features, including clawed hands and feet and leathery gray skin, and conceal a pair of limbs with sucker-like extremities within the chest cavity. They bleed dark green and apparently breathe oxygen, have no recognizable gender differentiation, "don't see well in daylight," live in tunnels, and devote themselves to gold-mining—by means indicated but unclear—and experimenting on their captives. Their motives are obscure. Wilde's character, revealed to be from a race destroyed by the creatures, says gold is "as rare to them as it is to you"—without explaining what they do with it—adding that "[T]hey're studying your weaknesses.... They will come back with more, and there will be no survivors." On the whole, however, the aliens are shown as entirely unknowable; the human characters respond only to their violence and cruelty, determining that, if the "scouting party" is destroyed, the aliens will leave Earth in peace thereafter. Although this invasion is on a distinctly local scale, the character descriptions echo *The War of the Worlds*:

> A big greyish rounded bulk, the size, perhaps, of a bear, was rising slowly and painfully out of the cylinder. As it bulged up and caught the light, it glistened like wet leather.
> Two large dark-coloured eyes were regarding me steadfastly. The mass that framed them, the head of the thing, was rounded, and had, one might say, a face. There was a mouth under the eyes, the lipless brim of which quivered and panted, and dropped saliva.

Coproducer and joint author of the screenplay Roberto Orci states that they were "loosely based on the Babylonian legend of the Anunnaki," who, as interpreted by Russian author Zecharia Sitchin, apparently first visited Earth 450,000 years ago searching for gold. Director Jon Favreau, however, refers to "the whole Conquistador thing" as well as to a recurring theme of aliens being in search of gold—a subject much discussed in UFOlogy circles. The alien character also incorporates deliberate inversion of the concept of "manifest destiny," which took for granted the rights of settlers to spread across what is now the United States and remake the country to their requirements, disregarding its original inhabitants. ILM representative Roger Guyett remarks, "[T]he irony of all this was that the aliens turn up and [the peril] could be more exaggerated for them. They're frontiersmen in a way: travelling to another place and having to deal with the adversities of the climate. And in our case, we played up the fact that they weren't comfortable in our world."

Turning the tables on 19th-century American characters and showing them as an invaded and threatened species underlies and emphasizes a series of redemption narratives in the text. Where characters survive, they are almost all changed for the better; Ford's cattle baron forms a stronger relationship with his son, for example, and Craig's outlaw is allowed to leave town unhindered. It can also be inferred that Ford's character has learned to live in peace with the Apache, but apart from the safe return of their missing people it is less easy to see what the Apache gain from the experience. They have cooperated with their white neighbors to drive off a common enemy, but their position is still ambiguous—are they, in fact, "cowboys," or are they "aliens"?—and they are apparently excluded from the celebrations at the end of the film.

*Fiona Pickles*

See also: *Alien* (Series); *War of the Worlds, The*; *Way of Thorn and Thunder, The*.

**FURTHER READING**

Jacobs, David M. "Aliens and Hybrids." *Alien Discussions: Proceedings of the Abduction Study Conference*, edited by Andrea Pritchard, David E. Pritchard, John E. Mack, Pam Kasey, and Claudia Yapp, North Cambridge Press, 1994, pp. 86–90.

Miller, Cynthia J. "The Woman Who Fell from the Sky: *Cowboys and Aliens'* Hybrid Heroine." *Heroines of Film and Television: Portrayals in Popular Culture*, edited by Norma Jones, Maja Bajac-Carter, and Bob Batchelor, Rowman and Littlefield, 2014, pp. 115–28.

Witmer, Jon D. "Once Upon a Time in the West." *American Cinematographer*, vol. 92, no. 8, August 2011, pp. 58–71.

## *Critters*

The original *Critters* (1986–1992), directed by Rupert Harvey and Barry Opper, has gained a sizable cult following since its release in 1986. Dominic Muir's original screenplay for *Critters* was actually written before the theatrical release of *Gremlins* and was later rewritten by director Stephen Herek and star Don Keith Opper to downplay any overt similarities to the earlier film. The finished picture sees a horde of tiny extraterrestrials arrive on a rural farm in Grover's Bend,

Kansas, where the Brown family—including mother Helen (Dee Wallace), father Jay (Billy "Green" Bush), elder daughter April (Nadine van der Velde), and courageous younger brother Brad (Scott Grimes)—must do battle with the menace from outer space with the help of a pair of shape-shifting bounty hunters working for the Intergalactic Council, a peacekeeping organization. Ultimately, it is a narrative that has less in common with *Gremlins* than it does with several other alien-invasion movies of the 1980s, such as *The Deadly Spawn* (1983), *Lifeforce* (1985), or *Killer Klowns from Outer Space* (1988), in which carnivorous life-forms arrive on Earth and begin to consume human victims for sustenance.

*Critters* went on to spawn three sequels: *Critters 2: The Main Course* (1988), *Critters 3* (1991), and *Critters 4* (1992). All of these films feature the eponymous critters as their primary antagonists. After their attack on the Browns' farm in the original film, the first sequel sees the creatures resurge in Grover's Bend, where Brad Brown must once again attempt to stop them, with the help of alien hunters Ug (Terrence Mann) and Lee (Roxanne Kernohan). In *Critters 3*, a new family unwittingly transports critter eggs to their home in Los Angeles, where the monsters take up residence in the basement of their dilapidated apartment building. There, teenagers Annie (Aimee Brooks) and Josh (Leonardo DiCaprio) attempt to do battle with the aliens. In the final film, the last remaining critters wreak havoc in deep space in the year 2045 when a pod containing their eggs is brought onboard a space station for examination.

Critters—Crites, or Krites, as they are known to the Intergalactic Council—are small, carnivorous creatures measuring only a few feet. They normally work in packs of varying numbers, from only three in *Critters 4* to thousands in *The Main Course*. They are covered in black, brown, or dark gray fur, have glowing red eyes, and possess hundreds of razor-sharp teeth, which they use to devour any organic material they come into contact with. They also possess a number of special abilities, though these vary from film to film; at various points in the series they are seen to fire sharp spines at their victims, grow to a huge size, and even join together to form a giant rolling sphere—a "critter ball"—that destroys everything in its path. One thing that remains constant is their relentless hunger; Crites will simply continue eating until they are destroyed. It is for this reason that they are hunted by the Intergalactic Council, which treats the critters as an extremely dangerous form of vermin with the potential to destroy entire planets if left unchecked.

The Crites, then, are the ultimate consumers: they maliciously devour everything they come into contact with—including human beings—with absolutely no regard for the consequences of their actions. The first two films in the series linger on the subtext implied by this instinctual behavior; the aliens are rendered as an especially potent allegory for the explosion of American consumerism throughout the 20th century and particularly for the culture of greed fostered by the Reagan administration, which espoused the virtues of consumption and material wealth in a free-market system. These creatures begin to eat from the moment they land on Earth in the original *Critters*, first feeding on livestock and then surrounding the Browns' farmhouse, effectively usurping humankind's position at the top of the food chain. This subtext is compounded in *The Main Course*, where the Crites run amok in Grover's Bend, home to a corporate fast-food chain named the "Hungry Heifer." By the end of the film, they have attacked a Hungry Heifer restaurant and its supply warehouse, devouring both dead meat and live flesh in the process. So both *Critters* and *Critters 2* criticize the capitalist attitudes of the 1980s by using their insatiable monsters to create a sharp satire of rampant consumerism.

Filmed back-to-back, *Critters 3* and *Critters 4* continue the series' fixation on the ills of capitalist modernity, though they expand the series' subtext beyond a critique of consumer culture. By transferring the Crites from a rural space to an urban—a tenement block that is soon to be demolished and replaced with luxury housing for the rich—*Critters 3* develops the allegorical connection between the aliens and corporate attitudes. Hostile to both tenant and landlord, here the Crites function as a form of vengeful vermin and underline the social injustice brought upon residents who are soon to be made homeless in the name of profit. Once the series' action has moved to outer space, *Critters 4* takes aim at capitalist involvement in governance and defense; a surprising development in the final film is that the Intergalactic Council—which spends the entirety of the first three films attempting to destroy the Crites—has become TerraCor, a corporation that has now set its sights on using the creatures as a biological weapon. This twist decisively connects *Critters 4* with its cultural moment: a film made during the Gulf War, it reshapes the anticapitalist themes of its forebears to indict the military-industrial complex.

The *Critters* series, then, uses its insatiable aliens to take aim at rampant consumerism, dangerous capitalist attitudes, and corporate greed. Sadly, beyond a well-received fan film—*Critters: Bounty Hunter* (2014)—and a web series that has now been in development for some years, a fifth entry in the series has not yet materialized.

*Craig Ian Mann*

See also: *Alien* (Series); *Body Snatchers*; *Prometheus*.

## FURTHER READING

McCarron, Chris. Review of the blu-ray editions of *Critters* 1–4: atthamovies.com/critters-1-4-blu-ray-review/

# D

## *The Dark Crystal*

Directed by Jim Henson and Frank Oz, *The Dark Crystal* (1982) features groundbreaking animatronics and beautiful concept design by fantasy artist Brian Froud, who would later collaborate with Henson and Oz again on *Labyrinth* (1986). The film took approximately five years from conception to release, and Henson believed in it so deeply that he paid $15 million to purchase the film from the studio, who lost faith in it after negative screenings. Henson's instincts proved sound, as *The Dark Crystal* has evolved into a cult classic that still attracts new audiences and has expanded into other media, such as books, comics, clothing, and collectible figures.

Because *The Dark Crystal* was made before digital effects could create "realistic" aliens, the creatures and humanoids of Thra are all puppets, some of which are complex enough to require six or more puppeteers to manipulate them. Regardless of where the story takes place or whether aliens are friends or foes, humans almost always appear in alien films, and their response to the other shapes and informs the audience's view, as we see the events unfolding through the eyes of characters we can bond with and relate to. However, no humans appear on-screen during *The Dark Crystal*. Not only would their presence be jarring and disrupt the film's strong artistic and concept design, it would inevitably draw the focus from the puppets and from Jen's quest to the journey of the human who steps in to help the indigenous people overcome their alien oppressors.

The film's protagonist, Jen (performed by Jim Henson and voiced by Stephen Garlick), has grown up believing he is the last living Gelfling, a race of small, slender elf-like folk with large eyes and pointed ears. When his people were enslaved and killed by the evil Skeksis, he was hidden, protected, and raised by the peaceful UrRu (the Mystics). Jen's mentor, the ailing Wisest of the Mystics, gives him a task before he dies: leave the valley he has called home and seek out Aughra (performed by Frank Oz and voiced by Billie Whitelaw), the astronomer, who possesses the shard of the broken Dark Crystal. If Jen can find the shard and use it to heal the Crystal when the planet's three suns are in alignment, the despotic rule and power of the Skesis will be broken. Pursued by an exiled Skesis and the corrupted creatures spawned from the Crystal, Jen finds the shard and discovers he is not the last of his people when he encounters Kira (performed by Kathryn Mullen and voiced by Lisa Maxwell), a female Gelfling who joins him in his quest to make the crystal and their world whole again.

At first glance, *The Dark Crystal* might seem more at home in a collection focused on fantasy creatures rather than one devoted to the alien. Thra is a preindustrial world that includes magic, and Brian Froud's creature designs, heavily influenced by Celtic lore, give the planet's indigenous peoples a look that resonates with classic depictions of the fairy folk. The elf-like Gelflings and diminutive Podlings, who raised the orphan Kira and have round, doughy faces and tiny black eyes, look like they could have stepped out of a field guide to folklore. The same applies to the ancient Aughra, who resembles the "ogre" that can be heard in her name.

However, Thra, a planet with three suns, is clearly an alien world, one with its own history, cosmology, and ecology. Thra's native creatures have an organic look and feel; their skin and fur are natural colors: browns, blacks, amber, tans, creams, and grays. Some notable examples include the tall, long-legged landstriders Jen and Kira use as mounts. They have wispy fur, a tentacled mouth, and a face reminiscent of a beakless squid. The grub-like amphibian nebrie live in Thra's swamps. The Skesis consider their flesh a delicacy. Then there is Kira's pet/companion, Fizzgig (performed by David Goelz and voiced by Percy Edwards), a round creature with wild fur, bright amber eyes, and a large mouth with sharp teeth.

These creatures stand in stark contrast to the unnatural ones created by the power of the Dark Crystal. The most imposing are the hulking Garthim, with deep purple crustacean carapaces and a pair of large frontal claws. Skittering, clicking sounds accompany them when they move. Crystal bats, winged spies with Gothic-styled wings, have bodies that seem to be chunks of purple crystal rather than anything organic, natural, and alive.

*The Dark Crystal* is more than just a film about an alien world. It is also a film where that world is, itself, invaded by another alien race. When the three suns of Thra align in the First Great Conjunction, the UrSkeks arrive, exiled from their own world because of their conflicted souls. They discover the Crystal of Truth, a colorless crystal that is the heart of Thra in tangible form, and plan to use it to purify themselves during the Second Great Conjunction. Their attempt succeeds, but not as they'd intended. It splits each UrSkek into two bodies: one Mystic (peaceful and contemplative) and one Skesis (greedy and cruel), each possessing a different part of the UrSkek's soul. Because the two bodies share a single soul, if one of the pairing is injured or dies, the same fate befalls the other. It is the Skesis who shattered the Crystal out of rage, staining it a deep amethyst purple. When Jen restores the Crystal, the Mystics and Skesis meld together, and the UrSkeks leave Thra, which has already begun to heal in the white light of the Crystal of Truth.

The museum at the Center for Puppetry Arts in Atlanta, Georgia, houses a permanent Henson collection of puppets from a number of films and television series. Their collection from *The Dark Crystal* includes the puppets for Aughra, Jen, Kira's companion Fizzgig, Podlings, and a Garthim soldier.

*Barbara Lucas*

See also: *Avatar*; *Farscape*; *Warhammer 40,000*.

## FURTHER READING

Finch, Christopher. *The Making of the Dark Crystal: Creating a Unique Film*. Holt, 1983.
Froud, Brian. *World of the Dark Crystal*. Knopf, 1982.
Gaines, Caseen. *The Dark Crystal: The Ultimate Visual History*. Insight Editions, 2017.

## Dead Space

*Dead Space* is a series of third-person horror games designed by Visceral Games/Electronic Arts for PC, Xbox 360, and Playstation 3. The main series includes *Dead Space, Dead Space 2*, and *Dead Space 3*. The first *Dead Space* (2008) limited player movement and had low-damage weapons, making the game closer to a survival horror game where resource management is critical. Sequels (2011 and 2013) made the player character more mobile, increased and diversified weapons, and added cooperative play. All three main series games received mostly positive reviews, but *Dead Space 3*'s changes in favor of action shooting and co-op play were polarizing among critics who appreciated the horror elements. Spin-off games venture into other genres and styles, such as puzzle games and rail shooters.

*Dead Space* follows the journey of Isaac Clarke (whose name is a reference to Isaac Asimov and Arthur C. Clarke), an engineer tasked with investigating a signal from the USS *Ishimura*, a planet-cracking ship used to harvest energy. Clarke boards the ship to discover the crew has been attacked by Necromorphs, combinations of reanimated tissue. Clarke discovers the Marker, a power source that creates Necromorphs, and destroys it. Later games find Clarke locked up in an insane asylum as human society attempts to deny the Necromorphs. After an outbreak of Necromorphs on a moon base that Clarke escapes after destroying another Marker, he accompanies a team to investigate and destroy a Marker on the ice world of Tau Volantis, home of an alien race also dominated by Markers and Necromorphs. Clarke ends the last game by sacrificing himself to destroy Tau Volantis and stop the existing threat of the Markers and Necromorphs.

The Markers help a species to grow in order to create problems of overpopulation and high energy demands. These demands require a species to travel in space to find sufficient energy to sustain their population. The Marker will reveal itself and implant instructions into the minds of the most intelligent members of a species. These instructions will allow a species to replicate Markers, thus helping them increase their energy production. The duplicate Markers, likely positioned in different parts of a species' homeworld and colonies, act as a transmitter for a signal that converts all life into Necromorphs. After a sufficient number of a species are converted, the Necromorphs are pushed into space to form a moon in a process called a Convergence Event. This moon absorbs all organic material, then leaves the planet to find new material.

The process of selective advancement, stratification, and annihilation resembles the ideal plan for an extractive colonizing force. The Marker is an alien that effectively colonizes by manipulating and stratifying a society for its own purposes in three stages. First, the Marker cultivates a desire for growth beyond the normal potential of a species. Second, it harnesses the likely leaders of a group by implanting its own designs and replicating them. The Marker selects those individuals who believe themselves to be above their species, promises those members a way to transcend their species, and ensures the method of transcendence sells out the other members of an elite's species. Finally, the less intelligent members of a species are turned into a mob that kills the former elites, themselves, and the entire civilization. After the extraction is complete, the colonizer moves to another species to start anew.

*Dead Space* offers an answer to the Fermi Paradox, claiming that Markers have converted all intelligent life reachable by humans into Necromorphs. Any civilization intelligent enough for humans to contact might have been affected by Markers, meaning anything of sufficient intelligence in the known universe would be absorbed. Because the Necromorphs are "dead," any search for life might miss a large collection of nonliving organic matter. An audio log in *Dead Space 3* claims the known universe is all "dead space" because Markers had ended all life as humans understand it. *Dead Space* claims the search for alien life might not be possible on terms understandable to humans.

Humans in *Dead Space* are unable to cope with their origins or the existence of a superior species. Humans respond to alien life in *Dead Space* with a mix of denial, religious fervor, or insanity. Most of the world of *Dead Space* denied the existence or problems of the Markers and Necromorphs until there were larger attacks. The Unitologists, people who believed converging is humanity's purpose, renounced human civilization in favor of complete surrender. People like Isaac Clarke who encounter the Markers and survive are traumatized and driven mad. His trauma is both personal (the loss of his girlfriend) and existential, because he becomes aware of the fact that humans and human civilization were created for mere harvesting.

The games themselves deliberately place the player in the position of Clarke, an engineer whose only goal is to survive. Clarke faces the enormity of a large entity different to and beyond most categories of human understanding. His movements are clunky and maladapted to handle the Necromorphs. His ingenuity allows him to survive, but it is beyond his ability to manage the Necromorphs alone. *Dead Space*, as a series, posits that the ordinary person is ill-equipped to manage large cosmic entities. Clarke's encounters with the Necromorphs force him to contend with the origin of people and their potential future. Encountering the alien in *Dead Space* involves humanity being completely unready for the knowledge encountering a large, godlike species would require.

*Dead Space* games require steady shooting and navigating from a third-person perspective. Scholars unfamiliar with third-person shooters, or video games in general, will find *Dead Space* games often have a steep learning curve. Lowering the difficulty settings can make any of the games easier, but players still need some basic skills with third-person shooting. Scholars who are unskilled in third-person shooters looking to explore the series can benefit from watching any of numerous "let's play" videos or having a colleague control the game, but managing the fear of encountering the overwhelming alien is essential to the *Dead Space* experience.

*Ian Derk*

See also: *Alien* (Series); *Half-Life 2*; *Halo*; *Mass Effect* (Trilogy); *X-COM*, *XCOM*.

## FURTHER READING

Lane, Rick. "*Dead Space* Is the Sequel *Resident Evil 4* Deserved." *Eurogamer*.Net, www.eurogamer.net/articles/2017-02-12-dead-space-is-the-sequel-resident-evil-4-deserved.

Yelmo, Silviano Carrasco. "Nicole is dead: ciencia ficción, terror y fantástico en *Dead Space*/Nicole is dead: sci-fi, terror and fantastic in *Dead Space*." *Brumal: Revista de Investigación sobre lo Fantástico*, vol. 3, no. 1, 2015, pp. 13–33.

## Dick, Philip K.

The imagination of Philip K. Dick (1928–1982), according to Patricia S. Warrick, "spills out a rich variety of alien forms—the vugs from Titan; Count Runnymede [sic], the slime mold; live vermin traps; commercial bugs" (20). To some extent, this is parodic scene-setting: the U.S.–Soviet Cold War displaced onto a world government fighting an alien civilization. Earth under threat is saturated with propaganda and paranoia. For example, in *Now Wait for Last Year* (1966), Earth finds itself drawn into a war due to an alliance with Lilistar. Eugene Warren argues that the "Starmen" "are human but treacherous; their enemies, huge insects called Reegs, are repulsive but good" (165). Earth's leader, Gino Molinari, has to adopt high-risk strategies to avoid humanity's being subsumed into another species' ideology. Whenever a member of his staff falls ill, Molinari shares the symptoms, buying time for negotiation.

Appearances are deceptive in Dick's novels, where, alongside the political commentary and satire he explores two themes: what is real and what is human? Protagonists and antagonists alike find themselves in worlds of doubtful authenticity—drug trips, dreams, simulated environments, conspiracies, media lies, fake news, and so on. It becomes unclear what is real and that might include the appearance of aliens, such as the possibly fictionalized mice who attempt to invade Earth in "We Can Remember It For You Wholesale" (1966).

In his first published story, "Beyond Lies the Wub" (1952), largely set on a spaceship returning from Mars, Peterson feeds his newly purchased wub, a vast, pig-like animal. Captain Franco decides he wants to eat it, even after it starts speaking via telepathy. At the end of the story, it turns out that the wub's consciousness has possessed Franco, and the wub has eaten itself. In a loose sequel, "Not by Its Cover" (1968), fur can survive the death of its wearer and also has a strange impact on anything it covers: the text of a wub-fur–bound edition of Lucretius's *De Rerum Natura* is revised, revealing a new eschatology.

Dick sometimes depicts aliens as a means of questioning what it is to be authentically human. In *Clans of the Alphane Moon* (1964), the death of Ganymedan slime mould Lord Running is the most moving in the novel. More often, Dick uses characters such as robots, androids, drug addicts, or the insane as a means of testing the definition of the human.

Sometimes the alien functions in the narrative in a similar manner to Dick's patriarchal characters—either a father or father figure to the male protagonist, often a boss, but certainly with power over him and at best ambivalent, morally speaking. A key example would be Palmer Eldritch in *The Three Stigmata of Palmer Eldritch* (1964), who has returned from an extra-solar space mission fused with an alien being from the Prox system. His false eyes, metal teeth, and artificial arm offer a perversion of the crucified Christ, and his drug Chew-Z will transport its imbibers into an alternate reality. In *Our Friends from Frolix 8* (1970), Thors

Provoni returns from outer space with a 90-ton protoplasmic slime, Morgo Rahn Wilc, who helps him bring down the dystopian system on Earth. It is not clear that humanity will be better off.

The quasi-god Glimmung in *Galactic Pot-Healer* (1969) summons a group of artisans including Joe Fernwright to raise a sunken cathedral on Plowman's Planet, offering as reward eternal life through infusion into himself. The Glimmung is well-meaning but incompetent; its nemesis the Black Glimmung is more dangerous. Dick recycled the Glimmung from a (posthumously published) children's novel, *Nick and the Glimmung* (1988), which also featured wubs, trobes, printers, spiddles, and father-things, all lifted from earlier short stories. Here the aliens offer exotic color as the background to the protagonist Nick Graham's attempt to protect his illicit cat, Horace, on a different version of Plowman's Planet.

If, in the first two decades of Dick's life, his characters resist assimilation into alien transcendence, in the last they welcome it. In a series of mystical experiences in February and March 1974, Dick encountered something he could never explain: God; the prophet Elijah; the late Bishop James Pike; scientists in Leningrad experimenting with telepathy or aliens. In *VALISystem A* (posthumously published as *Radio Free Albemuth* in 1985), Dick was to transform his theophany into an account of an attempt to overthrow a Nixon-like dictator with the aid of an extraterrestrial being called VALIS. After some editorial queries, Dick heavily rewrote the novel as the more realistic *VALIS* (1981), in which Dick's alter ego Horselover Fat wishes to return to the intimacy he felt with whatever VALIS was; this is in stark contrast to the revulsion felt by Fernwright or the horror created by Eldritch in relation to fusing with the alien. As Christopher Palmer argues, "A thing can't be a real thing unless it is in some sense an individual thing" (94). In *The Divine Invasion* (1981), a science-fictional sequel to *VALIS*, Herb Asher is forced by an alien deity Yah to help pregnant Rybys Rommey get to Earth. He is helped by a humanoid incarnation of Elijah. The Science Legate and Christian-Islamic church may wish to defend Earth from this alien invasion, but the alien child, Emmanuel, is skeptical about Yah's ethics.

Perhaps Dick's most significant observation on the alien occurs in *The World Jones Made* (1956), in which the oppressive world government that insists on all ideas being accepted as relative is threatened by Floyd Jones's precognition. Jones uses mysterious aliens, Drifters, who have started appearing on Earth as the focus for his resistance. At the end of the novel, government agent Doug Cussick and his family are relocated to a dome on Venus; there it is *they* who are the aliens.

*Andrew M. Butler*

See also: Hitchhiker's Guide to the Galaxy, The; Mœbius; Simak, Clifford D.

## FURTHER READING

Palmer, Christopher. *Philip K. Dick: Exhilaration and the Terror of the Postmodern*. Liverpool University Press, 2003.

Warren, Eugene. "The Search for Absolutes." *Philip K. Dick*, edited by Joseph D. Olander and Martin Harry Greenberg, Taplinger, 1983.

Warrick, Patricia S. *Mind in Motion: The Fiction of Philip K. Dick*. Southern Illinois Press, 1987.

# District 9

The film *District 9* (2009), written by Director Neill Blomkamp and Terri Tatchell, is an expansion and remake of Neill Blomkamp's *Alive in Joburg* (2006), set in and around Johannesburg. An alien ship had broken down over the city in 1982 and had been found to contain a large number of starving insect-like aliens who were transported down to an internment camp known as District 9. In 2010, the South African government employ Multinational United to move them to a new location against their will, led by Wikus van de Merwe, the son-in-law of an executive. Van de Merwe is infected with an alien fluid, begins to transform into an alien, and tries to persuade an alien known as Christopher Johnson to change him back. To do this, Christopher has to return to his home planet.

The reviewer Joshua Clover suggests that the film is "a neat allegory of apartheid, with the marooned race of repulsive and sad-sack aliens standing for the dispossessed" (8), while Eric D. Smith argues it "at first seem[s] an allegory for the suspension of constitutional law during the officially declared South African State of Emergency in the latter days of apartheid policy (1985–1990)" (149). Apartheid was a system intended to prop up white minority rule in what had been British and Dutch colonies. Before 1923, the various African populations had mainly been rural, but industrialization and the demand for domestic servants required that there should be a conveniently situated workforce in segregated townships. The 1950 Group Areas Act designated four racial groups—white, black, colored, and Indian—although in practice the last two groups were treated as one. The real-world District Six was a racially mixed suburb on the port side of Cape Town, consisting of workers, immigrants, freed slaves, and merchants, predominantly colored but often visited by whites in search of music or other recreation. Standing between Cape Town and the coast, it became an inconvenience to the white elite, who between 1964 and 1966 decided to relocate its inhabitants despite understandable resistance. In the process, devastation was caused to the community, and white settlers were unwilling to move into the area after the clearances.

In the film, the aliens have been left to scavenge in what has become a shantytown, separated from the rest of the city due to crime and violence, whether real or feared. The aliens have been nicknamed "prawns" by humans and are regarded as savage; we do not know what the species calls itself, and only one of the aliens is actually named. Of course, the English-sounding "Christopher Johnson" suggests that it is a name forced on him in the same way that colonial masters had renamed their slaves or servants in previous centuries. The gender and characteristics of the aliens is not clear; Christopher has a child that van de Merwe assumes is his son, but viewers are imposing masculinity on the two aliens they have gotten to know best. The aliens are subtitled—much like the so-called Nigerians who have moved into District 9 to exploit this market—although van de Merwe can understand their Xhosa-like language of clicks, and Christopher can understand his English. Christopher's name seems to evoke the "JC" of "Jesus Christ," and he is to become a potential savior to his people, ascending to the alien mothership at the climax of the film—although van de Merwe offers a version of the white savior seen in a number of texts about colonial and postcolonial struggle, including *Avatar* (2009).

Despite our growing sympathy for Christopher, his son, the aliens who have become subjects in scientific experiments, and the metamorphosing van de Merwe, we are also made to feel disgust at the process: Van de Merwe's loss of hair, teeth, and fingernails, his hemorrhaging of black fluid, the vomiting of black liquid and self-defecation, as well as his growing insectoid appearance and his taste for—like the aliens—cat food. The abject horror we feel at the challenge to the pure and proper body is fully experienced. The alien culture is insufficiently evoked to allow full empathy; relating to the prawn or the insect remains a big leap.

If the aliens offer an allegory for a subjected ethnicity in apartheid-era South Africa—the colored population if the parallel with District Six is followed—then this lack of development is potentially racist. If the aliens are allegorical versions of the black population, then we have to recall that this was the indigenous ethnicity of the area rather than immigrants/aliens. It is the white population doing the displacement.

The film certainly depicts racism in its characters. The majority of alien technology we see aside from the spaceship and landing capsule is military, whether weapons or armor. While they seem not to have been an invasion force, there is perhaps a sense of danger. Armond White argues that "*District 9* stops making sense and becomes careless agitation using social fears and filmmaking tropes Blomkamp and Jackson are ill-equipped to control," adding "*District 9* confirms that few media makers know how to perceive history, race and class relations." In the film's satire, underplaying the real struggle and real suffering of real people, nonwhite agency is trivialized. Adilifu Nama has argued that "the process of allegorical displacement [in SF cinema] invites audiences to affirm racist ideas, confirm racial fears, and reinforce dubious generalizations about race" (146). The specifics of the film work against the detailed allegorical reading that the film invites.

*Andrew M. Butler*

See also: *Alien Nation*; *Avatar*; Okorafor, Nnedi.

## FURTHER READING

Butler, Andrew M. "Human Subjects/Alien Objects? Abjection and the Constructions of Race and Racism in *District 9*." *Alien Imaginations: Science Fiction and Tales of Transnationalism*, edited by Ulrike Küchler et al., Bloomsbury, 2015, pp. 95–112.
Clover, Joshua. "Allegory Bomb." *Film Quarterly*, vol. 63, no. 2, 2009, pp. 8–9.
Nama, Adilifu. *Black Space: Imagining Race in Science Fiction Film*. University of Texas Press, 2008.
Smith, Eric D. *Globalization, Utopia, and Postcolonial Science Fiction: New Maps of Hope*. Palgrave Macmillan, 2012.

## Doctor Who

*Doctor Who* (1963–1989; 1996; 2005–present), created in 1963 by BBC's head of drama, Sydney Newman, distinguished itself from its inception with innovative programming and production. Despite Newman's initial resistance to "bug-eyed monsters," *Doctor Who* has manifested its interest in aliens throughout its 50-plus-year history. Although settings vary, the program's emphasis on alien invasion in Britain suggests a continuation of invasion narratives—a genre that responded to British anxieties resulting from conflicts near the end of the 19th century. Early invasion narratives, like H. G. Wells's *The War of the Worlds*, were alarmist in tone, often privileging technology's role on the side of the victor. While *Doctor Who* manifests these themes, it also stresses new values and new solutions. To this purpose, the Doctor is the ultimate weapon, using superior intelligence more often than superior might to defeat invaders. *Doctor Who* reveals British concerns regarding alien invasion and demonstrates that invasion anxiety is still present in 21st-century Britain. A continued lack of confidence in the United Kingdom's ability to respond is also perhaps indicated: Wells relied on bacteria to defeat the aliens, while the first line of defense against the alien in *Doctor Who* is the Doctor himself, an alien from the planet Gallifrey.

In essence, *Doctor Who* embodies change. Newman's controversial choice of female producer Verity Lambert and British-Indian director Waris Hussein contributed to the success of the longest-running science-fiction series in television history. Despite its cancellation in 1989 due to declining ratings, and lukewarm reception of a jointly produced Fox/BBC television movie in 1996, the serial was relaunched in 2005 by Russell T. Davies and Julie Gardner. Steven Moffat replaced Davies in 2010, with Chris Chibnall taking over in 2018. The serial's longevity has been credited to the titular character's mysterious ability to "regenerate," allowing for recasting the role, refreshing the face of the program every few years. To date, 12 male actors have headlined the series, with Jodie Whitaker, the first woman, assuming the role in 2018.

There are at least 99 different monsters in *Doctor Who*, as listed in Sleight's *The Doctor's Monsters*. Undoubtedly the best known are the Daleks. Created by Terry Nation and Raymond Cusick, Daleks directly reflect the *blitzkrieg* invasions of Nazi Germany. Daleks are daunting foes in any environment, but their presence on landmarks like Westminster Bridge ("The Dalek Invasion of Earth") and Canary Wharf ("Doomsday") demonstrate how fears about invasion continue to resonate. The military response to Dalek invasion is underscored by the Doctor's line-in-the-sand attitude toward his ancient enemy. From time to time, however, this staunch attitude is complicated by something reflective—the Fourth Doctor questions his "right" to exterminate his foe ("Genesis of the Daleks"); the Twelfth Doctor is told he is a "good Dalek" ("Into the Dalek"). Such moments recognize that fighting monsters may make monsters of us all.

Alternately, the Cybermen signify anxieties associated with bodily invasion and humanity becoming post-human. Created by Kit Pedler and Gerry Davis, Cybermen propose to "upgrade" humanity into perfectible cyborg bodies, suppressing all emotion and feeling. Over time, Cybermen have increased in strength, speed, and cyberconversion, specifically illustrating a relationship between rapid changes in technology and changes to the body. As with the Daleks, military force has little effect on Cybermen; however, some recent examples from the relaunched series suggest that resistance to cyberconversion is mental and emotional ("Closing Time," "Nightmare in Silver," "Death in Heaven"). Yet again, "The Doctor

In this scene from the episode "Closing Time" (2011) from the sixth season of the relaunched version of *Doctor Who*, the 11th Doctor (Matt Smith) is held captive by the Cybermen. (BBC/Photofest)

Falls" interrogates the suggestion that cyberconversion is part of an inevitable human evolution and reflects anxieties about the dehumanizing potential of technologies.

Also signified in *Doctor Who*'s attitude toward aliens are anxieties regarding indigenous peoples and refugees. The reptilian Silurians, created by Malcolm Hulke ("Doctor Who and the Silurians"), are native to Earth and predate human civilization. Prehistoric yet scientifically advanced, Silurians emerge from hibernation to discover humankind as the interlopers. In each successive encounter, peace negotiations often end in violence. The failure to establish peace reflects anxieties about Earth's shared inheritance and who can rightly claim ownership of the planet. Similarly, anxieties about refugees and their assimilation into British culture are also addressed. The Zygons, created by Robert Banks Stewart ("The Terror of the Zygons"), flee their home planet's destruction, intending to use their shape-shifting powers to infiltrate and subdue Earth's inhabitants. Alternately, some less aggressive Zygons wish merely to assimilate peacefully into Earth's culture ("The Zygon Invasion," "The Zygon Inversion"). The Zygons' ambiguous nature and ability to hide in plain sight reflect mixed feelings regarding the treatment of refugees as aggressors or victims.

Key shifts in tone between the classic and the relaunched series put the power to resolve conflict in human hands. Authority on all things alien, Doctors of both the classic and current eras oppose violence and encourage peace, but current

Doctors are more likely to make missteps due to anger or pride. In such cases, the Doctor's companion may step up to decide the fate of the future.

In a world subject to acts of terrorism, the difficulty of identifying and understanding the source of a threat creates its own level of anxiety. This fear is a recurring motif, as demonstrated by the Autons and the Weeping Angels, where objects as innocuous as mannequins or statues can suddenly turn threatening. However, sympathetic portrayals of classic aliens, once reviled, demonstrate that the program itself is reframing its narratives: individual Daleks are depicted with some sympathy ("Dalek," "Into the Dalek"); the integration of displaced aliens into human society is emphasized ("The Day of the Doctor"). All of which suggests that *Doctor Who*, unlike past invasion narratives, advocates alternative responses to invasion and invasion anxiety.

*Tanja Nathanael*

See also: *Quatermass* (Series); *Torchwood*; *War of the Worlds, The*.

### FURTHER READING

Bradshaw, Simon, Anthony Keen and Graham Sleight, editors. *The Unsilent Library: Essays on the Russell T. Davies Era of the New* Doctor Who. Science Fiction Foundation, 2011.

Brown, J. P. C. "Doctor Who: A Very British Alien." *Galaxy Is Rated G: Essays on Children's Science Fiction Film and Television*, edited by R. C. Neighbors and Sandy Rankin, McFarland, 2011, pp. 161–82.

Sleight, Graham. *The Doctor's Monsters: Meanings of the Monstrous in* Doctor Who. I. B. Tauris, 2012.

## Donaldson, Stephen R.

Although Stephen R. Donaldson (1947–) is best known for his fantasy, particularly his first two *Thomas Covenant the Unbeliever* trilogies, science fiction forms a significant part of his corpus. Born in India to American missionary parents, Donaldson moved permanently to the United States when he was 17. During college, he encountered the writings of French existentialists, particularly Jean-Paul Sartre and Albert Camus, and their themes helped motivate one of the abiding tensions in Donaldson's work: existentialist principles of absolute freedom and personal responsibility alongside a clear belief in universal human nature. According to a famous formulation by Sartre, existentialism holds that existence precedes essence; no objective moral system or set of constraints lessens our freedom (or responsibility) for free choice. Sartre categorizes "human nature" as one of those prior sets of constraints; as such, his thought entails a radical denial of human nature. Donaldson clearly accepts the existence of human nature, though, despite his high regard for existentialist freedom and responsibility; his work makes frequent appeals to "what makes us human" (the title, even, for one of his short stories). For Donaldson, standard features of human nature include emotion, creativity, and pain. One of the characters from Donaldson's five-volume *Gap* cycle (1991–1996) captures this tension between existentialism and essentialism pithily when he thinks, "Anguish and terror and excruciation were humankind's essential legacy: every child born inherited them" (*Gap into Ruin*). On the one hand, such a statement seems to echo Sartre's contention that the human situation is comprised of despair, anguish, and forlornness; on the other hand, Donaldson presents this situation as an essential and unavoidable inheritance.

The alien Amnion from the *Gap* cycle might be the single creation that best reinforces Donaldson's commitment to the idea of human nature. In the series, the Amnion and humankind have been locked in a decades-long stalemate struggle for supremacy in the *Gap* universe. Humanity knows very little about the Amnion (Donaldson deliberately heightens their otherness by revealing nothing about their culture or customs), except for one thing: their insatiable drive for "genetic imperialism," the assimilation of all intelligent beings *into* Amnion via genetic mutation. The Amnion are masters of biotechnology. Not only have they mutated and assimilated all previously encountered forms of sentient life, they relentlessly tinker with their *own* DNA, even on the individual level. Rarely do any two Amnioni look alike; as the text says, they "played with their shapes the way humans played with fashion, sometimes for utility, sometimes for adornment" (*Gap into Vision*). Although the Amnion have no concept of individuality, much like the Borg in *Star Trek,* their advanced genetic science otherwise suggests a racial liberation from the tyranny of nature, perhaps the ideal existentialist standpoint. Donaldson's other works have experimented with similar standpoints before. In *The Chronicles of Thomas Covenant the Unbeliever*, for example, the Waynhim and Ur-Viles are both creatures made rather than born. Since their existence precedes their essence, they must choose what "essence" they would have for themselves. The Waynhim, by and large, choose the way of law, healing, and nurture; the Ur-Viles, in contrast, choose the opposite.

Two factors distinguish the Amnion from the Waynhim or Ur-Viles. The first is Amnion genetic imperialism, which deprives others of their freedom of choice. The second factor might matter even more: how their mutagens rip the humanity from their human victims. No more terrifying fate exists for a person of the *Gap* universe than to fall prey to Amnion mutagens. Donaldson ties human nature to our DNA, and human genes might be considered the one sacred object in an otherwise secular literary universe. Although many human characters happily use mechanical means to augment their personal abilities, and weapons are even added to the human-turned-cyborg Angus Thermopylae, humanity—in stark contrast to the Amnion—draws the line at disrupting its fundamental DNA sequencing. Donaldson even coins a term, "genophobia," to describe the nearly gothic horror evoked by fear of mutating into an Amnion. Thus, while Donaldson repeatedly emphasizes individual freedom in his *Gap* books, that freedom has its limits. No human can morally choose not to be human. The monstrosity of the Amnion lies precisely in their willingness to change their essential DNA at will.

Since Donaldson completed his *Gap* cycle, rapid advances in genetics and biotechnology have only made the issues of humanism and posthumanism raised by Donaldson—that is, the possibility that humanity will someday become obsolete or even replaceable—more relevant. The Amnion and their genetic imperialism represent a posthuman future at its darkest; even worse, the greatest human villain in the *Gap* universe, Holt Fasner, deliberately seeks to harness Amnion biotechnology in order to more quickly usher a new posthuman era of humanity. Donaldson, though, is not the only voice to raise concerns about changing "what makes us human." In *Our Posthuman Future* (2002), for example, Francis Fukuyama argues that, since all political science is founded on some conception of human nature, any radical alteration of that nature threatens to render obsolete what we know about political society. Likewise, German critical theorist Jürgen Habermas has argued in *The Future of Human Nature* (2002) for our right to an unmanipulated genetic heritage, which he considers essential to democratic freedom. Others strike a more positive note, however. Science-fiction author Vernor Vinge and futurist Ray Kurzweil have both argued that the moment of "singularity" is imminent—scary, perhaps, but unavoidably soon. Regardless of where one falls, however, the Amnion in Donaldson's *Gap* cycle represent a fundamental caution about biotechnology from the standpoint of classical humanism and existentialism.

*Dennis Wilson Wise*

*See also*: Reynolds, Alastair; Sterling, Bruce; Vinge, Vernor.

**FURTHER READING**

Alder, Emily. "Ruined Skin: Gothic Genetics and Human Identity in Stephen R. Donaldson's *Gap* Cycle." *Gothic Science Fiction: 1980–2010*, edited by Sara Wasson and Emily Alder, Liverpool University Press, 2011, pp. 116–30.

Laskar, Benjamin. "Suicide and the Absurd: The Influence of Jean-Paul Sartre's and Albert Camus's Existentialism on Stephen R. Donaldson's *The Chronicles of Thomas Covenant the Unbeliever*." *Journal of the Fantastic in the Arts*, vol. 14, no. 4, 2004, pp. 409–26.

Wise, Dennis Wilson. "Science Fiction, Fantasy, and Social Critique: Stephen R. Donaldson's Gap into Genre." *New Boundaries in Political Science Fiction*, edited by Donald M. Hassler and Clyde Wilcox, University of South Carolina Press, 2008, pp. 290–98.

# Dr. Xargle

Dr. Xargle (1988–1997) is a character in a series of books written by Jeanne Willis and illustrated by Tony Ross. In each book and episode, Dr. Xargle is an alien expert on earth studies who instructs alien schoolchildren about Earth and its inhabitants. Dr. Xargle first landed on Earth in 1988 in *Dr. Xargle's Book of Earthlets*, a picture book that offers a primer on human babies from the misguided perspective of a furry green alien. Three decades after its initial publication, Willis reports that it remains a popular gift for new parents in the United Kingdom. Dr. Xargle features in a six-book series that concluded in 1993, followed by a 13-episode animatronic television show in 1997. According to Andersen Press, the series has collectively sold over half a million copies worldwide and has been translated into 14 languages. The third book, *Dr. Xargle's Book of Earth Tiggers*, in 1990 was a runner-up for the Library Association's annual

Kate Greenaway Medal for the best children's book illustration by a British subject.

The humor of the Dr. Xargle series develops between the words and the visuals. Dr. Xargle's narration is always incorrect or odd, while the images allow the reader to see familiar subjects in a new way. This counterpoint relationship functions in two ways. First, it points directly to language and its arbitrariness—making the words alien. The text invites readers to wonder why words have fixed meanings and to think about metonyms and other wordplay. For instance, readers can wonder if it would be more accurate to refer to train conductors as the "Tickets Please," as in *Dr. Xargle's Book of Earth Mobiles*.

Second, the gap between what is said and what is portrayed encourages the reader to delight in knowing the right interpretation and to consider their own group membership as an Earthling. The first page of each book points Dr. Xargle's five-eyed gaze right at the reader while the text reads, "Good morning, class." The alien students are never visible on this page; instead, this set up invites the reader to play at being one of his students. Unlike in many classrooms, the rest of the book encourages the child to correct the teacher. Sometimes Dr. Xargle's interpretation of an object or action is humorously wrong: "After soaking, Earthlets must be dried carefully to stop them shrinking." At other times, the words sound strange but the idea is humorously accurate: "To stop them leaking, Earthlets must be pulled up by the back tentacles and folded in half. Then they must be wrapped quickly in a fluffy triangle with paper and glue." Occasionally, the illustration depicts what would happen if Dr. Xargle's peculiar word choices were taken literally, such as when the image shows a befuddled baby who has actually been wrapped in paper and tape. The joy of these books lies in the opportunity to correct a supposed expert, validating young readers as authorities on their own planet.

This commentary on expertise also offers a lesson about perspective. Dr. Xargle gets everything wrong simply due to being an alien. Children can apply this concept of outsider misinterpretation to perceptions between cultures, religions, nationalities, and other major human divisions. Due to the broad applicability of this lesson, these books from the late 20th century remain applicable to contemporary children, enough to be reprinted in 2011.

The Dr. Xargle series depends on the idea that outsider perceptions risk being deeply flawed, alluding to the history of anthropologists confidently misinterpreting native cultures. At the same time, the books fall short of their own message due to their extremely limited, white, and Western portrayal of humanity. The only clear nod to the wide human difference of the Earth appears in the second spread of *Dr. Xargle's Book of Earthlets*. The verso page reads "They come in many colours . . . but not green," while the illustration shows four babies with four different skin tones: pink, light brown, dark brown, and yellow. However, even this point is undermined in the American edition, *Earthlets, as Explained by Professor Xargle*. In this edition, the third baby's skin is such a pitch black that only its eyes are distinguishable, while the fourth baby is egregiously yellow. This coloring harkens to old standards of stereotyped skin in publishing. While the concept has good intentions, the color choice is unfortunate, since this one page contains the only nonwhite skin in the entire series. Thankfully, the newest edition, reprinted in 2011 under the British title, opted for the original dark brown and reasonable yellow skin, and these versions are now readily available in the United States.

Finally, each story concludes with a subtle nod to alien-invasion tropes and the darker side of colonial anthropology. Each lesson concludes with a field trip to Earth. These scenes depict a huge, numberless army of aliens wearing identical, vapid human masks and school uniforms. This uncanny duplication ends the books on a note reminiscent of alien invasion via imitation or even cloning, with a hint of colonial invasion. While ostensibly just a field trip, a countless host of identical schoolgirls descending on Earth is daunting. The final page glosses over this horror by giving the reader the last laugh since Dr. Xargle always gets something crucially wrong. In *Dr. Xargle's Book of Earth Tiggers*, for instance, they go to pet a real Earth Tigger, while the illustration shows them approaching a huge tiger with only one sardine each. These concluding pages highlight how Dr. Xargle, as an alien, represents the risks of misinterpretation and the risks of being misinterpreted through a humorous lens for the audience of young children.

*Emily Midkiff*

See also: *Aliens Love Underpants*; *Clangers, The*; *Teletubbies*.

## FURTHER READING

Mendlesohn, Farah. *The Inter-Galactic Playground: A Critical Study of Children's and Teens' Science Fiction*. McFarland, 2009.
Nikolajeva, Maria and Carole Scott. *How Picturebooks Work*. Routledge, 2006.
Nodelman, Perry. *Words about Pictures: The Narrative Art of Children's Picture Books*. University of Georgia Press, 1988.

# E

## Ellison, Harlan

Harlan Ellison (1934–2018) was an American science-fiction and speculative fiction author best known for short stories such as "I Have No Mouth and I Must Scream," "A Boy and his Dog," and "'Repent, Harlequin!' Said the Ticktockman." He began writing in the mid-1950s and wrote over 1,700 pieces of work, including short stories, screenplays, novellas, memoirs, and comic-book scripts. He has also edited anthologies of science-fiction stories, most famously *Dangerous Visions* (1967), and has won multiple awards, including the Hugo and Nebula Awards.

While a common trope in Ellison's work involves placing people in strange worlds (such that the human being becomes the "alien"), a few of his works explicitly and directly involve aliens. Tensions surrounding alienation and displacement, and what it means to be human and inhuman, regularly infuse Ellison's work inspired by post–World War II.

Ellison's series of stories about the "Kyben war" refer to an intergalactic war between humans and the Kyben, a "golden-skinned and tentacle-fingered" type of alien (Weil and Wolfe, 58); however, these stories are not obviously connected, despite taking place in the same universe. For instance, his story/novella, "Run for the Stars" (1957) centers on the Kyben war and involves a human hero, Tallent, a drug addict who is turned into a bomb by the military, with the intent of killing the Kyben. He is essentially dehumanized and "alienated" by his own people, causing him to seek revenge and, ironically, lead the Kyben against Earth.

In the short story "The Wind Beyond the Mountains" (1962), an alien named Wummel narrates as he watches a spaceship invade his peaceful homeland. Wummel is eventually captured by the Earth spaceship's crew and dies when they take him away from his home. This short story highlights Ellison's use of an alien perspective to help highlight humanity's own flaws and to illustrate and problematize human behavior. For instance, he questions the need for human beings to act as colonizers, with unending and creeping capitalistic tendencies, even in space.

In "I'm Looking for Kadak" (1974), only 10 Jewish aliens remain on a planet (Zsouchmuhn), but one of them dies. Similar to the concept of a minyan (the need for 10 Jewish people for a service), the aliens also need 10 to perform their death ritual. The story revolves around searching for Kadak. The story is infused with many Yiddish phrases, which are necessary in order to understand the text but perhaps alien to many who do not speak the language.

Ellison worked with media beyond literature. He wrote for television (e.g., *Star Trek*), comic books, and film, some of which involved aliens and other science-fiction tropes. For instance, Ellison worked as a writer and conceptual consultant on *Babylon 5*, a series that focuses on different alien cultures intermingling on a spaceship hundreds of years in the future. One of the episodes he wrote, "A View from the Gallery," is notable because it takes on a new perspective on the inner workings of the Babylon 5 space station. Typically, the show focuses on the perspective of the captain and other top officers (such as Delenn and G'Kar), each of whom is from a different alien race. However, in this "stand-alone" episode, which is an aberration within the typical format, the show explores the perspective of two civilians who work as maintenance workers ("outsiders" from the main cast). Through this perspective, we also see the main characters in a new light—for instance, how Delenn treats others or how the captain deals with the crisis of an attack from an unknown alien race. This "other" perspective gives us new insight into the main characters, their personalities, their flaws, and their humanity. Additionally, it helps decenter the notion that the main characters (the top officers) are all who matter, underlining that each individual has their own unique perspective that matters and that everyone can at various times be the insider and outsider, or familiar and alien. This relates strongly to themes that pervade the *Babylon 5* series—such as taking on new perspectives by inhabiting new bodies, or even new alien races, in order to better understand the other (e.g., when Minbari Ambassador Delenn metamorphoses into a hybrid human and Minbar).

Ellison also helped create other forms of media—notably, a game based on his work, "I Have No Mouth and I Must Scream," which was a 1995 point-and-click adventure game created by Cyberdreams. One of his most famous works, "I Have No Mouth and I Must Scream" (1967) builds on the theme of human beings (and their creations) as an alienated and monstrous other. In the short story (and in the video game), a computer programmed for war, AM (Allied Mastercomputer), becomes sentient and ends up killing the other computers and all the people on Earth except for five people. These five people are loosely related to war efforts and include Ted (the story's narrator); Ellen, a computer programmer; Gorrister; Benny, a military officer; and Nimdok, a doctor involved in Nazi experiments. The five people are stuck inside AM in a kind of limbo between being alive and dead; victimizer and victim; human and alien (Schrier, 2014). AM, likewise, is a machine and living creature as well as god and a devil (Harris-Fain, 1991). These tensions are furthered in the video-game version, where the five people (playable characters) are trapped in a cage in an otherworldly space and cannot escape until they solve puzzles in different levels of a virtual world (for instance, Ellen's level involves an Egyptian-themed technology hive). Ellison seems to suggest that perhaps the process of alienation and dehumanization does not necessarily require one to live on other planets but may simply entail the entering of artificially created virtual realms as well.

*Karen Schrier*

See also: *Babylon 5*; Dick, Philip K.; *Star Trek*.

## FURTHER READING

Harris-Fain, Darren. "Created in the Image of God: The Narrator and the Computer in Harlan Ellison's 'I Have No Mouth, and I Must Scream'." *Extrapolation*, vol. 32, no. 2, 1991, pp. 143–55. Reprinted in *Critical Insights: Harlan Ellison*, edited by Joseph Francavilla, Salem Press, 2011.

Schrier, Karen. "The Weird Humanity of *I Have No Mouth and I Must Scream*." *Well-Played: A Journal on Video Games, Value and Meaning*, vol. 3, no. 2, 2014, pp. 139–60.

Weil, Ellen and Gary K. Wolfe. *Harlan Ellison: The Edge of Forever*. Ohio State University Press, 2002.

## *Enemy Mine*

*Enemy Mine* (1985) is based on Barry B. Longyear's Hugo and Nebula Award–winning novella of the same name, originally published in *Isaac Asimov's Science Fiction Magazine*, September 1979, and later rewritten as a novel and expanded into a trilogy. It is Wolfgang Petersen's U.S.-debut film direction, after his international breakthrough with the German World War II movie *Das Boot* (1981), which received six Academy Award nominations, and the well-received fantasy film *The NeverEnding Story* (1984). After the studio had stopped filming because of creative differences with director Richard Loncraine, Petersen took over production and started from scratch. He insisted on a redesign of the alien and decided against on-location filming, instead moving to Bavaria Studios in Munich for most of the film and building a full-blown set, extending both production costs and time. The cost of $40 million was not recovered, as the film could convince neither critics nor audiences, with a gross income of $1.6 million on opening weekend at the box office.

The film, like the novella, tells the story of two space fighter pilots at war becoming stranded on a hostile planet without hope for rescue. After initial hostilities, Willis "Will" Davidge, the human, and Jeriba "Jerry" Shigan, the Drac, realize that they must band together in order to survive in the harsh environment. Overcoming their original prejudices, they form an intimate friendship with each other, and when Jeriba dies in childbirth (Drac are hermaphrodites), Will cares for the child, Zammis, as his own, even rescuing it from enslavement by other humans later in the film.

The Drac are a reptilian-humanoid species from planet Dracon, with horny protrusions and plates covering head and body, speaking a complex language consisting of clicks, snarls, and gurgles and reproducing via parthenogenesis, without partners or sexual activity. In their visual representation, they are similar to the Gorn from the "Arena" episode of the original *Star Trek* (S01E18). Their culture is formalistic and driven by honor, adhering to traditions, rituals, and recitations. The most important factor defining a Drac's identity is its lineage, which is passed on orally and must be presented by its parent in a rite of passage before acceptance of the new member into Drac society.

Far from subtle, *Enemy Mine* is a story about the alien as a stand-in for human otherness, especially in the context of war and the dehumanization of the enemy. As reviewers have pointed out, the film (and most likely the novella) were strongly inspired by John Boorman's film *Hell in the Pacific* (1968), about an American and a Japanese fighter pilot marooned on an island, struggling with each other, before learning to cooperate and escaping the island on a raft. Not only the similar story line hints at this conflation of the Japanese with the alien, but also *Enemy Mine*'s emphasis on the rigorous hierarchy of Drac society and its belief system of ancestry. The film starts out with Will delivering racial slurs ("toadface," "lizard") and typical war propaganda about his enemy, highlighting their obvious differences: "I knew they were completely inhuman, not even male and female, but both, bundled together, in a scaly reptilian body."

But over the course of the film, Will, as a stand-in for the audience, comes to the deeply humanist understanding that the Drac is essentially human underneath its scales. Instead of struggling with the unbridgeable divide of language that alienates the Japanese and American soldiers in *Hell in the Pacific*, Jerry and Will easily find each other by Jerry's ability to learn English. Jerry's conversations with Will about religion, tradition, and family ultimately reveal the similarities of the two protagonists, the alien race becoming nothing more than humans in different skins. The film makes use of alien characteristics as excuses for plotlines to develop, emphasizing not the acceptance of difference but rather the commonality of a humanity hidden in the alien.

At the end of both film and book, Zammis is captured by human slavers, and Will is recovered by a human patrol ship. His connection with Zammis drives Will to rescue the child and help it gain entrance into Drac society. But whereas the literary form here stresses the need to understand the alien culture, by letting Will translate scripture and proving his knowledge of Drac traditions and Zammis's lineage, the film sidetracks this cultural education in favor of an action-filled finale that includes a shoot-out with the slavers in order to rescue Zammis. The reading of the lineage before the Drac's elder council is transmuted to the epilogue, performed out of feelings of duty rather than a strong understanding of its value for the alien culture.

The film did not have a strong impact on its audience in the 1980s, perhaps due to its too-early and too-blunt attempt at humanizing the alien, which in the Reagan era would more easily have been read as Soviet than Japanese and stood at odds with the shoot-first zeitgeist better portrayed in the contemporary *Aliens* (Cameron 1986). Nonetheless, in the years since, *Enemy Mine* has had a noteworthy impact on the portrayal of aliens in science-fiction television, for example in the *Stargate* episode "Enemy Mine" (season 7, episode 7), in which an alliance between humans and Unas needs to be formed. The film finds its most famous influence in the *Star Trek: The Next Generation* episode "Darmok" (season 5, episode 2), where Captain Picard and his Tamarian counterpart Captain Dathon find themselves alone on a desolate planet and desperately need to find a means of communication with each other. Both TV shows use reptilian-humanoid aliens, language barriers, and the ultimate resolution of conflict via cooperation and cultural understanding inspired by *Enemy Mine*, making its portrayal of the Drac an important influence on today's science fiction.

*Lars Schmeink*

*See also*: *Arrival*; *Avatar*; *Contact*; *Star Trek*.

**FURTHER READING**

Muir, John Kenneth. "Cult Movie Review: Enemy Mine (1985)." *John Kenneth Muir's Reflections on Cult Movies and Classic TV,* December 11, 2009, reflectionsonfilmandtelevision.blogspot.com/2009/12/cult-movie-review-enemy-mine-1985

Pourroy, Janine. "Behind the Lines of *Enemy Mine*." *Cinefex*, no. 25, February 1986, pp. 4–37.

Rabkin, William. "*Enemy Mine* (1984): Interview with Wolfgang Petersen." *Science Fiction Filmmaking in the 1980s*, edited by Lee Goldberg et al., McFarland, 1995, pp. 111–32.

## *E.T. the Extra-Terrestrial*

Released in the summer of 1982, Director Steven Spielberg's *E.T. the Extra-Terrestrial* has become one of the most beloved American science-fiction films of all time. Featuring a score by John Williams and creature effects by Carlo Rambaldi (both of whom earned Academy Awards for their work on the picture), *E.T.* was a barnstorming critical and commercial success—earning over $600 million worldwide on a modest budget of only $10.5 million—and the film's cuddly protagonist swiftly became an icon of popular culture.

The concept for *E.T.* originates in a screenplay for a horror film. Spielberg was developing the idea (titled *Night Skies*) with screenwriter John Sayles in response to Columbia's demands for a sequel to *Close Encounters of the Third Kind* (1977). Opting to pursue a more family-friendly film, Spielberg shelved *Night Skies* and worked up a new script with Melissa Mathison, partially based on elements of the previous project and inspired by Spielberg's childhood memories of his parents' divorce. The resultant screenplay was titled *E.T. and Me*; three drafts later, it had become *E.T. the Extra-Terrestrial*.

The film's narrative centers around Elliott (Henry Thomas), a lonely ten-year-old boy who befriends an extraterrestrial stranded on Earth. Dubbed E.T. by Elliott and his siblings, Michael (Robert MacNaughton) and Gertie (Drew Barrymore), the alien quickly bonds with the children and develops a telepathic connection with Elliott, who feels its emotions. After the child successfully helps E.T. contact its mother-ship, they both fall sick, and—when government scientists capture and quarantine the pair—their connection is broken. But, with the help of Michael and his friends, E.T. escapes to the forest where its spacecraft has returned, and, after an emotional goodbye, it leaves to be with its own kind.

In common with its chosen companions, E.T. itself is depicted as distinctly childlike. In the opening scene, in which small creatures with large eyes toddle through Californian woodland collecting botanical specimens, the aliens are rendered innocent and vulnerable: their chests glow with a warm red light, they appear awestruck by their surroundings, and all of them—save E.T.—stay close to the security of their mother-ship. This idyllic scene is interrupted by the arrival of a team of government officials who are filmed from waist height, obscuring their faces and creating the point-of-view of a frightened child. They chase the terrified E.T. through the woods as its family flees to safety, inadvertently leaving it behind. Alone, E.T. lets out a cry like "a newborn child's" (Morris, 86).

*E.T. the Extra-Terrestrial* (1982), directed by Steven Spielberg, and starring Henry Thomas (shown here with E.T.). (Universal Pictures/Photofest)

But despite its childish demeanor and relatively humanoid form, E.T. does possess physical attributes that render it distinctly alien, including its glowing heart, telescopic neck, and elongated, seemingly miraculous fingers, as well as its near-magical abilities. As the film's narrative progresses, E.T. heals a cut on Elliott's finger simply by touching it, brings pots of geraniums back to life, and—at the film's climax—resurrects itself before transporting Elliott and his friends to its spaceship. This sequence became one of the film's defining moments, as E.T. uses telekinesis to raise the children and their bikes into the air, flying them to safety to avoid the gun-toting agents on their tail.

As a result of E.T.'s miraculous abilities, a number of readings have discussed the film as a religious allegory and have suggested that E.T. can be seen as a Christ-like figure; Dennis Fischer notes that the alien is dogged by the authorities before it "ascends to the heavens while being watched by the people who have become [its] figurative disciples." However, Fischer's observation that E.T. is perpetually hounded by establishment forces is perhaps less proof of its religious connotations and more an indicator of its cultural context. This is, after all, a film produced under Ronald Reagan's conservative administration, and one that purposely subverts the usual bad-alien scenario of SF film.

*E.T.* was released as Reagan reignited the Cold War and attempted to reestablish America as a superpower on the world stage, creating an antagonistic opposition between the United States and the USSR. According to the nation's dominant ideology, E.T. should have been figured as a foreign invader; instead, the film delivers "a message of love and acceptance of difference" to combat Reagan's militaristic aggression (Morris, 87). While the alien's otherworldly appearance, strange vocalizations, and lack of gender render it ostensibly "other," E.T.

assimilates into a close-knit family that learns to accept it as one of their own; they come under attack from establishment forces rather than the benevolent alien. It is federal agents that bring wanton violence to suburbia, while E.T. wants nothing more than to return to its home planet.

During the film's initial theatrical run, Spielberg and Mathison considered a sequel to be titled *E.T. II: Nocturnal Fears*, in which Elliott would be abducted by evil aliens and turn to E.T. for help. The project was quickly abandoned for fear that it would cheapen the original; the same cannot be said for a notoriously awful video game produced by Atari. Much more successful, however, was William Kotzwinkle's sequel novel *E.T.: The Book of the Green Planet* (1985), in which E.T attempts to return to Earth. The film was remastered in 2002, where the guns held by shadowy agents are infamously replaced with walkie-talkies in a move that undermines its original message. After all, as James Kendrick notes (61), "in *E.T.* it is humankind itself that turns out to be dangerous."

*Rose Butler*

*See also*: *Arrival*; *Avatar*; *Close Encounters of the Third Kind*.

## FURTHER READING

Fischer, Dennis. *Science Fiction Film Directors, 1895–1988*, McFarland, 2000, p. 561.
Gordon, Andrew. *Empire of Dreams: The Science Fiction and Fantasy Films of Steven Spielberg.* Rowman and Littlefield, 2008.
Kendrick, James. *Darkness in the Bliss-Out: A Reconsideration of the Films of Steven Spielberg.* Bloomsbury, 2014.
Morris, Nigel. *The Cinema of Steven Spielberg: Empire of Light*, Wallflower Press, 2007, pp. 84–94.

# F

## *Farscape*

Coming out of the Jim Henson Productions stable from Creator Rockne S. O'Bannon, the television series *Farscape* (1999–2003, 2004) takes all the excesses of science fiction—the aliens, the strangeness, the spaceships and megalomaniac villains, and the melodrama—and turns them up to 11. This series charts what happens to NASA astronaut John Crichton (Ben Browder) when his attempt to slingshot his small ship around the sun goes totally wrong, resulting in the opening of a wormhole that throws him across the universe to a place where humans have never been. There, he is taken on a living bio-mechanoid spaceship (known as a leviathan) named Moya, where he eventually becomes friends with its occupants: Ka D'Argo (Anthony Simcoe), Pa'u Zotoh Zhaan (Virginia Hey), Dominar Rygel XVI (voice: Jonathan Hardy), and Pilot (voice: Lani Tupu). The crew soon expands to include Aeryn Sun (Claudia Black), as well as Bialar Crais (Lani Tupu) and Chiana (Gigi Edgley), among others, all of whom work against the villain Scorpius (Wayne Pygram), who attempts through various means to extract the wormhole knowledge he believes Crichton harbors in his brain. This is done in particular through a chip that eventually malfunctions and turns into hallucinations that take Scorpius's shape—which Crichton names Harvey, after the titular *púca* in the Mary Chase play and the James Stewart film of the same name. As is often the case when misfits and criminals are placed in a small space and forced to work together, the characters—with the possible exception of Scorpius—become close friends and even lovers by the series' end. *Farscape* out-Whedons Joss Whedon's creations for pop culture references and character-embedded wit and reworked science-fiction and fantasy tropes, as episodes like "Jeremiah Crichton," "I, E.T.," "John Quixote," and "Kansas" attest.

The treatment of the alien here is constant and multifaceted. Although Crichton is the only "real" human seen in the show, there are several species that look similar to humans. Most significant is the Sebacean species, which looks rather similar to humans and can cross-breed with them, but has an unusual intolerance to heat that can kill them. The Sebaceans are most often seen as the so-called peacekeepers, a purpose-bred military police force that is more feared than respected, though there are Sebaceans who are not part of the military. *Farscape* manages to use science-fiction television's preference for humanoid aliens in its favor, and many of the show's aliens are quite literally people of color, including the monochromatic Chiana and the blue priestess, Zhaan, who is a humanoid plant. Scorpius, meanwhile, is the result of a forced mating between a Sebacean and a Scarran—a thick-lipped, pale-skinned species that look like bipedal reptiles and radiate extreme heat. Scorpius's presentation therefore includes a cooling rod that inserts into his brain and a costume of black leather—not entirely unlike a gimp suit—that keeps his temperature at a consistent level. The final major humanoid alien character is D'Argo, a member of a warrior race, the Luxans, who are not entirely unlike the Klingons from *Star Trek*. The Luxans are reasonably humanoid but have long tentacles coming out of their temples and long, tattooed chins that serve as secondary sex characteristics and erogenous zones. Rygel and Pilot, however, are not humanoid and are not played by human actors but animatronic puppets. This allows for minimal CGI in their portrayal but also, as the actors mention in interviews, something "real" to interact with on set. This provides an interesting and deliberate confluence of the real and the alien—the minimal CGI means the aliens are physically present in a way they wouldn't be if they were computer generated, even if they look less photo-realistic than they might otherwise.

*Farscape* also takes the suggestion that setting can be a character quite literally; the ship this group lives on is Moya—not exactly a machine, not exactly an animal, but a Leviathan, a biomechanical living ship that forms a symbiotic relationship with a pilot. Aware of the tendencies of science-fiction television to simply present actors in funny suits, *Farscape* deliberately engages with and undermines this trope with humanoid aliens on some occasions, aliens that are visually identical to humans in others and completely unlike humans in yet others. Sometimes this results in a trend toward an "alien of the week," as is the case early on in the series, but more often than not undermining this much-maligned trope. The Scarran costumes, for example, are merely large masks and claws over a black PVC suit, while members of the Sebacean Breakaway colonies in "Look at the Princess" in all three parts are differentiated through particularly pink makeup—but in both cases, the new alien characters are important and carry entire narrative arcs.

Given the considerable number of aliens—and the single human—Crichton's interaction with aliens is one of overwhelming and constant estrangement: physical, mental, emotional, and intellectual. As Crichton says in the episode "Unrealized Reality," "Ah, screw it. But I am not Kirk, Spock, Luke, Buck, Flash, or Arthur frelling Dent. I'm Dorothy Gale from Kansas." Like Dorothy, Crichton makes friends, and this ship of prisoners becomes a family, but the otherness here is undeniable and constant. It is also seen in reversal—Crichton is as alien to those he meets as they are to him. The episode "Crackers Don't Matter," for example, reverses the typical human savior as superior to alien races: only because Crichton's senses are so dull can he withstand the light from T'raltixx with minimal ill effects. Humans, as Pilot quips in this episode, are "deficient," and much of the series is spent with Crichton renegotiating his position in the universe from one of dominance and privilege as a white, educated American male to that of a hunted convict—and just one more alien among many. In the largely post–9/11 context of the series (which the episode "Terra Firma" faces head on), such a maneuver seems an obvious attempt to reconsider not only the alien in light of such a watershed but also the place of science fiction itself.

*Amanda Dillon*

See also: *Babylon 5*; *Dark Crystal, The*; *Firefly/Serenity*; *Star Trek*.

## FURTHER READING

Battis, Jes. *Investigating Farscape: Uncharted Territories of Sex and Science Fiction.* I. B. Tauris, 2007.

Ginn, Sherry. "Exploring the Alien Other on *Farscape*: Human, Puppet, Costume, Cosmetic." *The Wider Worlds of Jim Henson: Essays on His Work and Legacy Beyond* The Muppet Show *and* Sesame Street, edited by Jennifer C. Garlen and Anissa M. Graham, McFarland, 2013, pp. 228–40.

Ginn, Sherry, editor. *The Worlds of Farscape: Essays on the Groundbreaking Television Series.* McFarland, 2013.

## *Firefly/Serenity*

Prior to *Firefly* (2002–2003), creator Joss Whedon had written demons (in the television show *Buffy the Vampire Slayer*), mutants (in the Astonishing X-Men comic series), and aliens (with the script for the film *Alien Resurrection*). Across the collective worlds of *Firefly* and *Serenity* (2005), known as "the 'Verse," the most monstrous aspects of all three of these species are distilled into the Reavers: a cannibalistic, self-mutilating, pirate race of humans from the outlying planet Miranda.

The Reavers operate on the edge of "civilized" space, that is, space brought under the regime of the Alliance. Whereas the Alliance are shown within the series to be sterile, strict, and conservative, the Reavers represent the other extreme of the spectrum, breaking all human taboos and corrupting all they come into contact with. As Zoe explains it, the Reavers are not afraid to inflict brutal violence on others with little regard for other living beings.

*Firefly* is a science-fiction Western with an overlaid analogy to the American Civil War from the perspective of the losing side. As such, with the crew of the *Serenity* occupying a compromised middle territory, both geographically and morally, the Alliance and their authoritarian doctrines can appear to be almost as alien and disruptive to their way of life as the Reavers. Therefore, the 'Verse, being subjectively presented from the viewpoint of a small crew, is constantly reoriented for the viewer. On a broad level, the liberal use of Mandarin within a contemporary American dialect—itself indicative of a more enmeshed social understanding between superpowers in the speculative future—may also present itself as an alien, cultural barrier to viewers of the U.S.-made show. Within the 'Verse itself, these same knowledge gaps are also critical in the unpacking and comprehension of narrative events. In "Safe" and "Objects in Space," for example, when people are discussing the skills that River has acquired through cutting-edge Alliance research, she is ignorantly branded a witch rather than a psychic, with Kaylee also offering that "nobody can shoot like that, that's a person" ("Objects in Space," *Firefly*). The Reavers occupy that same critical terrain of being considered nonhuman or alien. At the first mention of them, Jayne states, "Those people ain't human" ("Serenity," *Firefly*), a sentiment echoed later in "Bushwhacked," when in response to Book offering that "whatever acts of barbarism, it was done by men. Nothing more," Jayne firmly repeats his mantra: "Reavers ain't men."

*Firefly* (2002–2003), featuring (from left) Adam Baldwin as Jayne, Nathan Fillion as Captain Malcolm "Mal" Reynolds, and Gina Torres as Zoe. (FOX/Photofest)

To characters from the Alliance Core Worlds, the Reavers are understood to be "Campfire stories . . . Men gone savage at the end of space" ("Serenity," *Firefly*). Beyond the auspices of civilization, where the Border Worlds reside, they are more akin to "the bogeyman from stories" (*Serenity*), showing up sporadically from Reaver Territory to forcibly remind people that they exist. The people from the far-flung Colonies are simply their prey. Yet, only appearing in two episodes of the 14-episode series, the Reavers are not presented as the central antagonists of *Firefly*, and they're not exclusively the most bloodthirsty. Crime syndicate boss Niska is also a recurrent character capable of demonstrating how much violence he is willing to inflict on captives in order to gain a thrill and meet their "true self" ("War Stories," *Firefly*).

In "Bushwhacked," the episode is split into two parts, focusing on the Alliance and the Reavers in equal measure, with a brief yet bloody disagreement between the two competing schools of thought taking place primarily aboard Captain Mal's ship, caught uneasily in the center. *Serenity* the film amplifies this connective tissue as the Reavers are brought to the foreground of the 'Verse in direct comparison with the Alliance. The parallels and stark contrasts between their identities are most vividly seen in the final confrontation between the two opposing fleets, but the emotional impact and moral certainty of the conflict is virtually upturned when it is revealed that the Alliance accidentally created the Reavers in a planet-sized experiment to "make people better" (*Serenity*). By injecting gas into the air processors of the Alliance-civilized planet of Miranda, their plans to "calm the population, weed out aggression. Make a peaceful" world worked, but it not only made them overly sedated to the point of 30 million people allowing themselves to die, "about a tenth of the population had the opposite reaction to the Pax. Their aggressor response increased . . . beyond madness" (*Serenity*).

In *Firefly* and *Serenity*, the aliens are made real by the human race. The Alliance created an alien species of nonhumans—one that is not only antithetical to their own beliefs but those of humankind. It is only when faced with this reality, stripped of ideological rhetoric by the endangered people in the middle of the contested space, that the Alliance begins to concede their position on the limitations of government control. The narrative conceit of terraforming explains why there are no extraterrestrial life-forms in the 'Verse: every planet is literally a variation on *terra*, or the "Earth-That-Was." What was before has now been erased by human interference. In the 'Verse, cows are moved between planets, while geese, beagles, and dinosaurs are casually referenced. In the episode "The Message," the "proof of alien life" is a mutated cow fetus suspended upside down in a jar within a sideshow booth: proof that the only aliens to humanity are the ones that they create themselves and fail to understand from an uninformed perspective.

*Carl Wilson*

See also: *Babylon 5*; *Farscape*; *Star Trek*.

## FURTHER READING

Hadyk-Delodder, Gareth and Laura Chilcoat. "'See What's Inside': Understanding the Reavers' Posthuman Identity and Role in *Firefly* and *Serenity*." *Firefly Revisited: Essays on Joss Whedon's Classic Series*, edited by Michael Goodrum and Philip Smith, Rowman and Littlefield, 2015, pp. 37–52.

Pateman, Matthew. "Deathly Serious: Mortality, Morality, and the Mise-en-Scène in Firefly and Serenity." *Investigating Firefly and Serenity: Science Fiction on the Frontier*, edited by Rhonda V. Wilcox and Tanya Cochran, I. B. Tauris, 2008, pp. 212–23.

Whedon, Joss. *Firefly: A Celebration*. Titan, 2010.

## Flammarion, Camille

Nicolas Camille Flammarion (1842–1925) was a French astronomer and writer best known for several texts that simplified and popularized astronomy for the general reading public, for several science-fiction novels incorporating his astronomical research, and for a lifelong advocacy of spiritualism. His fusion of spiritualism and science caused controversy, particularly in his early career (he was fired from the observatory he worked at after publishing his first book on the subject), but such were his skills as a mathematician and popularizer of science that he was soon reemployed and eventually founded his own observatory. Flammarion was the editor of several scientific journals, the founder of the Société Astronomique de France, and a Legion of Honor recipient. He named the moons Triton (Neptune) and Amalthea (Jupiter) and in turn has a lunar crater, Martian crater, and several asteroids named after him and his writings.

Flammarion first lays out his speculations on the possibility of alien life in two early works—*La pluralité des mondes inhabités* (*The Plurality of Inhabited Worlds*) (1862) and *Les mondes imaginaires et les mondes réels* (*Imaginary Worlds and Real Worlds*) (1865)—while also conducting a historical survey of earlier speculations on the possibility of alien life, both in science and fiction. Then, in *Lumen* (1872) and *Uranie* (Urania) (1890), he presents fictive dialogues that illustrate these conceptions. Flammarion's most important conclusions were: (1) that the vast majority of worlds should be capable of supporting life, because it is a mistake to assume that the conditions that make life on Earth possible are the only conditions in which life may emerge; (2) that it is a mistake, stemming from anthropocentrism, to assume that alien life must be built on the human template, and instead alien forms of life should possess bodies and constitutions adapted to the conditions of their particular worlds; and (3) all worlds are psychically connected and all sentient alien races essentially human (in spirit though not in form), because souls continuously reincarnate from one planet to another. The first two points would prove important revisions to the contemporary state of science fiction going forward.

Flammarion makes the case for the existence of life on just about every celestial body in the solar system (and beyond), whether other planets, moons, asteroids, or even the sun itself. He bases this claim, first, on the sheer diversity of life on Earth (a planet Flammarion considers imperfect due to its axial tilt and other such "flaws"), even in areas humans would find inhospitable, which to him demonstrates that life is tremendously adaptable. Secondly, Flammarion believes in a creator deity who would desire sentient life to appreciate the full scope of Creation. To Flammarion, the conditions of the universe so favor life that the existence of aliens must not be *proven*, but rather *disproven*. As such, aliens often appear in Flammarion's works, since he thought it only natural for other worlds to be inhabited, but some of these appearances can be perfunctory, and from his perspective they require neither explanation from the author nor the amazement of the characters and readers. For instance, in his 1893 geological epic *La Fin Du Monde* (The End of the World), Martian astronomers enter contact with Earth to warn humanity of a coming comet but are never mentioned before or after this incident. As such, aliens were often little more than convenient plot devices in his fiction, stand-ins for the authority of the author himself.

Flammarion's refutation of anthropocentrism in the conception of aliens is his most important contribution to the field. Whereas before, aliens tended to be conceived as basically human, or close variants thereof (often inspired more by medieval legends than scientific speculation), Flammarion demanded that we imagine creatures adapted to their surroundings, whether extreme heat or cold, constant sunlight or darkness, etc. Although he provides a few examples of potential adaptations in his earlier works, it is not until *Lumen* that he imagines full alien beings and their ecosystems. Many are human analogs (in order to criticize contemporary human society), but his descriptions also include a planet populated by sentient trees, another by a species that escapes immediate description but combines various animal and vegetable parts into its own unique physiology; then later, in *Uranie*, he introduces an insect-like species and winged, six-limbed Martians. These aliens are described rather than encountered; they exist as thought exercises, rather than characters. Nonetheless, Flammarion's ecosystems would provide important direction for future science-fiction writers who strove to create physical templates for aliens beyond the normative human model.

Grounded in the spiritualist movement of the late 19th century, Flammarion's assertion that all alien cultures were essentially different humanities based on metempsychosis—the migration of souls, upon death, to new bodies (on other planets, per Flammarion)—has not had the profound impact on science fiction that his other revisions did. However, some of the ideas ancillary to metempsychosis survived even as the theory itself reverted to obscurity. Flammarion believed that all worlds followed the same basic life cycle from formation to a frozen death. The length of this progression varied according to the size of the celestial body—so, compared to the Earth, the moon and Mars had already undergone their most fruitful ages, while Jupiter's was only beginning. As such, there were alien species younger than humanity—and therefore at an earlier stage of cultural development—but also species much older, and consequently more advanced. While most aliens, to this point, had been close analogs to contemporary human society (or slightly more advanced, in the case of alien worlds employed as utopias), Flammarion encouraged writers to think both of more primitive alien societies and (anticipating Wells) aliens whose cultural and technology so far surpassed our own that their highly advanced state made them just as alien as any difference in physiology.

Flammarion's legacy is most keenly felt in the generation of science-fiction writers who immediately succeeded him; H. G. Wells and George Griffith in England, J.-H. Rosny aîné in France, and Edgar Rice Burroughs in America all cite his influence on their work.

*Steve Asselin*

*See also*: Burroughs, Edgar Rice; Cavendish, Margaret; Stapledon, Olaf.

**FURTHER READING**

Lundwall, S. J. "Omega: The Last Days of the World." *Survey of Science Fiction Literature* 4, edited by Frank N. Magill, Salem Press, 1979, pp. 1592–95.
Stableford, Brian. "Lumen." *Survey of Science Fiction Literature* 3, edited by Frank N. Magill, Salem Press, 1979, 1294–98.
Stableford, Brian. *The Plurality of Imaginary Worlds: The Evolution of French Roman Scientifique*. Blackcoat, 2016.

## Fort and Forteanism

Charles Fort (1874–1932) was born in Albany, New York, in 1874 and, apart from a trip in 1896 to South Africa and Britain and several years researching in the British Museum (between 1921 and 1928), spent his entire life in New York City. He initially made a living as a journalist and a short-story writer. At the age of 25 he wrote his autobiography and after that finished several novels, of which one was published: *The Outcast Manufacturers* (1909).

Two of his unpublished novels (both destroyed in manuscript by Fort himself) heralded some of the ideas for which he would become celebrated. *X*, which he completed in 1915, postulated that humanity was incapable of free will because it was under the control of more powerful minds: *X* located these on Mars. The rays transmitted from Mars produced many strange phenomena on Earth (the sort of phenomena Fort would explore in his last four books). While his friend and patron

Theodore Dreiser, the celebrated novelist, was trying to find a publisher for *X*, Fort was already hard at work on *Y*.

*Y* treated much the same sort of material as *X*, but Fort shifted his attention from Mars to the North Pole. The advanced alien race that lived there was also influencing the rest of humanity in various ways. These books seem to have balanced uneasily between fiction and nonfiction. At this time, Fort became financially independent; thanks to a small legacy, he was able to give up on fiction and turn to what fascinated him. In July 1918 he wrote to Theodore Dreiser that he had discovered *Z*.

*Z* was later renamed *The Book of the Damned* and was published in December 1919 by Boni and Liveright, up-and-coming New York publishers (responsible also for the prestigious Modern Library series). By "the damned," Fort meant the data that science had excluded: the data that he had collected, mostly in the New York Public Library, and written out on small rectangles of paper, some 40,000 by his reckoning, that he stored in pigeonholes in his apartment. He went on collecting material throughout the 1920s, and the results of his researches were published in four books. After *The Book of the Damned* came *New Lands* (1923), *Lo!* (1931), and *Wild Talents* (1932): they were published together as *The Books of Charles Fort* by Henry Holt (New York) in 1941, with an introduction by his disciple Tiffany Thayer. (Page references are to this edition, which is online at www.sacred-texts.com.)

Fort was always much more interested in attacking the dogmas of science than in establishing his own dogmas. He reserved some of his choicest abuse for scientists of various kinds, astronomers above all: "the supposed science of astronomy is only a composition of yarns, evasions, myths, errors, disagreements, boasts, superstitions, guesses, and bamboozlements" (714). He distrusted authority to such an extent that he distrusted himself, and it is always difficult to calculate the level of seriousness in what he writes. Ben Hecht, one of his earliest reviewers, probably had it right in the *Chicago Daily News*: "Charles Fort is an inspired clown who, to the accompaniment of a gigantic snare drum, has bounded into the arena of science and let fly at the pontifical sets of wisdom with a slapstick and bladder" (Steinmeyer, 181). It was Hecht who first declared that he was a "Fortean."

As an example of Fort's approach, we may take his examination of gelatinous substances found on the ground. These substances seem to have fallen from the sky. Perhaps, suggests Fort, there is a gelatinous layer, far up; the twinkling of stars may be the result of light penetrating this quivering substance. Perhaps fragments of this substance are torn down by storms or by meteors. "I think, myself, that it would be absurd to say that the whole sky is gelatinous; it seems more acceptable that only certain areas are" (47). One imagines Fort smiling, or laughing outright, as he wrote that.

*The Book of the Damned* has much to say about things falling from the sky: blood, frogs, fish, pebbles. Fort suggested that gravity extends only for a few miles above the surface: beyond that there is a Super-Sargasso Sea, which gathers objects up and occasionally deposits them once more upon Earth. Such depositions may occur when cylindrical-shaped flying machines pass through the Sea: Fort collects together instances of lights in the sky, or mysterious flying machines. He is the prophet of what, after 1953, came to be called Unidentified Flying Objects, or flying saucers. He was, however, much more adventurous than most later UFOlogists in terms of his perception of UFOs. He imagined giant wandering planets, unseen by human eyes or by the telescopes of incompetent astronomers. The inhabitants of some of these interfered in human history, such as those who lived in the blue world of Azuria, or Cyclorea, a great wheel-shaped world or "super-construction" (162). In the course of his discussion of such super-constructions he came out with his most famous statement about the relationship between aliens and humans: "I think we're property" (163).

Fort was writing in the period before the so-called Golden Age of science fiction in the United States, but he was read by most of those writers. His impact on science fiction has yet to be properly investigated, but it was very significant, above all in the 1930s and 1940s. The very first issue of John W. Campbell's magazine *Unknown*, in 1939, began with a serialization of *Sinister Barrier*, a novel by the British writer Eric Frank Russell, who was an enthusiastic Fortean. Moreover, not only Theodore Dreiser, but other well-known figures proclaimed their fascination. The Fortean Society was founded in January 1931 (Fort had to be inveigled into attending the inaugural meeting). Tiffany Thayer published the *Fortean Society Magazine* (later named *Doubt*) from 1939 until his death in 1959, and *Fortean Times* (originally *The News*) has been published in Britain since 1973, now appearing monthly.

*Edward James*

See also: Aliens Did Not Build the Pyramids; Grays; Roswell (Place).

**FURTHER READING**

Gardner, Martin. "The Forteans." *Fads and Fallacies in the Name of Science*, edited by Martin Gardner, Dover, 1957, pp. 42–54.
Knight, Damon. *Charles Fort, Prophet of the Unexplained*. Doubleday, 1970.
Steinmeyer, Jim. *Charles Fort: The Man Who Invented the Supernatural*. Tarcher/Penguin, 2008.

## *FTL: Faster Than Light*

*FTL: Faster Than Light* (2012) is a strategy game depicting ship-to-ship combat for PC, OSX, Linux, and iPad iOS. The game was developed by Justin Ma and Matthew Davis (Subset Games), who self-funded the initial development but turned to Kickstarter after the game's increased publicity demanded longer development. Kickstarter backers exceeded Ma and Davis's request twentyfold, and the game's subsequent success showed the potential for independent studios to find support through crowdfunding. *FTL: Faster Than Light's* critical reception was extremely positive, with the few complaints focusing on the game's punishing difficulty and use of random elements.

*FTL: Faster Than Light* is a rougelike strategy game with narrative elements that allow for some player choice. A "rougelike" is a procedurally generated game where events and challenges vary on each play-through. The strategy element comes from resource management and tactical decisions during combat. The game opens with the player acting as captain for the *Kestrel*, a small Federation ship carrying vital information just ahead of a Rebel armada. The player sends the *Kestrel* into various encounters across the galaxy, hoping to earn scrap (currency) to upgrade the ship or purchase upgrades and crew from a shop. The most common way to earn scrap and weapons is through ship-to-ship combat, where the player must staff various systems on the *Kestrel*, send power to those systems, and juggle offensive and defensive strategies. The journey across the galaxy has the player upgrading the *Kestrel* from a small ship staffed entirely by humans to a ship teeming with alien crew and advanced systems necessary to face the Rebel Flagship. Successful runs or side quests can unlock ships with different weapon and crew compositions. However, each play-through is randomly generated, meaning the player will have unique encounters and options in each play-through. Survival is about resource management, careful strategy, and understanding the various alien races.

The alien races in *FTL: Faster Than Light* include the robotic Engi, the insect-like Mantis, the fire-resistant Rockmen, the energy-based Zoltan, the telepathic Slug, the hidden Crystal, and the scavenging Lanius. Each race has its own particular abilities as crew, providing variety from the Humans, who are described in-game as "common and uninteresting" and have no unique abilities beyond learning skills slightly more quickly than other races. Humans comprise most of the Federation and all of the Rebellion, implying the Rebellion's mission includes a Human-centered agenda. Aside from the Engi, the Federation has strained relationships with most alien races. *FTL: Faster Than Light* posits a universe where aliens are aware of humans but treat them as nothing special.

When the player unlocks new ships, the default systems demonstrate the strengths or force the player to cope with the weaknesses of a particular alien race. The Shivan cruiser of the Rockmen has no way to vent oxygen, forcing Rockmen to fight fires and boarders hand-to-hand. The Engi Vortex allows for numerous automated drones but has limited crew to handle boarders and staff systems. Players will spend their time building up the ships by looking for the sectors of other races. A player selecting the Shivan might look for Lanius as alternative firefighters because their presence removes oxygen from the room, and the player selecting the Vortex might need some Rockmen or Mantis to supplement the Engi's poor performance in repelling boarders. Ship design and loadout seem to reflect the biological and cultural components of each species, and players must grapple with the inherent designs of alien ships. Successful play likely includes diversifying the crew, meaning that all ships are more effective with a mix of alien species.

*FTL: Faster Than Light* is a game where every encounter is like the first encounter, thus the universe is alien each time the player leaves the hangar. *FTL: Faster Than Light* encourages players to approach aliens on a species level rather than individually. Rougelikes encourage players to learn system rules rather than memorize levels, and the behavior of each alien species becomes another set of system rules. Composing an effective crew of aliens and humans requires balancing the strengths and drawbacks of a species rather than individuals. Any crew member can develop a skill by successfully completing a task, but the limitations of a species can slow skill development in some areas. For example, Engi are likely to develop repair skills quickly thanks to faster repair speed, but their poor hand-to-hand damage output makes them unlikely to defeat a boarder and gain experience. A player needs to balance these traits out and has a variety of options, from recruiting crew members that could compensate, investing in drones, or planning to open the airlock and suffocate any boarders. Although the player has numerous options, the player is best served by viewing aliens as a species with particular traits rather than individuals.

*Ian Derk*

*See also*: *StarCraft*; *Warhammer*; *X-COM, XCOM*.

## FURTHER READING

Cooper, Holland. "*Faster Than Light* Review." *GamesRadar+*. www.gamesradar.com /faster-than-light-review/.

Croshaw, Ben. "*FTL: Faster Than Light* (Zero Punctuation)." *Escapist Magazine*. www .youtube.com/watch?v=d7DT1Z5523s.

## *Futurama*

*Futurama* (1999–2003, 2007–2013) is an animated television show created by Matt Groening with executive producer David X. Cohen and originally aired by the Fox network from March 28, 1999, until August 10, 2003. Throughout its four seasons on Fox, *Futurama* was subject to an erratic airing schedule, resulting in many preemptings and schedule changes. During the production of *Futurama*'s fourth season, Fox stopped purchasing episodes of the show, effectively canceling it. Four years after this initial cancellation, however, Comedy Central resurrected the series in four direct-to-video feature-length movies: *Bender's Big Score* (2007), *The Beast with a Billion Backs* (2008), *Bender's Game* (2008), and *Into the Wild Green Yonder* (2009). Comedy Central later repackaged these films as 16 televised episodes, constituting a fifth season, which aired between March 23, 2008, and August 30, 2009. These episodes were followed by seasons 6 and 7 (June 24, 2010 to September 4, 2013), at which point, due to its tumultuous airing and cancellation history, Futurama concluded with its *fourth* series finale, "Meanwhile." Within the larger *Futurama* universe, there is also a long-running set of comic books, a video game, and a mobile game.

The show itself is about Philip J. Fry, a pizza-delivery boy from 1999 who accidentally falls into an open cryogenics chamber after a delivery goes wrong and is frozen and preserved until the 31st century, at which point he tracks down his great-grandnephew 30 times removed, Professor Hubert J. Farnsworth. Farnsworth, a mad scientist of advanced age, owns Planet Express, an intergalactic delivery company, and Fry begins assimilating into this new century by resuming his position as a delivery boy.

The animated cast of FOX TV's *Futurama* (1999–2003). Shown from left: Kif Kroker (voice: Maurice LaMarche), Zapp Brannigan (voice: Billy West), Turanga Leela (voice: Katey Sagal), Philip J. Fry (voice: Billy West), Bender Bending Rodriguez Bending Unit 22 (voice: John DiMaggio), Nibbler (voice: Frank Welker), and Amy Wong (voice: Lauren Tom). (Fox Network/Photofest)

While the series nominally focuses on Fry's adventures in the future, the main cast includes other employees of Planet Express: Turanga Leela, an orphaned alien cyclops; Bender Bending Rodríguez, a sentient, self-interested robot whose main function is to bend objects; Doctor John A. Zoidberg, an incompetent, continually down-on-his-luck lobsterlike physician; Hermes Conrad, a workaholic accountant and limbo champion; Amy Wong, a doctoral student in applied physics and heir to half of the planet Mars; and Professor Farnsworth.

Although the series rests on the well-worn foundations of a relatable outsider encountering an alien world, *Futurama* complicates this formula through its normalization of the alien. Humanoid and nonhumanoid beings exist alongside terrestrial humans, such as Kif Kroeker, a mild-mannered amphibious alien and lieutenant in the military arm of the Democratic Order of Planets (DOOP). Kif becomes Amy's love interest in the second season ("A Flight to Remember"), and eventually they solidify their relationship as Amy becomes Kif's "smizmar," a parental figure to the hundreds of tadpole-like offspring Kif births after an accidental exchange of genetic material with Leela ("Kif Gets Knocked Up a Notch"). While the pregnancy and birth rituals are infused with humor, the episode focuses on Amy's fear of losing her independence and freedom rather than fear of Kif's biology or the alienness of their children.

Even during true extraterrestrial threats, such as those posed by the Brain Spawn ("The Day the Earth Stood Stupid"), the Brain Slugs ("A Head in the

Polls"), Omicronian rulers Lrrr and Ndnd ("The Problem with Popplers"), and many-tentacled Yivo ("The Beast with a Billion Backs"), the main characters do not express fear of the other. Instead, they attend to the situation at hand—such as Lrrr and Ndnd's threat to eat humans in retaliation for humans eating their offspring—and its potential consequences. For those aliens who pose threats from within *Futurama*'s main terrestrial setting, such as Morbo the Annihilator, a hostile reptilian creature of extraterrestrial origin, characters' reactions to dangerous otherness are even more muted. For instance, Morbo, host of many in-universe news and entertainment shows, including *Channel $\sqrt{2}$ News*; *Good Morning, Earth*; *Entertainment and Earth Invasion Tonite*; *Who Dares to Be a Millionaire?*; and *Tea with Titans*, peppers his on-air performances with promises to destroy humanity, yet his co-anchor and viewers never react to these overt threats.

With the exception of Fry, Farnsworth, and Hermes, the main characters all exist as nonhuman or alien beings. Bender, a robot, and Zoidberg, an alien from Decapod 10, are the most obvious others, but Leela and Amy also fit in this category. With her purple hair and single eye, the orphaned Leela is presumed to be an alien, but Amy, who does not exhibit any extraterrestrial features, is an alien by virtue of being from Mars. *Futurama* thus undercuts the strangeness of the other by presenting one of the most mundane of its cast as a Martian. The show also plays with the idea of the strange existing within the familiar when Leela discovers in "Leela's Homeworld" in season 4 that she is a sewer mutant: her parents left her at Cookieville Minimum-Security Orphanarium in order to provide her with a better life above ground, as aliens experience less discrimination than mutants.

Leela's experience, as the extraterrestrial who becomes terrestrial, is a microcosm of Fry's journey within the show. In contrast to the ease with which all extraterrestrials integrate into the 31st century, Fry's 20th-century beliefs set him apart as a living artifact. His memories of the past do not fit the interpretations of the future, as represented by the Lunar Park on the moon ("The Series Has Landed") and the dangerous traditions of "Xmas" ("Xmas Story"), and his behaviors are misinterpreted by those around him. Yet despite these othering characteristics, *Futurama* fundamentally provides Fry with a sense of belonging in an alien landscape. Episodes containing flashbacks, including "The Luck of the Fryrish," "Jurassic Bark," and "Game of Tones," contrast Fry's past failures with the love of his family and serve to bolster the importance of his moderate successes in the future. Ultimately, Fry finds a new family among the aliens of the future, fitting in with them because of his innate strangeness. *Futurama* thus shifts the alien other away from a traditionally marginalized position to a centralized and hopeful futuristic vision where the strange becomes the familiar.

*Eden Lee Lackner*

See also: *Galaxy Quest*; *Hitchhiker's Guide to the Galaxy, The*; *Lilo and Stitch*; *Oddworld*.

## FURTHER READING

Geraghty, Lincoln. "'Welcome to the World of Tomorrow': Animating Science Fictions of the Present and the Past in *Futurama*." *Channelling the Future: Essays on Science*

*Fiction and Fantasy Television*, edited by Lincoln Geraghty, Scarecrow Press, 2009, pp. 149–64.

Lewis, Courtland and Shawn Young, editors. *Futurama and Philosophy: Bite My Shiny Metal Axiom*. Open Court, 2013.

Schlegel, Christian. *Futurama: Looking Backward at Present Day America*. Anchor Academic Publishing, 2015.

# G

## Galaxy Quest

The primary alien stars of director Dean Parisot's *Galaxy Quest* (1999), an affectionate and metareferential parody of the *Star Trek* franchise, are the Thermians. They are an intelligent, peaceful, but intensely literal group who intercept old reruns of the *Galaxy Quest* television show and mistake them for factual "historical documents." When they are threatened by alien warlord Sarris (Robin Sachs), they contact the now out-of-work actors from the show to help, believing them to be the intergalactic heroes portrayed on-screen. As the aliens shower the crew with fawning adulation while demonstrating a distinct social awkwardness, it is impossible not to see the parallels between the starstruck residents of the Klaatu Nebula and the hardcore fans that Jason (Tim Allen) and his fellow actors deal with at their convention appearances.

John Tulloch and Henry Jenkins have explored how this kind of fandom has been represented and how the stereotype of the "Trekkie" has been perpetuated, resulting in a construction of "the fan as extraterrestrial; the fan as excessive consumer; the fan as cultist" (4). What better way to embody these exotic and irrational beings than as literal aliens with an unshakable belief in the fictional Protector crew? The concept of fiction-for-entertainment is incomprehensible to Mathesar (Enrico Colantoni) and his fellow Thermians, even when presented with the truth about the *Galaxy Quest* "historical documents." Indeed, when Alexander (Alan Rickman) enquires whether they have television, theater, or film on their homeworld, they respond by calling such things "lies" and "deception." Like the stereotypical science-fiction fan, the Thermians are unable to find enjoyment in simply watching these forms of entertainment without heavily engaging with it on an extratextual level. They have gone to the extreme of building the starship and recreating every aspect of the show in a way not dissimilar to fans building models of the *Enterprise* and learning Klingon. That *Galaxy Quest*'s primary alien race is just one step further removed from reality, that they cannot even comprehend narrative fiction, suggests it is this extratextual engagement, recreation, and role-play that fans really enjoy, rather than the textual artifacts themselves.

The Thermians being presented as an audience of "Trekkies" is also crucial to understanding the character of Sarris, their ruthless alien enemy. Reportedly named after noted film critic Andrew Sarris, who had disliked producer Mark Johnson's previous film *The Natural* (Barry Levinson, 1984), Sarris has a dismissive contempt for the Thermians and an unusually eloquent language that place him firmly in the position of the critic who wants to destroy these "fans" because they prevent his world, his narrative fiction as the ruthless alien warrior, from being taken seriously. Some of his dialogue reads like a scathing review, for example when he tells Mathesar, "At every turn you demonstrate the necessity for your extermination" and when he mockingly praises the actors' performances using the specifically theatrical term "bravo."

Sarris clearly reflects prevalent critical and academic attitudes to the specific form of science fiction represented by *Star Trek*. As Tulloch and Jenkins point out, many critics consider the franchise to represent the most trivial and banal aspects of the genre, with Teresa Ebert labeling it "Parascience Fiction" and dismissing it as an update of old-fashioned space-opera science fiction designed for the middle classes' love of gadgets. It has also been claimed by a number of critics that media science fiction is infantile, which is certainly reflected in the way Sarris sees the Thermians as infants. During Jason's attempt to explain television to Mathesar, Sarris says, "He doesn't understand. Explain to him as you would a child."

Nevertheless, *Galaxy Quest* does not use that parallel to diminish the importance of the fandom, or of the entertainment products that formed it. Once Jason's initial meeting with the Thermians is played for laughs and he eventually realizes the ship is real, we are given a much more serious glimpse at the aliens' background. Mathesar talks about how Thermian society was in disarray and on the brink of collapse before they found the *Galaxy Quest* footage. The show then became not just a technological blueprint for creating the ship and advancing their scientific achievement, but also a social and moral core around which to rebuild their culture. This raises a much more profound question about the role of entertainment media in our own society and is particularly relevant to a film that is so eager to reflect specifically on the *Star Trek* franchise. NASA's first space shuttle, *Enterprise*, was named explicitly after the fictional vessel, and the show even provided the earliest depictions of modern technology such as flat-screen TVs, tablet computers, and Bluetooth communication.

Beyond this, the liberal humanist ideology of the show had considerable influence on identity politics and social attitudes for an entire generation of viewers exposed to a multigender, multi-ethnic ensemble of characters who had left the 20th-century obsession with money and borders behind in order to focus on bettering themselves as a unified "federation." So while the Thermians can be read as stereotypical "Trekkies" who have taken their obsession with an old TV show too far, they also allow us to reflect on the impact science fiction and media more generally have on our own way of life and the way we engage with the world around us. Such wide-reaching cultural influence is not so easy to dismiss as the purview of a niche fandom.

*Jonathan Mack*

See also: *Futurama*; *Hitchhiker's Guide to the Galaxy, The*; *Star Trek*.

## FURTHER READING

Duncan, Jody and Estelle Shay. "Trekking into the Klaatu Nebula." *Cinefex*, no. 81, April 2000, pp. 108–23.

Kaveney, Roz. "Comedy 1: *Galaxy Quest*." *From* Alien *to* The Matrix: *Reading Science Fiction Film*, edited by Roz Kaveney, I. B. Tauris, 2005, pp. 21–35.

Tulloch, John and Henry Jenkins. *Science Fiction Audiences: Watching Doctor Who and Star Trek*. Routledge, 1995.

## Grays

Grays, or gray aliens, are a specific species of extraterrestrial most closely associated with encounter and abduction stories among English speakers. Sightings of grays are most frequent in the United States of America, although they are also popularly reported as present in other North American and European encounter reports. Non-English-speaking cultures historically report encounters with substantially different alien species than the grays, but with the continued globalization of media, the number of reports of grays has significantly increased among all alien reports across the world within the late 20th and early 21st centuries.

Individuals who have seen grays generally report that they are short, usually no taller than an elementary-aged child, and completely hairless, with gray skin, long, spindly limbs, oversized heads, large black oval eyes, and an almost complete lack of other facial features. Although it is not a universal experience, much of the time grays appear naked, and as with their small or missing facial features, they do not have visible genitalia. While humanoid in shape, their proportions are exaggerated, emphasizing their essential otherness. They are technologically advanced and intelligent beyond human understanding, enhancing their status as dangerous, unknowable others. Gray abduction accounts often include intense interrogation and invasive medical exams, usually accompanied by bright, blinding lights, and both abductions and sightings generally involve witnesses' memory loss (partial or full) and missing time.

Grays in literature predate records of real-world encounters with them. In 1891, Kenneth Folingsby published *Meda: A Tale of the Future*, in which the narrator encounters small gray-skinned humanoids with balloon-shaped heads. Two years later, H. G. Wells posited what humanity would look like in the future in his article "The Man of the Year Million," evoking similar imagery of future humans as no longer having mouths, noses, or hair on their bulbous, oversized heads. He refined his vision of humanity's descendants in *The Time Machine* (1895), where humans have split into two distinct evolutionary lines: the Eloi and the Morlocks. Wells's Eloi share many characteristics with his "Year Million" men and grays, as they are short and delicate, with small mouths and ears and large eyes. Although they are not as technologically developed or intelligent as the grays, the Eloi do also exhibit physical androgyny. *The War of the Worlds* (1898) continues Wells's interest in otherworldly beings, as his Martians, while far larger than his earlier conceptions and now sporting tentacles, strengthen the link to modern grays. He moves their origin off-world, gives them advanced technology, and further exaggerates their skin color, the size of their eyes, and the shape of their mouths. Gustav Sandgren, writing as Gabriel Linde, further refined the literary predecessors of grays in his 1933 novel, *Den okända faran* (*The Unknown Danger*). Sandgren's aliens solidify the appearance of grays, as his description is the template upon which the popular conception of these beings rests.

An exhibit of "grays," based on descriptions from numerous alien encounter and abduction stories, at the International UFO Museum and Research Center in Roswell, New Mexico. (Palms/Dreamstime.com)

However, it is the Betty and Barney Hill abduction account that brings the grays fully into public consciousness as a real-world threat. The Hills claimed they had seen and been abducted by aliens over the night of September 19 and the morning of September 20, 1961. Their account features many of the major characteristics of gray sightings: missing time, memory loss and partial recovery, physical examinations, and interrogation. Betty described the aliens as small, gray-skinned humanoids with large noses and lips, black hair, and dark eyes; and under hypnosis, Barney added his own experience of nonconsensual sodomy (via a thin tube or cylindrical object) to their individual accounts of medical examinations. As knowledge of the Hills' experiences spread, so too did sightings of grays. This included the addition of grays to popularized accounts of the 1947 Roswell UFO incident.

Grays occupy a space in modern Western mythology previously held by the fae. Fairies, elves, gnomes, dwarves, brownies, leprechauns, and other folk-tale creatures share similar physical characteristics, from size and proportions to skin color, facial features, and movements. Just as with the grays, these mythological individuals display knowledge and magical abilities beyond human capacity, and encounters with them include memory loss and missing time. Both fae and grays also leave similar evidence of their passing in their wake. For fairies, rings of mushrooms or flowers indicate they have been present, whereas grays leave behind crop circles.

Traditionally, elves and fairies present danger to those that encounter them, often kidnapping mortals and replacing human babies with changelings. Gray sightings and abduction stories are a natural outgrowth of folktale abduction narratives, shifting from the fantasy underpinnings of the fae to science-fiction tropes while maintaining the figure of the strange, unknowable other. Indeed, in both fae and gray encounters lies significant fear of the unknown. The most dangerous sightings of both occur at night in isolated spaces; individuals encountering them are witness to private rituals—such as fairy dances—or specimen collection and experimentation—such as levitation for the purpose of abduction and medical procedures performed on livestock. When they become aware they are being watched, they react with hostility, violence, and overwhelming control over their unlucky witnesses, often culminating in abduction.

Yet past the fear of kidnapping, embedded in fae-encounter narratives is the loss of identity and control; victims lose their connection to their friends and families, and their ability to think for themselves, as they are seduced or enslaved in Faerie for impossible lengths of time before returning to society. These losses are mirrored in gray encounters, with victims experiencing similar disconnections in time and physical and psychological scarring, often being subjected to highly sexualized examinations. For victims of gray encounters, the anxiety around their loss of autonomy is further heightened by this sexualization; certainly, there is an embedded fear of sodomy within reports of gray encounters, which begins in the 1940s with the Hills' accounts and parallels the backlash against rising social movements relating to sexual freedom. As with the fae, grays occupy a space in western mythology in which anxieties regarding contemporary life and the uncertainty of the unknown are expressed.

*Eden Lee Lackner*

See also: Aliens Did Not Build the Pyramids; Condon Report, The; Fort and Forteanism; *X-Files, The.*

### FURTHER READING

Clancy, Susan A. *Abducted: How People Come to Believe They Were Kidnapped by Aliens.* Harvard University Press, 2007.

Hansen, George P. *The Trickster and the Paranormal.* Xlibris, 2001.

Sagan, Carl and Ann Druyan. *The Demon-Haunted World: Science as a Candle in the Dark.* Ballantine, 1997.

## Green Lantern

The original Green Lantern, Alan Scott, first appeared in *All-American Comics* from DC in 1940. He fought terrestrial villains using a magic ring until 1949. Ten years later, during the Silver Age of comics, Green Lantern was brought back as Hal Jordan, a former test pilot. His ring was no longer magical, but an all-purpose tool given to him by a dying alien who worked as an officer for an interstellar police force called the Green Lantern Corps. The Green Lantern rings respond to the will of the user, but other rings' colors correspond to other emotions, including Red (rage), Yellow (fear), Orange (greed), Black (death), White (life), Indigo (compassion), Blue (hope), and Violet (love). Whenever a Green Lantern is about to die, he passes his ring to a new job candidate, who must be "utterly honest and without fear." Charged by the Guardians, a race of immortals, with policing the entire universe, the Corps spans three billion years and boasts some 7,200 active members of many different species, highlighting a diversity of body types.

Hal Jordan first appeared in *Showcase* #22 in 1959. The Silver Age *Green Lantern* took the series in a particularly science fiction–based direction, going beyond the traditional concepts of the individualized alien conqueror and aliens as monsters and bringing such common science-fiction tropes as the galactic council and the multispecies police force into the realm of comic books. Green Lantern comics highlight interspecies diversity, portraying aliens as part of a well-structured, working organization. Aliens in the series function as both Lantern allies and antagonists. Sinestro, a continued threat to the Lantern Corps and founder of the Yellow Lanterns, was born on the planet Korugar. Parallax, the alien embodiment of fear, is also a primary villain who works with Sinestro to corrupt Hal Jordan. While these aliens are the major villains of the comics, the Guardians are creators of technology and bringers of order and enlightenment, while other nonhuman Green Lanterns make appearances in various issues of the comic book, leaving no consistency in alien representation in the comics. It is likely that Green Lantern's backstory was influenced by the Grey Lensman stories of E. E. "Doc" Smith, the most popular science-fiction writer of the 1930s and the chief purveyor of the rip-roaring, high-concept fiction later called space opera.

In the explicitly political issues of the early 1970s, beginning in *Showcase* #76, Green Lanterns such as Guy Gardner and African American John Stewart act as knights with a code, oath, and hierarchy established by the Guardians. Yet the individual Lanterns patrol their assigned sections of the galaxy without much oversight by the larger organization, making both human and alien lanterns true colleagues with similar levels of autonomy and responsibility. The Green Lantern Corps, with its universal perspective, functions as a counterculture that allows Hal and the other Lanterns some intellectual distance from the problems of American culture in the 1970s, which the comics use to engage in discussions of social justice.

In 1994, Kyle Rayner replaced Hal Jordan as the human Green Lantern. Though he fights many of the same villains as Hal Jordan, his primary enemy is the human Major Force, who murdered Kyle Rayner's girlfriend. The 2011 New 52 series adds the Lebanese American Simon Baz and the Hispanic American Jessica Cruz to the Lantern Corps. While the diversity of human Lanterns expands, the Green Lantern comics have always valued diversity by depicting humans as a small fragment of a larger universal system and society.

*Sara Austin*

*See also*: Martian Manhunter; *Nemesis the Warlock*; Superman.

## FURTHER READING

Johns, Geoff. *Green Lantern: Brightest Day.* DC Comics, 2012.
Moore, Jesse T. "The Education of Green Lantern: Culture and Ideology." *The Journal of American Culture*, vol. 26, no. 2, 2003, pp. 263–78.
Palmer-Mehta, Valerie and Kellie Hay. "A Superhero for Gays? Gay Masculinity and Green Lantern." *Journal of American Culture*, vol. 28, no. 4, 2005, pp. 390–404.

## Gwyneth Jones's Aleutians

*White Queen*, the first book of the Aleutian trilogy (*White Queen*, *North Wind*, *Phoenix Café*), is a first-contact novel. It opens in 2038, when a party of Aleutians—named for the site of their first landing on Earth in an invented African nation—are identified by the book's protagonist, Johnny Guglioli. As news spreads of the aliens' presence, the three Aleutian parties on the planet approach what they think is the world government, an international conference on women's rights taking place in Thailand.

The Aleutians have only one biological sex, and have trouble distinguishing between male and female among humans. Conversely, humans have trouble gendering the aliens, seeing some as masculine and others as feminine: the chief alien character, Clavel, is introduced in the novel with the line, "It was the girl." The alien protagonist of the second novel *North Wind* (Bella) is seen by humans as female, but considers himself male most of the time (and is treated as such by the other Aleutians). Jones uses the single-sexed Aleutians to argue that gender is both performance and at the behest of the individual. The Aleutians consider masculine and feminine to be merely behavioral: "The Aleutians recognize among themselves a spectrum of personality traits, which seem to match quite closely what humans regarded as 'masculine and feminine qualities'" (*North Wind*). This argument is brought to a savage point in *White Queen* when Clavel rapes Guglioli, after the Aleutian maps his own alien romantic notions onto the human.

The aliens' arrival on Earth also ignites a series of Gender Wars. *North Wind* takes place some 100 years after *White Queen*, during an uneasy truce in the Gender Wars. Humanity has split into two blocs, Women and Men, or Reformer and Traditionalist. Some men are Women, and some women are Men; the split is not exclusively on biological sex lines and there is a third group, the halfcastes, who surgically alter themselves to resemble Aleutians and follow some Aleutian practices. By the time of the events of the final book, *Phoenix Café*, set a further hundred or so years in the future from North Wind, gender in human society is dependent on which bloc a person belongs to: Men believe in traditional gender roles and presentation, which means females wear chadors and display very feminine characteristics. The Women do not perform gender.

Another way in which the Aleutians differ from humanity, and which also has a profound effect on human society, is in their technology. The aliens use biotechnology, most of which is grown from "wandering" cells of their own bodies. Some of these cells are used for communication, like pheromones but with much higher informational content, while others, "commensals," might grow into furniture or errand creatures or even weapons. By *Phoenix Café*, the Aleutians' biotech has destroyed Earth's technological base. However, there is one piece of human technology the Aleutians need: the Buonarotti Device, an instantaneous, that is, faster-than-light, drive. In *White Queen*, Guglioli uses the device to travel to the Aleutian worldship to destroy it in revenge for his rape. Knowledge of the device is then lost, and in *North Wind*, Bella, an alien hybrid with some genetic material from Guglioli, is believed to be capable of "remembering" where Buonarotti hid her drive. And in *Phoenix Café*, the Aleutians are preparing to leave Earth using the Buonarotti Device, which has proven mostly ineffective for humans.

The protagonist of *Phoenix Café*, Catherine, is an Aleutian who has been genetically engineered to be human. The Aleutians are serial reincarnators and Catherine is an incarnation of Clavel. Because of this ability to reincarnate—it is partly genetic and partly learning from the vast store of knowledge they keep about their former selves—the named Aleutian characters in the trilogy exhibit the same personalities. For example, Clavel is the "Pure One," a romantic tragic hero; Rajath is the Trickster; and Kumbva is the gifted scientist/engineer. Throughout the three books, Jones swaps the narrative from human point-of-view characters to Aleutian point-of-view characters. She shows the aliens from the inside, and successfully differentiates them from humans in sensibilities and outlook. She also demonstrates how they are a product of their biology; serial reincarnation, single sex, the wandering cells they use to communicate.

*Ian Sales*

*See also*: Butler, Octavia E.; Le Guin, Ursula K.

## FURTHER READING

Jones, Gwyneth. *Imagination/Space. Essays and Talks on Fiction, Feminism, Technology, and Politics*. Aqueduct Press, 2009.

Pearson, Wendy G. "Postcolonialism/s, Gender/s, Sexuality/ies and the Legacy of *The Left Hand of Darkness*: Gwyneth Jones's Aleutians Talk Back." *The Yearbook of English Studies*, vol. 37, no. 2, 2007, pp. 182–96.

Vint, Sherryl. "Double Identity: Interpellation in Gwyneth Jones's Aleutian Trilogy." *Science Fiction Studies*, vol. 28, no. 3, 2001, pp. 399–425.

# H

## Half-Life 2

*Half-Life* (2004), a game designed by David Speyrer, opens with a transdimensional alien invasion of the Black Mesa Research Facility from Planet Xen. It is directly indebted to the scenario of first-person shooter *Quake* but also inspired by Stephen King's novella *The Mist*, in which an alien force has escaped from a military installation, and an episode of *The Outer Limits* entitled "The Borderland," in which a scientist mistakenly invents a machine that can create a doorway into the fourth dimension,

The events of *Half-Life* feature scientist Gordon Freeman as he battles Xen's own refugee life-forms from other worlds, including an enslaved race of bipedal, four-armed creatures called the Vortigaunts and the Headcrab, a parasitic life-form visually comparable to the face-hugger of the *Alien* film franchise but functionally comparable to the zombifying Cordyceps fungus. This disparate force is led by the gigantic, fetus-like Nihilanth: a Lovecraftian cosmic horror and the last of its race until dispatched by Freeman at the conclusion of the game.

*Half-Life 2* reveals that, with the death of the overlord, Freeman released the Vortigaunts from their bonds with some of them choosing to remain on Earth as allies. However, Freeman also unwittingly allowed a further race to follow through the now expanded dimensional aperture: the Combine.

In the 20-year gap between the events of *Half-Life* and *Half-Life 2*, the Seven Hour War took place, with the Combine successfully taking over the Earth to install a totalitarian regime. The tone of *Half-Life* is essentially a B-movie exploration of the consequences of ambitious scientific enquiry gone wrong with an added critique of U.S. military safeguarding measures. With *Half-Life 2*, the invasion narrative is more sophisticated, incorporating and reflecting upon broader national ideologies and historical precedents.

The game is filled with overtly communist and fascist resonances, ranging from the Nazi-inspired uniforms of the peacekeepers through to the cold, sleek, alien architecture that literally expands to indifferently consume and reshape the culturally layered Eastern European setting; much as the Combine themselves systematically harvest the general populace and enforce their own dominant agenda as "benefactors" to a biologically neutered species, now reduced to cogs in the expansionist machine.

Elements of *Half-Life 2* are comparable to Robert A. Heinlein's *Starship Troopers*. There are the same fascistic overtones of the ruling military elite, but more notably, the Soldier Bugs and the Brain Bugs of Heinlein's novel and Paul Verhoeven's film adaptation are visually and functionally analogous to *Half-Life 2*'s Antlions and Combine Advisors—all in a world where hive minds, telekinesis, and proboscis-induced memory extraction are also possible. Expanded upon in *Half-Life: Episode 2*, the Advisors are also influenced by the Guild Navigators of Frank Herbert's *Dune* universe, with the inference being that they are equally super-evolved to the point of no longer requiring limbs but still reliant upon a largely subjugated workforce.

Alternatives to the alien invaders are presented throughout the narrative. Father Grigori is emblematic of the Church but also beset by mental instability as he violently exorcises his possessed congregation. The G-Man is more enigmatic, seeming to exist outside of space and time. He bookends the narrative with motives that could be construed as almost benevolent but are clearly corporate in nature; he refers to his "employers" while carrying out their shadowy orders, often literally in the background.

By contrast, the Combine represent a faceless yet omnipresent Empire, with *Half-Life 2*'s position within an incomplete trilogy of games affecting the dissemination of backstories and intentions. Both the player and the characters within the game never find out who the Combine are, where they are from, what they look like, or what their future plans are. Here, all information is suppressed, with any explanation of otherworldly motives channeled through Interim Administrator Wallace Breen, who perversely sees the aliens as saviors to the weaker human race.

The main reason for the Combine being so unknown is that they have co-opted the human race in a similar way to those that have been conquered before them. The Combine are adroit at literally combining and exploiting other alien species. Alien Dropships and Gunships are "Synths"; they are ambiguously both organic and technological in their form and function, with no explanation given to their extraterrestrial origins or any indication of sentience. Likewise, the towering tripod Striders echo the imposing Martian invaders from H. G. Wells's *The War of the Worlds* but function more as comparatively unsophisticated, irritable drones.

According to David Hodgson, the "very early version of the Combine Soldier moved like a snake or worm. Eventually it was decided to avoid any direct representation of human-scale enemies and instead visually depict the Combine as a more transparent force" (107). The "Transhuman" Metro Cops and Combine Soldiers epitomize this transparent threat, figuratively conjoining the Alien Grunts and Human Marines of *Half-Life* to make it obvious both that an invasion has taken place and also that the ongoing subjugation is so effective precisely because it enables and utilizes the worst traits of humanity.

Because of the protective clothing that they wear, it is never clear how augmented and culpable the Transhumans are, yet as an exact counterpoint to the societal order enforced by the Combine, the returning Headcrab Zombies also emphasize the brutal self-harm that can come from giving oneself over to a pernicious, parasitic intruder. Victims can be heard screaming for help as they relentlessly claw at the player protagonist, and the scene of any prior conflict that the player stumbles across is always horrifically visceral and terribly conclusive.

In *Half-Life 2*, alien Headcrabs make humans into unwilling slaves, while some people would prefer to be dormant slaves to the Combine. The case is made that these invaders are the same except for one crucial difference: one can at least try to fight back as a "Freeman" against an oppressive regime.

*Carl Wilson*

See also: *Dead Space*; *Halo*; Heinlein, Robert A.; *Mass Effect* (Trilogy); *X-COM, XCOM*.

## FURTHER READING

Hodgson, David. *Half-Life 2: Raising the Bar. A Behind the Scenes Look. Prima's Official Insider's Guide*. Prima Games, 2004.

## *Halo: Combat Evolved*

*Halo: Combat Evolved* (2004) is a first-person shooter game set in the 26th century, in a universe like ours. It tells the story of Master Chief, a cybernetically improved human who belongs to an elite military force. After his ship is attacked by the Covenant (a coalition of devout aliens against humanity), he is left stranded on a mysterious artificial world that is shaped as a halo. As it turns out, this halo is in fact the homeworld of the Flood, an alien race of parasites that feed upon the living and will eventually end all life in the universe.

The player's first encounter with the covenant is at the end of the tutorial. While Master Chief is readjusting to life (as he was frozen cryogenically), a member of the Covenant breaks down the door of the monitoring room and kills the technician there in cold blood, thus implanting the idea of aliens being the enemy. The player then roams through the *Pillar of Autumn* searching for the captain of the ship and finds several instances of human soldiers fighting these aliens, thus reinforcing the idea of them being against humanity.

Apart from the obvious physical differences between humans and aliens, another element that enhances the differences between them is the color of their blood: while soldiers bleed in red, the aliens' plasma is blue, purple, or orange. Every time that Master Chief slays one of these hostile creatures, they bleed in different colors, suggesting that, although most of them have humanoid shapes, these creatures do not have a human internal structure, thus enhancing their otherness.

There are also differences between the races in their technology. While the United Nations Space Command utilizes weapons based on human technology (that is, enhanced pistols and rifles that shoot bullets), the Covenant's weapons are designed to shoot raw energy. Players can utilize both human weapons and energy weapons, provided that they take the latter (in almost every case) from the dead body of a Covenant alien. These weapons offer a different kind of gameplay, as they lack magazines and instead may overheat. Furthermore, players cannot find any way to recharge these weapons (except for the needler, a weapon that shoots sharp crystals), so they are disposable, and players will need to swap weapons if they want to keep using them. The weapons are like their intended users: lethal, alien, and disposable. Players using these weapons need to be more cautious, not shooting frantically at the enemy, instead trying to hit them with one lethal shot. These differences further reinforce the idea of otherness insofar as they relate to a completely different first-person shooter experience: by creating two different ways of fighting the Covenant (with their own weapons or with those of the UNSC), the ludology further enhances the differences between the aliens and the UNSC.

In this story-world, the difference between humans has been eradicated: there is no human racism, whereas aliens are ultimately racist not only toward humans, but toward other aliens. The Jiralhanae despise the Shangheili, who at the same time consider the Unggoy inferior (they are the lowest in the Covenant hierarchy). While it is true that most of the characters are white (especially those in control), racism among humans has been, allegedly, overcome by the threat of the Covenant, and the game presents characters from different ethnicities, such as Private Mendoza. Furthermore, Master Chief's ethnicity is not shown throughout the entire game, as he is always wearing a full combat suit and helmet. The only instance in which Master Chief's ethnicity is shown is at the end of *Halo 4*, and then for less than a second. This suggests compatibility between avatar and player: because Master Chief's ethnicity is neither stated nor actually shown, players can imagine Master Chief as they want.

In short, narratologically the game presents a relationship with the alien as the enemy. While it is true that the other is focused in the story-world on religiousness and spirituality against the pragmatic approach of the UNSC, this is shown as an approach that leads to violence and devotion. The UNSC is always presented as saviors of the universe, defending themselves: because Halo is destroyed, the universe is not swarmed by the Flood and therefore allowing it to survive. With that, and regardless of the obvious, conflictive implications of Western versus Eastern perspectives, the game suggests a focus on the difference that offers a ludologic ambivalent functionality between both perspectives, although the narrative presents itself as being as simple as humanity versus the other. It is there where *Halo*, contrary to similar games (like the *Call of Duty* franchise) offers a better perspective, since both game styles are both similar enough and different enough to work.

*Jaime Oliveros*

See also: *Dead Space*; *Half-Life 2*; *Mass Effect* (Trilogy).

## FURTHER READING

Cuddy, Luke, editor. *Halo and Philosophy: Intellect Evolved*. Open Court, 2011.
Harvey, Colin B. *Fantastic Transmedia: Narrative, Play and Memory Across Science Fiction and Fantasy Storyworlds*. Palgrave Macmillan, 2015.

## Heaven's Gate

On March 26, 1997, police officers entered a house in the Rancho Santa Fe area of Encinitas, California, and found the bodies of 39 members of the Heaven's Gate group. They were found lying neatly on bunk beds, faces covered with purple cloths. All but two women had plastic bags over their heads. All 39 victims were dressed in black shirts, sweat pants, and Nike trainers; all carried a five-dollar bill and three quarters in their pockets. In a reference to the influence that science fiction had on their belief system, each wore an armband with a patch reading "Heaven's Gate Away Team." The members of the "Heaven's Gate" group had consumed phenobarbital mixed into apple sauce, washed down by vodka, and plastic bags were used as a way of inducing asphyxia, guaranteeing death. They had died over a period of three days, with their founder, Marshall Applewhite, committing suicide on the third day, leaving two female members to tidy up before they too killed themselves.

The suicides were justifiable in the minds of the "crew" due to a belief that planet Earth was to be recycled and the only chance to survive was to leave it immediately and enter "The Next Level." By volunteering to abandon their "vehicles," as their bodies were called, they could enter "The Evolutionary Level above Humans" (TELAH). Once this was achieved, a spaceship following the Hale-Bopp Comet would gather the members that had reached the next level.

The Heaven's Gate belief system was first developed when its founders, Marshall Applewhite (1931–1997) and Bonnie Nettles (1927–1985), met at a psychiatric hospital in 1972. Nettles was a psychiatric nurse with an interest in religious prophecy, and Applewhite had become a patient after the University of St. Thomas in Houston had fired him for an alleged homosexual relationship with a student. The pair formed a bond over their beliefs, reading the Bible and books about asceticism and Christianity. At this time Applewhite was also reading science fiction heavily. Soon referring to themselves as "The UFO Two," they came to believe that they had superior minds to other humans and had been chosen to fulfill biblical prophecies. They began producing pamphlets that implied that Applewhite was a reincarnation of Jesus and that they were the two witnesses mentioned in the Book of Revelations who would be killed and restored to life on a spaceship. It was in 1975 that Applewhite and Nettles, now calling themselves "Do" and "Ti," gathered a "crew" of disciples at an Oregon hotel. Like the followers of the Reverend Jim Jones the year before, the crew went underground, leaving families and jobs behind.

Around this time a belief was developing within the group that God was a highly developed extraterrestrial who had planted the seed of humanity on Earth. This theme is a familiar one in science fiction, with the earliest occurrence appearing in the 1896 unofficial sequel to Wells's *War of the Worlds*: Garrett P. Serviss's *Edison's Conquest of Mars*. Combined with this "ancient astronaut" concept was the idea of a group of aliens called Luciferians who falsely represented themselves as gods to mankind, in order to ensure that humanity was thwarted in their development to the next level, with Satan as the main protagonist. At this point it was suggested that Applewhite was a direct descendant of Jesus and that Applewhite and Nettles were the two witnesses to the end of times, linking them strongly to biblical prophecy and further strengthening their authority.

As the philosophy of the group developed, more science-fiction tropes were added, such as "walk-ins," seen in a number of alien-invasion films such as *Invaders from Mars*. A "walk-in" allowed an entity to occupy a body that had been vacated by the original soul. In the case of the Heaven's Gate group, these

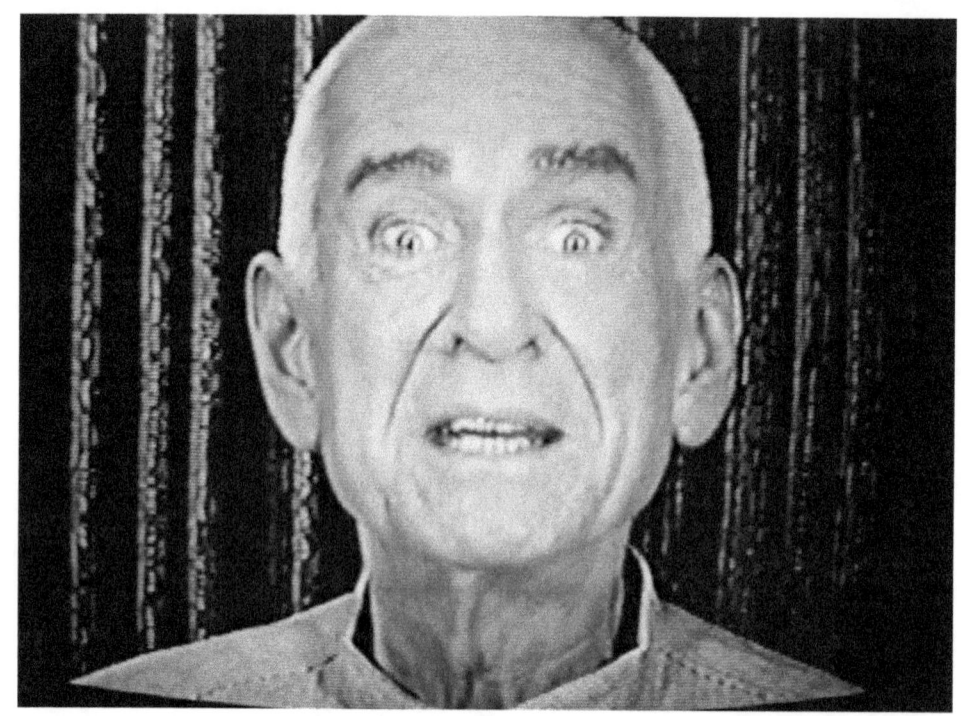

Marshall Herff Applewhite, founder of the organization known as Heaven's Gate, speaking in a videotaped recording shortly before leading 38 followers in a mass suicide near San Diego, California, in 1997. (Brooks Kraft LLC/Sygma via Getty Images)

walk-ins were extraterrestrial and benign in origin. The argument was that Applewhite and Nettles were new beings who had left their previous lives behind and therefore were beings of a higher level, again adding to their authority.

There was a radical philosophical readjustment after the death of Bonnie Nettles in 1985. Originally, it was understood that group members would be collected by the extraterrestrials, who would land their ship on Earth. Group members would receive new bodies in what could be considered a form of Rapture. To qualify would require sacrifice and sequestering themselves from the human condition; later, several of the male members of the group, including Applewhite, had themselves castrated as a show of dedication. After Nettles's death, the requirement to be "crew" was that you needed to leave your body behind, either by natural death, as in the case of Nettles, or by suicide, or random death, accident, or violence. Conformity was paramount, and as with many cults a strict set of rules were in place: for the men there was even a prescribed way of shaving.

After the massacres at Jonestown and Waco, Applewhite was particularly worried about possible government attention, a fear that was unfounded. Nonetheless, the group guarded their privacy. Their public face was an IT company called "Higher Source," which designed webpages. Clients considered them hardworking and courteous and were not aware that the company had links to the Heaven's Gate group.

With the appearance of the Hale-Bopp comet, Applewhite started putting his "evacuation plan" into place. The "Away Team" had a final, identical, dinner at a local diner, where a farewell message was taped. Then, over the next three days the Heaven's Gate Away Team killed themselves.

Heaven's Gate was mostly ignored during its existence, although the Heaven's Gate website is still currently maintained. The real legacy of Heaven's Gate is that it is considered to be the first "cyber-cult." Its evolving mix of religious philosophy and science-fiction tropes has had a major effect on popular culture, with references in music and television; in particular, it has reignited an interest in the idea of ancient astronauts and savior aliens.

*Mike Rennie*

*See also*: Aliens Did Not Build the Pyramids; Fort and Forteanism; Grays; Sun Ra.

**FURTHER READING**

Chryssides, George D., editor. *Heaven's Gate: Postmodernity and Popular Culture in a Suicide Group*. Routledge, 2011.
Lewis, James R., editor. *Violence and New Religious Movements*. Oxford University Press, 2011.
Zeller, Benjamin E. *Heaven's Gate: America's UFO Religion*. NYU Press, 2014.

## Heinlein, Robert A.

Robert A. Heinlein (1907–1988) was one of the most influential writers in modern science fiction. He is best known for his early juvenile novels, such as *Rocket Ship Galileo* (1947), *Space Cadet* (1848), and *Tunnel in the Sky* (1955) and for his major political novels, *Double Star* (1956), *Starship Troopers* (1959), *Stranger in a Strange Land* (1961), and *The Moon Is a Harsh Mistress* (1966). Heinlein's other major contribution to SF is his series of Future History stories, which project events of the galaxy running hundreds of years into the future. Heinlein's aliens often differ based on the intended audience of the novels. His young-adult fiction depicts friendly, benevolent races that wish to help humans (most notably children) evolve and become better citizens of the universe, as opposed to confronting social ills.

In the 1954 novel *The Star Beast*, Lummox, a friendly, sentient creature, is brought back by a scientist returning from an interstellar voyage. Over many years the amiable beast, which is treated as a beloved pet, is inherited by one of the scientist's descendants, John Thomas Stuart XI. Eventually it is discovered that Lummox is a baby Hroshii, one of a hitherto unknown alien race who appear on Earth demanding their child's return. Lummox is eventually identified as royalty and admits that she, never having seen herself as a pet, has instead had a long-term passion for raising several generations of John Thomases and is not willing to part with her current human.

The Vegans from Heinlein's juvenile *Have Space Suit—Will Travel* are telepathic, marsupial bipeds with large eyes and musical voices. One such being, called the Mother Thing by the human characters, Kip and Peewee, rescues them from alien kidnappers called Wormfaces and brings them to her native planet, Vega 5, where the wrongdoers are punished by an intergalactic tribunal. This intergalactic organization's role is to patrol space, protect member civilizations from predatory species, judge new species' ability to coexist with others, and destroy those that cannot. Enormously powerful, they exterminate the xenophobic Wormface civilization.

Heinlein's best-known adult work often plays with the definition of "alien" beyond that of the wholesale other life-form and moves the discussion of the alien to consider the ramifications of colonization throughout the solar system. In his earlier works featuring alien races' interactions with humans, however, the aliens are an invading and colonizing force that Heinlein uses to criticize elements associated with communism during the Cold War.

*The Puppet Masters* is a 1951 novel featuring parasitic invaders from outer space. A clear product of the Red Scare of the late 1940s and early 1950s, the novel postulates an invasion by slug-like creatures who arrive in flying saucers and take over people by attaching themselves to their backs under their clothes and using them as puppets.

The Bugs or Pseudo-Arachnids, are insectoid creatures native to the planet Klendathu in Heinlein's *Starship Troopers*. They are not the seemingly mindless warriors ruled over by a brain bug, as portrayed in the 1997 film version of the novel (and sequels), although they do have a caste system, and they possess advanced technology that is not merely an evolutionary outgrowth of their own bodies, including starships and a variety of dangerous weapons. Moreover, they have attacked other planets before engaging with humanity and have formed an interstellar "Arachnid Empire." In the novel, the protagonist Juan "Johnnie" Rico joins the Mobile Infantry to fight the Bugs to his pacifist father's great dismay and goes through a series of military campaigns, behaving heroically and ending up as an officer. The book, although exciting, is a heavily didactic exploration of civic and military virtue, with significant discussion of such issues as earning the right to vote, the value of corporal punishment, and the importance of military preparedness.

In later works, Heinlein's aliens blend elements of his young-adult and early-adult fiction by presenting themselves as wise, elder races who generally have humanity's best interests at heart and either peacefully enter human civilization or incorporate colonial humans into their own.

The Martians of *Double Star* are Heinlein's highly successful attempt to portray an alien species that doesn't look or think in a manner that is even remotely human. The Martians appear to be mobile vegetables, and they reproduce by fission. The novel involves a clear-sighted, charismatic politician who is fighting to bring both the Martians and the Venusians into Earth's empire as full citizens and as part of that attempt has agreed to become a somewhat more-than-honorary Martian.

The Martians of *Red Planet* (1949) and *Stranger in a Strange Land* (1961) differ significantly from those in *Double Star*. *Red Planet* assumes the successful colonization of Mars. The novel's protagonists, Jim and Frank, are boarding-school students who uncover political corruption but are saved by the three-legged

Martians, who eventually cause the corrupt human beings to simply disappear. In *Stranger in A Strange Land*, Valentine Michael Smith, the first human born on Mars and raised by Martians, comes to Earth and, naive but endowed by the Martians with psychic powers, transforms our planet through the introduction of healthy Martian values. While it isn't clear that *Red Planet* and *Stranger in a Strange Land* take place in the same universe, the Martians in the two books are very similar, sharing a three-part life cycle, the ability to make people disappear, and an emphasis on becoming "water friends" or "water brothers."

*Daniel Creed*

*See also*: Card, Orson Scott; Clement, Hal; Smith, E. E. "Doc."

**FURTHER READING**

Clareson, Thomas D. and Joe Sanders. *The Heritage of Heinlein: A Critical Reading of the Fiction*. McFarland, 2014.

Mendlesohn, Farah. *The Pleasant Profession of Robert A. Heinlein*. Unbound, 2019.

Patterson, William H. Jr. and Andrew Thornton, editors. *The Martian Named Smith: Critical Perspectives on Robert A. Heinlein's* Stranger in a Strange Land. Nitrosyncretic Press, 2001.

## *The Hidden*

*The Hidden* is a 1987 film directed by Jack Sholder set in Los Angeles. In the film, a seemingly ordinary and law-abiding citizen named Jack DeVries (Chris Mulkany) has embarked on a violent crime spree. After robbing a bank and killing several bystanders, he makes a high-speed getaway from the police in his newly stolen Ferrari before coming to an abrupt stop by way of bullets and a police blockade. DeVries is taken to the hospital and, once alone, rises from his bed to vomit a slug-like parasite into the mouth of his comatose roommate, Jonathan Miller (William Boyett). Detective Thomas Beck (Michael Nouri) and FBI Special Agent Lloyd Gallagher (Kyle MacLachlan), who has recently arrived in Los Angeles, travel to the hospital only to find DeVries dead and Miller gone.

Gallagher explains to Beck that he is actually an extraterrestrial lawman, pursuing the alien responsible for the death of his wife, child, and partner across the galaxy. Meanwhile, the body-hopping alien continues to acquire and discard new host bodies before setting its sights on Senator Holt (John McCann), a presidential candidate. Gallagher and Beck engage in a brief shootout with the alien, during which Beck is severely injured. At the climax of the film, Gallagher runs through a hail of gunfire before reaching the now-possessed senator and killing him with a flamethrower. As the senator's body burns, the alien leaves his mouth, and Gallagher, having previously demonstrated that his alien weapon is ineffective on human physiology, is able to end the parasite's rampage. The final moments of the film are heart-warming if ambiguous, with Gallagher transferring his life-force into a dying Beck after he witnesses the emotional turmoil of Beck's wife and daughter. This finale leaves it unclear whether Gallagher has sacrificed himself to save Beck's life or whether he will now reside in the body of a deceased Beck.

The two aliens in the film, Gallagher and the unnamed evil alien, both have an ability to possess humans. However, while the latter resembles a slug that physically crawls inside human bodies, Gallagher's true form appears to be made of pure light. Similarly, while Gallagher is able to occupy a host for several weeks with no sign of outward deterioration, the evil alien burns through host bodies quickly. The evil alien is also less adept at mimicking human behavior, with most of his dialogue being abrupt and unreasonable demands. Gallagher, on the other hand, has learned to blend in effectively, but his responses still have an uncanny quality to them. For example, when Beck asks him how he can afford a Porsche on a special agent's salary, Gallagher openly admits that he stole it. In fact—apart from masquerading as an FBI agent—Gallagher is disarmingly honest. For example, during his conversations with Beck's wife, Barbara (Catherine Cannon), Gallagher admits that he is chasing the person that murdered his family and partner. When Barbara asks him where he was born, he ominously points skywards, which Barbara assumes to mean "North."

While Gallagher is more eloquent in conversation than his evil counterpart, he is still puzzled by everyday human items. When Beck gives Gallagher an antacid and a glass of water to ease a hangover; Gallagher proceeds to bite straight into the tablet. This scene is referenced again later in the film, when Gallagher is offered aspirin and water. Having remembered what his human companion taught him about seltzer, he drops the aspirin into the water and waits for something to happen, earning a withering look from a passing Beck.

Written by Bob Hunt (a pen name for Jim Kouf) and produced by New Line Cinema at a time where yuppie culture was at its peak, it is possible to see the evil alien of *The Hidden* as a representation of the "me first" mantra of the late 1980s and the consumerist greed that characterized the Reagan era. As Gallagher explains to Beck in reference to his extraterrestrial adversary, "If he sees something he wants, he takes it. If someone gets in his way, he kills them." This greed is shown early in the film when the alien, at this point in the guise of Miller, is confronted for stealing a cassette tape from a music store. His response is to beat the store owner to death before pausing to fixate on a poster advertising a ghetto blaster. Seemingly compelled by this advertising, Miller smashes the store's display cabinet to claim his own. The alien rampantly consumes material possessions, and has a taste for fast, expensive, prestige cars. The excesses of the decade are also evident in a scene set in a car salesroom, where a salesman encourages his client to partake in more cocaine while he draws up a contract for the sale of a new Ferrari. The alien goes on to steal the vehicle, stating "I want that car" repeatedly.

This interpretation, however, is counterbalanced by the film's ambiguous ending and the growth of a strong bond of friendship between Beck and Gallagher, which supports a reading of the film that places themes of emotion, friendship, loss, and sacrifice at its core. Beck warms to Gallagher considerably after discovering that he has suffered the loss of his family and is quick to let Gallagher know that he will protect him during confrontations with his otherworldly nemesis. Similarly, Gallagher, whose expressions and demeanor are almost uncannily still and understated during the majority of the film, appears completely grief-stricken after Beck is gravely injured, holding the man's hand to his forehead and kneeling as if in the throes of emotional turmoil.

Although a sequel, *The Hidden 2*, followed in 1993, it performed poorly at the box office and—unlike its forebearer—has not found a home in cult fandom. Ultimately, *The Hidden* stands as a unique alien-invasion thriller with a *Miami Vice* (1984–1990) flavor, replete with fast cars, a rousing late-1980s rock soundtrack, and, at its heart, a rumination on the workings of human nature.

Shellie McMurdo

*See also*: *Alien* (Series); *Invasion of the Body Snatchers*; *V*.

**FURTHER READING**

Gilpin, Kris. "The Hidden." *Cinefantastique*, 18(2/3), March, 1988, pp. 102–103.
Kirst, Brian. "Director Jack Sholder remembers 'THE HIDDEN,' playing Chicago this weekend." *Fangoria*, April 16, 2015. http://fangoriaarchive.com/director-jack-sholder-remembers-the-hidden-playing-chicago-this-weekend/.
Kitka, Lorry. "Interview: Director Jack Sholder for The Hidden." *Nightmarish Conjurings*, June 12, 2018. http://www.nightmarishconjurings.com/interviews/2018/6/12/interview-director-jack-sholder-for-the-hidden.

## *The Hitchhiker's Guide to the Galaxy*

*The Hitchhiker's Guide to the Galaxy* is a series that includes novels (by Douglas Adams); radio plays (by Douglas Adams and John Lloyd, first and second phases; and Dirk Maggs, John Langdon, and Bruce Hyman, third and fourth phases); a television series on BBC 2 (Douglas Adams and John Lloyd); and a film directed by Garth Jennings. The dates are as follows: novels (1979, 1980, 1982, 1984, 1992), radio plays (1978, 2003, 2004), television series (1981), and film (2005).

In the most technical and literal of senses, to the natural world everything "unnatural" is effectively alien. In a strange way, this is the key to understanding the presentation of the alien in Douglas Adams's transmedia, multistranded, and constantly rebooted/readapted creation *The Hitchhiker's Guide to the Galaxy*. This approach is seen most clearly in the 2005 film that was made after Adams's death in 2001, and this adaptation provides a useful method of reading the alien in Adams's best-known work. This film charts the usual story of the adventures of Arthur Dent (Martin Freeman) and Ford Prefect (Mos Def) in the familiar fashion, moving from the destruction of Earth to make way for a hyperspace bypass, to their miraculous escape from the vacuum of space to the spaceship *Heart of Gold* and their eventual return to a newly minted Earth. (Earth is commonly mistaken for a planet, but is in fact a biomechanical supercomputer designed to find the question of life, the universe, and everything—the answer to which is 42.) The novel, television show, and radio versions (but not the film) make literal the idea that humans themselves are alien colonizers. This complex layering of natural and unnatural, terrestrial and extraterrestrial sets up Adams's parodic approach to the use of the alien commonly seen in science fiction. Here, the alien characters are

*The Hitchhiker's Guide to the Galaxy* (2005), directed by Garth Jennings. In this scene, Prostetnic Vogon Jeltz (voice: Richard Griffiths) tortures (from right) Arthur Dent (Martin Freeman) and Ford Prefect (Mos Def) by reciting his Vogon poetry. (Touchstone Pictures/Photofest)

not merely like the human characters because they are meant to parody them; instead, the humans themselves are aliens. This inflects Adams's parody of the nonhuman alien characters with a rather unusual tone and allows the underlying theme of conservation of the natural world to come through with more force.

The central nonhuman characters in *Hitchhiker's Guide* include Ford Prefect, a researcher for the titular Guide who became stranded on Earth, and Zaphod Beeblebrox, the Galactic President (a rather prescient vision of a mediated presidency given events at the time of writing this piece). Both Prefect and Beeblebrox are humanoid, and while Prefect largely passes for an eccentric human that blinks just slightly too little, Beeblebrox has a second head and third arm, which certainly marks him out as different, though there the film departs from previous visual incarnations: instead of the obviously prosthetic head and arm seen in the television series, Jennings's version of Beeblebrox (Sam Rockwell) shows his second head and third arm only occasionally. This serves to remind the audience of his alienness at specific points in the narrative rather than setting him apart from Dent—and the audience—at all times. Indeed, the film plays up the comedy and parody of the political rather than Beeblebrox's otherness to a considerable degree, and his extra body parts are seen as evidence of his insanity rather than as anything particularly extraterrestrial.

Other aliens are less well-developed, but the majority do not feel particularly other: Slartibartfast, one of the architects who creates Earth One and Two, is also humanoid and marked out only by being extremely long-lived. Similarly, Wowbagger the Infinitely Prolonged may be seen as alien only because of his extraordinarily long life. Indeed, the most alien thing about many of the humanoid aliens in Adams's work is not how they look but their names. Tricia McMillian, whom Beeblebrox effectively abducts from Earth several years before its destruction and who eventually takes the name "Trillian" because, according to the Quintessential Phase of the radio series, it sounds more "space-like," becomes alien through the adoption of a new name. Such an effect is more obvious in the novels than the visual adaptations, particularly given the juxtaposition of letters in many of these names, and has a clear comedic effect.

Among the more visually "other" aliens are the Vogons, an extremely litigious species and a clear parody of English middle-management culture. In the Vogons, we see Adams's most fully formed direct parody of the alien, and this makes them a source of laughter rather than fear. The Vogons' response to the population of Earth's shock at their planet being destroyed is clear: "All the planning charts and demotion orders have been on display in your local planning department in Alpha Centauri for fifty of your Earth years, so you've had plenty of time to lodge any formal complaint and it's far too late to start making a fuss about it now." Indeed, despite their appearance, the Vogons are probably the least othered alien in Adams's work, full of very human—and specifically English—flaws and tendencies.

The most interesting aliens here actually look nothing like aliens in the usual sense: both dolphins and mice are aliens, the latter only the physical manifestation of a race of aliens that exist across dimensions and the former representing those who commissioned the building of Earth itself. These aliens are easily forgotten, but they are possibly the most alien of all, even though human beings had rarely realized their intelligence. After all, the dolphins had tried to warn humans about the hyperspace bypass, and the mice "spent a lot of their time in behavioral research laboratories running round inside wheels and conducting frighteningly elegant and subtle experiments on man." They are alien posing as natural, again fitting into Adams's complex layering of natural and unnatural, as seen in his presentation of human beings.

Indeed, apart from the linguistic othering and very occasional physical othering, the majority of aliens in Adams's work are all too familiar, and this is where Jennings' cinematic adaptation comes into play. The ending of *The Restaurant at the End of the Universe* and the beginning of *Life, The Universe, and Everything* make it clear that the humans on Earth are themselves alien, having been sent from the planet Golgafrincham because they were "a load of useless bloody loonies." Adams's parody slips into sharp, conservationalist satire here: the Earth is a literal supercomputer that human beings have invaded, virus-like. The environmental philosophy here is clear: human beings are aliens and do not belong here. The true alien, at least from a conservationalist point of view, is actually the human. Jennings softens this reading, however, and instead embraces the less radical notion that humans are an essential part of the running of the planet, whether as supercomputer or natural phenomenon, and "rebooting" the Earth means everything goes back to the way it was at the moment of its destruction—human beings, dolphins, bulldozers, and all. The film leaves the audience with a sense of the alien that is more linguistic and visual than conservationist, a not unsubstantial departure from the presentation of the alien in most of the *Hitchhiker's Guide* franchise.

*Amanda Dillon*

See also: *Futurama*; *Galaxy Quest*; *Men in Black*.

## FURTHER READING

Gaiman, Neil. *Don't Panic: Douglas Adams and the* Hitchhiker's Guide to the Galaxy. Titan Books, 2009.

Harwood-Smith, Jennifer. "Destroying Arcadia: Undermining Literary Britain in *The Hitchhiker's Guide to the Galaxy*." *Revisiting Imaginary Worlds: A Subcreation Studies Anthology*, edited by Mark J. P. Wolf, Routledge, 2017, pp. 294–309.

Kropf, Carl R. "Douglas Adams's "Hitchhiker" Novels as Mock Science Fiction." *Science-Fiction Studies*, vol. 15, no. 1, 1988, pp. 61–70.

## Invasion of the Body Snatchers

Adapted from Jack Finney's *The Body Snatchers* (1955) by screenwriter Daniel Mainwaring, *Invasion of the Body Snatchers* (1956), directed by Don Siegel, is perhaps the most famous alien-invasion film ever made: a paranoid science-fiction thriller in which the residents of a Californian town, the quaint Santa Mira, come to believe that their neighbors, friends, and family have been replaced by someone—or something—else. It follows Dr. Miles Bennell (Kevin McCarthy), the community's general practitioner, as he begins to suspect that what he thought was a mass delusion spreading among his patients is actually a full-blown alien invasion. He enlists the help of his high-school sweetheart Becky Driscoll (Dana Wynter), old friends Jack and Teddy Belicec (King Donovan and Carolyn Jones), and colleague Dr. Dan Kauffman (Larry Gates) to help him investigate the conspiracy. Together, they discover that their town is being overrun by "pod people": otherworldly invaders posing as human beings.

The pod people have begun to infiltrate human society even before the main action begins. Bennell's first contact with them occurs when he sets out to investigate the claims of his hysterical patients, unknowingly communicating with the aliens that have silently supplanted beloved uncles and doting mothers. But the extraterrestrials are not humanoid in their true form; the doctor comes to discover that they are actually a vegetal species that initially arrived from space in the form of seeds, quickly growing into enormous pods that serve as incubators for the perfect human replicas that form within them. The body snatchers develop as their victims sleep and emerge as perfect copies of the people they have replaced—save for their total inability to feel genuine emotion.

For these doppelgängers are unable to express true joy, anger, hate, or happiness. In fact, they have no aspirations or dreams beyond the survival and continued proliferation of their species. They can mimic human behavior, but a fundamental lack of humanity subtly betrays their alien nature. Bennell sees behind their façade when he visits his nurse, Sally Withers (Jean Willes), and catches the townspeople gathered in her home, stoically discussing how and when they will replace him with an impostor. And once they have taken Santa Mira—both Kauffman and the Belicecs have become pod people before the film's final act—the body snatchers quickly set about harvesting more pods to be transported to surrounding towns by the truckload, their aim to spread as far and wide as possible.

Both *Invasion of the Body Snatchers* and Finney's source novel were produced at the height of the Cold War, and much of the existing writing on the film attempts to negotiate the cultural links between the pod people and American society in the

*Invasion of the Body Snatchers* (1956), directed by Don Siegel and starring Dana Wynter and Kevin McCarthy. (Allied Artists Pictures Corporation/Photofest)

mid-1950s, particularly in relation to the Second Red Scare, Joseph McCarthy's crusade against communist subversion and the House Un-American Activities Committee, then chaired by Francis E. Walter. Two readings have historically been the most dominant. The first suggests that the film is a work of acute conservative paranoia, in which the emotionless extraterrestrials symbolize the insidious spread of anti-American ideology in sleepy suburbia. Kim Newman, for example, suggests that the body snatchers are just one example of "hive-minded, godless 1950s monsters" that "bluntly represent Soviet communism" in science-fiction cinema of the era.

A second and starkly opposed interpretation posits that the body snatchers are stand-ins for the conservative majority, their invasion a metaphor for the pressure to conform in a nation increasingly concerned for the sanctity of the American (i.e., capitalist) way of life. After all, the aliens gradually merge with the establishment, seizing control of the telephone exchange and even the police department. And it is difficult to escape the fact that by the film's climax, when even Bennell's beloved Driscoll joins the pod people, the doctor finds himself hounded by a relentless mob made up of former patients, neighbors, and even close friends. As Stuart Samuels notes, "All have betrayed him. All have become his enemy." As Bennell flees into the hills surrounding Santa Mira, his pursuers come to epitomize a herd mentality, which, as in the HUAC hearings of the period, roots out those who, like Miles, are deemed dissenters.

Siegel's original cut gives weight to this interpretation. In it, Bennell escapes the aliens and descends from the California hills onto a busy highway. He runs among the traffic, shouting grave warnings, before discovering that trucks carrying fresh pods are heading for the state's biggest cities. The film concludes with the doctor screaming "They're here already! You're next!" Of course, this sequence survives in the theatrical cut. However, producer Walter Wanger famously requested that Siegel shoot two wraparound scenes, turning the majority of the film into a flashback. Wanger's reassuring epilogue sees Bennell in hospital, trying to persuade skeptical staff to take the alien threat seriously. Just then, news comes in of a road accident involving a truck filled with seedpods. Convinced, the doctors contact the FBI. This safe ending avoided a potentially controversial conclusion that might have been too pessimistic.

The final film ultimately supports both readings—and many others. For example, Natania Meeker and Antónia Szabari suggest that it anticipates the ecological horror of later decades by having its vegetal monsters erode the imagined boundary between nature and the human world. Furthermore, later remakes have reculturalized the film's narrative for new eras: *Invasion of the Body Snatchers* (1978) sees the aliens take over San Francisco and farm pods on an industrial scale in a scathing satire of consumer capitalism; *Body Snatchers* (1993) has the pod people infiltrate an army barracks to indict popular support for military interventionism in the aftermath of the Gulf War; and *The Invasion* (2007) imagines the extraterrestrial invader as a parasitic fungus to play on a 21st-century fear of infectious disease. These rich and varied adaptations of Finney's novel are all culturally significant in their own ways, but they are not quite as multilayered as the original *Invasion of the Body Snatchers*.

*Craig Ian Mann*

See also: *Invasion of the Body Snatchers*; *Hidden, The*; "Who Goes There?"

## FURTHER READING

LaValley, Al., editor. *Invasion of the Body Snatchers*. Rutgers University Press, 1989. Rutgers Films in Print.

Meeker, Natania and Antónia Szabari. "From the Century of the Pods to the Century of the Plants: Plant Horror, Politics, and Vegetal Ontology." *Discourse*, vol. 34, no. 1, 2012, pp. 32–58.

Newman, Kim. "Unearthly Strangers." *Sci-Fi: Days of Fear and Wonder*, edited by James Bell, British Film Institute, 2014, p. 92.

Samuels, Stuart. "The Age of Conspiracy and Conformity: *Invasion of the Body Snatchers*." *American History/American Film: Interpreting the Hollywood Image*, edited by John E. O'Connor and Martin A. Jackson, Frederick Ungar, 1979, pp. 198–207.

# L

## Le Guin, Ursula K.

Ursula K. Le Guin's (1929–2018) Hainish novels and stories are extended meditation upon the encounter with the alien, in which the alien ranges from different types of humans developed from Hainish genetic engineering to nonhuman species such as the Shing. The key Hainish novels are *Rocannon's World* (1966), *Planet of Exile* (1966), *City of Illusions* (1967), *The Left Hand of Darkness* (1969), *The Word for the World Is Forest* (1972), *The Dispossessed* (1974), and *The Telling* (2000). Stories have been collected in editions such as *The Wind's Twelve Quarters* (1975), *Four Ways to Forgiveness* (1995), and *The Birthday of the World: and Other Stories* (2002). Le Guin's concern with encountering the alien is an interrogation of the motivations for and effects of colonialism, out of which she envisions a colonialism that relies upon dialogue, mutual benefit, recognition of difference, and autonomy instead of exploitation, dominance, and self-interest.

In Le Guin's future, the Hain long ago seeded many worlds with colonies, which explains the evolution of humans on Earth (or Terra). Yet, when Hainish civilization broke down, colonies became unaware of each other. Eventually, a League of Worlds emerges; when the League is defeated by the Shing, it reforms as the Ekumen, which comes to include more than 80 planets. Le Guin's narratives of alien contact tend to center upon setting aside ego and materialist interests for the more utopian dynamic of communication, sharing, and empathy. The ansible exemplifies this dynamic as a technology that allows instant transmission across any distance in space with another ansible. As Keng says to Shevek in *The Dispossessed*, after he offers the Terran ambassador the physics to make the ansible, "We can talk—at last we can talk together" (ch. 11).

Such talking together well describes the relationship forged between Genly Ai and Estraven in Le Guin's most significant alien contact novel, *The Left Hand of Darkness*. Genly, representing the Ekumen as an Envoy to the planet Gethen, hopes to convince Gethenians to join the Ekumen; Estraven, a political figure in Karhide, one of the principal nations of Gethen, proves vital to Genly achieving his goal. As a Terran, Genly struggles with overcoming the alienness of the Gethenians, but also with his own position as "alien and isolate" (ch. 10) on the world. What makes the Gethenians so alien to Genly is their "sexual physiology" (ch. 7), which is explained in chapter 7 in the field notes of Ong Tot Oppong, who visited Gethen several years before Genly. Once a month, Gethenians go through *kemmer*, when they can become sexually male or female, which means an individual can be both a mother and a father in their lifetime; otherwise, Gethenians are androgynous. Ong Tot Oppong identifies the challenge of contact with Gethenians: a Gethenian is not a man or a woman, but a "manwoman" (ch. 7); moreover,

"One is respected and judged only as a human being," which is "an appalling experience" (ch. 7); and Gethenians do not rely upon the dualisms so inherent to "bisexual" (ch. 7) humans. Thus, Genly must constantly be aware of how he perceives and defines Gethenians with regard to sex/gender, for "man" and "woman" are "categories" ultimately "irrelevant" to a Gethenian's "nature" (ch. 1).

The failure to talk together with the alien is addressed in *The Word for the World Is Forest*, the events of which occur historically before those of *The Left Hand of Darkness*. Terrans have come to New Tahiti, a planet covered by forests, to harvest and ship lumber back to a "worn-out Earth" (ch. 1). Captain Davidson exemplifies the conventional colonialist attitude, enslaving the native "creechies" (or, Athsheans) and believing the planet "was intended for humans to take over" (ch. 1). Short, their bodies covered in a green fur, Athsheans can dream while awake; like Gethenians, they resulted from Hainish genetic experiments. When the Athsheans revolt against the occupying "yumens," Davidson disobeys orders and carries out a program of genocide until he is caught. Events on New Tahiti are the spur for the very different approach to alien contact taken by Genly Ai.

Conversely, the short story "Vaster than Empires and More Slow" (1970) deepens the idea of unity in difference signified by Genly's yin and yang symbol. The 10 "misfits" of the spaceship *Gum* come upon World 4470 and proceed to explore it. Osden, who possesses a "supernormal empathic capacity," realizes the entire planet is sentient and connected and fears the aliens who have arrived upon it. Ultimately, Osden chooses to stay on World 4470, surrendering himself "to the love of the Other," an act that cannot be fully accounted for by "the vocabulary of reason." While the rest of the crew leave World 4470, Osden stays as a colonist. Le Guin not only resists traditional colonialism in this story, but she also stresses the necessity of an entirely new language to define the sort of "love" Osden (and Genly Ai) discovers for the alien—which requires a thorough redefinition of "colonist." Osden is not an egoistic, xenophobic Social Darwinist like Captain Davidson. Instead, he is a "colonist" in the sense of a pioneer, acting by compassion and not the "reason" responsible for a long history of violent, exploitative human colonialism.

Le Guin wrote and published the greater part of her Hainish novels and stories from the mid-1960s to the mid-1970s, during the height of both the Cold War and the space race between the United States and USSR. In the context of events such as the Cuban Missile Crisis in October of 1962 and the manned landing of Apollo 11 on the moon in July 1969, Le Guin's focus upon narratives of space exploration and colonialism suggests her effort to proffer a structure for confronting the Other that does not involve a power struggle for dominion and superiority.

*Michael Johnstone*

*See also*: Butler, Octavia E.; Gwyneth Jones's Aleutians; Tepper, Sheri S.; Tiptree Jr., James.

## FURTHER READING

Freedman, Carl, editor. *Conversations with Ursula K. Le Guin*. University Press of Mississippi, 2008.

Le Guin, Ursula K. *The Language of the Night: Essays on Science Fiction and Fantasy*, edited by Susan Wood. Putnam, 1979.

Le Guin, Ursula K. *Words Are My Matter: Writings about Life and Books, 2000–2016*. Small Beer Press, 2016.

## Lem, Stanislaw

The work of the prolific Polish writer Stanislaw Lem (1921–2006) is typified by philosophical rumination and futurological speculation; central to his oeuvre is an expansive exploration of advancing technology, alongside investigations of both organic and artificial evolution. Lem depicts a myriad of evolutionary trajectories in his first-contact novels, which engage with distinctly nonhumanoid aliens. Fundamental to all his first-contact novels are pessimistic encounters, which emphasize the impossibility of communication between humans and aliens of absolute otherness. Thus, Lem's writing offers some of the most compelling depictions of alien otherness, and the subsequent problems it poses for the human subject, found throughout the science-fiction canon.

The first of Lem's contact novels, the dystopian *Eden* (1959), is inhabited by large, gelatinous aliens with retractable thoraxes, an incomprehensible doubleness of form that leads a human spaceship crew to dub them "doublers." At the center of *Solaris* (1961), his masterpiece, is an amorphous planet-sized alien. In *The Invincible* (1964), a spaceship crew are stymied by "the Cloud," a conglomeration of self-organizing alien microautomata that resemble insects and operate in a cybernetic pack. Another highly regarded work, *His Master's Voice* (1968), provides a protracted series of speculations upon the meaning of an intercepted alien transmission. *Fiasco* (1986) charts the meeting of humanity with the reclusive Quintans, an alien civilization seemingly in a perpetual state of global warfare. Although these texts deal with alien entities differently, their fundamental exploration is interwoven due to the consistent attention given to the dilemma of alien intentionality.

Throughout Lem's first-contact novels, the failure to recognize alien behavior, or the mistaken ascription of intentionality to it, causes conflict that undermines attempts at communication. In *Eden*, a spaceship crew fail to recognize the language of the "doublers," mistaking their intentional attempt at communication as "coughing," a mere physiological reflex. Upon realizing the erroneousness of their anthropomorphic assumption, the spaceship crew develop a computer program to make partial translations between them and the "doublers." Although this is the closest that any of Lem's novels get to direct communication between humans and aliens, the technological intercessor can only achieve limited success. Due to semantic slippages and the anthropomorphic bias inadvertently built into the machine, the resulting translations feature more extraneous noise than relevant information.

In *Solaris*, humans' inability to distinguish between information and noise is inexplicably bound to the unclassifiable evolutionary trajectory of the ocean. As it is impossible to ascertain whether the "thinking colossus" (ch. 11) is geological, biological, or technological in origin, its modes of thought and the (un) intentionality of its actions remain similarly unfathomable. When a group of scientists studies the ocean, it materializes their innermost dreads and desires as human simulacra called "phi-creatures." It is never determined whether these phi-creatures are an instinctual response, a natural extrusion, technological programming, or an intentional attempt at contact. Humankind's inability to categorize the Solaris life-form within preexisting taxonomies points toward the insufficiency of preestablished scientific frameworks to encompass alien phenomena.

In *The Invincible*, the programming of ancient technology has adapted over millennia into the Cloud a "black crystal brood" (ch. 9) of artificial life, which has integrated into the local ecosystem. This evolution has mutated programming into an instinctual, reflexive imperative to survive. The crew of *The Invincible* misidentify the Cloud's actions as intentionally aggressive and respond with a fatuous chain of military escalation. Only once they conceptualize the cloud as the result of "necro-evolution . . . the development of inorganic matter" (ch. 9) do they realize the futility of their retaliations. Thus, they acknowledge the emergence of autonomous artificial life, representing a radically new form of speciation outside of human experience and necessitating revisions to how intent is understood in relation to complex behaviors.

The question of intention is the unanswerable conundrum at the center of *His Master's Voice*. Here it is impossible to ascertain whether an alien missive was intentionally directed at earth or whether we are mere interlopers. This confusion is further complicated when it is postulated that the communiqué could in fact be a natural emission, a unintentional by-product of a large alien entity—perhaps here obliquely referencing Solaris—thus further reinforcing the uncertainty around intention arising from the ontological unknowability of the alien and the crisis this causes for human regimes of knowledge.

*Fiasco*, Lem's final contact novel, follows the repeated anthropomorphic misinterpretation of alien intentionality, leading to military escalation. The evolution of intelligent life is understood to move beyond the physical plane at a certain level of technological sophistication; hence the spaceship crew of *Fiasco* arrive at the planet Quinta in order "to catch a civilisation before it flew out the window" (ch. 5). The crew's swift recourse to inflicting large-scale environmental damage in order to force contact with the Quintans serves to emphasize humanity's bellicosity and irrationality when interpreting alien intentions. In the final disastrous moments of the novel, a human ambassador realizes the Quintans are "defenceless warts" (ch. 16). Here, as throughout Lem's alien encounters, it is only through moments of surrender, capitulation, and vulnerability that the human is open to communication with the alien. Although still highly ambiguous, the relinquishing of assumed models of behavior and the suspension of conventional modes of thought result in fleeting reconciliatory moments with alien otherness.

Rather than expanding human knowledge and extending human reach, Lem's encounters with alien otherness serve to emphasize the insufficiency of human imagination when engaging with the nonhuman. Thus, attempts to assimilate alien otherness into preexisting models of thought preclude, rather than enhance, the possibility of communication. The attempt at conditioning the alien to the knowable is also a futile attempt at preserving the validity and universalizability of human rationality. Offering scant redemption and no resolution, Lem's aliens are enigmatic invitations to peer over the edge of thought into the vastness of the unknowable alien other.

*Rachel Hill*

*See also*: Dick, Philip K.; *Solaris*; Strugatsky, Arkady and Boris.

**FURTHER READING**

Enns, Anthony. "Mediality and Mourning in Stanislaw Lem's *Solaris* and *His Master's Voice*." Science Fiction Studies, vol. 29, no. 1, 2002, pp. 34–52.
Kandel, Michael. "A Freudian Peek at Lem's *Fiasco*." *The Art and Science of Stanislaw Lem*, edited by Peter Swirski, McGill-Queen's University Press, 2006, pp. 72–80.
Swirski, Peter. "Stanislaw Lem: A Stranger in a Strange Land." *A Stanislaw Lem Reader*, edited by Peter Swirski, Northwestern University Press, 1997, pp. 1–20.

## *Lesbian Spider Queens of Mars*

*Lesbian Spider Queens of Mars* (2011), designed by Anna Anthropy, started as a browser-based game. Anthropy took inspiration from *Wizard of War* for gameplay, meaning Anthropy's game involves navigating a single-screen maze while capturing enemies. The player controls a Spider Queen whose all-female "slaves" have escaped and need to be captured. The Spider Queen is armed with a constantly firing web (thus allowing the game to be played with one hand) to capture the "slaves" and earn points. More advanced levels include "slaves" with projectile attacks and "slaves" that can only be approached from behind. The final boss is the Tarantula Queen, a spurned lover of the Spider Queen, who started the "slave" revolt. The most popular version is browser based, but Anthropy also sells an uncensored version that includes exposed nipples. A sequel, *Lesbian Spider Queens of Mars 2: Tarantula's Turn*, includes a two-player competitive experience.

"Slaves" is used in quotation marks because the narrative appears to include a kind of sexual play rather than actual enslavement. During the "attract" screen sequence (a series of screens including a demo and title cards), a card appears with the Spider Queen and a bound "slave" shaking hands with the phrase "All power exchange must be consensual." Aside from a bondage-flavored parody of the public-service announcements common in traditional arcade games, the card places the game's characters as agreeing to a particular kind of exchange. While it is possible to read the game as an actual slave revolt, the card points toward a game-within-a-game where the Spider Queen and "slaves" are playing for their own amusement.

*Lesbian Spider Queens of Mars* offers a view of alien sexuality as playful and nonprocreative. Sexual activity among aliens is usually depicted as a kind of biological power where forced impregnation is a common trope. Power differences between aliens and humans are meant to elicit terror and anxiety about those who are different. Instead, *Lesbian Spider Queens of Mars* exists in a world where power exchange and subordination offer a cathartic pleasure. Video games frequently create tension by using an unequal balance of forces that allows a player to overcome the challenge with her skills. Where *Lesbian Spider Queens of Mars* differs is that the joy coming from disempowerment is explicitly coded as fun rather than as terrifying.

The encounter with nonprocreative sexuality reconsiders the alien idea of a world without work. *Lesbian Spider Queens of Mars* depicts a world where there is little war or strife beyond romantic conflicts. Martian society is apparently uninterested in industrial production, staying within a monarchy powered by magic. The only goal of Martian society is play, showing an alternate version of a society without material scarcity. When struggles for material scarcity have been eliminated, contests move toward power dynamics. *Lesbian Spider Queens of Mars* shows a world that is neither sexually reproductive nor industrially productive.

The lack of production and reproduction, along with the idea of losing agency as "play," pushes on notions of queer representations of aliens. Pearson argues that science fiction could chart a course outside of heteronormative structures, including texts that place gay and lesbian characters into heteronormative versions of the past or future.

*Lesbian Spider Queens of Mars* also depicts sexual games between different species of female aliens. The playful nature makes the subversion less threatening to a heteronormative audience. The arcade-style gameplay moves away from heavily immersive narrative, but moving from narrative allows for subtle forms of queer subversion. The style of an arcade game depicts a conflict *in media res*, meaning items like motivations or origins are less relevant. A planet full of magical spider women and their "slaves" is less likely than an arcade game to find challenges, because narrative questions are subordinate to gameplay during early play-throughs. Players might resist the queer structure upon reflection, but the game simply posits a queer structure and demands the player accept the premise of the domination game. *Lesbian Spider Queens of Mars* is significant because a queer alien sexuality is presented as a given rather than as something that requires explanation.

As of this writing, *Lesbian Spider Queens of Mars* is available as a free browser-based game. Any scholar with access to a PC can find it online. Scholars could also download the uncensored version if they have concerns about using a third-party website or want consistent access. Anthropy intended for the game to be accessible, which inspired the always-on web attack. The game can be controlled with one hand, much like arcade and early console games from which *Lesbian Spider Queens of Mars* draws inspiration. Scholars might need some quick finger movements to succeed and earn high scores, but the game allows for continues that sacrifice the player's score in exchange for preserving their progress. Scholars looking for narrative will find that, like most arcade games, the story of *Lesbian Spider Queens of Mars* is told in the margins. Showing the experience of marginalized sexualities in the margins of an arcade game is appropriate, given it shows the conceptual depth in an arcade B-movie tribute about spider women tying down half-naked "slaves."

*Ian Derk*

*See also*: *Oddworld*; *Space Invaders*.

**FURTHER READING**

Anthropy, Anna. "Lesbian Spider Queens of Mars." auntiepixelante.com/?p=1034.

Anthropy, Anna. "Lesbian Spider Queens of Mars. Uncensored." auntiepixelante.com/?p=2336.

Pearson, Wendy. "Alien Cryptographies: The View from Queer." *Science Fiction Studies*, vol. 26, no. 1, 1999, pp. 1–22.

## *Lilo and Stitch*

*Lilo and Stitch* (2002), thus far Disney Animation's only foray into animated science-fiction feature films, presents a complex knot of discourses surrounding the alien and the other that can be only partly unraveled here. Directed by Chris Saunders and Dean DeBlois and centering around two orphaned Hawaiian girls, teenage Nani and six-year-old Lilo, the film presents what happens when the genetically engineered alien Stitch—formerly "Experiment 626"—lands in their backyard and becomes part of their family. After escaping his captors several systems away, Stitch crash-lands in Hawaii and is taken to an animal shelter after having been run over by two tractor-trailers. The next day, Nani, in an attempt to win her sister's favor and please social worker Cobra Bubbles, takes Lilo to this same shelter to adopt a dog. Fleeing creator Jumba and Earth specialist Pleakley, who the unnamed Galactic Grand Councilwoman sends to fetch him, Stitch transforms his six-limbed, spiney, and antennaed body into something like a dog's, and—of course—becomes Lilo's choice of pet. The majority of the film's action follows Stitch's new life with Lilo and Nani, the girls' own problems living without their parents, and the increasing pressure from Bubbles once Stitch causes Nani to lose her job as a waitress at a tourist luau. The film also details Jumba and Pleakley's fascinated observations of the changes in Stitch's behavior—along with a number of Elvis Presley songs over a montage as Lilo tries to improve Stitch's behavior and Nani looks for a new job. These changes climax when the United Galactic Federation sends Captain Gantu (who lost Stitch to begin with) to collect him, resulting in Stitch believing himself part of Nani and Lilo's family. After a high-altitude battle, it is decided that, due to Hawaii's adoption fees at the animal shelter, Stitch is officially deemed Lilo's property, and the Grand Councilwoman declares Stitch to be exiled on Earth—with his new family.

*Lilo and Stitch*'s cast of aliens is small, limited to Stitch (small, blue and black, and six-limbed, with spines on his back), his creator, Jumba (a rotund, four-eyed mad scientist type), the "Earth specialist" Pleakley (a thin, green cyclopsian alien with a single antenna), Captain Gantu (an enormous gray and black bipedal hippopotamus-like alien), and the Grand Councilwoman (who looks like a classic Gray with ungulate legs). There are minor alien characters on Gantu's ship, some of which look like anthropomorphized versions of Earth animals, including armadillos, pigs, pumas, hammerhead sharks, and, in one case, a dinosaur. The character design of the aliens is therefore two-fold: simultaneously uncanny, particularly in the cases of the minor alien characters and the councilwoman, but also round and almost cuddly—particularly in the case of Gantu, Stitch, and Jumba. Much of the art direction here deliberately makes the characters—and sometimes the spaceships—round and bottom heavy, a technique that undermines any potential scariness for child audience members (a technique also seen in Sauders's other projects, such as *How to Train Your Dragon*). This softness when so many familiar cinematic aliens are more angular and insectoid provides a warmth to the characterizations: Jumba, who could be menacing, is simply a bumbling fool, and even Gantu's enormity becomes nonthreatening. Stitch, of course, changes his body shape to appear more familiar, but as the film goes on, his body language becomes more rounded and "cute"—and thereby less threatening.

*Lilo and Stitch*'s truly fascinating element is its layering of the other and the alien with its central issue of family. Stitch is the most obviously alien, but Lilo and Nani—and Nani's not-quite-boyfriend David and a handful of minor characters—are all native ethnic Hawaiians. While Stitch and the other extraterrestrials are all aliens to the human characters, it is worth considering the level of "otherness" that these people of color present to the audience. This is seen on a small scale with Lilo and her "friends"—who are all white girls—that Lilo says "deserve to be punished." It is unlikely that Lilo speaks racially, and the film in no way engages directly with the institutionalized racism that native Hawaiians face—indeed, the film presents it without comment—but this clear division between natives and invaders may be seen throughout. What is interesting is that this embedded "otherness" is not immediately seen with Stitch: indeed, until the final act, no one has realized that Stitch is an alien. Until Jumba and Pleakley reveal themselves to Nani—who attacks them, Basil Fawlty-style, with a tree branch—everyone in the film sees Stitch as a rather unusual and particularly mischievous dog, but no more. Only at this point do any of the characters see Stitch as alien, and Lilo's age and own oddness makes her oblivious to Stitch's less canine qualities: his penchant for destruction, his ability to ride a tricycle, his construction of a replica of San Francisco to destroy as Godzilla, and so on. She accepts him as is because she feels a kinship with him, which is, in effect, the film's overriding concern: the formation of a family and, with some archetype shorthand support from "The Ugly Duckling," the finding of one's real family. The alien, thus, is categorically *not* metaphorical in this film.

The film's centrality of the term *ohana* therefore may be seen as an attempt of a broken family to form itself on its own terms despite all attempts to break it apart, but it also opens itself up to a wider understanding of the universe as one family. And, as the audience is reminded throughout: "*ohana* means family, and family means no one gets left behind—or forgotten." This seems to be true regardless of whether one is a six-year-old Hawaiian girl or a destructive, blue, genetically engineered alien who just needs a family to call his own.

*Amanda Dillon*

See also: *Futurama*; *Mork & Mindy*; *Steven Universe*.

## FURTHER READING

McKnight, Utz. "The African in America: Race and the Politics of Diaspora." *African Identities*, vol. 6, no. 1, 2008, pp. 63–81.

Pallant, Chris. "Neo-Disney: Recent Developments in Disney Feature Animation." *New Cinemas: Journal of Contemporary Film*, vol. 8, no. 2, 2010, pp. 103–117.
Scherman, Elizabeth L. "Monsters Among Us: Construction of the Deviant Body in Monsters, Inc. and Lilo and Stitch." *Galaxy Is Rated G: Essays on Children's Science Fiction Film and Television*, edited by R. C. Neighbors and Sandy Rankin, McFarland, 2011, pp. 15–30.

## Liu, Cixin

As of 2014, Cixin Liu (1963) is the best-selling science-fiction author in China—making him a minor celebrity in the most populous country in the world and renowned in the United States as one of the few Chinese science-fiction authors to have their work exported to the Western world. For American readers particularly—many of whom are unaccustomed to cultural narratives that deviate from what the Western media-entertainment complex feeds them—Liu's novels are an unusually detailed peek into contemporary Chinese cultural values and politics, while his aliens align with a reductive view of human history as epitomized in Cold War politics.

The astounding details with which Liu explicates the politics of both alien and human societies are possible in his trilogy because the story takes place over a long arc. *Remembrance of Earth's Past* begins in 1960s China and ends with the heat-death of the universe—and throughout all of history, Chinese cultural hegemony remains intact. In the span of this time, Liu describes the ongoing political, technological, and social issues of each future epoch, often with more detail than the emotions and actions of the characters themselves. Interestingly, contemporary sociopolitical doctrines remain relatively intact throughout the trilogy's timeline, including the political power of private capital, our current class system, and the existence of a China-esque semi-authoritarian government with a strong social welfare state. In one politically telling scene, a 22nd-century particle accelerator is constructed—via a public-private partnership. Neoliberalism, evidently, is interstellar and eternal.

The first two books of the *Three Body Problem* trilogy (*The Three Body Problem, The Dark Forest, Death's End*) establish the big existential question that characterizes the trilogy at large: what if humanity were doomed by a fleet of invading aliens, yet they were four centuries from arrival? And here's the catch: the aliens, known as Trisolarans, have a technology called a sophon that allows them to see and hear everything that happens on Earth. And while they can see and hear everything that happens on Earth down to the molecular level, the Trisolarans cannot manipulate anything, aside from sending a few stray photons here and there. It sounds harmless enough, yet these stray photons are enough to doom fundamental progress in the sciences—as they render particle accelerators useless by allowing the Trisolarans to spoof data.

There are characters in Liu's books, certainly, but the bulk of the action—and the plot—concerns political systems and technologies. How might humans organize their political systems under this kind of existential threat? How does one plan ahead if all conversation, e-mail, and paper is instantly visible to the approaching Trisolarans, and only human thought is invisible?

In Liu's slow plotting of future human technologies and societies, it is hard for the reader not to see his future as a natural one.

Every time a new human epoch comes to pass, Liu devotes a few pages to explaining how society changed, and why. In the "Deterrence Era," in which humans have established a detente with the distant yet approaching Trisolaran fleet, civilization is characterized by a peace so literal that the built environment resembles an enormous tree. Moreover, the humans of the Deterrence Era have feminized appearances, which shocks protagonist Cheng Xin, who had been hibernating since the 21st century. "What happened to the men?" she asks after awakening from decades of induced slumber. The answer is that they all look like women: "Half a century of peace" had accelerated the trend toward a "society and fashion [that] preferred men who displayed traditionally feminine qualities" (*Death's End*).

If humanity's peaceable eras are defined by feminized men, the eras of conflict are defined by men who epitomize toxic masculinity. In humanity's "Bunker Era," an epoch in which human civilization devotes much of its resources to concealing itself from alien threats, masculinity returns. "The men who had disappeared during [earlier epochs] had returned. . . . This was another age capable of producing men," Liu writes (*Death's End*). The message is clear: peace feminizes humanity, conflict masculinizes it.

Unfortunately for those who don't want to be masculinized, the nature of the trilogy's universe is one of conflict, as the inherent hostility of all alien life is discovered to be a universal (pun intended) law. The second book, *The Dark Forest*, marked the characters' discovery of "cosmic sociology," the sociological principles that link all alien civilizations throughout the universe. As Gerry Canavan wrote of that book:

[Liu] suggests the first two axioms of cosmic sociology: "First: Survival is the primary need of civilization. Second: Civilization continually grows and expands, but the total matter in the universe remains constant." The two, taken together, flatten the idea-space of science fiction dramatically into a strictly Darwinian and imperialist paradigm: civilizations *need* to expand to gather more resources if they hope to continue to survive. And thus one of the first conclusions of cosmic sociology is that all other civilizations must be, more or less, exactly what ours has been: ravenous, violent, expansionist, shortsighted, and devoted to its own continuation at any cost. . . . In the cosmic scheme of things, the true material core of all sociality, everywhere in the universe, is robbery and murder."

*Keith A. Spencer*

See also: Reynolds, Alastair; Stapledon, Olaf; Vinge, Vernor.

## FURTHER READING

Canavan, Gerry. "Quiet, Too Quiet." *Los Angeles Review of Books*, February 12, 2016, lareviewofbooks.org/article/quiet-too-quiet/.

Liu, Cixin. "The Worst of All Possible Universes and the Best of All Possible Earths: Three Body and Chinese Science Fiction," *Invisible Planets: Contemporary*

*Chinese Science Fiction in Translation*, edited by Ken Liu, Tor, 2016, pp. 361–68, and at www.tor.com/blogs/2014/05/the-worst-of-all-possible-universes-and-the-best-of-all-possible-earths-three-body-and-chinese-science-fiction.

Lyau, Bradford. "Many Paths, One Journey: Cixin Liu's Three Body Problem Novels." *Dis-Orienting Planets: Racial Representations of Asia in Science Fiction*, edited by Isiah Lavender III, University Press of Mississippi, 2017, pp. 160–74.

## Lovecraft, H. P.

H. P. Lovecraft (1890–1937) was an American writer of the early 20th century. Although a celebrated writer of what has been termed "weird fiction," much of it concerning ancient aliens, Lovecraft has become a controversial figure, polarizing readers due to the racist tendencies and prejudices that characterize his writing, yet he remains influential in many areas of popular culture.

The stories of H. P. Lovecraft are replete with malevolent aliens. Encounters with them are generally not weighted in favor of humanity. After his early work, fantasies styled after the works of Lord Dunsany, his middle period, characterized by his most famous story, "The Call of Cthulhu" (1926), is when Lovecraft began exploring science-fictional elements, introducing alien presences, and in the 1930s his interests shifted from isolated encounters with horrific, eldritch aliens to expositions of the detritus and horrors remaining from alien societies in Earth's primeval past. These aliens illustrate Lovecraft's sense of "cosmic horror," where a true consideration of time and the immensity of the universe, of infinity, throw into contrast the insignificance of life.

Lovecraft's tales of these aliens are wrapped in a patina of the Gothic tradition, but the "sins of the past" his characters confront are not humanity's. His tales brim with the "haunted house" trope, except it is the Earth itself that is haunted. Maintaining strong overtones of horror, Lovecraft stories utilize tropes from science fiction: ancient-alien civilizations and invasions, extradimensional portals, deathless aliens and contamination, to explore the unease generated by the confrontation with the unknown. The world's towns and villages contain families shunned as a result of miscegenation with aliens; evil reputations cling to geological, geographical, and topographical features. Surrounded by religiosity and ritual, Lovecraft's aliens infect remote wilderness and urban areas alike with the uncanny, their presence hinted at through high rates of social ills such as incest, inbreeding, and poverty, as exemplified in "The Dunwich Horror" (1928) and "The Shadow over Innsmouth" (1931); as with "The Whisperer in Darkness" (1930), these are tales situated in rural communities, which increases the helplessness coloring the encounters. "The Thing on the Doorstep" (1933) and "The Haunter of the Dark" (1935) are sited in urban areas, ideal for surreptitious alien intrusion. Three of his best-known novellas—"The Call of Cthulhu" (1926), "At the Mountains of Madness" (1931), and "The Shadow Out of Time" (1934–1935)—are situated in liminal landscapes such as the South Pacific Ocean, Antarctica, and the Pilbara Desert in north-western Australia.

Each tale presents a different alien, often subtly linked in what became known as the "Cthulhu Mythos," but all his tales contain aliens that speak to the wide terror of the unknown universe. Representing both an existential and epistemological crisis, Lovecraft's aliens evince an indifferent or hostile universe, perhaps reflecting Lovecraft's own existential problems with the world he confronted. Lovecraft's mastery in varying the descriptions from hints to broad, sweeping brush strokes or to highly focused detail continues to inspire artists and writers and fascinate readers. Some of his aliens, such as Cthulhu, exist only in rumor and hearsay. The alien of "The Colour Out of Space" (1927) can only be described in terms of light or its effects. In "The Shadow over Innsmouth," the townsfolk are contaminated by a bargain made generations before: human only for a short time, they take on piscine features before returning to the depths as "Deep Ones," a race of submarine aliens never described apart from the effect on the townsfolk. The aliens of "The Whisperer in Darkness," fungoid creatures in the shape of crustaceans, will indulge in "brain-napping" to conceal their existence. "The Dunwich Horror" concerns the intersection of humanity and interdimensional aliens, one a visible travesty of a human, the other an invisible, destructive force. This is one of the few tales where humanity was able to push back: three scholars sent it back to its own dimension—at least for a time.

H. P. Lovecraft in June 1934. Although he was virtually unknown during his lifetime, Lovecraft is now widely considered to be one of the most significant and influential horror writers of the 20th century. (Archive PL/Alamy Stock Photo)

Lovecraft's later tales concentrated on the aliens' social structures, although the aliens themselves were "inhumanely" unconcerned with other life: the Great Race of Yith from "The Shadow out of Time" were bodiless minds traveling space and time via the displacement of the minds of other beings with their own, including a man in Lovecraft's contemporary time. These aliens fled the civilization they founded before tectonic changes turned the area into desert, leaving behind their own doom to terrorize coming ages. The "elder beings" in "At the Mountains of Madness" were also alien invaders who manipulated terrestrial life for their own ends; the ruins of their city conceal massive, sentient shoggoths, a form of artificial life grown by the "elder beings." Shoggoths developed their own agency, overwhelmed their creators, and now wait on the fringes of the known world to devastate humankind.

Lovecraft's aliens represent the outside threat, assuming a mythological resonance that poisons the Earth in subtle ways. They are never proven or accepted, despite the author propelling his characters into the objective reality of the aliens' existence. With few exceptions, the protagonists are unable to mount a successful challenge; survivors report dire warnings to authorities of a mounting danger in vain. Even if sane after their encounters, the survivors sink into silent helplessness, keeping their terrible knowledge secret.

Lovecraft wrote in the time between two world wars, a time of scientific enquiry and exploration; he did not live to see the changes wrought by World War II but resented much of the social change confronting him, a resentment prominent in his writing: resentment about changes in immigration is reflected in his racism, and resentment about changes in society as a whole is displayed in his elitism. He bumped up against the emergent modern, and it disagreed with him. As a self-styled "antiquarian," often reflected in his prose, his sense of loss at the world he was born into in the late 19th century is almost palpable. The future, in Lovecraft's world, is a place of terror, with humanity subjected to the horrors from "outside," a legacy from ancient-alien presences extant within the earth's crust.

*Keira McKenzie*

*See also*: Fort and Forteanism; Polar Aliens.

## FURTHER READING

Joshi, S. T. *H. P. Lovecraft: A Life*. Necronomicon Press, 1996.
Lovecraft, H. P. *Collected Letters, Vols. 1–5*. Arkham House, 1965–76.
Oakes, D. A. *Science and Destabilization in the Modern American Gothic: Lovecraft, Matheson and King*. Greenwood, 2000.

# M

## *The Man Who Fell to Earth*

*The Man Who Fell to Earth* (1963) is the best known of Walter Tevis's science-fiction novels, an account of Thomas Jerome Newton, a humanoid alien from a dying species who comes to Earth in search of asylum for his people. Producer David Cammell read the novel and brought it to the attention of his brother, Donald, and Nicolas Roeg, who had codirected *Performance* (1970); in response, Roeg directed a typically elliptical film version in 1976. In 1987 a pilot was made for a television series, directed by Robert J. Roth, although the series was not subsequently made. David Bowie adapted the material with his own songs as a musical, *Lazarus* (2015), and a further remake has been announced.

Newton fits into the alien messiah tradition best demonstrated with Klaatu in *The Day the Earth Stood Still* (Robert Wise, 1951): the solitary alien with technological superiority who wants to help humanity but is treated with suspicion by politicians and the military. Published at the height of the Cold War and the Space Race, Tevis's novel draws attention to Newton's messianic nature through his recognition of a painting of Christ, and later in a comparison voiced by a scientist, Nathan Bryce. Newton realizes he can save humanity and his own species through technology. Both American business and the CIA are suspicious, doubting whether he is an alien, and Newton is blinded by the secret service. It is tempting to read the novel as an exploration of the possibilities for international cooperation over ecology—Rachel Carson's *Silent Spring* had been published the previous year—and how this could be scuppered by politics.

Newton's alienness is equated to queerness: Bryce notes that Newton's "way of walking reminded Bryce of the first homosexual he had ever seen. . . . Newton did not walk like that" (77), while Newton's human companion Betty-Jo wonders "maybe he was queer—anyone who sat around reading all the time and looked like he did. . . . But he didn't talk like that" (57). Nonetheless, his difference from normative models of male behavior is emphasized.

It is perhaps this that led Roeg to cast Bowie as Newton: the singer had come out as bisexual and had cultivated a sense of alienness. The film also features homosexuals whose sexuality is incidental to the plot, an interracial relationship and a sex scene between Newton and Mary-Lou (the film's version of Betty-Jo). Roeg pushes at the taboos of cinema. A few U.S. states had decriminalized homosexuality, and the American Psychological Association and the American Psychiatric Association had only just removed homosexuality from their registers of mental disorders.

As in Roeg's other films, he chooses to tell the narrative in a kaleidoscopic way: there are flashbacks and flash-forwards, and it isn't always possible to be clear

*The Man Who Fell to Earth* (1976), directed by Nicolas Roeg and starring David Bowie (right) and Rip Torn. (Cinema 5 Distributing/Photofest)

what is real and what is dream or fantasy. By locating Newton in front of dozens of televisions, it almost feels as if Newton witnesses all of the film's scenes, even if he was not physically present. As viewers we are forced to construct the diegetic world of the film just as Newton constructs his view of Earth through television; it is an estranging experience.

Throughout his mission—possibly even from his crash-landing on Earth—Newton has been under surveillance, and he is blinded. This leaves him powerless. He has come to Earth to save us and his people, but he is barely able to save his friends, and they can hardly save him. However, it may be that he is still in contact with his own people through other means. This feels in tune with other films of the early 1970s, both within and outside of the genre, although with the emergence of the SF blockbuster in 1977, American family values and straightforward heroism were firmly reinscribed.

The television film was made during Ronald Reagan's second presidential term. The Anthean, renamed John Dory, makes his way to New York to establish his patents and inventions, taking an apartment by the World Trade Center. He forms a relationship with Eva Milton and her shoplifting son, Billy. This is a version of the relationship of Klaatu and Helen Benson and her son Bobby; it is made explicit that Dory has a son who has needs, so it is made to seem natural that Dory is paternal, advising and providing economically for his dependents. Billy shifts from wearing a leather jacket, a recurring signifier of the rebel, to a rather more homely check shirt. The program celebrates the nuclear family.

Lewis Smith's alien is more assured than Bowie's, able to leap between buildings despite vertigo and more explicitly aware that he is the target of espionage. His disguise as a human rather than Anthean is made more explicit; the film's reveal involves the removal of nipples during a sex scene; here it is rather more comic shock. While the book and film depict the use of alcohol—Betty-Jo/Mary-Lou is alcoholic, and drink has an increasing effect on Newton—here tomato juice is established as something that removes Dory's inhibitions. As the series never followed, it is unclear where the narrative would have continued. Dory's attempt to leave Earth in a spaceship is frustrated, and this was likely to be a continued plot point.

The two adaptations of the novel offer very different versions of the alien messiah. Roeg's version makes us feel the alienness through his editing techniques and the strong performance of Bowie. The murky role and interconnections of the secret services, the military, and large corporations, with their willingness to kill, allowed Roeg and scriptwriter Paul Mayersberg some space for political commentary. Dory is easier to identify with as a protagonist, albeit as a fish out of water in less comic mode than *Mork & Mindy* (1978–1982). As the 1989–1990 television version of *Alien Nation* (Graham Baker, 1988) was to later explore, the format would allow for moments of critique of contemporary society, but it is the human bourgeois family that is being saved and valorized rather than the alien Anthean society.

*Andrew M. Butler*

See also: *Alien Nation*; Bowie, David; *Mork & Mindy*.

## FURTHER READING

Ruppersberg, Hugh. "The Alien Messiah in Recent Science Fiction Films." *Alien Zone: Cultural Theory and Contemporary Science Fiction Cinema*, edited by Annette Kuhn, Verso, 1990, pp. 32–38.
Sinyard, Neil. *The Films of Nicolas Roeg*. Letts, 1991.
Tevis, Walter. *The Man Who Fell to Earth*. Pan, 1976.

## Martian Manhunter

J'onn J'onzz, the Martian Manhunter (1955–), was created by writer Joseph Samachson and artist Joe Certa for DC Comics. J'onzz first appeared in *Detective Comics* #225 in November 1955 and was also one of the original members of the Justice League of America. Possessing many of the same powers as Superman, including super strength, flight, invisibility, precognition, and the ability to read minds, the Martian Manhunter would often stand in for the Man of Steel in Justice League adventures without risking the overexposure of one of DC's most popular characters. J'onzz also mirrors Superman's alien identity as an immigrant, an identity that evolves over the course of the comics.

The Manhunter's origin story, in "The Strange Experiment of Dr. Edel," features a bald, green, heavily muscled humanoid accidentally brought to Earth by an experimental teleportation beam. Dr. Edel dies instantly from shock and is unable to send J'onzz back to Mars. Stuck on Earth, J'onzz decides to take on a secret identity, John Jones, and work as a detective. J'onzz takes the perspective of an immigrant. Separated from his family and culture, he tries to assimilate to his new home. Though J'onzz was taken from Mars against his will, he focuses on building new relationships with the Justice League rather than trying to return home, trusting that eventually technology will advance and allow him to return.

The emergence in the 1950s of visibly different characters such as the Martian Manhunter emphasizes the importance of accepting racial diversity in order to unify society against the truly alien threat of communism. Yet the fact that J'onzz is green rather than black points to how these comics dramatize the difficulty in being a cultural outsider. J'onzz eventually became one of the few DC superheroes to give up his secret identity and operate openly as himself. A mainstay of *The Justice League of America,* J'onzz's place in the JLA was eventually largely usurped by the more popular Superman. J'onzz's individual stories were transferred to *House of Mystery* in June 1964. His run in that magazine ended in 1968, when, readers were told, he had been able to return to Mars.

In 1984 the Martian Manhunter returned to Earth, reestablished his secret identity as John Jones, private detective, and rejoined the Justice League of America, continuing with the organization and gaining more prominence after the comic was relaunched as *Justice League International* in 1987. He also starred in a four-issue miniseries, *Martian Manhunter,* in 1988. At this time the books' authors, J. M. DeMatteis and Mark Badger, revealed that J'onzz's mostly human appearance was the result of the violent psychic trauma he had undergone when the entire Martian race was exterminated. J'onzz's identity shifted from the assimilating immigrant to the refugee who could never return home, a backstory similar to Superman's. It is possible that DeMatteis and Badger were influenced to rewrite the character by the Refugee Act of 1980, which allows special consideration for immigrants based on humanitarian reasons.

J'onzz's appearances continue in Grant Morrison's *DC One Million* (1998), Frank Miller's *The Dark Knight Strikes Again* (2001–2002), and Morrison's *Multiversity* (2014–2015). J'onzz is also featured in 2004's *DC: The New Frontier*, which reimagines characters in their original 1950s settings. The book reflects 1950s culture through a contemporary social lens: J'onzz watches *Invaders from Mars* and wonders aloud about integration and the American fear of difference, "If Americans react this violently to people for a difference in skin color, then I fear they'll never be ready to accept me" (Cooke book 4). J'onzz has appeared in the animated films *Justice League: The New Frontier* (2008) and *Lego DC Comics Super Heroes: Justice League: Attack of the Legion of Doom* (2015); on television in the live-action *Smallville* (2001–2011) and *Supergirl* (2015–), the animated shows *Justice League of America* (2001–2004), *Batman* (2004–2008), and *Justice League Unlimited* (2004–2006); and in video games such as *Justice League: Chronicles* (2003), *Justice League Heroes* (2006), *Mortal Kombat vs. DC Universe* (2008), and *Injustice: Gods Among Us* (2013). J'onzz also appears in two novels: Alan Grant's *DC Universe: Last Sons* (2006) and Kevin Anderson's *The Last Days of Krypton* (2007).

*Sara Austin*

*See also*: Green Lantern; Mekon, the; Superman.

**FURTHER READING**

Gruenwald, Mark. "The Martian Chronicles: Chapter 3 in the Continuing Guide to Confusing Continuity." *Amazing World of DC Comics* 3, no. 13, October 1976, pp. 7–9.

Ndalianis, Angela, editor. *The Contemporary Comic Book Superhero*. Routledge, 2009.

## *Mass Effect* (Trilogy)

The Canadian *Mass Effect* trilogy (Bioware 2007, 2010, 2012) remains one of the most critically acclaimed science-fiction titles in the games medium. Unlike many other game series, whose sequels depend on the critical and commercial success of previous installments, *Mass Effect* was conceived as a trilogy with a continuous narrative and a conclusion, largely preempting any future attempts at continuation. *Mass Effect: Andromeda* (2017), the most recent addition to the franchise, is set in the same universe but explores a completely different narrative trajectory.

*Mass Effect* is set in 2183, when humanity has made contact with other spacefaring races and joined the Citadel Council, a UN-like entity based on the Citadel, which was a city-sized space station as well as a mass relay allowing for instantaneous travel to the farthest reaches of the galaxy. The player role-plays Commander Shepard, whose avatar can be customized with regard to gender, race, appearance, and backstory. At the beginning of the opening game, Shepard becomes the first human Spectre, an elite operative given broad authority to neutralize threats to galactic order in the galaxy. In a variety of Council- and self-sanctioned missions, mostly combat or recovery in nature, Shepard is accompanied by a diverse crew whose loyalty needs to be won. Throughout his/her adventures (since players have control over Shepard's body, gender, and sexual orientation—especially in *Mass Effect 3*) in the *Normandy*, Shepard's ship, the player will find out that the Rogue Spectre that was being chased has been indoctrinated by Sovereign, an ancient synthetic life-form, whose main goal is to wage war against the living. Two years after this, Shepard is attacked and almost killed by a mysterious race called the Collectors. Thanks to the efforts of Cerberus, a secret human organization that fights for humanity over any other race, Shepard comes back to life and is tasked to fight the Collectors. One year after this, war is brought to Earth, and (unless the player finishes *Mass Effect 2* catastrophically) Shepard must find a way to fight back against these synthetics with the aid of the rest of the galaxy. Once the whole story has unfolded, Shepard will have to decide for all sentient beings.

The main narrative engine of the trilogy is a galactic war erupting every 50,000 years in which a machinic-organic race of starships known as Reapers cleanse the galaxy of high-intelligence organic life. The current iteration of this war provides the narrative scaffolding for the third game, with the first two parts serving as preludes. At the same time, the trilogy features numerous other threads not directly related to the Reaper invasion.

The presence and character of alien races is a major contribution to the depth of the trilogy's gameworld. Apart from humans, the games feature over 20 extant races, a dozen of which are meticulously described either in the games themselves or their paratexts and the in-game encyclopedia-like Codex, as well as a number of other extinct races and non-sapient species. A significant portion of the trilogy's textual layer is committed to the construction of biology, customs, and belief systems of at least some of the races as well as complex histories and relations between them, many of which predate human contact. Visually, the major sentient races can be mapped along the broad spectrum of human verisimilitude, ranging from human-like (Asari) and strongly anthropomorphic (Turians, Salarians, Quarians, Drell) to those resembling various mammals (Krogan, Elkor, Volus) and other animals (Hanar, Rachni). Specific iconographies vary broadly (Salarians resemble the archetypal alien Grays, while Rachni owe much of their physiology to the insect species of *Starship Troopers*), but the developers have managed to invest several of the major species with enough detail to achieve individuation of various characters.

The most noticeable aliens are the three that rule over the Citadel, the massive space station, which is central in the games. These races are the Asari, a mono-gender blue-skinned race that mates with other races, and in fact considers intraracial mating negatively; the Salarians, a matriarchal race of short-lived, inventive amphibians; and the Turians, bipedal avian raptors whose culture is essentially militaristic, the rogue Spectre from the first game being a member of this race. Players may recruit characters from these alien races to aid them in their task and can even engage in a romantic relationship with them. In the first game, only Liara T'Soni, an Asari, can be an alien romantic interest for Shepard (either male or female), but in *Mass Effect 2*, Garrus, a Turian, can also be a romantic interest. Salarians, however, cannot be romantic interests, since, due to their short life span, they are not interested in such relationships. Instead, Mordin Solus, the *Normandy*'s scientist, will oversee ship improvements and provide medical support. The main enemy of the trilogy are the Reapers, a synthetic life-form determined to terminate organic life. To do this, they enslaved the Geth, another synthetic life-form. The conflict broadly suggests a fight between organic life and synthetic life. In *Mass Effect 3*, the main premise is to unite the whole galaxy against the Reapers, leaving aside conflicts among races. Nevertheless, not all synthetics are presented as enemies in the game. EDI, the Artificial Intelligence of the Normandy, appears as an ally and a Squad member in the third installment of the trilogy.

As is common in science fiction, individual alien races can be read as reflections or metaphors of various demographics or types: Salarians are master scientists with very few ethical and moral checks, Turians form a Spartan-like militaristic culture, and Batarians and beastly Vorcha are customarily associated with organized crime. A number of species are also capable of biotic powers using force fields somewhat reminiscent of the demystified Force in the *Star Wars* universe.

The race that has attracted the most attention is the Asari, a purple- or blue-skinned, strongly human-like species that occupies a central position in *Mass Effect*'s gameverse. Presented as mono-gendered, Asari characters claim to have no concept of gender differences (although they can recognize them in other races) and can mate and reproduce with any gender or race thanks to a parthenogenesis-like process. While the physiological status partly locates them in the genre tradition of single-sex societies, Asari are visually represented as distinctly female, with breasts and voices generally emblematic of human women. Almost all Asari characters are referred to as "she," bear honorifics such as "matriarch" or "huntress," and refer to their offspring as "daughters." More problematically, they are consistently depicted as being sexually alluring and are often seen in game locations as entertainers and sex workers of various types. Their presentation has led some critics to denounce them as a stereotypical representation of bisexuality and "space hookers."

Despite all these differences, the trilogy's major alien races are at best portrayed as "an extension of humanity, rather than its foil" (Zekany 70) and at worst as unevolved, primitive cultures. The true alienness is only represented by the Lovecraftian Reapers, whose logic eludes comprehension because of their genocidal brutality as well as time scales within which they operate.

Paweł Frelik and Jaime Oliveros

See also: Lovecraft, H. P.; *StarCraft*; *Warhammer*.

## FURTHER READING

Bizzocchi, Jim and Joshua Tanenbaum. "*Mass Effect 2*: A Case Study in the Design of Game Narrative." *Bulletin of Science, Technology & Society*, vol. 32, no. 5, October 2012, pp. 393–404.

Jørgensen, Kristine. "Game Characters as Narrative Devices. A Comparative Analysis of *Dragon Age: Origins* and *Mass Effect 2*." *Eludamos. Journal for Computer Game Culture*, vol. 4, no. 2, April 2010, pp. 315–31.

Zekany, Eva. "'A Horrible Interspecies Awkwardness Thing': (Non)Human Desire in the *Mass Effect* Universe." *Bulletin of Science, Technology & Society*, vol. 36, no. 1, February 2016, pp. 67–77.

## *Masters of the Universe*

*Masters of the Universe* (1982–) is a franchise primarily intended for a preteen male audience, ages 9–15. The franchise was created in 1982 by Mattel Inc. and was shortly followed by the first animated television series in 1983, colloquially known as *He-Man*. The premise of the series follows He-Man (real name Prince Adam) and his associates as they fight to protect their planet, Eternia, and Castle Greyskull from the evil Skeletor and his minions. *He-Man* would be followed by a spin-off series aimed primarily at the female preteen market, *She-Ra*, where He-Man's titular sister attempts to save the universe. Both series are notable for their particular brand of techno-fantasy, combining traditional sword and sorcery tropes with the technology commonly seen in space Westerns, such as *Star Wars*. The *Masters of the Universe* franchise would act as a trendsetter, as its particular brand of science-fiction fantasy would be replicated in *Thundercats* (1985–present).

While the animated series uses its episodic format to maintain the status quo between He-Man and Skeletor—with He-Man remaining primarily in power and the victor—the live-action film (*Masters of the Universe*, 1987, dir. Gary Goddard) takes a different approach to their conflict. At the outset of the film, Skeletor has successfully taken Castle Eternia and imprisoned the Sorceress, beginning the process of siphoning off her power. He-Man and his two cohorts, Man-At-Arms and Teela, are part of a rebellion to retake the castle, though they are seriously outnumbered. They eventually encounter Gwildor, who has created the Cosmic Key, which can open up portals to nearly anywhere. They transport to Castle Grayskull, where they are, again, outnumbered. They find that Gwildor has made this device before, and Skeletor has the original prototype. He-Man and the others hold off the enemy forces until Gwildor can open another portal; this one sends the heroic quartet to Earth. When they arrive, though, they have lost the device. It has been found by a teenage couple, Julie and Kevin. They play with the device and see it as an advanced synthesizer. Skeletor sends his bounty hunters—Beast Man, Blade, Karg, and Saurod—to recover the device. They accost Julie at her high school; she no longer has the Cosmic Key, however, as Kevin has taken it elsewhere. She is eventually saved by He-Man, forcing a retreat of the bounty hunters. Skeletor kills one and sends Evil-Lyn in his place to recover the device. By manipulating both Kevin and Julie, she recovers the device and summons Skeletor to Earth. He-Man recovers the device, but, eventually, the heroes are overwhelmed. He-Man is taken prisoner and the Cosmic Key is damaged; through some technological manipulation and Kevin's musical skill, they are able to return to Eternia. Skeletor and He-Man have their final showdown, with He-Man as the victor, and the humans return to Earth.

The aliens in the film can be split into three separate groups. The first group is the "good" aliens: He-Man, Man-At-Arms, Teela, and Gwildor. For the most part, this group is visually human in stature and appearance. He-Man wears barbarian-style garb, while Man-At-Arms and Teela wear sleek silver outfits with gunbelts for their weapons. Gwildor is the only one who is literally alien in appearance, a short, elfin creature that is some combination of gremlin, gnome, and elf. The second group of aliens is what could be termed "evil": Skeletor, Evil-Lyn, the bounty hunters Karg, Beast Man, Blade, and Saurod, and Skeletor's army of minions. They are visually opposed to the "good" aliens, as most of them are alien in appearance. Skeletor, Evil-Lyn, and Blade are human-like; the other three are all various interpretations of animal-like humanoids, while the army is made up of faceless, black, robotic humanoids. The third group of aliens are the humans themselves; when they travel to Eternia at the end of the film, they become the aliens who do not fit into the society or environment of that planet.

The film itself can be seen as an exploration of the difference between "good" aliens and "bad" aliens, in which good is aligned with patriarchal values and hegemonic masculinity, while bad is aligned with the other and femininity. He-Man has always been seen as a bastion of extreme hyperbolic masculinity. While the animated series works to create a thoughtful contrast between his effete prince appearance and his heroic masculine superhero form, the film presents him only as the latter. His masculinity is both a boon—as he controls almost every action scene—and a hindrance—as Skeletor sees his masculine iconography as something that needs to be conquered for Skeletor's success. Each of He-Man's cohorts also represents positive masculinity: Man-At-Arms as the expert weaponmaster, Gwildor as technological progress, and Teela herself as representing asexual female warrior masculinity. On the other hand, the film positions the "evil" aliens as othered and feminine. First, their appearance is nonhuman and monstrous; second, most of them speak sibilantly, so that even their use of English is othered; third, they work to manipulate, control, and twist the good of He-Man and the named human characters. By creating these oppositional representations of aliens, the film posits that it is aliens who are sufficiently like humans—physically, emotionally, and in terms of masculinity—that humans can connect with, learn from, and be upgraded by them. Aliens who are unlike humans are there to manipulate, control, and kill. The film also directly connects femininity to the alien, as Evil-Lyn, the most obviously feminine of all the aliens, uses that femininity as a weapon. The film actively others femininity and sanctions masculinity.

*Nathaniel Fuller*

See also: *Dark Crystal, The*; *Tenchi Muyo!*.

## The Mekon

Five years after the end of World War II, the United Kingdom reached for the stars. Instead of gleaming Spitfires soaring through the skies over Europe, valiant Englishmen went in search of glorious adventure in the distant corners of the solar system. Rather than facing the fading twilight of the empire, Britain now had its own space fleet, which was the envy of every other planet. All of this, of course, took place only in a comic strip, albeit the most popular one of its time. *Dan Dare, Pilot of the Future* was the flagship serial of the *Eagle*, a weekly publication that, between the years 1950 and 1969, sold millions of copies and captivated the imaginations of entire generations of youngsters. The iconic face of the *Eagle* was the lantern-jawed visage of Dan Dare himself, a dashing, unflappable chap who looked more like a stolid veteran of the Battle of Britain than a daring astronaut.

If Dan Dare was, as the screenwriter Wolf Mankowitz once proclaimed, the "Hero of Our Time," he needed to be pitted against a truly dastardly villain. Fortunately for the readers of the *Eagle*, they didn't have to wait very long to see Dare meet the figure who was to become his greatest nemesis. On November 2, 1950, *Eagle* issue number 30 introduced the world to the Mekon, a character who eventually became every bit as famous and popular as Dare himself. Hailing from Mekonta, a region of the northern hemisphere of Venus, above its vast volcanic fire belt, the Mekon was the lord of the Treens, a race of fearsome green-skinned warriors.

The ghastly result of a disastrous genetic experiment, the Mekon was born with super-intelligence as well as an all-consuming desire to become the universe's supreme ruler. After Dare foiled the first of his campaigns for galactic domination, the Mekon swore that he would have his revenge. An immediate and enormous hit with readers, the character was subsequently resurrected to torment Dare in every second story line the *Eagle* published. Their seemingly eternal duel was later played out not only in the pages of *2000 AD*, but also on radio and even in a short-lived television series.

Dan Dare has often been thought of as the British counterpart of Flash Gordon or Buck Rogers, but the Mekon was certainly a far more original and chilling villain than either Ming the Merciless or Killer Kane. Indeed, it is difficult to convey the exact nature of his menace. Physically small and feeble, with an enormous bulbous skull, the Mekon had spindly limbs that necessitated a levitating chair to move around. What made him absolutely deadly was his gigantic brain, alive with countless diabolical schemes and plans for ever more fiendish weapons. The result of a collaboration between the talented and innovative illustrator Frank Hampson and editor Marcus Morris (who was also an Anglican priest), the *Eagle* was conceived as a means of communicating Christian values to a younger audience in an exciting and colorful fashion. In the fantasy universe they created together, the Mekon fulfilled the role of Satan, an implacably evil being who would stop at nothing in order to achieve his goals.

Like all great fictional villains, the character of the Mekon lends itself to an intriguing multiplicity of interpretations. With his heavily hooded eyes, cruel and vaguely simian features, and distinctive skin color, he is a rich composite of racial stereotypes and most obviously embodies the enduring xenophobic anxiety about the "Yellow Peril" and the threat of the inscrutable Oriental. If Dan Dare himself was in many ways a throwback to an older phase of British literary heroes, like Horatio Hornblower and even Allan Quatermain, the Mekon can equally be seen as the distillation of an earlier vintage of villainy. He combined the wickedness, power hunger, and abominable otherness of Dr. Fu Manchu, the perverted cerebral brilliance of Professor Moriarty, and the masterful deviousness and indestructibility of James Bond's arch enemy, Ernest Stavro Blofeld.

The Mekon was also an expression of the British public's growing distrust of the power wielded by science. In an essay in an 1893 issue of the *Pall Mall Budget*, a youthful H. G. Wells had made the first of his many scientific prophecies. In "The Man of the Year Million," he glowingly predicted that technology's beneficial influence on evolution would ultimately see the human race become a species of pure intellect, with huge brains and shrunken, atrophied bodies. The sketch of a frail, balloon-headed creature with withered arms and legs that accompanied Wells's essay eerily anticipated the image of the Mekon. However, what the character exemplified was the worst kind of futuristic nightmare. Some of the most terrible atrocities of World War II had been committed in the name of science and progress, leading to a profound distrust of the utopian vision they had once promised. In this respect, the Mekon symbolizes the horror of a world run along perfectly rational, scientific lines, the entire cosmos as one colossal mechanism from which the last traces of love, compassion, and individuality have been expelled.

As well as harkening back to the monstrous figures of a previous era, the Mekon can also be seen as foreshadowing some great villains of more recent science-fiction texts. Davros, the mad scientific genius and inventor of the Daleks in *Doctor Who* is his foremost descendant. Indeed, when Terry Nation decided to introduce the character in the classic story "Genesis of the Daleks," the show's producer Philip Hinchcliffe specifically instructed sculptor John Friedlander to base his design on the shriveled, dome-headed appearance of the Mekon. With their pitiless combination of logic and technological might, the Time Lord's other great foes the Cybermen also resemble him, as does the sinister Imperious Leader of the Cylons in *Battlestar Galactica*. However, his most obvious contemporary equivalent is the Borg Queen, the avatar of that terrifying cybernetic race in *Star Trek*. It has now been some years since the Mekon himself last made an appearance, but it can only be a matter of time before he returns to plague humanity once again.

*Edward O'Hare*

See also: *Doctor Who*; *Nemesis the Warlock*; *2000 AD*.

**FURTHER READING**

Crompton, Alistair. *The Man Who Drew Tomorrow*. Who Dares Publishing, 1985.
Higgs, Mike, editor. *Dan Dare: Pilot of the Future. The Deluxe Collectors Edition*. Patrick Hawkey, 1987.
James, Edward. "The Future Viewed from Mid-Century Britain: Clarke, Hampson and the Festival of Britain." *Foundation*, vol. 41, 1987, pp. 42–51.

## Men in Black

Produced by Steven Spielberg and directed by Barry Sonnenfeld, *Men in Black* was released in July 1997 to significant critical acclaim and financial success; it earned three Academy Award nominations—best art direction, best original score, and winning for best makeup—and finished as the year's third-highest-grossing film. Starring Tommy Lee Jones as deadpan MIB veteran Agent K and Will Smith as streetwise rookie Agent J, it is loosely based on Lowell Cunningham and Sandy Carruthers's short-lived *Men in Black* comic books (1990–1991), in which elusive government agents monitor and police all manner of paranormal activity on Earth.

The film condenses the comic's scope to focus solely on extraterrestrials, inspired by a conspiracy theory insisting that real men in black exist, either secret agents or aliens in disguise dedicated to maintaining the secrecy of UFO knowledge (certainly an irony considering the success of the franchise). They are said to have the ability to psychically control human beings, communicate telepathically, and induce amnesia in those who have had a close encounter with extraterrestrials. Usually appearing in groups of two or more, they are called "men in black" for their austere attire: black suits and ties (with white shirts), but sometimes with black hats and sunglasses, too. They are also the inspiration behind the "Observers," who appear, mostly peripherally, in Fox Broadcasting's television series *Fringe* (2008–2013).

In the film *Men in Black*, it is revealed that Earth was designated an "intergalactic apolitical zone" in the 1960s for creatures without a home planet. Decades later, Earth now secretly harbors a multitude of alien species, most of which inhabit the New York City area disguised as humans. Some of the aliens Agents K and J encounter are criminals actively hostile toward humans, but most "are just trying to make a living."

*Men in Black* is an inversion of space opera. In particular it challenges the space-opera variant most commonly associated with *Star Trek*. Here humanity achieves a united, rational, egalitarian "good society" and extends it into space, where Earth leads the formation of a community of species sharing these values

*Men in Black* (1997), directed by Barry Sonnenfeld and starring Will Smith (left) and Tommy Lee Jones. (Columbia Pictures/Photofest)

(as in *Star Trek*'s United Federation of Planets). The order of events may vary, space travel and alien contact prompting or following the good society on Earth, but one typically goes with the other.

*Men in Black* breaks the connection between space and progress. The aliens did not meet a spacefaring human species but landed on Earth *before* the first manned space flight. Additionally, given the decades between the aliens' arrival and the film's events, it is clear that first contact did not spur *Star Trek*–style progress. Indeed, the sole reference to advance of any kind is to technological transfer from the aliens, and even this is an ironic commentary on the trivia of consumerism, including Velcro, microwave ovens, liposuction, and a new recording device to replace CDs, seeing which Agent Kay expresses dismay that he must buy "The White Album" again.

Humanity's lack of progress is matched by the galaxy's lack of progress. Earth's openness to refugees does not win it the respect of other species. Instead, Agent Kay characterizes the planet as merely an "apolitical zone," comparing it to Casablanca in the 1943 film, a place where other powers intrigue and war is a constant possibility, "an Alien Battle Cruiser . . . or a Korlian Death Ray . . . [always] about to wipe out life" on the planet.

The aliens depicted in the film are not universally flawless beings: they each come with their own share of foibles and virtues. There is Jeebs (Tony Shalhoub), a shifty pawnbroker who is able to regenerate his head; Reggie (Joseph Breen), a nervous recent father of a squid-like alien, hurrying to flee Earth; and Frank, an irascible MIB informant resembling a talking pug (voiced by Tim Blaney), among many others who mostly serve as sight gags. Threatening their otherwise innocuous existences, however, is the crash-landing of a "bug" alien—the film's chief antagonist. A ferocious insectoid creature, the bug forcefully inhabits the skin of a belligerent farmer (with a brilliantly demented performance from Vincent D'Onofrio) before it proceeds to wreak havoc in its search for a galactic energy source. Should the bug purloin this precious item, Earth will be destroyed. With its ill-fitting guise and generally repugnant demeanor, the bug is redolent of the fears of those who oppose immigrants.

Central to the film, however, and to the compassionate ideology of MIB, is the principle that in order to avoid war and destruction, we must put our cultural—though, in this case, intergalactic—differences aside and learn to coexist peacefully. As bigotry is far from a thing of the past, MIB enables anonymous sanctuary for alien life on Earth. As such, the responsibility of the knowledge of extraterrestrial activity is not bestowed upon anyone outside of MIB for fear of social chaos.

Following its critical and commercial success, *Men in Black* has thus far spawned two sequels: *Men in Black II* (2002) and *Men in Black III* (2012), both of which have seen Jones and Smith reprise their roles. While the sequels brought further box-office takings—elevating the series' overall earnings to well over US$1 billion worldwide—they were not met with the same significant critical acclaim as the original film.

*Liam Hathaway and Nader Elhefnawy*

See also: *Galaxy Quest*; *X-Files, The*.

## FURTHER READING

Chapman, Aneta. "Real Men Wear Black: The *Men in Black* Films." *The Science Fiction Film Reader*, edited by Gregg Rickman, Limelight, 2004, pp. 390–96.

Engelhardt, Tom. *The End of Victory Culture: Cold War America and the Disillusioning of a Generation*. University of Massachusetts Press, 2007.

Pierson, Michele. *Special Effects—Still in Search of Wonder*. Columbia University Press, 2002.

## *Metroid*

*Metroid* (1986) is a game series of exploration platformers developed in Japan by Nintendo, specifically by R&D1. *Metroid* follows the adventures of Samus Aran, a bounty hunter sent on various missions on behalf of the Galactic Federation. Commonly encountered on these missions are Metroids, intelligent and aggressive organisms that drain the life out of anything they encounter. The term "Metroid" is a portmanteau of "metro" and "android": most of the games take place underground, like a subway, and the original concept was an android instead of a woman in a suit of armor. Samus is prepared to fight the Metroids because she was raised by the Chozo, a species of bipedal birds with strong interests in technology and genetic engineering, and the Chozo provided her with a power suit that could be modified with various upgrades that are scattered around the planet. The four games that fans consider to be the "main series" games (*Metroid, Metroid II: Return of Samus, Super Metroid, and Metroid Fusion*) will be the focus of this entry. Game journalists now use "Metroid" as a shorthand for various kinds of video games based on exploration.

Samus often starts off as fairly weak and ineffective against the various aliens she encounters, and she is unable to traverse the entire world at the start. During the course of the game, Samus discovers various additions and modifications to her power suit that allow her to access new areas. For example, Samus can locate the Ice Beam that freezes enemies and turns them into platforms, allowing her to access new areas of the game. The sectioning of the game through items and abilities rather than by levels allows *Metroid* to have a more cohesive and continuous feel when compared to other games that use levels or maps to contain challenges. The ability to explore an entire world rather than levels gives the sense of exploring an alien planet rather than completing a series of tasks.

All four of the main series games have the player navigate Samus through a hostile world full of various aliens. After Samus defeats a group of Space Pirates and their sentient computer Mother Brain in *Metroid*, she is hired to wipe out all of the Metroids on their homeworld in *Metroid II: Return of Samus*. She succeeds in exterminating them all except for a single baby Metroid that imprints on her and treats her as its mother. Samus delivers the last Metroid in *Super Metroid*, but the baby is stolen and weaponized by the space pirates. The baby Metroid sacrifices itself in defense of Samus against Mother Brain, thus ending the species. Samus accompanies an expedition to the Metroid homeworld in *Metroid Fusion*, only to be attacked by a parasite known as X. The X parasite was originally contained by the Metroids, but the X spread after losing their only natural predator. Samus is treated with an experimental treatment derived from the baby Metroid, making her the last Metroid. After destroying the station containing the X parasite to prevent it from leaving the station, Samus exists as the last Chozo, the last Metroid, and the last X.

Narratively, the *Metroid* series claims xenocide might be the best option for galactic peace. Metroids became powerful weapons in the hands of space pirates, meaning they could not be left to exist on their homeworld. *Metroid II: Return of Samus* includes a counter to ensure every Metroid on their homeworld is wiped out. After the last Metroid is killed in *Super Metroid*, Samus discovers that the Galactic Federation attempted to clone Metroids and the X parasite. She realizes the danger in letting these species exist. Failing to contain two deadly intelligent parasites would present an obvious problem, but successfully harnessing them would destabilize galactic order as well. Humans would become the conquerors of the universe and would threaten stability. The Chozo instilled a need for balance and harmony in Samus, and she decides that destroying all the clones and going into exile will stabilize the galaxy. The more alien Samus becomes the more she recognizes humans as a threat to peace. Samus retains her alien rather than human nature by declining to start a genocide, thus breaking with the species-ending habits the *Metroid* series claims are part of human beings. Even parasites like

Metroids remain in harmony with their environment, showing that something that appears alien and aggressive has a particular role in the universe. The Metroid series argues against meddling with the cosmic balance.

The *Metroid* series, especially *Metroid* and *Metroid II: Return of Samus*, immerses players in the experience of being lost on an alien world. The lack of a clear map or guide means the player will be constantly disoriented and confused about their direction. Some critical paths in the game are hidden in walls, are perched in high places, or require specific items to reach. While some players might enjoy the experience of wandering an alien world, others might find the complete lack of direction in the early games a little too frustrating. The cryptic nature of the early games was replaced by a more linear style in *Metroid Fusion*, which meant players were less likely to get lost. *Super Metroid* likely has the best balance of feeling lost on an alien and unfamiliar world while providing enough clarity to avoid looking online for a map. Remakes like *Metroid: Zero Mission* and the 2017 remake of *Metroid II: Return of Samus* allow players to experience the core portions of the first two games while getting better guidance and objectives when compared to the originals. The series allows players to experience a world of alien rules and paths, but there are also options that are a little less cryptic.

Ian Derk

*See also*: *Mass Effect* (Trilogy); *Star Trek*; *StarCraft*.

**FURTHER READING**

Meslow, Scott, "Why Nintendo Needs to Save the *Metroid* Franchise," *GQ*, March 2017. https://www.gq.com/story/why-nintendo-needs-to-save-the-metroid-franchise.
Muncie, Julie. "How *Metroid* Fans Made a Better Game than Nintendo," *The Wired*, September 2017. https://www.wired.com/story/metroid-ii-remake-fan-vs-nintendo/.
Webster, Andrew. "The Enduring Influence of *Metroid*." *The Verge*, September 2017. https://www.theverge.com/2017/9/14/16303016/metroid-nintendo-influence-legacy.

## Miéville, China

Only one of China Miéville's (1972–) novels to date has conspicuously featured aliens as aliens (the peoples of his New Crobuzon sequence are all indigenous). His 2011 novel *Embassytown* presents the Ariekei, or Hosts, as intensely alien physiologically, socioculturally, and linguistically. In the novel, Avice Benner Cho tells the story of the consequences of the arrival on the planet Arieka of EzRa, "the impossible new Ambassador" (5), sent to the planet specifically to serve as a translator with and for the Hosts. Such Ambassadors are needed because the Ariekei speak "Language" (26) by means of "an intertwining of two voices" (53) known as "the Cut and the Turn voices" (56); moreover, they can understand Language spoken only in this way, and thus Ambassadors are genetically engineered twins trained to speak empathetically with two voices yet a single mind. This dynamic has evolved owing to the peculiar nature of the Hosts' Language, which can tell just the truth in a parallel of Adam's naming of the beasts in Eden before the Fall. "Everything in Language is a truth claim" (56), Avice explains, as

English fantasy fiction author and political activist China Miéville in 2012. (SFX magazine/Getty Images)

"Language for Ariekei was speech and thought at once" (273). Importantly, the Hosts cannot lie. For the Hosts, Language cannot say what is not known or what has not been witnessed, which means they employ similes to describe their experiences. However, EzRa proves defective, as their facility with Language acts upon the Ariekei like "'a drug'" to which they become addicted, such that "'EzRa are infecting *every, single, Host*'" (170). To save the Ariekei, Avice and other humans of Embassytown teach the aliens to lie through discovering metaphor. Avice succeeds, and the Ariekei undergo a profound and even traumatic social and linguistic change as they enter the postlapsarian world of signification, abstraction, and thought. While some Ariekei remain locked in Language, others called the Absurd develop forms of communication such as gestures and even writing, and others called the New Ariekei begin learning French and developing the new language "Anglo-Ariekei" (343). Yet this fall of the Ariekei into metaphor and sentience carries distinctly colonial implications, encouraged as it is by humans. Avice hears "minds reconfigured" (336), and she notes with satisfaction that the humans of Embassytown replaced "Language" with "language" (310), bringing the Hosts linguistically into "the world we live in" (312). This outcome represents a victorious "coup" (343), with humans and Ariekei together achieving self-determination and establishing an "explorocracy" (345) as "the last outpost" (344) of known space.

Within a novel focused on the tension between truth and lying, reference and signification, the alien Ariekei are a perpetually ambiguous form. Avice at no point provides a single, extensive description of a Host. Instead, the reader must visualize a Host from disparate clues: they walk with "crablike precision" (13); the Cut and Turn mouths are on separate stalks (79); they have "giftwings" (25) and "fanwings" (83); they have a "carapace" (86), "eye-corals" (88), and "spiky fibrous limbs" (133); they are "insect-horse-coral-fan things" (121). Physiologically and textually fuzzy, they constitute what Istvan Csicsery-Ronay Jr., identifies as the science-fictional "grotesque" (146). For Csicsery-Ronay Jr., the grotesque refers to the "familiar" and "intimate" physical world "undergoing surprising transformations" that unsettle our "sense of rational, natural, and desirable order" (146–47). Grotesque bodies are "constantly opening up, metastasizing" (192) as they produce "excrescences, protuberances . . . pimples, tumors, genitalia" (194). Such acute, unrelieved otherness explains the humans' perpetual "discomfort" (Miéville 14) in the presence of the Ariekei. Also, the lack of a complete, definitive physical portrait of the Ariekei amplifies their alienness: they remain a constantly shifting and indeterminate signifier, contrasting the condition of Language, in which lying, polysemy, and ambiguity are "impossible" (Miéville 295). Avice and the humans of Embassytown steering the Ariekei out of Language and into metaphor and lying, therefore, serve in part (ironically) to resolve the open-endedness of the alien by making the Ariekei think and communicate more like humans. Not quite precisely colonial assimilation, perhaps, but the Hosts' "minds" are in the end "reconfigured" (Miéville 336) according to human norms of language and signification.

This reconfiguring of the Hosts is seen as good by both aliens and humans. Spanish Dancer, one of the Ariekei, says, "Before the humans came . . . we were mute. . . . We speak now or I do, and others do" (336). Avice casts the new relationship between humans and Ariekei as a dynamic of mutual political and economic self-determination: "we can run ourselves" (344); "to survive and rule ourselves, we have to explore" (345). Yet the ending of *Embassytown* strangely leaves the potentially troubling colonialist implications of the Hosts' fall into metaphor unexplored—or, at least, ambivalent. Adam Głaz observes that at the end, "the feeling of human superiority over non-humans is nearly palpable" (336). For Abigail Nussbaum, the closing "note" of a "bright future . . . doesn't quite work," as "the eradication of Language . . . by alien interlopers is ultimately held up as a good thing." On one hand, in the aftermath of the 2008 financial crisis and concurrent with the Occupy movement of 2011, the restructuring of the Ariekei/human relationship in *Embassytown* can constitute a united resistance to the socioeconomic interests of the centralized interstellar government of Bremen. On the other hand, Avice appears so wholly invested in the necessity, correctness, and success of leading the Hosts out of Language that either she is a satire of an unwitting colonialist or the novel sincerely tenders the radical shift of the alien into human thinking and language as desirable (and so the Hosts experience a Fortunate Fall). The former reading is plausible, but the latter proves difficult to disregard, which, finally, might undermine the novel's impressive presentation of the Ariekei as so truly alien.

*Michael Johnstone*

*See also*: *Arrival*; Banks, Iain M.; Reynolds, Alastair.

## FURTHER READING

Csicsery-Ronay Jr., Istvan. *The Seven Beauties of Science Fiction*. Wesleyan University Press, 2008.

Głaz, Adam. "Reversals and Paradoxes: China Miéville's Anti-Language." *Extrapolation*, vol. 56, no. 3, 2015, pp. 335–52.

Miéville, China. *Embassytown*. Del Rey-Ballantine, 2011.

Nussbaum, Abigail. "*Embassytown* by China Miéville." *Asking the Wrong Questions*, November 27, 2011, wrongquestions.blogspot.ca/2011/11/embassytown-by-china-mieville.html.

## Mœbius

For considering aliens in the Mœbiusverse, one may separate the work of Jean Giraud "Mœbius" (1938–2012) as writer and artist of his own works and as an artist bringing to life other writers' visions. Mœbius writes and illustrates in the mythic mode, so his characters, including aliens, and the worldbuilding in general, are generally expressions of mythic archetypes and symbols. Furthermore, since many of his works are set in the future, even human characters with their biological modifications are often just as estranging as any alien species.

The first significant science-fiction work that brought Mœbius's artistry to the spotlight was the comic work "Le bandard fou" ("The Horny Goof: The Devilishly Clever Story of a Syldanian Wild Pecker"; 1974). There are two parallel stories in this narrative, which explore different aspects of being alien. In one half, there is a wordless story of a man who visibly mutates after snapping his fingers: melting into a blob, then reshaping into an egg, and finally, from that egg emerging as a tiny bespectacled human. In the other half, we have the story of the "Horny Goof," a humanoid alien who suddenly finds himself in an illegal state of priapism ("wild pecker") on a conservative desert planet. He is rescued by the Lady Kowalsky, an alien who is interested in mating with him, and taken to the pleasure asteroid Flower. This early story already displays some of the typical characteristics of Mœbius's alien environments and characters. The presentation of the desert as an alien landscape and site of transformation was largely the result of Mœbius's own experiences traveling in Mexico, interacting with indigenous people, and being exposed to the work of the anthropologist and shamanist Carlos Castaneda. Visually, the preponderance of yellow and brown shades to represent desert colors, from character clothing to the landscape, is typical of Mœbius's style both in his non-SF works such as the Blueberry series as well as his SF works. The transforming humanoid, the crumbling shell or egg, the character of the fool, and finally, the sexualized alien female who leads the hapless hero through a journey of self-knowledge as lover and/or as predatory threat may also be seen as regular features of Mœbius's works.

Some of these features appear in the cult *Arzach* stories as well as *The Airtight Garage*, first published in *Métal Hurlant*, which Mœbius cofounded in 1974 with Philippe Druillet and others. *Arzach* is for the most part a wordless series, featuring a cloaked alien warrior, Arzach, who travels through a mostly desert landscape atop a mechanical pterodactyl. The stories are suffused with a surrealist vibe and portray archetypal scenarios in a negative light. The alien landscapes are ruined and postapocalyptic, featuring crumbling towers, mountains of skulls, ravenous wild creatures, naked humanoids who walk aimlessly through the ruins, and the purposeful heroic figure of Arzach, who seems to wander the landscape looking for a mate. Arzach often spies upon female figures as they undress, but unlike the goof, he never seems to be able to be intimate with them, because their alienness does not match his own: one of these women, although she has a female human body, bears the face of a different species from Arzach's own, while another one appears to be human and thus also, for Arzach, alien. This postapocalyptic desert planet seems to be devoid of normal life, and any attempt at communication is bound to fail. These stories also introduce some of Mœbius's other signature themes, especially concern about communication with other species and a general eco-sensitive attitude toward landscape. Several other minor tales featuring aliens, such as "The Long Tomorrow" (written by Dan O'Bannon, 1974, and a key visual influence for *Blade Runner*), "It's a Small Universe," (1976), and "The Ballade" (1977) also display these concerns, in addition to reusing a color palette similar to his other stories.

These features, however, are most prominent in Mœbius's largest cycle of SF stories, *Le Monde d'Edena* (translated as *The Gardens of Aedena* or *The World of Edena*, between 1983 and 2001). The story originally began as a promo for the automobile maker Citroën, entitled "Upon a Star" (1983) and featured the protagonists Stel and Atan, but Mœbius kept on developing the world, adding a prequel ("Repairs") and then adding four further stories. In the initial adventure, intergalactic repairmen Stel and Atan end up repairing an intergalactic vessel that carries them, and specimens from all species (who do not really feature in the story at large), to the utopian planet Edena. The stories in the cycle deal with the mythos of this planet as the genderless "alien" protagonists are slowly transformed back into humans who consume natural foods instead of artificial foods, befriend local fauna, become healthy, discover lust and love for each other, lead their own descendants out of their complacent mechanized existence, and achieve a kind of apotheosis after fighting a symbolic, but also physical, darkness. The stories are the best illustration of Mœbius's ecological outlook, which had been developing further under the influence of the French new-age guru and UFO enthusiast Jean-Paul Appel-Guéry. The stories render the ancient astronaut theory directly into the SF idiom, where Stel and Atan become the Adam and Eve of the new planet. In Mœbius's Edena mythos, humans themselves are the aliens, estranged from their own bodies, desires, and needs, cut off from nature and its offerings, and they need to be remade into humans. The message is rather simple, even if the visual portrayal is complex and multilayered. A significant part of the action once again takes place in the desert, and the recurrent theme of transformation and communication finds its place. Unlike *Arzach* or his other narratives, however, the Edena cycle offers a positive resolution and hope.

Similar hope and ideas are also expressed in *The Incal* (1980–1988) and *After the Incal* (2000), the result of a collaboration with Alejandro Jodorowsky (b.1929) that began with the failed film project *Dune* but which received a life of its own in the surrealist comic. Spanning several dimensions, planets, and universes, the story visually recreates many of Mœbius's signature landscapes and themes: the alien desert planet, the battle between light and dark, the masculine and feminine principles creating a balance, transformation of the goofy protagonist into hero through contact with the feminine, and so on. Even though the story is credited to Jodorowsky, the reappearance of many of Mœbius's concerns highlights the process of cocreation.

Mœbius's work has been a huge direct and indirect influence on the visual imaginary of SF in general, especially through the work published in *Métal Hurlant* and his Hollywood collaborations. Notable instances include *Tron* (1982), the Star Wars universe, the *Alien* films, *Blade Runner* (1982), *The Fifth Element* (1997), and the films of Hayao Miyazaki, among others. Perhaps his most significant legacy is not so much in creating the figure of the alien as character but in the estranging effects of world-building, in particular the postapocalyptic alien landscape and the industrial city wasteland.

Bodhisattva Chattopadhyay

*See also*: Dick, Philip K.; *Saga*; *2000 AD*.

**FURTHER READING**

Giraud, Jean. *The Collected Fantasies of Jean Giraud*. Vol. 0, Dark Horse, 1987; Vol. ½, Graphitti Designs, 1991; Vols. 1–9, New York: Epic Comics, 1987–1994. 11 volumes.
Giraud, Jean. *Mœbius-Giraud. Histoire de mon double*. Numéro 1, 1999.
Jodorowsky, Alejandro and Jean Giraud. *Incal*. Humanoids, 2001.

## Moore, C. L.

C(atherine) L(ucille) Moore (1911–1987) published her first short story featuring an alien life-form in 1933 at the age of 22. "Shambleau," the story of an alluring, Medusa-like extraterrestrial who drains vitality from humans in exchange for an addictive ecstasy, would remain Moore's most famous work of science fiction throughout her lifetime and beyond. Like "Shambleau" itself, several of Moore's numerous other fictions featuring extraterrestrials belong to the same series of short stories starring the raygun-wielding interplanetary outlaw Northwest Smith, whose exploits most often appeared in the pages of *Weird Tales* (also the usual home of Moore's other major recurring protagonist, the sword-and-sorcery heroine Jirel of Joiry). Northwest Smith's eerie close encounters were a perfect fit for Farnsworth Wright's *Weird Tales*, sometimes sharing an issue with Lovecraft himself and regularly with other members of the so-called Lovecraft Circle.

Many of Moore's nonhuman extraterrestrials evoke qualities of unknowable menace, cosmic dread, and immemorial antiquity that one might be tempted to term generically Lovecraftian today. And yet Moore's interests in extraterrestrial elder gods and things from beyond deviate from those of Lovecraft in certain respects, not least important of which is her characteristically frank treatment of gender, sexuality, and desire, more broadly conceived of as these might intersect with the otherness of the alien. The tentacle-haired humanoid predator Shambleau, for instance, is a universe-traveling incarnation of deep myth—and also a woman.

The gender politics and other larger significances of the intentionally cryptic "Shambleau" have been much debated, but Moore's wider body of work reveals a sustained obsession with similar figures. For example, in "Black Thirst," published in the April 1934 issue of *Weird Tales* just a few months after "Shambleau," Northwest Smith finds himself facing an alien threat familiar in its inscrutability. The Alendar, a kind of age-old Minotaur at the center of the story's literal and figurative labyrinths, appears perfectly human at first but later deliquesces into primordial black slime upon his psychic defeat. The Alendar had been breeding a race of beautiful women to be sold throughout the solar system, but unlike his creations he turns out to be an elemental horror older than humanity, originating on some distant planet. A being that feeds on beauty, the Alendar identifies himself as akin to aliens like Shambleau that feed on life-force. While it would be reductive to describe this figure as simply a gender-reversed Shambleau, the threat of the alien here acquires a definite undertone of homoeroticism: the Alendar's desire to taste and consume male beauty for the first time in the person of Smith is far more striking than the vague and unseen threat of other Lovecraftian "black beasts" that we are told also lurk in his halls.

Northwest Smith's adventures usually take place on Venus or Mars, with an excursion to a Jovian moon in "Yvala" (*Weird Tales* February 1936), where the dominant life-form turns out to be a physical incarnation of beauty that can take the shape of women in order to ensnare and "devolve" its human prey, in a process that reminds Smith of Homer's Circe. In contrast to the impersonal alien entities against which Smith so often struggles, the various Venusian and Martian "races" to which Moore alludes throughout these stories, while distinct in their physical characteristics, temperaments, and cultures, seem to belong to the same human species. Some other notable alien encounters of Smith's include "Scarlet Dream" (*Weird Tales* May 1934), in which a mesmerizing pattern on a strange shawl transports the outlaw to a dream world covered in vampiric grass and dominated by a formless alien presence; "Dust of Gods" (*Weird Tales* August 1934), in which Smith is tasked with recovering the literal residue of an obliterated elder god; "Julhi" (*Weird Tales* March 1935), a highly eroticized story of a cyclopean temptress reminiscent of Shambleau, always seeking new sensations on which to feed; and "The Tree of Life" (*Weird Tales* October 1936), in which yet another godlike interdimensional entity known as Thag has manifested in the form of a malevolent anthropophagous tree. At least two of Moore's other stories from this period—"The Bright Illusion" (*Astounding Stories* October 1934) and "Greater Glories" (*Astounding Stories* September 1935)—contain encounters with powerful and incomprehensible alien beings of the kind that might have featured in Northwest Smith's adventures, had the plots of these stories not required the death or assimilation to godhood of their protagonists.

After her early success, Moore would later collaborate regularly with Henry Kuttner (they married in 1940), and it has proved difficult to ascertain where authorial credit for certain works should be understood to lie, as, for example, when the couple would publish pseudonymously. For one, the celebrated time-travel story "Vintage Season," originally published under the byline "Lawrence O'Donnell" in the September 1946 issue of *Astounding*, has sometimes been reprinted under Moore's name alone and, in other venues, as a product of the pair in collaboration. While "Vintage Season" does not feature extraterrestrial beings as such, the visitants from Earth's future strike the same chords of uncanniness as many of Moore's aliens do, hailing not from a deep past or distant star, but nevertheless distinguishing themselves as a strange race from an unknowable future that has grown apart from humanity as we know it. Similarly, the short novel

*Judgment Night* (serialized in *Astounding* in 1943) imagines a galactic empire constituted by far-flung "races" of humans whose differences from one another finally pale before more obviously alien presences, such as the godlike Ancients that wield unimaginable power and the ambiguously sentient *llar*, the latter of which, it is implied by the novel's end, may become the inheritors of the galaxy, with their superior collective consciousness, after humans have destroyed themselves. Moore's works written both before and during her marriage to Kuttner vary a great deal in their relative interest in genuine science-fictional extrapolation and the real possibility that extraterrestrial life might be discovered in the universe, but in so many of her narratives the alien remains a central figure, acting as bearer of often horrific difference but also deep mystery.

*T. S. Miller*

*See also*: Burroughs, Edgar Rice; Lovecraft, H. P.; Weinbaum, Stanley G.

## FURTHER READING

Bredehoft, Thomas A. "Origin Stories: Feminist Science Fiction and C. L. Moore's 'Shambleau'." *Science Fiction Studies*, vol. 24, no. 3, 1997, pp. 369–86.

Gamble, Sarah. "'Shambleau . . . and Others': The Role of the Female in the Fiction of C. L. Moore." *Where No Man Has Gone Before: Women and Science Fiction*, edited by Lucie Armitt, Routledge, 1991, pp. 29–49.

Gubar, Susan. "C. L. Moore and the Conventions of Women's SF." *Science Fiction Studies*, vol. 7, no. 1, 1980, pp. 16–27.

## *Mork & Mindy*

*Mork & Mindy* (1979–1982) was a spin-off of the TV show *Happy Days* (1974–1984) created by Garry Marshall, Dale McRaven, and Joe Glauberg. The show followed Mork (played by Robin Williams), an alien from the planet Ork, who came to Earth in a one-Orkan egg-shaped spaceship. Originally, the character of Mork first appeared in "My Favourite Orkan," episode 22 of season 5 of *Happy Days*. A riff on the 1960s sitcom *My Favourite Martian*, the episode involved Mork attempting to bring Richie Cunningham back to Ork as a human specimen, only to be foiled by Fonzie. While it was intended to be a dream sequence, Mork proved so popular that the ending was edited to show him wiping the cast's memories, and he was granted a spin-off. To explain the time difference, it was revealed that Mork could also travel in time, although he would return to the 1950s in "Mork Returns" (season 6, episode 24).

Set in Boulder, Colorado, in the late 1970s and early 1980s, *Mork & Mindy* follows Mork, who, it was then claimed, has been sent away from Ork, where humor is not permitted, by his superior Orson. He becomes the unlikely roommate for Mindy McConnell (Pam Dawber), who originally mistakes him for a priest, as he wore a suit backward, making it look like a priest's collar. In his innocence, Mork tells Mindy who he is, and she offers him a place to live in her attic. While her father doesn't approve of her roommate, her grandmother does, and Mindy and Mork settle in to what can only be described as wacky alien hijinks.

*Mork & Mindy* (1978–1982), starring Robin Williams (middle) and Pam Dawber. Famed comedian Jonathan Winters (left) joined the cast in the fourth season in the role of Mork and Mindy's son, Mearth. (ABC/Photofest)

In what has now become a trope of the genre, the "innocent abroad" approach to Mork allowed the show to make social commentary through the lens of the stranger without becoming overly didactic. At the end of every episode, Mork psychically reported what he had learned about life on Earth to the long-suffering Orson, reports often of a highly philosophical nature. In his report on loneliness, Mork declares that people on Earth "are so busy looking out for number one, there is no room for two" ("In Mork We Trust," season 1, episode 21); other report topics include losing a friend, the price of celebrity, and hugging. While the reports could have fallen into sentimentality, Williams's charming, innocent, and heartfelt performances carried the series. Unlike its successor *Third Rock from the Sun* (1996–2001), which in later seasons continued to reset the alien visitors' ignorance of human activities, Mork absorbed what he learned of humanity and carried it through. However, the innocent traveler trope was balanced by Williams's comedic improvisations, which were so popular that the showrunners began to leave time during filming for Williams to carry them out.

In addition to learning about humanity in general, Mork forms a relationship with Mindy that evolves throughout the run of the series. They eventually marry, and Mork lays an egg that hatches their son, Mearth; as Orkans age backward, Mearth was played by Jonathan Winters, who was much older than Robin Williams, though he was costumed like a small child. The series was also characterized by Mork's catchphrase "Na-Nu Na-Nu," and his greeting resembling a Vulcan salute mixed with a handshake. It was also extremely self-referential; in season 3, episode 14, "Mork Meets Robin Williams," Mork and Mindy find themselves interviewing Robin Williams, who unlike Mork is soft-spoken and quite humble.

Ork and Orson are never seen in *Mork & Mindy,* and Mork's claim that he was created in a test tube suggests that he is perhaps not a typical Orkan. This is reinforced by the small clues planted in his reports to Orson, such as in "In Mork We Trust," where Mork's report interrupts Orson's shower. Mork's line, "Oh, please don't shake yourself dry this time, Your Immenseness; last time it rained for weeks!" could indicate that Orson is extraordinarily large, though it remains unclear whether there are other Orkans of Mork's size. This ambiguity benefits the comedic nature of the show; the audience is free to imagine Orson as they will, and Williams was free to ad-lib whatever absurd claims he wished.

The series suffered in later seasons from changing time slots—intended to entice viewers away from popular shows on other networks—and the focus shifted from Mork's innocent exploration of Earth to his emerging romance with Mindy and, at one point, his search for a job. These changes caused the show to fall from the third-highest rating in 1978 to the sixtieth by its final episode in 1982. Nonetheless, the series remains timeless; Mork and Mindy's journey through the 1970s was a clear inspiration for *Third Rock from the Sun*'s much raunchier exploration of the late 1990s and remains an insightful yet hilarious view of the 1970s.

*Jennifer Harwood-Smith*

See also: *Futurama*; *Man Who Fell to Earth, The*; *Third Rock from the Sun*.

## FURTHER READING

Itzkoff, *Robin: The Definitive Biography of Robin Williams*. Sidgwick and Jackson, 2018.
Marshall, Garry. *My Happy Days in Hollywood: A Memoir*. Crown Archetype, 2012.

# N

## *Nemesis the Warlock*

*Nemesis the Warlock* (1980–1999) is a comic strip created by Pat Mills and Kevin O'Neill. Mills was one of the writers who created the British science-fiction comic *2000 AD*, while. Kevin O'Neill was a staff artist on the comic and had worked with Mills on strips such as *Ro-Busters* and *ABC Warriors*. *Nemesis* grew out of that work and debuted in *2000 AD* in 1981, after a couple of prequel strips in 1980.

Nemesis is a Warlock from a race of demonic sorcerers, perhaps the most distinctive alien people featured in the strip. Book 3 includes much information about the society and customs of the Warlocks, centered around the birth of Thoth, while a short episode, "The Secret Life of the Blitzspear," goes into the symbiotic relationship between the Warlocks and their living spacecraft.

*Nemesis the Warlock* combines science fiction with swords and sorcery and tells of an earth thousands of years in the future, now called Termight, that rules a galactic empire and pursues a fanatical crusade to exterminate all aliens. The word "crusade" is deliberately chosen: Mills and O'Neill depict a future that has very much taken up the aesthetic of medieval Christendom and its wars against Islam. Nemesis leads the resistance against Termight and its Terminators.

The intent is obvious; this is a parable about racial intolerance and genocide, with the aliens in the role of every persecuted minority that ever existed. Explicit parallels emerge not only with wars against Islam, but with persecutions of the Jews (the chief villain is called Tomas de Torquemada, after the leader of the Spanish Inquisition, and is a reincarnation of Adolf Hitler) and of Native Americans (Torquemada is also a reincarnation of U.S. Colonel John M. Chivington, perpetrator of the Sand Creek Massacre of 1864). The absurdity of intolerance is underlined in an episode when Termight is temporarily on better terms with aliens and so sets out to persecute people with freckles, just to give humans someone to hate. As the series developed, this message became less and less subtle, and the strip became hectoring, losing much of the humor that had once made it so enjoyable.

O'Neill's aliens are often grotesque and strange looking in appearance, but this generally belies a far more "humane" nature. For instance, Kremlin, the chief of the alien Vologs, insists on being polite to humans even as he kills them. The message is often put out that the aliens fight the humans only because the humans have attacked them, apparently without any reason beyond pure hate. (There are, however, some nasty aliens, such as the slave-owning Nagas.) In contrast to the depiction of aliens, the Terminators of Termight conceal their humanity behind equally grotesque uniforms, but these accentuate their savagery and cruelty.

In Book Two, drawn by Jesus Redondo, the reader is introduced to the Arachons, who run a prison for captured humans. They are giant spiders and so trigger the latent arachnophobia that many humans have—but they are kind and benevolent. Book Three introduces the Basilisks, who live in a world-tree and petrify when they die. The steampunk-themed Book Four (drawn by O'Neill and then Bryan Talbot) centers on the Goths, shape-changing aliens who model their appearance and society on Britain of the early 20th century, having received radio transmissions—their affinity for humans means that other alien races distrust them. Talbot does a good job of making them look like humans, though not quite right, through details such as the shape of their noses.

After Book 4, however, the strip becomes less interested in creating new and distinctive alien races and progressively becomes more and more about the personal struggle between Torquemada and the eponymous Nemesis, complicated by Nemesis's human associate Purity Brown and Nemesis's son Thoth, who seeks revenge against Torquemada for bringing about the assassination of his mother and Nemesis for not being there to prevent it. More and more, the comic becomes a character study of Torquemada, as Nemesis becomes an increasingly shadowy figure. Aliens en masse continue to have a role to play as the "other" that is the target for humanity's hatred. But individual aliens become less important, with the exception of Nemesis himself. Though Nemesis is leader of the resistance to Termight and has many human allies, he often seems indifferent, or even hostile, toward the fate of the race as a whole, more than once promising to exterminate humanity. It is progressively revealed that he fights Torquemada as much for the sheer entertainment of it all as for any moral imperative. He is often depicted as being no better than Torquemada, just as cruel and callous, indifferent to concepts such as "good" and "evil, and fundamentally unfathomable. This last aspect is developed as the strip goes on; in earlier books the reader is privy to what is going through Nemesis's mind, sometimes through thought balloons and captions. By Book Ten, the last in the series, the reader is told that it is impossible to comprehend what the Warlock is thinking.

The strip ends with the deaths of Nemesis and Torquemada, and with Purity Brown becoming president of a Termight that is open to aliens. The problems that ensue are explored in *Deadlock: Return to Termight*.

*Anthony Keen*

See also: Green Lantern; Martian Manhunter; Mekon, The; Superman; *2000 AD*.

## FURTHER READING

Mills, Pat. *The Complete Nemesis the Warlock*, Books 1–3. Rebellion, 2006–2007.

## Niven, Larry

Larry Niven (1938–) is among American science fiction's most prolific authors and has a talent for creating unusual and varied aliens. He is also one of science fiction's most honored writers, having received, to date, five Hugo Awards, four Locus Awards, and one Nebula Award. Niven's most famous work is the Hugo- and Nebula Award–winning *Ringworld* (1970), which has spawned many sequels and prequels. However, this is only part of a vast series titled Tales of Known Space, in which much of Niven's science fiction is based. The series is set within a volume of space 60 light-years in radius, with Earth at its center. Various characters and important species make multiple appearances within these stories. As part of this greater universe, the Ringworld series includes the title novel *Ringworld* (1970), *The Ringworld Engineers* (1979), *The Ringworld Throne* (1996), and *Ringworld's Children* (2004). To date there have also been 14 volumes of The Man-Kzin Wars, set in Niven's Known Space; Niven has himself written very few of these.

*Ringworld* is a story of the 200-year-old Louis Wu, who is recruited to join a crew of explorers. The team also includes a much younger woman named Teela Brown; Nessus, the Piersson's Puppeteer; Speaker-to-Animals, the Kzin. The Puppeteers and the Kzin are Niven's best-known alien species. These two species are very different, and this disparity is a vital part of the story. The Puppeteers, who are extremely long-lived, with Nessus being over 300 years old during the novel, are compulsive cowards despite being one of the most advanced species in the galaxy. The main reason behind their cowardice is that their culture has no belief in an afterlife, and therefore staying alive is of vital importance. As a species they are intensely manipulative, considering the rare, brave Puppeteer to be expressing signs of mental illness. They are herd animals and herbivores (which may also explain their cowardice), featuring three legs and two "heads," although their brains are housed within a protected thorax. Their heads contain their sensory organs and throats, but they also use them as a humanoid might use hands. Humanity has purchased much of its advanced technology from the Puppeteers. By comparison, the Kzinti are violent and warlike. They resemble eight-foot-tall pseudo-feline humanoid tigers with rat-like tails. The history of the Kzinti was influenced by a spacefaring race called the Jotoki, who themselves resemble giant starfish. Due to the warlike nature but relatively low technological experience of the Kzinti, they were given more advanced technology and recruited as mercenaries by the Jotoki. The Kzinti have a strong honor code based on heroism; unhappy with being enslaved by the Jotoki, they eventually rebelled and made their former masters into slaves. Once they had taken complete control of the technology, they used it to genetically enhance all the males, turning them into super-warriors and breeding out most of the intelligence from their females.

As the title implies, the expedition is given the goal of exploring a recently discovered ringworld, an enormous artifact that circles around a sun-like star, orbiting in a distance roughly equal to that of Earth's orbital radius. Centrifugal force gives it an approximation of Earth's gravity, and the inner surface of the ring, equivalent to three million Earths, is inhabitable. The ringworld is incredibly old, and its creators are unknown. This concept borrows from the idea of a Dyson sphere, but at the time fans noted some physics problems with the ringworld that Niven later addressed in *The Ringworld Engineers* (1979). Once at the ringworld, the expedition is shot down by automated defense systems and crash-lands. The crew then set off across the vastness of the ringworld hoping to learn more about the artifact and to find a way to return home. They discover a variety of sentient species, including humans and Kzinti, that appear to have inhabited the ringworld for centuries, which only adds to the mystery. From the evidence, it becomes obvious that many civilizations have risen and fallen on the ringworld. Some of the civilizations, such as those that left the automated defense systems, appear to be more advanced than even the explorers. However, the only examples of advanced technology that still seem to be operating are automated and nonsentient. Eventually, in part thanks to Louis's scientific ingenuity, the crew—except for Teela, who decides to stay behind—manage to escape the ringworld's gravity and return home. However, they are already planning a return expedition, which is described in later books.

It is a science-fiction adventure story exploring new races and would have been at home in the early pulp magazines. However, there is enough hard science fiction to separate it from most of them. What distinguishes Niven's stories are superior language skills and his ability to make aliens, alien landscapes, and alien technologies believable. Nessus and Speaker-to-Animals define their species' characteristics but are also engaging characters that encourage a reader to care about their stories. However, they are only two examples of Niven's many memorable alien characters.

Niven's work includes many other novels and story collections not part of the *Known Space* universe that feature aliens of varying importance, including *The Mote in God's Eye* (1974) and its sequel; *The Integral Trees* (1984), and *Footfall* (1986), all coauthored with Pournelle; the Heorot series, coauthored with Steven Barnes and Pournelle, beginning with *The Legacy of Heorot* (1987); and *Bowl of Heaven* and its sequel, coauthored with Benford.

*Michael J. Hollows*

*See also*: Brin, David; Card, Orson Scott; Cherryh, C. J.

## FURTHER READING

Kerslake, P. *Science Fiction and Empire.* University of Liverpool Press, 2007.
Niven, Larry. "The Alien in Our Minds." *Aliens: The Anthropology of Science Fiction*, edited by George E. Slusser and Eric S. Rabkin, Southern Illinois University Press, 1987, pp. 3–12.
Niven, Larry. *Playgrounds of the Mind.* Tor, 1992.

## Oddworld

The *Oddworld* video games, developed by Oddworld Inhabitants Inc., led by Lorne Lanning, were intended to be a pentalogy. To date, only two have been released (1997 and 2016), with two spin-off games. The first was *Abe's Oddysee*, in which the titular protagonist embarks on a quest to free his people, the Mudokons, from slavery and from becoming the newest processed-food product. It was popular enough that a sequel was commissioned and quickly released—*Abe's Exoddus*—in which Abe must stop the desecration of his people's burial grounds. The next official entry in the planned series was *Munch's Oddysee*, with Abe returning to help Munch save his own species, the Gabbits, from extinction. *Stranger's Wrath*, the second spin-off, was set in a different part of the world with little relation to the previous stories and followed a bounty hunter through a setting reminiscent of the Wild West. Reception of the games was generally very positive, and the fanbase remains devoted. At the time of writing there are over 1,100 reviews of *Abe's Oddysee* on Steam, and 92 percent are positive.

The games, especially the first three, are satirical, lampooning corporations and consumerism. Many elements resemble things from modern Earth, even though Oddworld itself is a distant planet and the residents are wholly alien. Examples include the business suits worn by the Glukkons, one of the antagonist species, and the title given to the richest and most successful of their kind: Glockstar. As another example, the Gabbits are an amphibious species that have been overfished such that Munch is the last one, and their eggs are sold as a delicacy called "Gabbiar."

Featured most predominantly are the Mudokons, Abe's people. They are blue/green-skinned humanoids, initially presented as a slave race and literally at the bottom of the food chain. One objective of the games, to unlock the "good" ending, is to rescue as many of them as possible. As such they are generally passive in-game, but Abe can instruct them to help him by pulling switches and opening doors.

Aside from the "slave race" aspect, there are some potentially problematic elements. Free Mudokons are frequently referred to as "native," for one, and resemble a mixture of various existing indigenous cultures. Helpful game hints in *Abe's Oddysee* are given in the form of stylized cave art, particularly in an area called "Monsaic Lines." In the same game Abe's guide is a Mudokon mystic he refers to as "Big Face" due to the large mask he wears, similar to various tribal masks and carvings from Earth. In *Munch's Oddysee*, hints and information are provided by a "shaman" who appears in places marked by concentric circles drawn in the dirt. Also in *Munch's Oddysee*, the subjugated Mudokons, including Abe, are mostly hairless but for a ponytail/topknot from the crown of their heads, while "native" Mudokons have feathers sprouting there, almost like a headdress, and they can be upgraded to weapon-using warriors called "Tomahawkers."

The Glukkons are a complete contrast. Rather than being a hodgepodge of existing cultures they are a blatant satire of capitalism and corporate corruption. They are first introduced as the ruling power of their part of Oddworld, the top of the food chain. Physically, they are tall, broad-shouldered figures in tailored suits that reflect their station, with Glockstars being very ornate. Primarily represented by the powerful Magog Cartel, they are ruthless industrialists whose only concerns are their own wealth and status. One of their businesses, the meat-packing plant RuptureFarms, has already wiped out one animal species and driven two more to the brink of extinction by the start of *Abe's Oddysee*. Faced with dwindling livestock and dropping profits, the CEO, Molluck, devises a new product line, code-named "New 'n' Tasty." This, it is soon revealed, will be made out of the Mudokons, which is the catalyst for Abe's quest to escape and free his people.

In *Abe's Exoddus* the Glukkons have created Soulstorm Brew, which they market under slogans like "Don't think. DRINK!" It's addictive, and Mudokons who get hooked are forcibly indentured to work in the brewery, to be paid with more Brew. Furthermore, one of the ingredients is bone from the Mudokon burial grounds, and the slaves assigned to dig there are blinded so they cannot see what they unearth.

Lastly, in *Munch's Oddysee* it is revealed that Glukkons smoke a lot of cigars and use Gabbits as a source of lungs for transplant. There is also an auction for the last can of Gabbiar, effectively all that remains of Munch's species. Not that the Glukkons care.

In all of this they are aided by a small army of gleefully violent Sligs they employ as enforcers, and they defend their facilities with vicious dog-like Slogs and numerous explosive mines.

Despite their financial and temporal power, the Glukkons are a hollow sham. They look impressive, but they have no visible arms, and their suits fit like a narrow sheath, so that they walk with a foot-shuffling gait. When at one point a Glukkon is electrocuted, his clothes comically disintegrate, revealing that underneath the sharp suit is a tiny, shrunken body with shriveled legs. His arms, however, are extremely long, so that he stands on his hands, which are in turn hidden in his shoes. Which, of course, is why they have others do their dirty work. They literally can't get their hands dirty.

The conflict between the Mudokons and the Glukkons (with Munch later helping Abe) boils down to "nature versus industrial," and the games give us an exaggerated look at the sort of thing that might happen if corporations are given too much leeway. That it's shown with funny aliens only makes it easier to take in.

*Jonathon Side*

See also: *Futurama*; *Hitchhiker's Guide to the Galaxy*; *Lesbian Spider Queens of Mars*.

## FURTHER READING

www.oddworld.com

# Okorafor, Nnedi

The American writer Nnedi Okorafor (1974) first became known as a young-adult (YA) writer, notable in particular for featuring women of color as the protagonists of her novels and novellas. Born to Nigerian parents and very familiar with Nigeria thanks to frequent visits, Okorafor combines her Igbo and American cultural heritages in her Afrofuturist fiction.

Okorafor's first publication in the YA field was *Zahrah the Windseeker* (2005), which won the Wole Soyinka Prize for Literature. Here, the adolescent protagonist, Zahrah Tsami, begins Okorafor's discussion of magic. Zahrah shows the connection of magic to West African traditions and the land, issues Okorafor continues to examine in the majority of her publications. The female protagonist's appearance and talents position her as the alien; but the alien proper appears in Okorafor's more recent work, which is clearly science-fictional, even if it retains elements of fantasy.

In *The Book of Phoenix* (2016), Phoenix is one of numerous speciMEN who live in Tower 7: people who have been genetically engineered to be super-beings. She is going to be a weapon. She also appears to be related to aliens, and there is a giant alien tree in Tower 7 itself. As she is escaping from Tower 7, she ventures down to the lobby and sees the tree (the Backbone); symbolically, the tree gives birth to a seed, which is enclosed in a box. Once Phoenix touches the alien seed, she envisions traveling to a blue planet, Earth: "I was hope sent from afar." Here, the unknown alien origin is meant to represent the Middle Passage and the Atlantic slave trade; the alienation and Phoenix's subsequent desire to seek understanding of her background analogizes the experience of the slaves. Notably, Phoenix's alien connection enables her to physically transport herself from space to space, especially when in danger. Phoenix feels alienated because she does not believe that she belongs anywhere, but once she understands her connection to this alien place and her purpose, to cleanse the world of the representation of colonization, the Big Eye, she no longer feels that she does not belong.

We find super-beings in *Lagoon* (2014) as well: each of the three people who witnesses the arrival of the aliens (a marine biologist, a soldier, and a singer) has superpowers. But the arrival of the aliens, in the sea off Lagos, is the central event of the novel, and we follow the varied reactions of different representatives of Nigerian culture. In part the book is a reaction to the normal approach of aliens in science-fiction books, which is to have them land in America or Britain. "If there were aliens," says one character to himself, "they certainly wouldn't come to Nigeria. Or maybe they would" (ch. 8). The alien takes the form of a beautiful Nigerian woman and takes the Yoruba name Ayodele. But she is a shape-shifter, her shifting signaled by the grinding noises of the metallic particles that take the place of cells in her/its body. It is through the alien, who wants to bring peace, but also wants to bring change, that the novel reveals some of the complexities of Nigerian society.

Okorafor's most recent science-fiction work includes three closely linked novellas: *Binti* (2015); *Binti: Home* (2017), and *Binti: The Night Masquerade* (2018). Binti is an extremely bright teenage Himba girl from Namibia who wins a place at the celebrated Oomza University, hundreds of light-years away. Okorafor has said that she wrote the story when she herself was displaced from her family, when she took up a professorship at the University of Buffalo. Binti is the first of the Himba people to leave home and family; the Himba's history, culture, and sense of self are all determined by their close connection with the land. Throughout the novella, when Binti needs to heal herself she rubs the clay mixture that she has brought from home—it is called *otjize*—onto her body and hair.

In *Binti*, Binti leaves her home and travels among foreigners, the Khoush, in order to reach the ship; her appearance, in particular her hair and her *otjize*, make her identifiable as an outsider. Many Khoush find fault in Binti; it is not until she reaches the ship that she finds friends. During her initial moments on the ship, Binti's behavior is like that of an ordinary adolescent: she is unsure of herself, and she feels isolated. Even before she arrives at her destination, however, an alien group called the Meduse attack the ship and kill everyone but Binti: she is apparently protected from the jellyfish-like aliens by her *edan*, a piece of unknown alien technology. Through self-acceptance, Binti is able to survive (she merges with the Meduse), ultimately arriving at the university for the next stage of her life as a biracial/bispecies character. Her hair has now been transformed into *otjize*-covered Meduse tentacles. Binti takes her Meduse friend, Okwu, home with her to meet her family and to learn how to accept her new self, one rooted in both human and alien cultures. Okwu is the first Meduse to go to Earth since the peace treaty with the Meduse was signed, and Binti's position as peacekeeper continues through the second and third novellas. As in *Lagoon*, meeting aliens has brought change to humans, who are mostly reluctant to accept it.

*Melanie A. Marotta*

*See also*: Butler, Octavia E.; Le Guin, Ursula K.; Thompson, Tade.

## FURTHER READING

Burnett, Joshua. "The Great Change and the Great Book: Nnedi Okorafor's Postcolonial, Post-Apocalyptic Africa and the Promise of Black Speculative Fiction." *Research in African Literatures*, vol. 46, no. 4, 2015, pp. 133–50.

O'Connell, Hugh Charles. "'We Are Change': The Novum as Event in Nnedi Okorafor's *Lagoon*." *Cambridge Journal of Postcolonial Literary Inquiry*, vol. 3, no. 3, 2016, pp. 291–312.

Whitted, Quianna. "'To Be African Is to Merge Technology and Magic': An Interview with Nnedi Okorafor." *Afrofuturism 2.0: The Rise of Astro-Blackness*, edited by Reynaldo Anderson and Charles E. Jones, Lexington, 2016, pp. 207–13.

# P

## *Pacific Rim*

*Pacific Rim* (2013) is a film directed by Guillermo del Toro. It was derived from the various mecha anime (in which humans pilot robots to fight monsters) and kaiju films ("strange beast," most famously *Godzilla*) of Japan. In this world, the Kaiju are giant aliens who cross over from an interdimensional breach deep in the Pacific Ocean and wreak havoc by attacking the shorelines of Australia, China, Russia, Japan, and the Western United States. The world responds with international cooperation to create Jaegers, thousand-foot-high mechas that are piloted by telepathically linked pairs. In "the drift" of linkage, pilots share memories and physical reflexes; they become the heroes and rock stars of the new world. As time passes and kaiju attacks increase, they start to lose influence in favor of massive protective walls. When the Jaeger program is summarily canceled by the World Council, British Marshal Stacker Pentecost (Idris Elba) collects the five surviving Jaegers and their pilots and pulls Raleigh Beckett (Charlie Hunnam) out of retirement. Raleigh and his brother Yancy had piloted the American Jaeger *Gipsy Danger* until five years before, when Yancy was killed. Pentecost wants him to pilot *Gipsy Danger* again and auditions a series of possible pilots for the purpose; Raleigh instead singles out Pentecost's adopted daughter, Mako Mori (Rinko Kikuchi), herself a survivor of a Kaiju attack in childhood. The pair are tested in the trials for drift linkage and are soon called to battle. Kaiju attacks are increasing in frequency and severity; an ill-advised partial drift by American scientist Newton Geiszler (Charlie Day) reveals that the Kaiju are themselves engineered by a race in another dimension to colonize the planet. The race's earlier effort millions of years ago spawned the dinosaurs, but the aliens could not thrive in Earth's climate; however, humanity's catastrophic impact on the environment has effectively terraformed the planet for them. The Kaiju attacks are meant to whittle away at the population and its decreasing resources, and then the real invasion can begin. A last-ditch effort to prevent the invasion is to destroy the breach itself with nuclear weapons in a suicide mission. Both Raleigh and Mako survive the final battle, successfully closing the breach and saving the world.

The film itself undercuts a number of familiar tropes utilized in the genre: Raleigh Beckett's role as the "maverick American hero" who disdains orders to save the day is completely rescripted so that his solo efforts result in tragedy, while international and interpersonal cooperation saves the day. Further, while set up for a plot in which Raleigh learns to trust/love again by overcoming his man-pain, he instead heals emotionally offscreen during the time skip and spends his time as a mentor to Mako, helping her to overcome *her* survivor's guilt and gain vengeance for her family. A romantic subplot between these two characters would

*Pacific Rim* (2013), directed by Guillermo del Toro. (Warner Bros./Photofest)

also be required in most genre films, and while there is a scene of Mako's physical interest in Raleigh (through a literalized female gaze in which Raleigh's naked torso is viewed through the peephole), the relationship remains nonsexual and nonromantic in a positive way.

In the United States, the film faced a critical backlash for its emphases on diversity and internationality. In a review for *The New Yorker*, July 22, 2013, Anthony Lane wrote that "even as the story hops between Alaska, San Francisco, Sydney, Vladivostok, and the Far East, you begin to realize that it could be happening anywhere, or nowhere. Small wonder that it ends up beneath the waves." It performed poorly at the domestic box office but was one of the highest-generating films in China and Asia (Mendelson). Nonetheless, it gained a cult following, and a sequel was greenlit for production in 2016; the sequel, starring John Boyega, will be released in 2019.

The Kaiju as aliens themselves are largely unexplored beyond being seen as a threat, though the revelation late in the film that they are engineered as biological counterparts to the Jaegers rather than ignorant destructive creatures is fascinating. That they plan to colonize the Earth after the destruction of humanity and reap its resources for themselves, and that humanity is largely presented by people of color on-screen, creates a colonial discourse that has gone without comment in the criticism (such as it is). "We always thought alien life would come from the stars, but it came from deep beneath the sea. Something out there had discovered us. . . ." Raleigh states both at the film's beginning and in the trailers. This is explicated a little more in the licensed novelization by Alex Irvine, in which the Kaiju's creators are called the Precursors, and their world is the Anteverse, which is described as "A great city made of flesh and bone and organ, grown and made over millions of years . . . the last gasping remnants of a planet they had come to from somewhere else and somewhere else before that. They had drained it of everything they could use and now if they could not move on, they would die. . . ." Director and creator Guillermo del Toro frequently returns to the themes of cultural violence (as in *Pan's Labyrinth*, 2006) and ecological disaster (*Hellboy II: The Golden Army*, 2008) in his works, but this is the first where those aspects are directly combined, and indeed, inextricably linked. The film's tagline in the trailers, and some posters, was "To fight monsters, we created monsters." The idea of the monster as savior as well as enemy is another of del Toro's penchants . . . and one seen in the original kaiju films from which this work derives.

*Cait Coker*

See also: *Cloverfield*; *Transformers*.

**FURTHER READING**

Coker, Cait. "The Mako Mori Fan Club." *Dis-Orienting Planets: Racial Representations of Asia in Science Fiction*, edited by Isiah Lavender III, University Press of Mississippi, 2017, pp. 204–17.

King, Sharon D. "The Apocalypse Will Not Take Place: Megamonster Films (*Cloverfield*, *Pacific Rim*, *Godzilla*) in the Postmodern Age." *The Last Midnight: Essays on Apocalyptic Narratives in Millennial Media*, edited by Leisa Clark et al., McFarland, 2016, pp. 165–73.

Mendelson, Scott. "*Pacific Rim* and More Domestic 'Flops' That Became Global Hits." Forbes.com. September 2, 2013. www.forbes.com/sites/scottmendelson/2013/09/02/pacific-rim-and-more-domestic-flops-that-became-global-hits/#56fe0b507c18.

## Polar Aliens

The closest thing to an actual encounter between humans and aliens in the Arctic occurred in 1818. The humans were a party of Arctic Highlanders, Inughuit, on the west coast of Greenland, as far as they knew the only humans in the universe; the aliens were members of a British Royal Navy expedition, led by Commander John Ross and Lieutenant Edward Parry, on the search for a sea route to the Pacific, the famous Northwest Passage. The encounter went happily; initially wary, the humans eventually summoned the courage to approach the alien ship and interrogate them, through an interpreter, about their impressively advanced technology. Subsequent encounters did not go so well. Ross and Parry noticed to their surprise that the Inughuit had iron-edged tools; a chunk of the iron, brought back to London, revealed that the Inughuit had made the jump into the Iron Age courtesy of a trio of nickel-iron meteorites. An 1894 expedition, led by Robert Peary, took all three meteorites with them, with colossal effort, back to New York. Fifty years after Peary, the Inughuit were deported to make room for Thule Air Force Base. The story of the Inughuit mirrors the ways in which the polar regions have been treated in imaginative literature.

First, the Arctic and Antarctic were *unexplored*. Wishful thinking, dubious oceanography, and Inuit legend led to a popular belief in Europe in the Open Polar Sea. Break through the barrier of ice, and you would sail into an area of open water, perhaps even warm; the ancient Greeks believed something similar, postulating the temperate land of Hyperborea beyond the origin of the North Wind.

From its origins, science fiction has been linked to the poles. *Frankenstein*'s framing story is that of an early polar explorer (very early; the story, written in 1816, is set in "17—"). Shelley's Captain Walton eventually decides, after hearing Victor Frankenstein's story, to turn back before reaching the hypothetical Open Polar Sea—Shelley didn't know that the Open Sea did not exist, but still uses

Walton as a parallel to Frankenstein; both embarked on an obsessive pursuit of knowledge that is eventually fruitless. The Brontë siblings, as children in the 1820s, were avid fans of polar exploration, which then had the same status in Britain as the Space Race in 1950s America, as a combination of strategic struggle, exploration, and national pride; they named two of their toy soldiers "Parry" and "Ross," and their real-life counterparts were universally lionized.

But some explorers were driven by far stranger ideas. John Cleves Symmes, a Cincinnati eccentric, decided in the early 19th century that the Earth was hollow, with an enormous hole, thousands of miles across, at each pole giving access to the interior surface (and possibly, he speculated, a smaller Earth inside, with its own access holes, and another inside that, and so on, a sort of planetary matrioshka doll). He managed to get 25 U.S. senators to vote in favor of funding an expedition to find the Great Boreal Manhole; eventually, after his death in 1829, the Great United States Exploring Expedition did actually set sail, its aims moderated somewhat by sanity.

A pseudonymous 1820 novel, *Symzonia*, peopled Symmes's interior with a race of humans whose racial superiority was symbolized by their extreme whiteness (echoing, perhaps unintentionally, the Greek idea of Hyperborea as a utopia surpassing even Atlantis). In 1836 Edgar Allan Poe wrote *The Narrative of Arthur Gordon Pym*, which ends with an encounter, near the South Pole, with a looming figure with skin as white as snow. The Mormon founder Joseph Smith assured his followers that the 10 lost tribes of Israel were at the Pole, perhaps inside Symmes's hole, waiting for him to melt the ice and lead them home. The interior of a hollow Earth was fertile ground for many pulp writers in the 19th and 20th centuries, and true believers still exist, pinning their hopes on a NASA conspiracy to airbrush out the hole from satellite images.

But the poles did not remain unexplored. True polar aliens start to appear in fiction in the early 20th century—and the essence of the poles in this second phase is not that they were *unexplored* (by this time they were anything but) but that they were *frozen*. Scott's last expedition in 1910–1912 had retrieved fossils, recovered from alongside his body, that proved that Antarctica had once supported cycad ferns the size of trees. Antarctica was no longer a *tabula rasa*; it was a place that had bloomed with subtropical life before being wiped clean. It was a disaster area.

H. P. Lovecraft took this scientific discovery a step further; his ancient Antarctica in "At the Mountains of Madness" (1931) had had prehistoric animals and plants but also an alien city, whose builders had been driven into hibernation by the cooling climate. The horror starts when one of the aliens is thawed out by curious scientists; the same mistake unleashes a visiting alien in John Campbell's 1938 "Who Goes There?," filmed in 1951 as *The Thing from Another World* and in 1982 as *The Thing*, and the conveniently indescribable Thing in *In Amundsen's Tent* (1928), which stalks and eats a retreating polar party. *The Blob* (1958) is eventually defeated by being frozen solid and is then dumped in the Arctic by the U.S. Air Force. That was never going to work; *The Blob Returns*, having been accidentally thawed, in 1972. Still more aliens, also unwisely revived, and an ancient city improbably preserved beneath the Antarctic ice appear in *Alien vs. Predator* (2004). The temple to Mike Mignola's Lovecraftian Ogdru-Jahad, in *Hellboy: Seed of*

*Destruction* (1994), is in Greenland rather than Antarctica; defrosting it still turns out to be a mistake, as does trying to retrieve a meteorite and its cargo of parasitic worms from beneath the Greenland ice in Peter Høeg's novel *Miss Smilla's Feeling for Snow* (1992). Horrors at the poles are common in fantasy as well; the *Warhammer* fantasy gaming setting (1987) gives over both poles of the world to the forces of Chaos, and George R. R. Martin's *A Song of Ice and Fire* (1994–) threatens Westeros with an encroaching winter and the icy, malevolent Others. The aliens associated with the *frozen* are without exception hostile—demons unwisely raised.

No unpleasant aliens have yet been defrosted by the melting induced by climate change, but John Wyndham runs things the other way round in *The Kraken Wakes* (1953), with aliens deciding to wipe out humanity by melting the ice caps and raising the sea level, though they hide in the deep sea rather than beneath the ice.

Anything still undiscovered at the poles is, if not frozen, also probably *hiding*; the 1939 German expedition to Antarctica has produced plenty of conspiracy theories about secret airfields, fugitive Nazis, flying saucers, mysterious Antarctic pyramids, meetings with aliens, and so on; elements of these, along with the inevitable frozen and unwisely thawed aliens, made it into *The X-Files: Fight the Future* (1998). And Lovecraft's Antarctic aliens reemerge in Charles Stross's *A Colder War* (1999), in company with various Cold War aerospace projects, the Burgess Shale creatures, and Oliver North.

In the real Cold War, the Arctic would be overflown by bombers, as featured in *Dr. Strangelove* (1963), and patrolled by nuclear submarines. Few more Lovecraftian objects exist than a modern ballistic missile submarine—the Cold War itself was pretty Lovecraftian, as Stross points out in his afterword to *The Atrocity Archives* (2001)—but *Strangelove*'s autonomous Doomsday Machine, buried in "the perpetually fog-shrouded wasteland below the arctic peaks of the Zhokhov Islands," must be one of them.

*Alexander Campbell*

*See also*: Lovecraft, H. P.; *Thing, The*; "Who Goes There?"

## FURTHER READING

Glasberg, Elena. "Who Goes There? Science, Fiction and Belonging in Antarctica." *Journal of Historical Geography*, vol. 34, no. 4, 2008, pp. 639–57.

Leane, Elizabeth. *Antarctica in Fiction: Imaginative Narratives of the Far South*. Cambridge University Press, 2012.

Spufford, Francis. *I May Be Some Time. Ice and the English Imagination*. Faber and Faber, 1996.

## *Prometheus*

Director Ridley Scott's *Prometheus* (2012) is a science-fiction/horror film that takes place within the same universe as Scott's *Alien* film franchise. *Prometheus* marks the return of Scott to the director's chair for the first time since *Alien* (1979). Although the screenplay was originally written as a long-promised prequel to the original film, in interviews Scott has suggested that it is better understood as a stand-alone film that takes place within the same universe as the original. Together with its eventual sequel, *Alien: Covenant* (2017), *Prometheus* expands the mythology of the original series by exploring the origins of the films' xenomorphs. The film is set in the 21st century and follows a group of scientists as they discover star maps in ancient cave drawings. Researchers Elizabeth Shaw (Noomi Rapace) and Charlie Holloway (Logan Marshall-Green) believe that these star maps hold the keys to humanity's origins and set out for the distant planet LV-233 in the hopes of coming face to face with the Engineers, the mysterious beings that they believe created humankind. However, unbeknownst to them, the project is funded the dying billionaire and CEO of Weyland Corporation, Peter Weyland (Guy Pearce), who has secretly journeyed on the spacecraft with them in an attempt to "meet his maker" and to discover the key to immortality.

The Engineers' relationship to the origins of humanity is revealed through a mysterious opening scene. An alien spaceship arrives on a prehistoric Earth and leaves behind a humanoid Engineer who appears dressed in ceremonial garb. The Engineer drinks a mysterious black liquid that causes him to become violently ill as the liquid thrashes under his skin and through his veins, eventually causing his body to decompose and collapse into the waterfall below. In a scene that blurs the boundaries between evolution and intelligent design, close-ups of his body parts show that his DNA mixes in the water, causing a biological reaction that establishes the genetic basis for life on Earth. Centuries later, the scientists arrive on the distant planet and discover an abandoned spacecraft, which holds a number of objects indicative of an advanced civilization, including cylinders loaded with black liquid, a large statue of a humanoid head, and the decapitated body of a well-preserved Engineer. The exploration of the spaceship confirms that the Engineers are genetically related to humanity. Taking the decapitated head back to the spaceship's laboratory for research, Shaw determines that the Engineers and humans have identical DNA.

The Engineers' creation of life on Earth parallels a subplot involving Weyland's creation of artificial life. The film's title (which is also the name of the expedition's spaceship) is a reference to the Greek god Prometheus, who stole fire from Olympus in order to create human life. Similarly, Weyland has created David (Michael Fassbender), an android that Weyland has turned into the company's servant. Drawing a connection to Mary Shelley's *Frankenstein; Or, The Modern Prometheus* (1818), Weyland has used the powers of science and technology to create life but has abandoned any concern for his creation. Likewise, the film suggests that Weyland's purpose on the trip is to continue his project of scientific investigation by programming David to experiment with alien life. During the exploration of the Engineers' spacecraft, David covertly steals one of the cylinders, which he brings back to the Prometheus, and intentionally infects Holloway. Holloway impregnates Shaw, which causes an alien creature to rapidly gestate inside her. However, using an automated surgery table, Shaw aborts the creature, removing a squid-like creature from her body. In the film's closing scenes, Shaw's alien offspring attacks an Engineer. Mimicking the chestbursters of the original films, an alien creature resembling a xenomorph bursts from the Engineer's chest, suggesting that David's experimentation is responsible for the origins of the alien creatures.

Weyland's godlike desire to create life leads him to the Engineers in an attempt to discover the source of immortality. During the exploration of the planet, David finds a sleeping Engineer remaining at the helm of the spacecraft and then leads Weyland and Shaw to the Engineer. David, who has mastered the Engineers' language, attempts to communicate with them; however, the Engineers hold too much disdain for their creations. The Engineer rips off David's head and uses it to bludgeon Weyland to death. Much like Weyland, the Engineers have become indifferent to their creations. After the Engineer kills Weyland and David, Shaw discovers that the Engineers intend to return to Earth in order to unleash a deadly virus that will wipe out the entire planet. The black liquid the Engineers created was originally intended as a weapon of mass destruction: it had evolved, taking on a life-form of its own and attacking the Engineers. Attempting to stop the Engineer from destroying Earth, Shaw tells the *Prometheus*'s Captain Janek (Idris Elba) to use the ship to destroy the Engineer's spacecraft, an act that both kills Janek and traps Shaw on the planet alone.

*Prometheus*'s engagement with questions around the origins of humanity, and the Promethean powers of science to create life, reflects ongoing concerns around developments in the techno-scientific and biotechnical fields. The film's focus on the experimentation with life closely resonates with recent projects such as the Human Genome Project, cloning, and artificial intelligence, which have all raised important questions regarding the possibilities of biogenetic creation. These developments have called into question anthropocentric understandings of humanity's place in the universe (see McWilliam). In detailing the possibilities of creating life, *Prometheus* draws from historical works such as Greek mythology and *Frankenstein* in order to highlight the dangers intrinsic to creating and manipulating life. It also highlights the ethical responsibilities humans have toward their creations.

*Zak Bronson*

See also: *Alien* (Series); Donaldson, Stephen R.

## FURTHER READING

Brinded, Nicolas. "Exceptionalist Discourse and the Colonization of Sublime Spaces: Alfonso Cuarón's *Gravity*, Ridley Scott's *Prometheus* and Thomas Cole's *The Oxbow*." *European Journal of American Culture*, vol. 33, no. 3, 2014, pp. 223–36.

Luckhurst, Roger M. "Darwin's Nightmares." *Sight & Sound*, vol. 24, no. 11, November 2014, pp. 34–38.

McWilliam, David. "Beyond the Mountains of Madness: Lovecraftian Cosmic Horror and Posthuman Creationism in Ridley Scott's *Prometheus* (2012)." *Journal of the Fantastic in the Arts*, vol. 26, no. 3, 2015, pp. 531–45.

## Quatermass (Series)

The four *Quatermass* (1953–2005) thrillers written for television by Nigel Kneale in the 1950s and 1970s were produced on low budgets and, in the first three instances, produced live. The alien encounters were mostly offscreen, with special effects often limited to filmed inserts and cutaways.

Kneale was employed by BBC Drama as an in-house scriptwriter, initially adapting plays and books for television, but in 1953 he was commissioned to write a six-part serial, *The Quatermass Experiment*. Its good ratings led to *Quatermass II* (1955), partly an attempt to compete with ITV. After Kneale did not renew his contract, he was commissioned to write *Quatermass and the Pit* (1958–1959). He rested Quatermass for a decade—aside from a Hammer remake—before he wrote a final serial in the early 1970s, although budgetary restraints meant it was made in 1979 on ITV, in four parts, with a 90-minute version for cinema. In 2005, BBC4 transmitted a live remake of *The Quatermass Experiment*.

The BBC was still establishing itself as the national television broadcaster after the interruption of World War II, with the 1953 coronation of Queen Elizabeth II as one of the factors that allowed its growth. It is no accident that the climax of *The Quatermass Experiment* takes place in Westminster Abbey, with a puppet alien manipulated by Kneale and his then-girlfriend, later wife, Judith Kerr (later to become famous as a children's author) in front of a photo of Poets Corner. It was still conceivable that there would be a British space mission. Three British astronauts have been possessed by an alien during their mission and their capsule has crash-landed on a house in Wimbledon. Such bombsites would still have been a familiar sight in 1953.

The shapeless alien absorbing people, plants, and animals owes a little to *The Thing* (Christian Nyby, 1951), which could be read as an allegory for communist infiltration, although Kneale disliked mass movements of any political persuasion. Unfortunately, only the first two episodes were preserved, so there is no footage of the alien. The serial was remade by Hammer as *The Quatermass Xperiment* (Val Guest, 1954)—the title exploiting the new X-Certificate—and their alien looks somewhat octopoid. The BBC4 remake relocated the climax to Tate Modern's Turbine Hall, merely showing the three spacesuited astronauts.

Alien possession also features in the plot of *Quatermass II*, with an invasion already underway. In the meantime, Kneale had adapted a version of *Nineteen Eighty-Four* (1949) for the BBC, and the vision of stifling bureaucracy and propaganda has seeped into this script, the events of the first serial having been covered up. Strange meteorites have crashed near an oil refinery, and Quatermass investigates. Some of those who come into contact with them have been possessed by an alien force.

Eventually Quatermass discovers a conspiracy to build an environment that is hospitable to the aliens, and he deduces that they have evolved on a moon of Saturn. Leading politicians and military figures, as well as big businesses, are implicated, as is the union, perhaps unwittingly. The aliens threaten British pluck and individualism and may be fought by the application of willpower. Quatermass frees the possessed by destroying the alien asteroid base. The tentacular aliens are glimpsed only briefly. Hammer bought the film rights while the serial was in production, and Kneale wrote the first draft of the screenplay. He also wrote a serialization for the *Daily Express*.

Dave Rolinson and Nick Cooper note that "If the first serial featured 'us' going to 'them,' and the second 'them' coming to 'us,' then the third is based on the equally fertile sci-fi trope of 'they've been here all the time.'" As workers prepare for a new building—in the Hammer version for an Underground extension—prehistoric hominid skeletons are discovered, along with an alien spaceship, although the authorities claim it is a Nazi rocket. Quatermass deduces it is part of a five-million-year-old Martian invasion that had directed human evolution. The aliens look like giant ants but have three legs and devil-like horns.

The relics influence human emotions, sparking panic and xenophobia. As violence breaks out on the streets of London, civilization is on the brink of collapse. The influence is stopped by earthing the alien with a steel cable—in the film a much bigger alien is wrapped around a metal crane. Inspired by race riots in Britain where white mobs were attacking immigrants, Kneale explored mass hysteria and suspicion of the other.

The final serial, *The Quatermass Conclusion* (1979), is the weakest of the stories, featuring aliens who harvest young people at Neolithic sites as British society falls apart. The always-patrician Quatermass seems like a relic from an earlier age, here ennobled by an act of self-sacrifice to save the young. The young, alternately missed and feared, are throwbacks to late-1960s hippies and seem alien in themselves to traditional British society; broadcast after the high-water mark of punk, the series felt dated at first showing. As perhaps was the case in earlier serials, Kneale is more interested in decrying mass hysteria and the mob than offering rich characterization of individuals.

The *Quatermass* serials demonstrated that there was a market for adult serials and that science fiction was a viable television genre. A scientist hero more in the mold of Arthur Conan Doyle's Professor Challenger than Mary Shelley's Frankenstein could even survive recasting; inevitably, this character was in the mix when Sydney Newman and Donald Wilson and C. E. Webber were creating *Doctor Who*. Kneale's narratives of possessed astronauts, surreptitious invasions, and excavated spaceships were repeatedly borrowed by *Doctor Who*, and aliens attacking the face influenced *Alien* (Ridley Scott, 1979). The success of the first two Quatermass films helped Hammer move into horror, and Kneale's work influenced *The X-Files*, *Fringe*, Stephen King, and John Carpenter, among many others. Most importantly, Kneale showed that even within budgetary limitations, the use of aliens to thrill, scare, and provoke thought was possible within a mass medium.

*Andrew M. Butler*

See also: *Alien* (Series); *Doctor Who*; *Torchwood*.

## FURTHER READING

Chapman, James. "*Quatermass* and the Origins of British Television SF." *British Science Fiction Television: A Hitchhiker's Guide*, edited by James R. Cook and Peter Wright, I. B. Tauris, 2006, pp. 21–51.

Murray, Andy. *Into the Unknown: The Fantastic Life of Nigel Kneale*. Headpress, 2006.

Rolinson, Dave and Nick Cooper. "'Bring Something Back': The Strange Career of Professor Bernard Quatermass." *Journal of Popular Film & Television*, vol. 30, no. 3, 2002, pp. 158–65.

# R

## *Repo Man*

Set in Southern California in the mid-1980s and directed by the Englishman Alex Cox, *Repo Man* (1984) is a science-fiction comedy that follows the misadventures of an 18-year-old named Otto Maddox (Emilio Estevez). Otto is a punk rocker looking for his place in the world, but he feels alienated even from the punk-rock subculture to which he belongs. Ultimately, Otto becomes involved with the Helping Hand car repossession company, where he is taught the life of a repo man, which, according to his mentor, Bud (Harry Dean Stanton), is "always intense."

The film begins with J. Frank Parnell (Fox Harris) being stopped by a police officer for driving his 1964 Chevy Malibu erratically. Parnell seems disheveled and dazed in the way he speaks but warns the police officer not to open the car's trunk. The officer does not heed Parnell's warning and, upon opening the Malibu's trunk, explodes from a blast of radiation that emanates from it. The next scene introduces Otto stacking cans in a grocery store, where he is fired for not paying attention to how he is stacking the cans. That night, Otto goes to a punk-rock party, where he goes to bed with Debbi (Jennifer Balgobin), whom he loses to his friend Duke (Dick Rude). Otto leaves the party and wanders the streets all night. He is approached by Bud (Harry Dean Stanton), who recruits Otto into the life of a repo man.

As a repo man working for Helping Hand, Otto meets other people in the business, each with his own philosophy of life. The most outlandish philosophy comes from the repo yard mechanic, Miller (Tracey Walter), who tells Otto that flying saucers are time machines taking dead bodies into the past. Otto also meets Leila (Olivia Barash), a young woman who shows Otto pictures of dead aliens in the back of Parnell's Malibu. Eventually, the repo men at Helping Hand see a flier that shows the Chevy Malibu is worth $20,000 to repossess. After a few missteps, Otto chases down the car, and Parnell invites him to ride with him. Soon after, Parnell dies from radiation poisoning leaking from the dead aliens in the trunk. After leaving Parnell's corpse on a bench, Otto takes the car to the repo yard. Otto meets Bud in a convenience store that Duke and Debbi try to rob. During the robbery, Bud gets injured by a bullet, and Duke is shot dead. With his dying words, Duke blames society for making him the way he is, to which Otto replies, "That's bullshit. You're a white, suburban punk, just like me." Soon, Otto is abducted by federal agents, who have been searching for the Malibu with the aliens in the trunk.

The repo men, the agents, Leila, and a televangelist, Reverend Larry (Bruce White), arrive at Helping Hand, where Bud arrives with the Malibu glowing. The agents kill Bud, and while there is a commotion, Miller gets in the glowing

Malibu and invites Otto into the passenger seat. Otto joins him, and the car flies into the air over the city and into space.

Even though there are aliens from outer space in the trunk of the Chevy Malibu, Otto is the metaphorical alien throughout the film. At the beginning of the story, he is a part of a punk-rock counterculture; however, he realizes that he does not truly fit into this culture, which is confirmed when he watches a punk band (The Circle Jerks) perform toward the end of the movie and states, "I can't believe I used to like these guys." His telling Duke that he is a white, suburban punk reaffirms that he does not fit into "normal" society either. Otto then finds himself in an unconventional job as a repo man, where the line between being an honest worker and being a criminal is blurred. When each repo man tells Otto his philosophy, Otto seems just to listen without agreeing with anyone except for Miller, because, like Otto, Miller does not entirely fit in with that culture either. Otto's own feelings of not fitting into any aspect of society come to fruition when he gets in the car with Miller and flies over Los Angeles, demonstrating that he is different than all earthlings except the quirky Miller.

*Brett Butler*

See also: *Cowboys and Aliens*; *Men in Black*; *They Live*.

## FURTHER READING

Cox, Alex. *Repo Man*, edited by Dick Rude, Faber and Faber, 1987.
Cox, Alex. *X Films: True Confessions of a Radical Filmmaker*. I. B. Tauris/Soft Skull, 2008.
Mendik, Xavier. "*Repo Man*: Reclaiming the Spirit of Punk with Alex Cox." *New Punk Cinema*, edited by Nicholas Rombes, Edinburgh University Press, 2005, pp. 193–203.

## Reynolds, Alastair

Alastair Reynolds (1966–) is best known for his Revelation Space sequence of novels and stories as well as for his dedication to hard science as the underpinning of his fictional universes. Holding a degree in physics and astronomy from Newcastle University and a PhD from St. Andrews, Reynolds is a scientist writer who melds traditional space-opera vastness with noir, gothic, and cyberpunk influences. He most often depicts extraterrestrials as having motivations beyond human comprehension, as being postbiological intelligences, or as being examples of the ancient-aliens trope. These three strands are combined and recombined not just in the Revelation Space sequence but also throughout the author's many stand-alone novels and his more recent Poseidon's Children trilogy. They are further apparent in *The Medusa Chronicles* (2016), which Reynolds wrote in collaboration with Stephen Baxter as a follow-up to Arthur C. Clarke's 1971 novella "A Meeting with Medusa."

Reynolds's major work, the Revelation Space sequence, comprises the trilogy of *Revelation Space* (2000), *Redemption Ark* (2002), and *Absolution Gap* (2003), the companion novels *Chasm City* (2001) and *The Prefect* (2007), and numerous novellas and short stories, the most important of which is "Galactic North" (1999), which, in spite of being one of the earliest entries, offers an ending to the narrative as a whole. The sequence follows humanity's conflict-ridden colonization of local space and how it eventually attracts the attention of an alien machine intelligence called the Inhibitors. Dedicated to the eradication of all sentient life above a certain technological level, the eons-old Inhibitors serve as the author's explanation for the Fermi Paradox (the apparent contradiction between the lack of evidence for extraterrestrial civilizations and the high-probability estimates for their existence): in the Revelation Space sequence, many alien races have either been destroyed by the Inhibitors or are in hiding from them.

A postorganic intelligence, the Inhibitors typically appear as relentless black cubes (one is reminded of the Borg from *Star Trek: The Next Generation*). The larger examples of these attack interstellar craft, the smaller ones the bodies and minds of their crews. Exemplifying the author's recurring depiction of alien consciousness not as a plateau to be reached but, instead, as the crest of a wave, the Inhibitors no longer exhibit sentience *per se*, except in the case of especially problematic exterminations for which a higher-order intelligence can be generated. Thus, for Reynolds, surviving their onslaught is the pitting of creativity (both human and alien) against Inhibitor brute force and perseverance. Indeed, many of the races in the Revelation Space sequence reflect responses to the Inhibitor threat that counterpoint humanity's own quest for technological improvement and superiority. For instance, the aliens nicknamed Grubs cower in the darkness between the stars, maintaining low energy and heat signatures to avoid detection. The Shrouders have chosen to wait out the Inhibitors within ferociously deformed regions of space-time sealed off from the outside universe (the "Shrouds" from which they take their name). Still others, such as the Pattern Jugglers (widely dispersed collectives of marine organisms capable of rewiring and occasionally absorbing the neural structures of humans) and the Nestbuilders (insectoids who, as with the Inhibitors, have lost their sentience, and whose bodies and technologies are now controlled by parasites) are generally depicted as beyond the grasp of human beings, in the fashion of Arthur C. Clarke.

Reynolds's stand-alone novels and short stories pursue similar themes. *Pushing Ice* (2005) further displays the influence of Clarke not only in the inscrutable motivations of extraterrestrial beings but also in its depiction of their gigantic space objects/interstellar zoos (reminiscent of *Rendezvous with Rama*, 1973, and its sequels). *House of Suns* (2008), though largely concerned with clones exploring the Milky Way, offers a mechanistic alien race (The First Machines) who have fled to Andromeda after almost being wiped out and who thereafter departed even that galaxy for greater challenges. As with aliens from both ends of Reynolds's oeuvre—*Revelation Space* to, say, *Poseidon's Wake*—they have left behind tests and superstructures in the hope that worthy races will emerge and, in time, matriculate to higher levels of not just scientific but also moral understanding. While this aim is overt in *Pushing Ice* and *House of Suns*, the alien influence is more accidental in Reynolds's most recent series, the Poseidon's Children trilogy of *Blue Remembered Earth* (2012), *On the Steel Breeze* (2013), and *Poseidon's*

*Wake* (2015). Again, the aliens here are of the ancient variety, but, in this case, it is their artifacts—ranging from inscriptions on the so-called Phobos Monolith to massive "wheels" rolling through an alien ocean—that offer evidence of their existence and, crucial to the progress of humanity, cheat sheets to their advanced technologies.

In terms of shorter pieces, merciless alien cyborgs recur in the Merlin novellas (*Merlin's Gun* [2000]; *Hideaway* [2000]; *Minla's Flowers* [2005]; and *The Iron Tactician* [2016]). Separate from the author's other fictional universes, these stories find humanity aboard fleets of ships once again fleeing extermination, this time by a race known as The Huskers. This relentless pursuit of humanity across the stars by an at least partially mechanistic race, let alone the highly episodic nature of the series, evokes *Battlestar Galactica* (the original series, 1978–1979, rather than the remake). Meanwhile, kinder aliens—literally "The Kind"—appear in "Understanding Space and Time" (2005), one of Reynolds's greatest short stories. Here, the last member of the human race is resurrected centuries after death by ancient and, again, machine-based aliens, who care about life above all else and who have "arrived to preserve and resurrect what we may." The Kind help the protagonist evolve "long past human" in an exaggerated version of the transformations that the Pattern Jugglers in the Revelation Space books are capable of performing. Over the course of millennia, the Kind transform this astronaut into a kilometers-high substrate of thinking crystal and, across subsequent millions of years, into a free-floating being of pure quarks. These aliens are enablers of the character's quest for ultimate wisdom about the universe, and the assistance they provide is, in many ways, a scientist writer's keenest desire.

*Val Nolan*

*See also*: Banks, Iain M.; Clarke, Arthur C.; Vinge, Vernor.

**FURTHER READING**

Herbe, Sarah. *Characters in New British Hard Science Fiction: With a Focus on Genetic Engineering in Paul McAuley, Alastair Reynolds and Brian Stableford*. Neckar Universitätsverlag Winter, 2012.

Kincaid, Paul. "Alastair Reynolds." *Call and Response*, edited by Paul Kincaid, Beccon Publications, 2014, pp. 269–76.

Slocombe, Will. "Ideas, Inspirations and Influences: An Interview with Alastair Reynolds." *Foundation*, no. 123, 2016, pp. 90–100.

## Roswell (Place)

The Roswell incident (1947) was one of a cluster of reports of UFOs in the United States in 1947. Although the purported crash site was approximately 75 miles away from Roswell, New Mexico, the investigation and subsequent conspiracy theories involved Roswell Army Air Field (renamed Roswell Air Force Base in 1947 and Walker Air Force Base in 1948).

Official reports in 1947 referred to a flying disc having crashed, a disc that was soon identified as a weather balloon. In 1994, an official government report was released, partly in response to the proliferating conspiracy theories. The 1995 version of the report included documents that had been declassified and revealed the retrieved object to be a balloon that was being used in relation to nuclear test sites. The report did not convince entrenched conspiracy theorists that aliens had not landed near Roswell in 1947.

The Roswell Incident has led to 70 years of articles, films, books, television series and episodes, a museum and research center, and theme merchandise:

> The myth carries generic expectations—the consumer expects his/her "reality" narrative to contain elements of science fiction, the occult, esoteric beliefs and conspiracy. To fulfil these needs and expectation, an entire mythology of narratives, a belief system, has evolved, all framed by one name: "Roswell." (Murphy, 125–26)

While we are accustomed to thinking of the alien as metaphor, the depiction of the Roswell aliens has been influenced by the unique documentary presentation of "evidence" constructed from narratives of people claiming to know through their connection with the investigation that a spaceship (or as many as three) crashed and that the ship and one or more aliens had been recovered. In some narratives the aliens were all dead; in others, one alien is said to have survived and to have been tortured—whether intentionally or not. The description of the aliens as smooth, green, child-sized humanoids wrapped in metallic cloth suits was reinforced by the dissemination of photographs that were later revealed to be a hoax. The black-and-white photographs show large, slanted eyes in a head like an inverted teardrop: broad and rounded at the top and tapering to a small mouth and chin. The bodies are emaciated, though it is unclear whether that is their natural state or the result of space travel or exposure to Earth's atmosphere.

The Roswell aliens are depicted in popular culture as dead on arrival or in transit to the military facility, or dead as a result of experiments and/or interrogation in a military facility. In 1947 the images might have resonated with the photographs that had surfaced of World War II concentration camp survivors. Against a backdrop of coalescing postwar tensions, a nearby World War II POW camp, and the U.S. military's nuclear tests in the New Mexico desert, elements of secrecy applied to the balloon research were interpreted as cover-ups related to the alien landing.

One of the complications of the victim alien narrative is that a dead alien is unknowable except through autopsy and artifacts. They remain fully alien and knowable only through the application of human science. These are the aliens depicted in the popular nonfiction Roswell conspiracy-trope literature by Stanton Friedman, Thomas Carey, Donald Schmitt, Charles Berlitz, and William Moore.

The trope of receiving a vision after an extended journey into the desert is realized by narratives of people going from Roswell to the crash site to find the truth about the aliens. Balancing the seemingly real existential threat of the "documented" alien is the commodified "kitsch" alien of Roswell. The real town promotes this interpretation, turning a modest city of 50,000 into a UFO-themed tourist destination. The alien figure is rendered as a graphic design, the image used for merchandising both in the real world and as a commentary in the popular culture depiction—surrounding the "real" aliens with their corrupted image. These images are attached to UFO-themed merchandise internationally. They also appear as social-media memes.

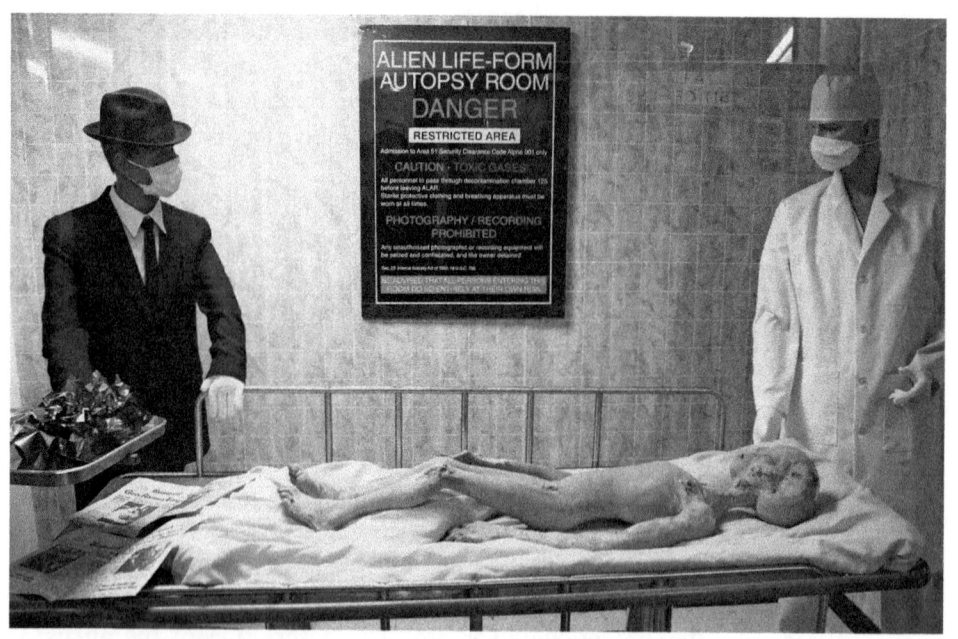

A "re-creation" of the aftermath of the Roswell UFO incident showing the body of an extraterrestrial in an autopsy room, at the International UFO Museum and Research Center in Roswell, New Mexico. (Conchasdiver/Dreamstime.com)

Roswell as proof of alien existence, or proof of government conspiracy, or proof of alien contact, is invoked in passing by many popular-culture products. Episodes of television series have been devoted to Roswell, including *The Simpsons* (1998), *Unsolved Mysteries* (1987), *Mystery Hunters* (2003), *Book of Secrets* (2016), *Living in America* (2011), *Secret History* (1995), *The X-Files*, and others. Many films and made-for-TV movies make direct or indirect references to Roswell, assuming that North American audiences will understand the reference because Roswell has become so entrenched in popular culture. Film and television characters have been named Roswell to suggest their alien nature, literal or otherwise, as in the 1999–2002 television series *Roswell*, created by Jason Katims.

The Roswell history allows the popular culture artifacts to shapeshift (like the full aliens of the 1999 television series) from conspiracy theory to reportage to science fiction to teen identity formation and beyond, giving it staying power in a changing popular-culture environment.

*Timothy J. Anderson*

See also: *Alien Autopsy (Fact or Fiction?)*; Aliens Did Not Built the Pyramids; Condon Report, The; Grays; *Roswell* (TV); *X-Files, The*.

## FURTHER READING

Murphy, B. Keith. "Little Green Secrets: The Growth of the Roswell UFO Myth in American Popular Culture." *Journal of the Georgia Association of Historians*, vol. 26, 2005–2006, pp. 123–152.

Pflock, Karl T. *Roswell: Inconvenient Facts and the Will to Believe*. Prometheus Books, 2001.

Weaver, Richard L. and James McAndrew. *The Roswell Report: Fact versus Fiction in the New Mexico Desert*. United States Air Force/U.S. Government Printing Office, 1995.

## Roswell (TV)

The TV series *Roswell* (1999–2000), created by Jason Katims, is based on the *Roswell High* book series developed by Laura J. Burns and written by Melinda Metz for Pocket Books (although optioned by the first draft of the first book, such that the novels launched contemporaneously with the show). It is now a cult classic, blending the sensibilities of a teen drama set in a high school with the slow-burn mythology of science fiction.

*Roswell* trades on the infamy of the supposed events of the 1947 Roswell crash (the world's best-known UFO incident) and the iconic lore sprung from it but gives it a sexy, young twist in establishing a world in which the Crash left behind three (later, four) human-alien hybrids who have all emerged from stasis-pods to make their way into the local high school alongside their unsuspecting small-town American peers.

When waitress Liz is shot at her family's alien-themed diner, Max is compelled to save her life, outing himself as an alien and putting his safety, and that of his friends and family, into her hands. This includes his sister Isabel and Michael, his brother, raised separately in foster care. As Liz soon lets her best friends Maria and Alex in on the secret, the six teens quickly bond and learn to trust one another, putting aside their fears and differences to work together to fend off the suspicions of law enforcement and alien hunters while seeking clues about the aliens' origins and destinies. The local sheriff and his son also become involved, moving from antagonists to allies and demonstrating how a group of people can come together through difference to combat xenophobia and keep each other safe. Through friendships formed and discoveries made, a Romeo-and-Juliet love story unfolds between Max and Liz and mutual best friends Michael and Maria, this emotional core of the story balancing romance with adventure and genre elements.

Max is relatively shy and quiet, deliberate and cautious, whereas Michael is an angry, rebellious loner and hothead and Isabel a popular girl who masks her vulnerabilities with an ice-queen persona. The alien "pod squad" are marked by their physical attractiveness and share a preference for foods that are extremely sweet or spicy (Tabasco bottles and sugar packets are frequent signs of their presence). The aliens have special powers, including molecular manipulation (the ability to change objects, to move them telekinetically, to heal injuries, to generate heat) and the ability to "dreamwalk" (observe, participate in, and manipulate others' dreams) and can sense each other's emotions and create psychic connections. These powers are a source of substantive drama but, as Isabel uses hers "recreationally," ensuring perfectly color-coordinating nail polish and lipstick, also breach the mundane.

The success of the show lies in its ability to merge the unbelievable with emotional honesty and familiar reality. Much of this harmony and richness is produced by the skillful tonal dissonance of the show, as "real" aliens and the reality of teen life and its growing pains are set against sci-fi kitsch. Max takes a job at a UFO museum, complete with hokey dioramas; Liz's family runs the Crash-Down Café, where even the waitresses' aprons are shaped like the heads of shiny silver alien grays, with matching antennae headbands, and Michael, an eventual cook there, serves up specials like orbit rings, ironic alien-encounter shakes, and Sigourney Weaver and Will Smith burgers. Maria's mother bulk-supplies alien bendy straws, blow-up balloons, keychains, and drink stirrers, and plot points are supplied by over-the-top convention and conspiracy touchstones.

Perhaps meddling with the tone and texture of the show, *Roswell* moved from the WB to UPN (later the CW) during its run, and while the early episodes have a marked YA *X-Files* feel, later episodes are diverted into soap-opera drama and sci-fi mumbo jumbo, the plot veering inconsistently into past lives, murder, secret babies, lost kings, a devious congresswoman, shape-shifters, time travel, government cover-ups, and a dying millionaire. Yet, the lessons it offers in balancing YA and genre conventions represents a line of influence evident in *Smallville* and *Supernatural* and traceable into *The Vampire Diaries* and much of the presentation of today's teen-targeted genre programming.

*Roswell*'s approach to the "aliens among us" story line is notable in how it seeks to erode the us-versus-them narrative, focusing on the hybrid's humanity and aligning audience sympathies firmly with their journeys. Indeed, the natural position of "alien" as outsider perfectly positions the show to explore the alien as metaphor for adolescent experience and its associated angst. With narration from Liz's diary structuring the narrative and a finale that culminates with high-school graduation and a speech where Max exhorts his classmates (and audience) to find their places in the world, embrace who they are and what they want to be, and celebrate identity and difference and self-discovery, *Roswell* is about growing up, growing into oneself and into the world. (For example, a school Fathers' Camping Trip provides cover for searching for a downed UFO in an episode that is also about water bras and girls/daughters becoming women). The show's handling of teen sexuality is particularly notable in uniting genre conventions to provide explanation and motivation: Max and Liz's make-out sessions provoke "flashes," memories or visions of the location of an alien artifact that both holds the key to the truth about the aliens' origins and, as a pulsing beacon and radio tower, replicates orgasmic potential. Both natural and supernatural, human connection proves the key to answers and route to success for aliens and humans alike.

As adolescence is an important developmental time, the human-hybrid concept also productively mirrors the teen condition: caught between childhood and adulthood and wanting to be both visible and invisible, to fit in while being true to oneself, to honor one's parents but follow one's heart, to conceal uniqueness, to downplay difference, and yet to learn to celebrate what makes one special. These are all typical, familiar tensions played out alongside the search for more supernatural truths. *Roswell* tackles the alienation of high school (here, even the guidance counselor is not to be trusted), the backdrop of aliens and adolescence, the experience of being outcast and seeking to find one's place and to feel seen and understood, ultimately arguing that shared experiences and emotions felt need not rely on shared DNA.

*Cassandra Bausman*

See also: *Alien Autopsy (Fact or Fiction?)*; *Men in Black*; Roswell (Place); *X-Files, The*.

**FURTHER READING**

Badmington, Neil. "Roswell High, Alien Chic and the In/human." *Teen TV: Genre, Consumption, Identity*, edited by Glyn Davis and Kay Dickinson, British Film Institute, 2004, pp. 166–75.

Banks, Miranda J. "A Boy for all Planets: *Roswell*, *Smallville* and the Teen Male Melodrama." *Teen TV: Genre, Consumption, Identity*, edited by Glyn Davis and Kay Dickinson, British Film Institute, 2004, pp. 17–28.

Garcia, Frank and Mark Phillips. "Roswell (1999–2002)." *Science Fiction Television Series, 199080004: Histories, Casts and Credits for 58 Shows*, edited by Frank Garcia and Mark Phillips, McFarland, 2009, pp. 200–209.

## Russell, Mary Doria

Mary Doria Russell's (1950–) pair of science-fiction novels, *The Sparrow* and *Children of God*, set between 2019 and 2096, take up questions of faith and forgiveness in order to explore the ways relationships among humans and aliens might clarify or complicate conceptions of good and evil. Rather than presenting a new planet as a new Eden, Russell's duology demonstrates the complexities of responding to alien cultures with human ideas about ethics and justice. Refracted through the practices of Catholicism, and to a lesser extent Jewish philosophy, Russell's novels seek to assert a role for the Divine far beyond the geographic scope of Earth.

*The Sparrow*, winner of several prizes including the Arthur C. Clarke Award, details the discovery of musical transmissions from a planet merely 17 light-years distant. Secretly, the Society of Jesus (the Jesuits) sends a mission to the planet, christened Rakhat; the crew includes Emilio Sandoz, a Jesuit linguist who serves as the novel's focal point, along with three other priests, an astronomer, an artificial-intelligence analyst, a doctor, and her husband. While first contact with the planet's inhabitants, called the Runa, is nearly ideal, the explorers eventually learn that Rakhat supports a second and more dangerous species, the Jana'ata. Despite their caution, most members of the team are killed within their first few months on the planet, and Emilio is sold as an exotic prostitute to the very Jana'ata poet whose music first enticed the explorers to the planet. Rescued by members of a second mission, Emilio returns to earth physically broken and spiritually embittered.

In the sequel, *Children of God*, Emilio begins to fashion a life for himself outside the clergy. His horror at being forced to participate in a new mission to Rakhat is ameliorated by the discovery that Sofia Mendes, one of his original crew mates, unexpectedly survived and can still be rescued. Arrival at Rakhat demonstrates, however, that the ideas introduced to the Runa through their initial contact with the explorers, as well as Sofia's leadership over several decades, have led to a revolution in the relationship between the Runa and the Jana'ata with far-reaching consequences.

In both novels, the explorers live primarily with the Runa, who are described as "large, vegetarian bipeds with stabilizing tails." They are gregarious and communitarian—almost herdlike in many of their behaviors. Although rarely inventive, the Runa are quick to adapt and modify ideas and practices. Emilio develops an especially strong relationship with Askama, a young female assigned the job of translator. The generous and unquestioning hospitality offered to the explorers by the Runa reinforces the Jesuits' belief that God has led them to make contact with these aliens.

The second alien species on Rakhat complicates matters. The Jana'ata are urban, feudalistic, and economically sophisticated. They are also capable of great ferocity, and the explorers depend upon the Jana'ata merchant Supaari to negotiate with the rest of his people. Supaari exhibits the curiosity, caution, and sharp intelligence they had expected to find among aliens whose broadcasts indicated both a rich artistic culture and a level of technological development.

Slowly the explorers realize many of their initial assumptions about the aliens of Rakhat were wrong. They have misunderstood simple biological facts about the Runa as well as the principles that govern relationships between the two species. The Runa and the Jana'ata do not simply trade goods; the Jana'ata manage, breed, and eat the Runa. One species has nearly completely domesticated the other, and the reproductive practices used to limit both species sustain an environmental balance between the predator and the prey populations.

Yet in Russell's second novel, as the ideas introduced by the explorers begin to take root among the Runa, like gardening and collective action, the social and ecological balance between the two populations is transformed. Within a single generation, the historically dominant Jana'ata stand on the brink of extinction.

The traditional relationship between the Jana'ata and the Runa horrifies the explorers even as it paints in stark relief a portrait of the ways powerful cultures and peoples on Earth have routinely preyed upon weaker and less technologically sophisticated populations. Like Swift in his infamous "A Modest Proposal," Russell's novels point out that the difference between unrestricted exploitation of a weaker cultural group and literally devouring them is more a matter of self-serving linguistics than a meaningful ethical distinction. Simultaneously, Russell's novels wrestle with problems raised by even the most conscientious approaches to colonialization. Distressing as the relationship between Rakhat's two alien species may be, it has fostered a sustainable pair of cultures while escaping both intransigent social problems like poverty and the physical degradation of the planet. Ultimately, the choices made by the Jana'ata are neither more admirable nor more terrible than those humanity has made as a species or those that Emilio and Sofia make themselves on a smaller scale as they struggle to survive on Rakhat.

Among all three cultures, grave social and personal injustices are ultimately transcended by a willingness to bear witness to the pain one has enabled, especially if the injustices are hallowed by confession and forgiveness. The transactions that underpin Christianity, rather than the specific texts and rituals of the faith, become the model for the relationships that triumph among all of them. As an inhabitant of Rakhat says, "Jana'ata and Runa and H'uman—children of a God so high that our ranks and our differences are as nothing in his far sight" (ch. 33).

*Megan Isaac*

*See also*: Butler, Octavia E.; Cherryh, C. J.; Le Guin, Ursula K.

## FURTHER READING

Butler, Andrew M. "First Contact: An Interview with Mary Doria Russell." *Vector*, no. 200, July/August 1998, pp. 11–14.

Butler, Andrew M. "1998: The Sparrow—Mary Doria Russell. Music, Food, Sex." *The Arthur C. Clarke Award: A Critical Anthology*, edited by Paul Kincaid with Andrew M. Butler, Serendip Foundation, 2006, pp. 141–52.

Khader, Jamil. "Race Matters: People of Color, Ideology, and the Politics of Erasure and Reversal in Ursula Le Guin's *The Left Hand of Darkness* and Mary Doria Russell's *The Sparrow*." *Journal of the Fantastic in the Arts*, vol. 16, no. 2, 2005, pp. 110–27.

# S

## Saga

As of late 2017, *Saga* (2012–) is an ongoing comic-book series, written and produced by Brian K. Vaughan and Fiona Staples. First published by American comic-book publisher Image Comics in 2012, *Saga* is best described as a space opera, or a fantasy epic set in space, that leans more toward the melodramatic and often hilarious aspects of the soap-opera subgenre rather than toward hard science fiction. Because it has the tone and style of a fantasy epic, the comic book has been compared to *Star Wars*, or Shakespeare's *Romeo and Juliet*, thanks to its initial plotline, but the distinctive use of surrealism paints a picture that is more reminiscent of *Doctor Who*, though with less time travel. *Saga* uses elements from both fantasy and SF and connects them cleverly through witty dialogue that often borders on the bizarre, as well as the heavy use of visceral and often surreal humor.

The plot follows the family of Hazel, a child born to parents from two societies at war with each other, and their pursuers. Hazel's mother, Alana, was born on Landfall, where she served in the army and, eventually, became a prison guard on Cleave. Her father, Marko, was born on Wreath, a moon orbiting Landfall, and served as a foot soldier in its military. The Landfall Coalition and the Wreath, along with the Narrative, are at war, even though the reasons for this armed conflict are not clear. Hazel's parents transgress the military code of conduct by fraternizing with the enemy, eventually eloping and committing what seems to be the ultimate transgression; that is, Alana gives birth to a child. Hazel becomes a symbolic manifestation of unity and cannot exist as such; thus, it is not surprising that the command of both planets wants her parents dead and Hazel herself delivered to them. As a result, *Saga* merges the quotidian family life with action and intrigue straight out of an adventure movie. Alana, Marko, and Hazel travel seemingly without a purpose, except to survive as fugitives.

As the family journeys through the galaxy, different species are introduced in the series, including robot humanoids with television heads, humans with a variety of animal features, and humanoid animals. Hazel, despite being arguably the most important character in the narrative, is perhaps not immediately recognizable as such. Because *Saga* features so many different alien species, it is hard to pinpoint the most important figures. The book is permeated with characteristic silhouettes of the female characters: Alana cuts a strong Landfallian figure, humanoid with insect-like wings and dark hair with green streaks. The Stalk, an ex-partner of the Will, one of the mercenaries sent after the family, is an arachnid who only vaguely and hauntingly resembles a human being. Gwendolyn, Marko's ex-fiancé; Klara, Marko's mother; and Izabel, a Horror, ghost of a teenage girl who had stepped on a landline and is missing the lower part of her body, complement this side of the cast of characters. The male protagonists include Marko, Hazel's father, with the ram-like horns and ears characteristic of his family; the very memorable Prince Robot IV from the Robot Kingdom; D. Oswald Heist, a Cyclopean man and author of the book that inspired the relationship between Hazel's parents; and a humanoid seal, Ghüs. To add to the surreal experience, the book also features a big Lying Cat, which, upon hearing untrue statements, loudly exclaims the word "lying," although it does not speak otherwise.

The representation of alienness depends on the circumstance; that is, there is no overarching rule for the types of alien encounters that *Saga* employs. As an example, not all Freelancers are as threatening and purely alien as the Stalk. She is juxtaposed with the Will, ostensibly human, with no discernible alien features. Furthermore, due to the fact that the narrative merges the homelands of Hazel's parents, neither the Landfallians nor the people of Wreath are ever depicted as entirely alien. However, they are often considered a threat, sending pursuers after Hazel's family. In fact, the characters in the book usually fit into one of three categories, even if the connection is not always immediately clear: they are either members of the family, their allies, or adverse parties, that is, their pursuers or enemies. Hazel, once born, is a symbol of her parents' desertion from service to their respective nations. They are viewed as traitors to their kinds, and thus the members of their races are simultaneously represented as an alien threat and something that is already familiar.

The alien in *Saga* seems to be used as a thinly veiled metaphor for racial and ethnic discourse, as so often happens in the works of fantasy, taking the examples of elves, dwarves, or, in this case, "moonies," as the citizens of the Wreath are pejoratively called. In a sense, the alien discourse in *Saga* is undoubtedly postcolonial, since both Landfall and Wreath colonize planets to wage war between each other without destroying their own home planets. One of the recurring themes in *Saga* is war and its romanticization. The series criticizes conflict between people who are essentially the same, with some minor differences, be it horns or wings. This critique of war is further underlined when Prince Robot IV, arguably one of the most alien creatures in the book, merging artificial embodiment with biological functions, witnesses a brutal event that causes him to suffer from a form of PTSD. Moreover, with its portrayal of the Robot Kingdom, *Saga* also touches briefly on the issue of class, where the members of the royal family have for heads TVs displaying colors, while the rest of the populace has black-and-white or single-color screens (e.g., green). *Saga* also provides material for analysis in terms of gender, considering that Alana assumes many traits culturally attributed to men, while Marko assumes the traditionally female passive stance for a significant part of the narrative.

*Patrycja Sokołowska*

See also: *Doctor Who*; Mœbius; *Star Wars*; *2000 AD*.

## FURTHER READING

Vaughan, Brian K. and Fiona Staples. *Saga*. Image Comics, 2012–2018, 9 volumes.

# Sawyer, Robert J.

Robert J. Sawyer (1960–) works where future-probable meets philosophical thought experiment. In a little less than 40 years, he has published 23 novels and two anthologies of short stories, alongside his scripts, nonfiction writing, and work on science/science-fiction documentaries. Beyond their mainstream success, what unifies (most of) Sawyer's many works is their Canadian setting and the optimism with which Sawyer depicts humanity's continued growth—including our eventual contact with the other. As a 2010 *Toronto Life* article notes, Sawyer has "built an empire on happy endings."

In his essay for the *Journal of Futures Studies*, Tom Lombardo argues that science fiction is the mythology of the future, creating "new myths for a new era." Sawyer has a similar understanding of his genre's place in contemporary culture: "science fiction should provide a range of possible futures so that we can choose the one we want. If all the visions are dystopian, the only thing we have to work toward is dystopia." As a self-described "thematically driven writer," Sawyer admits to fitting his plots and characters to "what [he] want[s] to say" and even maintains a list of over 30 motifs that recur in his writing. There, he identifies "First Contact" as a major theme in nine of his novels: *Foreigner* (1994), *End of an Era* (1994), *Starplex* (1996), *Illegal Alien* (1997), *Factoring Humanity* (1998), *Calculating God* (2000), *Hominids* (2002), *Rollback* (2007), and *Wake* (2009). Of these nine, *Hominids* and *Wake*—both the beginnings of their respective trilogies—feature "others" that are not technically aliens: *Hominids* centers on the discovery of a parallel Earth where Neanderthals are the dominant species, while *Wake* concerns the discovery of an Internet consciousness called Webmind. Though these books are consistent with Sawyer's other works, in terms of presenting an ultimately hopefully perspective on humanity's potential for growth, they are ultimately beyond the scope of this book. *Factoring Humanity* includes only limited direct contact with aliens, instead focusing on a shared human "overmind" accessed through alien technology, and is also of limited relevance.

*Foreigner* is the final book in the Quintaglio Ascension trilogy. Quintaglios are intelligent Nanotyrannuses (a dwarf form of tyrannosaur); in *Foreigner*, they discover another saurian race living on their planet/moon who are literally referred to as "Others." Initial meetings spark "dagamant," where the Quintaglio explorers enter a fierce territorial rage due to the Others' uncanny nature and kill several of them. The Others attempt an invasion and extermination by sea, but the Quintaglios save themselves by destroying this fleet with napalm—an extremely dark ending to first contact for a Robert Sawyer novel. This is partially redeemed by Toroca, a Quintaglio, saving and raising an Other child, as well as Sawyer's epilogue, in which the Quintaglios have achieved space flight and escaped their doomed moon.

*Rollback* also features interspecies adoption as a happy ending, this time with a human character. *Rollback*'s titular technology is a youth-restoring treatment offered to astronomer Sarah and her husband, Don, by a billionaire interested in Sawyer's second hypothetical: alien communications, the first of which Sarah decoded 38 years prior. When a new message is received, however, the "rollback" works only on Don. The novel's focus stays on Don's struggles with his new youth and the distance it puts between him and his wife of 60 years; however, *Rollback*'s happy ending is dependent on its alien element. Based on Sarah's answers to their original message, the aliens choose her to raise their ambassador, a biosynthetic member of their species that ends up in Don's care after Sarah's death—a second child for his second middle age.

Like *Foreigner*, *Rollback* posits an intellectual growth and moral redemption made possible through accepting the other as ourself. *Calculating God* poses a similar solution, from a more explicitly spiritual perspective. Hollus, a spider-like alien, comes to Toronto looking for paleontologist Thomas Jericho, because he believes Earth's fossil record will help Hollus prove the existence of God. When the novel's ultimate villain—an alien society that uploaded themselves into VR machines and initiated a supernova to kill nearby life-forms—is stopped by an unidentifiable force, even the atheist, cancer-stricken Thomas has to acknowledge God's existence. He then spends the final pages of the novel having his DNA fused with alien genetic material to create the next iteration of intelligent life in the universe.

Conflict between aliens and humans (or Other and Self) is not a central element in these novels—accounting for their extremely disparate plots and highlighting Sawyer's similar moral solutions. For Sawyer's final three "First Contact" novels, interspecies conflict *is* the focus. *End of an Era* is a time-travel novel featuring glowing blue parasites that use "gravity suppressor satellites" to create an Earth where their conflicts can be fought in surrogate dinosaur bodies. *Starplex* features five sentient species: the mysterious darmats and the Ib, Waldahud, and dolphins (not technically aliens), who are members of the Commonwealth, alongside humans. Finally, *Illegal Alien* follows the murder trial of Hask, one of eight Tosoks who have been touring Earth while their damaged ship is repaired—at which point Kelkad, their leader, will wipe out humanity, in accordance with their religious beliefs. Yet it is still through cooperation and growth that these three novels achieve hopeful outcomes: Brandon and Klicks bury the hatchet to crash the alien satellites; the Commonwealth takes a chance and forgives the darmats because of a belief that races can "grow up"; and after Hask and his defense attorney Dale Rice defeat the genocidal Tosoks, Dale travels with them to another planet to act as *their* lawyer.

*Meagan Black*

See also: Heinlein, Robert A.; Watts, Peter; Wilson, Robert Charles.

## FURTHER READING

Broege, Valerie. "Robert J. Sawyer's Place in Science Fiction." *Relativity: Stories and Essays*, edited by Robert J. Sawyer, ISFIC Press, 2004, pp. 289–94.

Lombardo, Tom. "Science Fiction: The Evolutionary Mythology of the Future." *Journal of Futures Studies*, vol. 20, no. 2, 2015, pp. 5–24.

Sawyer, Robert J. "The Profession of Science Fiction, 54: The Future is Already Here." *Foundation*, no. 80, Autumn 2000, pp. 5–18.

## Simak, Clifford D.

Clifford D. Simak (1904–1988) wrote science fiction commonly described as pastoral, suggesting an idealized and nostalgic view of the country. Because Simak spent his childhood in small-town Wisconsin, this view is tempting, but his perspective is complicated not only by the realities of rural America but also by Simak's long-time career as a newspaper writer and editor for the *Minneapolis Star* and *Minneapolis Tribune*. In fact, his portrayal of rural life recognizes its harshness as well as its beauties, and Simak confronts the growing corporatization and depersonalization of farming, along with the paranoia, isolationism, and nuclear danger that threatened both farm and city before, during, and after World War II. Simak's frequent and memorable use of aliens develops these concerns.

Simak uses the figure of the alien to find compassion, anger, and humor in the ways that totalizing and depersonalizing forces can be combated through effective communication and by imagining the view from the other side. A number of his short stories, and many of his novels—including *Cosmic Engineers* (1950), *Time Is the Simplest Thing* (1961), *The Werewolf Principle* (1967), *The Goblin Reservation* (1968), *Destiny Doll* (1971), *Mastodonia* (1978), and *The Visitors* (1980)—use the figure of the alien with varying degrees of seriousness and success. A few of his finest examples illustrate how Simak uses the trope of the alien to explore the issues outlined above: "Desertion" (1944; incorporated into the 1952 novel *City*), "The Big Front Yard" (1958), *They Walked Like Men* (1962), *Way Station* (1963), and *All Flesh Is Grass* (1965). Of these, *City* won an International Fantasy Award (1953), and "The Big Front Yard" and *Way Station* won Hugo Awards (1959 and 1964). For his body of work Simak was made an SFWA Grand Master in 1977.

"Desertion," a relatively early story, contains many of Simak's characteristic touches: a poetic style interlaced with humorous folksiness, deflation of heroic stereotypes, consideration of unexpected and alternate perspectives, and a dog. Here, humans confront what they see as a violent and terrifying Jupiter, "a hell of ammonia rain and stinking fumes" populated by monstrous aliens they call Lopers. When the viewpoint character and his dog transform into Lopers to explore the planet, they see Jupiter as gentle, fragrant, and beautiful. As natives, they feel smarter, stronger, and healthier than ever before, able to communicate with one another, fulfilling the dream of understanding the other, even the nonhuman (or non-dog) or alien. What is hell to the stranger may be beautiful to the native—or to whoever can adapt, transform, change perspective, and learn to communicate.

More commonly, Simak examines how the native accepts the stranger: "The Big Front Yard," *Way Station*, and *All Flesh Is Grass* use strikingly similar ways to do so. Each has a protagonist who, although a multigenerational native of a rural area, is nonetheless open to other viewpoints and another character who is disabled in some way but able to communicate with nonhumans. Each story presents a portal to alien worlds. While Simak also uses these stories to demonstrate the damage of corporatization to family farms and rural communities in general, through factory farming, monoculture, and GMOs (as they are called now), he also explores how to find peace in a universe of strangers. In all three stories, a crisis arises when human beings threaten the opportunity to form meaningful connections between native and stranger. In each of the three stories, the ability to communicate without xenophobia opens a portal to understanding between humans and aliens, natives and strangers. Simak does not belittle the dangers that surround such attempts, picturing everything from mob violence to nuclear war as responses to these portals. The result, achieved against many obstacles, and with no guarantee of permanent peace, is the kind of universal detente proposed during that same period by the United Nations and such SF authors as Arthur C. Clarke, part of the horrified response to the violent nationalism of the 20th century's wars.

Simak nevertheless also harshly criticizes the bland erasure of local cultures that occurs in globalization. Unlike the previous examples, *They Walked Like Men* takes place in a city (Minneapolis, perhaps), as alien entrepreneurs buy up all the real estate, driving out local families and businesses, causing prices to climb. The aliens follow the letter of the law but, like corporations, have no moral sense. Only communication among the human beings and these predatory invaders and other more benign aliens sends the invaders on their way. The novel's concerns seem remarkably prescient of 21st-century problems but remind us that alien pressures on local economies have been present for a long time.

Simak's use of aliens differentiates between universalism and globalization and honors both the local and the universal in its vision. In 1963, Emmanuel Levinas despaired that "one's attachment to *Place*, without which the universe would become insignificant and would scarcely exist" inevitably leads to "the very splitting of humanity into natives and strangers" (232; emphasis in original). Simak, also very conscious of post–World War II anxieties, uses science fiction to imagine a way beyond this impasse through communication and respect for individual difference, a solution that often seems beyond reach in the real world.

*Joan Gordon*

*See also*: Brin, David; Clarke, Arthur C.; Heinlein, Robert A.; White, James.

**FURTHER READING**

Levinas, Emmanuel. "Heidegger, Gagarin and Us." *Difficult Freedom: Essays on Judaism*, translated by Seán Hand, Johns Hopkins University Press, 1990, pp. 231–35.
Lomax, William. "The 'Invisible Alien' in the Science Fiction of Clifford Simak." *Extrapolation*, vol. 30, no. 2, 1989, pp. 133–46.
Westfahl, Gary. "The Marketplace." *The Oxford Handbook of Science Fiction*, edited by Rob Latham, Oxford University Press, 2014, pp. 81–92.

## Smash Martians

In 1999, *Campaign*, the U.K. advertising weekly, announced its "ad of the century." The winner was a television advertisement for Cadbury's Smash instant mashed potatoes, a prosaic product more normally advertised in a prosaic way. But this ad was different; it was the first and most successful U.K. television ad to use a science-fiction theme. Written by Chris Wilkins, with art director John Webster, it was directed by Bob Brooks for Boase Massimi Pollitt.

The advert shows a room full of metallic Martians discussing Earth. The script runs:

> On your last trip did you discover what the Earth people eat?
> They eat a great many of these [holds potato].
> They peel them with their metal knives, boil them for twenty of their minutes, then they smash them all to bits.
> They are clearly a most primitive people.
> [Martians laugh uproariously.]
> Jingle: For mash get Smash.

The ad was a critical and commercial success; Smash quickly took the top spot in the U.K. instant-mashed-potato segment and has remained there ever since. Several other ads followed, and the campaign has since been revived twice for new potato eaters. The Martians also spawned books and toys, as well as many impressions by various comedians.

The Martians had two main antecedents. Earlier BMP Smash ads had featured a spaceman eating a meal of meat and vegetable pills and Smash, introducing the potato as a "serious rival" to Smash. But the direct inspiration was Bob Newhart's "Tobacco" skit, in which a bemused Elizabethan takes a phone call about tobacco from Walter Raleigh. John Webster, the art director and the person credited with creating the Martians, described a conversation with writer Chris Wilkins in the pub. "But when you think about it . . . if someone from another planet came to Earth and heard that we could either make potatoes by peeling, boiling, mashing, taking ages, or just pour them out of the packet, and we chose the former, he'd think we were barmy" (Collister, 2013, 33:00). Wilkins quickly generated a script, and Webster designed grinning, metallic Martians with chest dials and pincer hands, then telephoned Dalek voiceover artist Peter Wilkins and asked him to "have a go at laughing like a Dalek" (Carter, 2012). Audience testing of ads was uncommon at the time, but animatics of the Martian ad were tested against two less unusual ads, with good results. The final ad was directed by superstar commercial director Bob Brooks. A serendipitous puppet collapse during filming served only to make the end result even funnier.

To understand the role of the alien here, it helps to look at Webster's other output. He had a long history of anthropomorphic ads, with characters including the Sugar Puffs Honey Monster, the Hofmeister Bear, the Prize Yoghurt Prize Guy and Cresta Bear. His use of these creatures is twofold: first, to appeal to the British love of animals, but second, to appeal very directly to simple emotions in the audience. The Smash Martians are just one in this series of anthropomorphic creatures. Although the Martians are presented as looking and sounding alien, they're not. They come from a fully realized world that is exactly like our world, apart from trivial surface trappings and a lack of whole potatoes. The Martians arrive home from work, kiss their spouses, put on their slippers, pet their cats, comfort their children, and eat Smash. Their stainless environment channels the early-1970s appeal of antiseptic futurism, into which instant mashed potato fits perfectly. The ads, perhaps inadvertently, say something profound about the modern human relationship with food and its origins. For potatoes, it's very funny. For sausages, it really wouldn't be.

The earlier ads in the series work because the Martians are presented as thinly disguised people mocking potato-related human foibles. But later ads derive most of their humor simply from the way the Martians look and talk. Some are "family around the kitchen table" situations, indistinguishable from other ads of their type except that the family is Martian. Further evidence for the theory that the Martians stand in for a more general sense of "the other" is an animatic for a second ad from the original set, never made. This one is a music-hall song about "good old Cadbury's Smash," featuring the Martians as a troupe of minstrel-style backing singers. Unlike the ads that aired, there's not even surface science-fictional content in this animatic apart from the bodies and voices of the Martians themselves. The intended humor arises solely from the othering of the Martians, making this animatic feel dated and uncomfortable to the modern viewer.

One of the Smash Martians, a family of "Martian robots" featured in a series of popular 1970s television advertisements in the United Kingdom for the Smash brand of instant mashed potatoes. (David Crausby/Alamy Stock Photo)

More recently, critics have started to question whether the Smash Martians damaged the standing of instant mashed potato in the longer term. The Martians indelibly and permanently associated the product with artificiality and metal. The tagline "98% pure potato," compelling in the 1970s, now inevitably raises the question of what the other 2% consists of. And although we now seek out more convenient versions of everything, instant mashed potato has become a symbol of taking that convenience a step too far.

*Alison Scott*

See also: Clangers, The; Futurama; Mork & Mindy; Oddworld.

## FURTHER READING

Delaney, Sam. *Get Smashed: The Story of the Men Who Made the Adverts That Changed Our Lives*, Sceptre, 2007, ch. 6.

The History of Advertising Trust holds an archive of material on the Smash Martians, including original animatics at www.hatads.org.uk. A documentary that includes all the adverts is available at www.youtube.com/watch?v=n9wEtGB0BZ0.

## Smith, E. E. "Doc"

Born in Wisconsin in 1890, E. E. "Doc" Smith (1890–1965) was an important early contributor to the science-fiction pulps and remained a popular writer throughout the "Golden Age" of SF. Smith's first major SF work, *The Skylark of Space*, appeared in Gernsback's *Amazing Stories* from August to October 1928. This story—written in collaboration with Lee Hawkins Garby, the wife of one of Smith's former classmates—was among the first to take humanity out among the stars. Previously, the most famous works depicting journeys to outer space, such as Wells's *The First Men in the Moon* (1901) or Burroughs's *Under the Moons of Mars* (1912), had largely confined themselves to the solar system. In the mid-1920s, however, authors such as Smith, Edmond Hamilton, and Ray Cummings began to produce more expansive works whose spatial frames of reference took in star systems, nebulas, and entire galaxies.

Of these interstellar works, Smith's *Skylark of Space* proved one of the most enduringly popular, earning Smith the retrospective title "The Father of Space Opera." *Skylark* tells the story of Richard Seaton, a gifted scientist who discovers a revolutionary new propulsion system and uses it to build a spaceship (the titular *Skylark*). Seaton's subsequent interstellar adventures, and his clashes with the evil genius DuQuesne, are chronicled in *The Skylark of Space* and its three sequels: *Skylark Three* (1930), *The Skylark of Valeron* (1934–1935), and *Skylark DuQuesne* (1965).

The *Skylark* works are imperialist in nature, a fact that conditions Smith's depictions of human-alien encounters. Just as much European fiction from the *fin de siècle* period drew upon colonial fantasies of European social and technological superiority, so early space operas drew upon similarly imperial fantasies of America's perceived technological dominance. The protagonists of *Skylark* occupy the role of the technologically superior imperial force, while the aliens they encounter are largely relegated to the position of "natives" awestruck by human technological might. Even in cases where alien technology proves superior to that of humanity—as with the "projectors" and synthetic foods of the "Norlamilians," a humanoid race featured in *Skylark Three*—it takes little time for the enterprising humans to master and then surpass the technological capacities of their alien counterparts.

At times, it hardly seems appropriate to refer to Smith's imagined beings as aliens at all. The green Kondals of the planet Osnome, for example, who feature throughout the *Skylark* series, are humans in all but name, as are the Mardonales, an immoral and violent race with whom the Kondals are at war. The imperial tone of the series is evident in the interactions between the humans and the Osnomian aliens. The emphasis is placed on similarity to Western humanity: the Kondals, resembling Seaton both in appearance and moral feeling, are portrayed as the more sympathetic of the two Osnomian races and so benefit from Seaton's advanced technical know-how in their long-standing war with the "evil" (that is, non-Western) Mardonales. Other alien races appear throughout the *Skylark* series—the Fenachrone (a race of warmongering bipeds), the Dasorians ("porpoise-men" with webbed feet), and others—but, like the Kondals and Mardonales, the majority of such aliens are broadly humanoid in thought and appearance. The alien races in *Skylark*, then, are portrayed from a heavily anthropomorphic perspective, figuring essentially as humans from other worlds.

In Smith's later *Lensman* series, this anthropomorphic bias is partially redressed. *Lensman* is Smith's best-known work, consisting of a series of serialized novels published between 1934 and 1948. The series centers on the Lensmen, an elite organization of law-enforcement officers whose jurisdiction spans the entire galaxy. Each officer is equipped with a Lens, a device that enables telepathic communication. Any kind of being can become a Lensmen, and the series demonstrates, to a much greater extent than *Skylark*, Smith's capacity to imagine genuinely alien worlds. One such world, Trenco, for example, experiences winds of 800 miles an hour and 40 feet of rainfall every night. Trenco is inhabited by a "flatly streamlined creature," its "highest life-form," armed with "long, hooked flippers" for pulling itself along in the violent winds (*Galactic Patrol*, ch. 10). Another race, the Palainians, are depicted as "frigid-blooded, poison-breathing" yet sympathetic beings who exist in more than three dimensions. As a result, Palainians appear to any "three-dimensional creature" as simply a "fluid, amorphous, ever-changing thing" (*First Lensman*, ch. 10).

Such inhuman beings help to rectify the anthropomorphism evident in *Skylark*: in *Lensman*, the human race becomes simply one more alien race among many. Indeed, Smith's repeated emphasis on the highly diverging understandings of what constitutes an attractive body among his many aliens perhaps offers an implicit argument against the racist divisions that divided U.S. society at the time that he was writing. To a being of radically different body type, Smith asserts, even the "trim and graceful human form" may constitute "the very quintessence of malformation and hideousness" (*Triplanetary*, ch. 10). By extension, we might assume that human types are equally relative and that none can therefore be said to constitute the objectively "best" version of the human form.

For all their bodily diversity, however, the aliens of the *Lensman* series nevertheless remain resolutely human in thought, feeling, and expression. Indeed, entry into the Lensmen is contingent upon the possession of a recognizably human set of moral and intellectual qualities that stress psychological similarity over bodily difference. The immediate telepathic rapport established between Lensmen of any race ultimately renders any physical disparity between the human and the alien merely superficial. As a result, the genuine differences that appear between humans and aliens—the completely nonaltruistic mind-set of the Palainians, for example, or the "sense of perception" possessed by certain aliens that allow them to comprehend their immediate surroundings without visual aid (*First Lensman*, ch. 12)—are flattened in the service of a well-meaning but recognizably humanist vision of universal identity.

Smith produced a number of other minor works, now largely forgotten, but following the same basic mold set down in his *Skylark* and *Lensman* works. Smith's depiction of aliens, although rarely xenophobic, never quite succeeds in imagining a *truly* alien world or being. Nevertheless, Smith deserves credit for expanding the spatial framework of SF to the stars, thus introducing a whole new set of worlds on which aliens may be encountered.

*Thomas Connolly*

*See also*: Burroughs, Edgar Rice; Heinlein, Robert A.; Stapledon, Olaf.

**FURTHER READING**

Clute, John. "E. E. Smith." *Science Fiction Writers*, edited by E. F. Bleiler, Scribners, 1982, pp. 125–30.
Ellik, Ronald and William Evans. *The Universes of E. E. Smith*. Advent, 1966.
Stableford, Brian. "The Lensman Series." *Survey of Science Fiction Literature* 3, edited by Frank N. Magill, Salem Press, 1979, pp. 1183–87.

## *Solaris*

*Solaris* (1972), directed by Andrei Tarkovsky, is adapted from the novel *Solaris* (1961) by the Polish writer Stanisław Lem (1921–2006). The alien in both versions of *Solaris* is best described as an attempt to imagine a planet-sized intelligence whose vastness and methods of communication are both incomprehensible. In the adaptation, as in the book, Solaris is a planet whose surface is covered by an ocean, and the ocean seems to be an intelligent life-form. In *Solaris*, there is no humanoid alien that one can identify whose alterity is one of degree rather than any fundamental difference. Most of the movie happens on the space station above the planet surface, from whose windows we see only small parts of this ocean. The ocean appears in different colors, green and pink being the most common. At the end of the film we can see some islands that have appeared on the surface of the planet. We also get several descriptions of the ocean by different characters, and we hear ocean sounds.

There are two main aspects of the alien that deserve consideration in terms of their impact on popular culture as well as their relevance in contemporary discussions. The first is the aspect of borders and limits of communication when faced with things that cannot be fully described. The second is the planet itself as the other, with the planet Solaris as a stand-in for Earth, which also would involve political critique regarding human intervention on planetary processes.

Communication, and its limits, is a central organizing theme in *Solaris*. Communication is connected to the things that can be used to communicate, such as language, gesture, and touch, all of which are within the range of human ability. Anthropomorphization requires a sharing of abilities between humans and alien species for communication. In *Solaris*, the planet communicates by materializing painful memories of the humans, seeking to communicate through their dreams. The protagonist, Kris Kelvin (Donatas Banionis), has his wife Hari/Rheya (Natalya Bondarchuk), who committed suicide, materialize exactly as he remembers her. His first attempt to destroy this apparition fails, and she returns yet again in the same form. Thus the planet-alien has access to at least parts of the human consciousness, but its tools for communication are a manifestation of human abilities rather than its own. The planet-alien begins to communicate only when humans engage in apparently hostile activity, either through nuclear bombardment or by sending military aircraft through its atmosphere (both of which could be historically contextualized as representations of Cold War anxieties). The planet-alien mirrors human communication, and its intents do not seem malicious per se, as we simply do not know for certain whether these apparitions are simply meant to haunt or be some form of interface between humans and the planet-alien. These apparitions do not voice any desires or even any ideas that come from the planet-alien, and the apparitions are initially even unable to maintain an independent existence, as they are the product of the memories that materialize them. As the story progresses, the apparitions gradually become free of those memories as well as the planet, taking on a life of their own. Thus, these creatures become a second class of aliens, presenting the alienness of one's own repressed traumatic memories as they return to the surface. These humanoid beings are composed differently from humans at a subatomic level, and they are able to heal spontaneously from most physical trauma.

The relevance of the alien in *Solaris* for the present is that it can represent the alienness of a/the planet itself and open the portrayal to new ecocritical readings. In current literature on the Anthropocene (for example, Haraway 2016), there is an attempt to move away from a model of the planet as a passive recipient of human activity to the planet as a complex system where humans and nonhumans interact in ways that cannot be mapped. Notwithstanding human activity and its impact, the way the planet and its other inhabitants respond, and how different kinds of new configurations are brought about through human activity, is fundamentally unpredictable. Statistical modeling and extrapolation of trends offer only limited foresight when most of the variables are unknown. In *Solaris*, this is presented through the difference between scientists at the station, who fail to communicate because they understand the planet in terms of data, classification, and description, and Kelvin, who is a psychologist, who focuses on interaction rather than classification. Kelvin's initial revulsion at these apparitions is born of ignorance, which leads him to incinerate the first apparition of his dead wife. This ignorance is gradually replaced by an acceptance of his own responsibility in his wife's suicide. Parsing through the different stages of "solaristics" (the study of Solaris) in order to understand the role played by humans in this exchange of trauma, Kelvin is able to face the apparition of Hari as trauma, just as the planet experiences anthropogenic activity as trauma, which links him and the planet in kinship. Furthermore, as Kelvin's brainwaves are beamed down to the planet surface in another attempt at communication, the traumatic apparitions disappear. By the end of the movie, Kelvin arrives at a new balance with the alien planet, even though it is ultimately beyond his understanding, surviving a fever in which the apparition of traumatic memory is replaced by a more benevolent apparition of his caring mother. After this realization, new islands appear on the planet surface to allow life, beginning, arguably, a process of spontaneous terraforming. Kelvin is left with a choice of living life on these terms in harmony with the planet-alien or returning to Earth.

As a landmark work in the history of SF, both the book and the film have been extensively studied in scholarly literature. The film's focus on radical otherness has made it particularly open to psychoanalytical readings (see Bird and Bould).

Bodhisattva Chattopadhyay

See also: Lem, Stanislaw; Strugatsky, Arkady and Boris.

## FURTHER READING

Bird, Robert. *Andrei Tarkovsky: Elements of Cinema*. Reaktion, 2008.
Bould, Mark. *Solaris*. British Film Institute/Palgrave Macmillan, 2014.
Haraway, Donna. *Staying with the Trouble: Making Kin in the Chthulucene*. Duke University Press, 2016.

## Space Invaders

Originally appearing in the Taito arcade game, created by Tomohiro Nishikado, the aliens in *Space Invaders* (1978) are nameless extraterrestrials consumed solely with the conquest of the player's homeworld (represented by a lunar backdrop on the playing field). The simplicity of the game's conceit is contained directly within the title: the aliens are invaders from space. The where and the why are not important in this case, and the threat is made explicit in the attack launched as soon as the game is started. Given the technical limitations of video-game hardware at the time, little importance was given to the narrative compared with the actual mechanics of gameplay. Like many other game designers at the time, Nishikado made reference to something that already existed in popular media as a way to make a conceptual shortcut for players and let their imaginations fill in the rationale for the endless waves of space invaders that could never be truly defeated.

The origin of the space invaders drew upon several different referents from popular culture. In the course of refining the original game design, after being inspired by Atari's *Breakout* (1972), Nishikado wanted to transform the *Pong*-style mechanics into a shooting game. Abandoning his original design of military vehicles and eschewing the idea of letting players shoot human-looking enemies, Nishikado adopted a space theme after reading a magazine article about *Star Wars*, which had yet to be released in Japan. As he later admitted in an interview, the look of the aliens themselves was inspired by George Pal's 1953 film adaptation of H. G. Wells's *The War of the Worlds* (1897). He created a bitmap (an image made of arranged pixels) of an octopus-like alien and then stayed with an aquatic theme by creating two more modeled after a squid and a crab. Nishikado wanted to call the game *Space Monsters* in reference to "Monster," a popular song in Japan at the time; the title was changed to *Space Invaders*, although the initial title resulted in the creation of a bipedal alien on the arcade game's side art, even though this creature is not featured in the game. A mothership-style UFO periodically moves across the top of the playfield, providing another target for the player to hit, although this opponent is completely optional; only the invaders marching down the screen must be destroyed. The technical sophistication of the game also featured a continuous music soundtrack, looped beneath the sound effects of the game. As fewer invaders were left on the screen they speeded up, and the music track increased its tempo. Another important feature was retaining the highest scores and presenting them as the achievement of the best players for other players to see.

Upon its release, *Space Invaders* created a major sensation in Japan across generations. While a popular, but unsubstantiated, industry legend says that the game was responsible for a shortage of 100-yen coins in Japan, this is likely due to the record number of machines produced (initially 100,000 in Japan by the end of 1978) and which produced a staggering (U.S.-adjusted) $600 million in gross revenue. Entire arcades, known as "Invaders Houses," were composed of nothing but *Space Invaders* machines. Through 1982, production of another 200,000 machines in Japan, along with 60,000 in the United States, would yield gross revenues of $2 billion in under four years.

Screen display from the arcade version of the *Space Invaders* video game, released in 1978. The pixelated enemy aliens (seen behind the game title) became iconic in pop culture. (Christina Jaramillo/Dreamstime.com)

The success of *Space Invaders* quickly led to multiple arcade sequels: *Space Invaders Part II* (1979), *Return of the Invaders* (1985), *Super Space Invaders '91* (1990), *Space Invaders DX* (1993), and *Space Invaders '95: The Attack of Lunar Loonies* (1995). Atari, hoping to boost low sales of its Video Computer System (VCS, also known more popularly as the 2600), licensed a port of *Space Invaders*, making a home version that became the first console "killer application" (a piece of software that is in such demand that consumers will purchase the necessary hardware to use it). In its first year of release, Atari sold two million copies of the game (the first home title to ever break the one-million mark). Atari reduced the number of aliens per wave but created six entirely new aliens that were still evocative of Nishikado's original designs, kept the UFO mystery ship, and retained a version of the distinctive heartbeat-like music loop. The success of the home version resulted in over 20 additional licensed *Space Invaders* titles made for over 30 different hardware platforms in the three decades since Atari's adaptation.

The popularity of the space invaders continues almost four decades after their creation. In the film *Pixels* (2015), the space invaders become actual invaders when an alien-invasion force mistakenly assumes the look of notable characters from various video games in response to what they perceive as a declaration of war from Earth. Of the three aliens from the original *Space Invaders*, the crab version has become iconic not only within its hardware generation of arcade games and consoles but also within the whole video-game industry, to the point where it adorns a wide variety of consumer products, from shirts to pint glasses to soap on a rope. Even the French urban artist Invader has adopted his moniker from the game as he creates ceramic mosaics of the space invaders, and other video-game characters, that have been installed in over 33 countries, creating a sort of art invasion as fans hunt for the public works. The once-ominous aliens have become ambassadors for the entirety of video-game culture.

*Stefan Hall*

See also: Lesbian Spider Queens of Mars; War of the Worlds, The.

## FURTHER READING

Burnham, Van. *Supercade: A Visual History of the Videogame Age, 1971–84*. MIT Press, 2003.

King, Lucien, editor. *Game On: The History and Culture of Videogames*. Universe Publishing, 2002.

Newman, James and Iain Simons. "Space Invaders." *100 Videogames*, British Film Institute, 2007, pp. 200–202.

## Stapledon, Olaf

Olaf Stapledon (1886–1950) garnered a reputation in two rather different quarters. As a moral philosopher and social reformer, his work on ethics, such as his first academic book, *A Modern Theory of Ethics* (1929), and the two-volume Penguin *Philosophy and Living* (1939), underpinned his campaigns for disarmament and world government after World War I, in which he served with the Ambulance Unit of the Society of Friends. On the other hand, as the author of novels such as *Last and First Men* (1930), *Last Men in London* (1932), *Odd John* (1935), *Star Maker* (1937), *Sirius* (1944), and *The Flames* (1947), Stapledon reached a wider public to become one of the great innovators of alien otherness in science fiction.

The two audiences are not, perhaps, as separate as might first be thought. Stapledon's concern was futurity (political futures arising from the clashes of ideology during his lifetime) but also the overarching evolutionary potentials of the human form and the human spirit. *Last and First Men* is narrated by a being from the far future, occupying the mind of one of the "First Men": an obscure English intellectual whose experiences on the Western front have jarred him into fusing the wartime clash between collective and individual ethics with a more existential concern with the position of humanity in a barely understood cosmos. The resulting future-history brings a genuine life to the cliché "*we* are the alien."

*We* vanish quickly. The "First Men" die out after the collapse of the first World State and the later rise and fall of a civilization based in Patagonia, which destroys itself in nuclear cataclysm. New species of humanity evolve—the titanic Second, the furred "Third Men," the artificially created "Great Brains" of the Fourth. The avian Sixth flourish on Venus after the disintegration of Earth's moon forces an exodus. Another "designed" Ninth human species populates Neptune as the sun expands. The Eighteenth "version" of humanity, multigendered, telepathic, with enhanced and extra sense organs, are in some ways the culmination of the evolutionary process, but in their own turn they are faced with destruction from the expanding sun. In a final act of affirmation, they disseminate spores into the universe in the hope that they will find some hospitable environment and reach back through history. Their message to "us" is to highlight the dynamic between the spiritual-yearning and pragmatic-materialist "poles" of human experience working itself out through the aeons of Deep Time.

There are other aliens, less human, in Stapledon's universe. In *Last and First Men*, the Second Men and their successors are weakened after a series of invasion attempts by semigaseous, telepathic Martians. Stapledon revisits the moral territory of Wells's *The War of the Worlds*, suggesting that the Martian "invaders" have a right to survive. This dilemma is recapitulated when the Fifth Men set about terraforming Venus while exterminating its ocean dwellers. Drawing upon a similar scenario in a chilling essay by his friend J. B. S. Haldane, Stapledon confronts the obvious point: does humanity have any "right," other than the *"might*-is-right" justification of racial survival, to exterminate the native "Venerians"?

It is in his masterpiece *Star Maker* that Stapledon most fully expands his imagination. We never experience any sense of viewpoint from the previous novel's Venerians. This is certainly deliberate—Stapledon is at pains to emphasize that *Last and First Men*, which contains barely a single named character and little dialogue and which swoops over millions of years in a single sentence, is a rather novel exercise in "myth creation," a message from the future designed to spur us into thinking about our individual and collective creation of it. In *Star Maker* (which Patrick A. McCarthy compares to Dante's *Divine Comedy*), Stapledon paradoxically tackles the problem of a culturally partial viewpoint by increasing the scale.

It begins with a simple domestic quarrel and becomes a vision of a universe of life-forms striving to understand their place in the cosmic dance. The consciousness of the narrator (again a version of Stapledon himself) expands to experience a "Diversity of Worlds." There are the humanoid "Other Men" whose particular sensory bias is toward *taste* rather than sight or hearing. There are avian life-forms, quasi-humans that do not share our usual duplication of organs, six-legged instead of quadruped models resulting in centauroids, and "humans" developed from starfish-like echinoderms. On large waterworlds, mollusc-like "nautiloids" evolve a membrane, which is used as a sail, and become living ships. "It was a strange experience to enter the mind of an intelligent ship," Stapledon writes. With fellow-"pioneers" our narrator follows the path of evolution beyond individualism, to planetary, collective consciousnesses, and to the fusion of galaxies into a godlike "Star Maker."

In these two novels, the building-blocks of science fiction—future-history itself, the invention of alien cultures as thought-experiment tools with which to compare our own, bioengineering the human form to meet new physical conditions—are almost casually presented before us. Elsewhere, the human/"other" relationship is explored in less overtly cosmic ways. *Odd John*'s "superhuman" mutation, the bioengineered superbright dog in *Sirius*, and the solar beings in *The Flames* offer different perspectives on human concerns. Throughout, from these more local instances to the apotheosis at the heart of *Star Maker*, Stapledon suggests that Humanity itself is simply a viewpoint. However we conceive of "us," that conception is only partial and parochial.

This sometimes chilly grandeur is perhaps the reason why Stapledon's work is so often mediated through the work of others. His tone and subject matter is echoed in writers like Arthur C. Clarke, Brian Aldiss, Stephen Baxter, and especially Doris Lessing, who found his "space fiction" a stimulus for her "Canopus in Argos" sequence. His deliberate refusal of "sides" in the ideological conflicts of his time brought him accusations of being a communist fellow-traveler, while novelist Naomi Mitchison, whose insight helped shape *Star Maker* and who later borrowed some of its aliens for her *Memoirs of a Spacewoman*, criticized an early draft of the novel for the "patriarchal" nature of the "Star Maker" deity-analog. Yet he remains one of SF's most valuable examples of how and why to imagine the alien.

*Andy Sawyer*

See also: Flammarion, Camille; Clarke, Arthur C.

## FURTHER READING

Bailey, K. V. "Time Scales and Culture Cycles in Olaf Stapledon." *Foundation*, no. 46, Winter 1989, pp. 27–39.

Crossley, Robert. *Olaf Stapledon: Speaking for the Future*. Liverpool University Press, 1994.

Lem, Stanislaw, "On Stapledon's *Last and First Men*." *Science-Fiction Studies*, vol. 13 part 3, no. 40, 1986, pp. 272–91.

## *Star Trek*

*Star Trek* (1967–1969) functions as a futuristic Western, following the Federation starship USS *Enterprise* as it explores the frontier of space and meets new alien species. Throughout the series, alien life creates weekly challenges for the *Enterprise* crew, but some species have particular valence as metaphors for particular cultural fears. The Federation, an organization of alien governments, functions as an analog for either the United States of America or the United Nations, depending on context. Aliens outside the Federation are the primary antagonists in the series. The Klingons were originally conceived as a stand-in for the Soviet Union, and so interactions between Klingons and the Federation largely follow the structure of proxy wars between the United States and the USSR. In the episode "Errand of Mercy," when the Klingons are first introduced, the crew of the *Enterprise* attempt to help a local population engage in guerrilla tactics to rid their planet of an occupying Klingon military. In a standoff similar to the Cuban missile crisis of 1962, the Federation and Klingon fleets are poised for war. In a literal deus ex machina, the local population turns out to be highly powerful incorporeal beings that force the two sides to sign a peace treaty, suggesting the need for a forced peace in the Cold War, similar to the plot from *The Day the Earth Stood Still*. Other alien species in the original series include recurring humanoid Vulcans and Romulans as well as one-off nonhumanoid races such as the Tribbles and Melkotians.

*Star Trek: The Next Generation* (1987–1994) shifted the Klingon character at a moment that perfectly coincided with Gorbachev's emphasis on glasnost. In *TNG*, a Klingon, Lieutenant Worf, is actually a crew member on the *Enterprise*. Worf is an orphan raised by humans Sergey and Helena Rozhenko, whom the scriptwriters of *TNG* specifically designated as "of Russian descent." Worf spends a large portion of the show trying to reconnect with this Klingon heritage and is often shown as disappointed in his son, who does not carry the same desire to be a traditional Klingon, illustrating a generational break between pre– and post–Cold War cultural values. In 1991's *Star Trek VI: The Undiscovered Country*, released the same year the Soviet Union collapsed, the Klingons are faced with an ecological disaster. At the beginning of *Star Trek VI*, Praxis, one of the Klingon moons, explodes after excessive mining (hearkening back to the Chernobyl disaster). The Klingon government seeks a long-term peace with the Federation to assist after the disaster, but elements within both the Federation and Klingon militaries conspire to undermine the peace efforts. However, the conspiracy is discovered, and an alliance is struck, setting the stage for the Klingon-Federation relationship that exists in *TNG* and the subsequent series, *Deep Space Nine*.

A new enemy introduced in *TNG*, the Borg, is a collective consciousness consisting of a Queen and drones from thousands of species who have been captured and assimilated. The Borg's goal is to forcefully assimilate all intelligent species into the Collective by implanting nanotechnology in their victims, linking them to the hive mind that controls their actions. Through this mixture of genetic variation and cybernetic enhancement, the Borg believe they are striving closer to perfection. While the Federation brands itself as a pluralistic society that celebrates diversity, the Borg, by contrast, actively suppress individuality in favor of the individual's utility to the Collective. This is visually depicted by the change in assimilated species' skin tones to a monochromatic gray. Whereas the Klingons were a depiction of an external threat (the Soviet Union), the Borg represent an internal threat, the danger of losing individuality to a technocracy that prioritizes digital interconnection at the expense of individual expression. A Borg drone is literally a cog in the machine. Other recurring alien species introduced in *TNG* include the Ferengi, a culture premised on male greed and the objectification of women, and the Q, a literal god-race that plays with other species for fun when they get bored. Indeed, the *Enterprise* first encounters the Borg because one Q wants to teach humanity a lesson about being too eager to explore.

Subsequent *Star Trek* series, including *Deep Space Nine* (1993–1999), *Voyager* (1995–2001), and *Enterprise* (2001–2005), use the Borg as villains and also introduce new antagonistic alien governments such as the Dominion. The Dominion comprises three species: (1) the Founders, a group of shapeshifters that rule as an oligarchy, (2) the Vorta, the bureaucrats who carry out the will of the Founders, and (3) the Jem'Hadar, the soldiers who are controlled through the use of drugs and

Scene from the episode "Scorpion (Part 2)" from season four of *Star Trek: Voyager* (1995–2001). Shown (from left) are Tim Russ as Lt. Cmdr. Tuvok and Jeri Ryan as a Borg. (UPN/Photofest)

a brutal training program. The Dominion poses both a military threat and a threat to the information security of the Federation, since the Founders' shapeshifting abilities allow them to pose as Federation officers and diplomats. The Founders' physical abilities also challenge boundaries of gender and physical identity.

Most recently, J. J. Abrams's reboot of *Star Trek* does not reuse the Borg or the Dominion. Instead, Abrams makes his villains individual terrorists. In *Star Trek*, the extremist is a Romulan who blames the Federation for not saving his planet. Abrams's subsequent films pull their villains from within the Federation itself, suggesting that the cultural fears of the late 2000s have shifted from external government and technological threats to individual terrorist actors.

*Sara Austin*

See also: *Babylon 5*; Ellison, Harlan; *Firefly/Serenity*; *Star Wars*.

## FURTHER READING

Asherman, Allan. *The Star Trek Compendium*. Pocket Books, 1986.
Bernardi, Daniel. *Star Trek and History: Race-ing toward a White Future*. Rutgers University Press, 1998.
Weldes, Jutta. *To Seek out New Worlds: Science Fiction and World Politics*. Palgrave Macmillan, 2003.

## Star Wars

The *Star Wars* film franchise, founded in 1977 with the release of George Lucas's *Star Wars* (later renamed *Episode IV: A New Hope* in the iconic crawl at the beginning of the 1981 release), is an epic space opera that spans generations and star systems and is responsible for some of the most iconic, best loved, and most reviled aliens in science fiction.

Planets in the *Star Wars* universe have their own animal and plant life. On the desert world of Tatooine, bantha, horned and furred herbivores, serve as favored mounts, companions, and beasts of burden for the Tusken Raiders, while sarlaac lurk under the sands waiting for prey to come close enough to snare it with their tentacles. However, on the frozen world of Hoth, tauntauns, large, bipedal creatures resembling heavy-set kangaroos with vaguely simian faces, horns, and shaggy fur, serve as mounts for Rebel patrols. Tauntauns have to worry about more than Hoth's unforgiving weather, as they feature prominently in the diet of wampas, predators resembling yeti with shaggy white fur, wickedly sharp teeth and claws, and small horns that hug their faces.

Even the vacuum of space supports its own ecosystem of silicone-based life. When the *Millennium Falcon* takes refuge from pursuit on an asteroid in *Episode V: The Empire Strikes Back* (1980), the cave the ship and its passengers hide in turns out to be the gullet of an exogorth, a giant gastropod resembling a lamprey eel. The exogorth also hosts mynocks, bat-like creatures that drain energy from starships. The presence of these creatures grounds the fictional worlds as surely as their sentient peoples, cultures, and architecture.

Because regular interplanetary travel exists in the *Star Wars* universe, sentient races move between worlds for business, politics, and pleasure. When Queen Amidala of Naboo addresses the Galactic Senate in *Episode I: The Phantom Menace* (1999), human and alien races are represented among the assembly, just as they compete against each other in the pod races Anakin Skywalker (Jake Lloyd) wins on Tatooine. Humans and aliens work together as part of the Rebel Alliance in *Episode V: The Empire Strikes Back* and *Episode VI: The Return of the Jedi* (1983), and they live with one another in the marketplace Rey visits to sell her scavenged wares on Jakku in *The Force Awakens* (2015). Thus, encountering the alien has, to a certain extent, been normalized in the *Star Wars* universe. Unless a person has led a very isolated life, she will have come in contact with alien humanoids.

One of the most iconic moments in all the films is the Mos Eisley cantina bar scene in *Episode IV: A New Hope*. While Luke Skywalker (Mark Hamill) has regularly dealt with the diminutive, golden-eyed Jawas and aggressive Tusken Raiders, the cantina sequence demonstrates the diversity of the worlds beyond his family's farm and Tatooine, and the audience shares his sense of wonder. As the camera's gaze pans across the bar, it reveals a variety of aliens, including a horned Devaronian who looks like he could have stepped out of a medieval print of a devil, a hammer-headed Ithorian, a walrus-faced Aqualish, a three-eyed, bovine-faced Gran, and a diminutive, furry, bat-faced Chadra-Fan. Bith musicians, who share a passing resemblance to the "gray" aliens of urban legend and conspiracy theory, provide an upbeat musical backdrop for the scene.

Bith musicians playing in the Mos Eisley cantina in *Star Wars* (1977), written and directed by George Lucas. (Lucasfilm/20th Century Fox/Album/Alamy Stock Photo)

In the *Star Wars* universe, alien races serve as more than a backdrop for world building. They are mentors and allies, rivals and antagonists. In the cantina scene, Ben Kenobi (Sir Alec Guinness) bargains with Chewbacca (Peter Mayhew), the tall, heavily furred Wookie who becomes one of the major characters in the films, and Han Solo (Harrison Ford) has a lethal encounter with Greedo (Paul Blake), a green-skinned Rodian bounty hunter with large, gleaming eyes and a tapir-like snout, who has been sent to capture him. The diminutive Jedi Master Yoda (Frank Oz) serves as a mentor to Luke, just as Maz Kanata (Lupita Nyong'o) helps Rey (Daisy Ridley) sense the Force.

Rather than construct elaborate alien words/language like *Star Trek*'s Klingon or *Avatar*'s Na'vi, *Star Wars* employs several techniques when representing alien language. One way it accomplishes this is by altering the structure of Galactic Basic (which is represented as English in the films) to lend the language an alien quality. For example, when Yoda speaks, his sentences follow an "object-subject-verb" order instead of the familiar English syntax that employs "subject-verb-object" order.

The films are also successful when they approach language as a matter of sound design, using real Earth languages and then distorting them through sound engineering. The whistles, whines, and beeps of Droidspeak that BB-8 and R2-D2 communicate in are the result of synthetically altered human vocalization, while Shyriiwook, the growling, roaring language of Wookies, is constructed by combining and distorting animal sounds, including those from walruses, camels, and badgers. Other languages, like Huttese (spoken by Jabba), take the sounds of non-English languages and use them to construct alien-sounding dialogue.

*Star Wars* succeeds in its representation of aliens in those areas where it normalizes the alien and celebrates the diversity of all sentient species. The films, however, use the device of having aliens speak in heavily accented English, a technique that proves problematic, as it combines with other stereotypical physical characteristics and behaviors associated with real-world cultures. For example, the miserly Toydarian merchant Watto has a large nose and Middle Eastern accent, whereas the cowardly and treacherous Nute Gunray and the Neimoidians of Trade Federation have the stereotypical Asian speech mannerism that reverses "r" and "l" sounds. Perhaps the single most problematic alien representation is that of Jar Jar Binks and the amphibian Gungans native to Naboo. While the Gungans are loyal warriors, they are presented as a simple people with childlike speech mannerisms and vaguely Caribbean accents. They lack advanced technology, and despite being indigenous to the planet, they are treated as second-class citizens.

*Barbara Lucas*

See also: *Close Encounters of the Third Kind*; Smith, E. E. "Doc"; *Star Trek*.

**FURTHER READING**

Brode, Douglas and Leah Deyneka, editors. *Myth, Media, and Culture in Star Wars: An Anthology*. Scarecrow Press, 2012.

Guynes, Sean and Dan Hassler-Forest, editors. *Star Wars and the History of Transmedia Storytelling*. Amsterdam University Press, 2017.

Lewis, Ann Margaret and Helen Keier. *Star Wars: The New Essential Guide to Alien Species*. Random House, 2013.

## *StarCraft*

*StarCraft*, designed by Blizzard Entertainment, is a real-time strategy game initially created for the PC and released in 1996. The expansion pack, *StarCraft: Brood War*, followed in 1998. After several years of development, a sequel was released in 2010 as *StarCraft II: Wings of Liberty*, set four years after the end of Brood War. Further chapters of *StarCraft II* followed: *Heart of the Swarm* in 2013 and *Legacy of the Void* in 2015. The original *StarCraft* game has also been updated with improved graphics, dialogue, and audio and released as *StarCraft: Remastered* in August 2017.

The story takes place far from Earth, in an area of space known as the Koprulu Sector. By the 25th century, Humans (otherwise referred to as Terrans) have colonized several worlds and formed a number of competing governments. The game begins when they become embroiled in a conflict between two alien species: the enigmatic Protoss and the monstrous Zerg. Each faction is featured in its own story arc, and the story takes place on a number of different worlds, providing a variety of settings.

Both of the alien species are depicted as other in some way, distinctly nonhuman, and almost as polar opposites. Terrans are at least somewhat familiar, reminiscent of modern Earth armies with infantry wielding guns and flamethrowers, albeit equipped with powered armor suits and heavier weaponry than we have now. Their fortifications consist of bunkers that must be manned to be effective, and their vehicles and artillery resemble those of modern Earth.

The Protoss are humanoid but otherwise have little resemblance to humans. Their legs are digitigrade, their skin is scaly, and their hands have two fingers with an opposable thumb on either side. They do not have a mouth, nose, or ears. Instead of hair they have long tendrils trailing from the back of their heads. These are the neural cords that help facilitate a communal psychic link they call Khala. This link binds them together, providing empathic connection and a unified purpose as well as being a philosophy and way of life. Those that follow it are known as Khalai. All Protoss are capable of mental communication, and some can manifest psychic blades and psionic storms for use in combat.

In addition to their psychic abilities, the Protoss are far more technologically advanced than the Terrans. Their achievements include warping space, allowing them to teleport injured warriors out of danger, and they can use beacons that allow them to quickly place whole buildings and other structures rather than building them. Several of their weapons are robotic machines with varying levels of intelligence. They are also the only ones able to use energy shields for protecting themselves, their machines, and their buildings. Their machines and architecture share the same aesthetics: metallic, elegant, brightly colored, almost ornamental.

As the story progresses, other groups of Protoss are introduced. The Nerazim rejected the Khala for fear of losing their individuality, severing their neural cords in the process. The Khalai exiled them, but the outcasts simply hid in the shadows and continued to protect their homeworld. Another group are the Tal'Darim, a brutal and more warlike sect who are not part of the Khala, instead serving and worshipping godlike beings called Xel'Naga. Last are the Purifiers, robotic bodies that house the spirits of ancient Protoss. Each group has its own signature colors, but all use similar technologies.

The Zerg, however, do not use technology at all, nor do they build. They are driven to adapt and evolve at all costs, and everything they create is entirely organic. Even their "buildings" are grown in place rather than constructed. Mostly insectoid in appearance, the Zerg can take on a variety of forms for different purposes. These forms are mutated from other life-forms that the Zerg Swarm has absorbed and consumed to gain useful genetic traits. In *StarCraft* they want to assimilate the Terrans because they have psionic potential, which would give the Zerg an edge against the Protoss. They eventually succeed with a human woman, Sarah Kerrigan, who is mutated into a Zerg hybrid referred to as "Queen of Blades."

A single creature rules the Zerg at first, the Overmind, making them a hive species. Lesser Zerg have little free will or intelligence of their own. The Overmind has divided the Swarm into a number of "broods," each with a different purpose. Control of the individual broods is delegated to "cerebrates." When a cerebrate is slain, the Zerg it controlled tend to run berserk. Eventually the Overmind itself is slain, and Kerrigan assumes control of the Swarm.

Using natural defenses such as claws and chitinous armor, the Zerg are not as durable as the Protoss or even the Terrans. However, they make up for it by being able to reproduce quickly, allowing them to overwhelm their enemies with greater numbers. One tactic is to field a large swarm of lesser creatures and destroy unprepared enemies before they can mount a defense. This is known among players as a "zerg rush," or simply "zerging."

In *StarCraft II* the "primal" Zerg are revealed. They were never dominated by the Overmind and remained on their home planet, Zerus. These Zerg are more intelligent and individual, forming packs under a strong leader rather than being a single hive mind. Their appearance is also different from the Swarm, more mammalian or reptilian, as the Overmind had been focused entirely on combat when breeding its Zerg.

Despite their differences, the Protoss and Zerg have one similarity: the Khala and hive mind connect the members of their respective species to each other. For the Protoss, many come together for a single purpose, while the Zerg is driven by one will in many bodies.

Both are distinctly alien in their own ways, and while they may become more understandable over time, they are still very much other.

*Jonathon Side*

See also: *FTL*; *X-COM, XCOM*.

### FURTHER READING

Choe, Steve and Se Young Kim, "Never Stop Playing: *StarCraft* and *Asian Gamer Death*." *Techno-Orientalism: Imagining Asia in Speculative Fiction, History, and Media*, edited by David S. Roh et al., Rutgers University Press, 2015, pp. 113–24.

## Sterling, Bruce

Bruce Sterling's (1954–) foray into science fiction began with his short story "Man Made Self" (1976) and his novel *Involution Ocean* (1977), which concentrates on Joe Newhouse's move to the planet, Nullaqua, which is predicated on his captivation with the alien drug Flare (syncophine). However, it was during the mid-1980s that Sterling attained notoriety with his contribution to the cyberpunk genre through his preface to and editing of *Mirrorshades: The Cyberpunk Anthology* (1986) and his continued examination of alien worlds. In *Schismatrix* (1985), Sterling offers his readers the everlasting battle for supremacy between the Shapers and the Mechanists. In this series, which is composed of a novel and a number of short stories, Sterling focuses on Abelard Malcolm Tyler Lindsay, a Shaper who, in his moments of brilliance, resembles Max Bialystock from Mel Brooks's *The Producers*. Throughout the novel, Sterling describes the war between the two human factions, the biodiverse and bacteria-free Shapers and the cyborg Mechanists. Each group asserts its ideology—the Shapers are biomechanism-free in order to retain their humanity but work tirelessly to reverse the aging process. In a tongue-in-cheek exploration of humanity's evolution, notably that humans now populate space, living on other worlds, Sterling asserts that devolution is occurring, as is shown through their detachment toward others, including members of their own species.

Early on in the novel, the Shapers become disbelievingly aware that humans are not the only species in the universe. They (and the Mechanists) believe that an association with the reptilian Investors is going to shift the balance of power in their favor. Both factions become aware that the Investors have no intention of choosing sides; rather, they are depicted as a capitalist species desirous of retaining their power. It is Lindsay, the intelligent and shrewd outsider (his Shaper training is considered passé among many of the younger Shapers), who, by asserting his individuality, uses the Investors to his advantage. He rises in position, starts and loses civilizations, and ends his physical life in the same place that it began, on his family's estate. By coming to the realization that humans should not be taking advantage of others for their own gain and then accepting this fact, Lindsay reaches his final stage of Shaper enlightenment and transcends his physical body, thereby being able to join the alien Presence in a quest for knowledge.

Having refused to write a sequel to *Schismatrix*, Sterling instead rereleased his Shaper/Mechanist short stories in *Crystal Express* (1989). Significantly, Sterling wrote these stories— "Swarm," "Twenty Evocations," etc.—before the novel and also includes the stories' chronology in *Schismatrix Plus* to clarify the progression of the Shaper/Mechanist's war. Readers will observe a change in emphasis from Sterling's earlier Shaper/Mechanist plots to that of the novel. In "Spider Rose" (1982), set in "the fringes of the solar system," Sterling focuses on the Mechanists rather than the Shaper figure he favors in *Schismatrix*. Female Mechanist Spider Rose/Lydia Martinez resides on a station alone. Like Lindsay, she is elderly; however, she lives with the notion that the Shaper assassins are hunting her and that her superior knowledge will assist in outwitting them. While she is engaged in the eternal battle with the Shapers, which she enjoys, she also revels in her infrequent negotiations with the alien Investors. Sterling centers the plot on Lydia's transformation, her transcendence, involving her alien pet, Fuzzy, obtained in trade from the Investors. The Investors contact Spider Rose/Lydia about a rare jewel; it becomes clear that this contact has been initiated by Spider Rose/Lydia and that she relishes bartering with the shrewd aliens. When they offer her their mascot and appear to suffer greatly when they relinquish it, it seems that she has the upper hand. She kills Fuzzy (and later eats it) in an attempt to save herself, and when she later emerges from her cocoon she becomes her own pet. The story closes with Lydia "eager for the leash" because it is she who is now the mascot of the Investors. In this story, and in "Swarm" (1982), Sterling portrays aliens as having the dominant position in their relationship with humans.

"Swarm," which Sterling observes is his most-republished work, follows the Shaper Captain-Doctor Simon Afriel in his quest to commodify the alien species known as the Swarm. As one of the agents of the Ring Council, it is Afriel's job to deal with various alien species, including the Investors. So that the Shapers may be victorious in the war against the Mechanists, the Shapers attempt to use the alien species, both Investors and Swarm, to their advantage. Before meeting with the representative of the Swarm and entering the Nest, one of the Investors tries to ascertain the reasoning behind the Shapers' interest in the Swarm. The Investor cites the Shapers' ignorance of the Swarm and of aliens overall as their motivation for the Swarm's study, a lack of knowledge that leads to the downfall of the two

Shaper representatives, Afriel and his partner and scientist, Galina Mirny. Sterling portrays the Swarm as resembling bee society, complete with a hierarchy that includes a queen at the helm. Dr. Mirny tries to warn Afriel about taking advantage of the Swarm, but he convinces her that they will be ignorant of his actions, that the Swarm will come to no harm. Ultimately, the aliens strike back at the Shapers, the story concluding with Afriel asserting that a new war is on the horizon. Sterling's loyal readers hope that he continues to find humanity as interesting as he has in the past; we look forward to his next venture.

*Melanie A. Marotta*

*See also*: Reynolds, Alastair; Vinge, Vernor.

## FURTHER READING

Call, Lewis. "Anarchy in the Matrix: Postmodern Anarchism in the Novels of William Gibson and Bruce Sterling." *Anarchist Studies*, vol. 7, no. 2, 1999, pp. 99–117.
Hollinger, Veronica, Daniel Fischlin and Andrew Taylor. "The Charisma Leak: A Conversation with William Gibson and Bruce Sterling." *Science Fiction Studies*, vol. 19, no. 1, 1992, pp. 1–16.
Raulerson, Joshua T. *Singularities: Technoculture, Transhumanism, and Science Fiction in the 21st Century*. Liverpool University Press, 2013.

## Steven Universe

Cartoon Network's first animated series solely created by a woman (Rebecca Sugar), *Steven Universe* (2013–) is an Emmy Award–nominated coming-of-age story about a human/alien hybrid named Steven Universe growing up on Earth with his three alien guardians. Steven joins the Crystal Gems, Amethyst, Pearl, and Garnet, on their magical adventures as he slowly learns about his developing gem powers. In the early episodes of the series the Crystal Gems seem unparalleled in power, but as Steven learns more about his gem identity he comes to understand that this is not the case.

More than 5,000 years before Steven was born, the Homeworld Gems, under the leadership of Pink Diamond, landed on Earth in order to use the planet to grow new gems. This process would destroy the planet, in turn killing humanity. To stop this genocide, Rose Quartz, one of Pink Diamond's soldiers, started a rebel group known as the Crystal Gems. They fought not only to protect the Earth and humanity, but also to live free of Homeworld tyranny. Each Crystal Gem's identity functions as a site of resistance, often in ways that are analogous to different queer experiences.

The aliens of *Steven Universe*, the gems, are a species of uniformity. All gems use she and her pronouns, and every gem's identity is based on the specific gemstone found somewhere on their body. It is their gemstone that gives the gem their name, specific physical and magical characteristics, and social class. Gems are not born but grown; their gemstones are planted in a planet's crust, where they incubate and grow, sucking the life out of the earth. Once grown, the gem projects her body from her gemstone like a physical hologram. Every gem is expected to project the same physical body as every other gem with the same gemstone, because each gem is grown for a specific purpose. This determines not only the gem's social role but also its place in a social hierarchy. There is a strict uniformity among gems of the same gemstone. Gems who do not, or cannot, meet the expectations of this uniformity either live in hiding for fear of being executed or join Rose Quartz's rebellion.

Amethyst resists the uniformity of gem bodies in a way that is analogous to queer gender identity and expression. Amethyst projects a unique physical body unlike any other gem, appearing differently than other Amethysts. She also spends a great deal of time shape-shifting. One of her most noteworthy transformations is the Purple Puma, a male wrestler who Amethyst initially turns into only in secret. Amethyst's body- and shape-shifting consistently resists gem norms regarding what her body should be and how she should present herself to others.

Pearl resists gem hierarchies by subverting her expected social role. A Pearl gem is grown to be a servant for high-ranking gems. The Pearl of the Crystal Gems is one of the first members of the rebellion and is infamous for her expert sword-fighting skills. Pearl often takes charge of situations and advocates for equality and teamwork.

Garnet resists the identity of gems as specific to those with particular gemstones by embodying forbidden love. Garnet is a fusion of an aristocratic Sapphire and a common soldier Ruby. A fusion is a gem created when two gems join together, combining their magical and physical attributes into a single entity. On the gem homeworld, only gems with the same gemstone fuse. When Ruby and Sapphire fuse, other gems consider them disgusting, and Ruby, being a lower class than Sapphire, is sentenced to execution. The two flee together, join the Crystal Gems, and continue to fuse into Garnet as an embodiment of their love.

Steven's very existence resists the ideologies that dictate a gem's purpose, embodying a position of liberation and freedom. After Rose Quartz defeats Pink Diamond, she falls in love with a human named Greg Universe and gives up her physical form to create Steven. While gems are grown for a purpose, Steven is born for no reason other than because he is wanted. This allows Steven to be whoever he wants and live his life as he chooses—the very aim of the Crystal Gems.

When Steven begins to develop gem powers at the age of 12, the surprising changes to Steven's hybrid body are analogous to queer puberty. The alien part of Steven's body and family history functions as a site of mystery, discovery, and growth. Steven's three Crystal Gem guardians have no idea how to raise a half-human, half-gem child or what kinds of powers he might develop. Amethyst, Pearl, and Garnet frequently try to guess what gem powers Steven will have, and very often they guess wrong. For example, the Crystal Gems expect Steven's tears to have healing powers, but instead Steven learns that he has healing saliva. It is not until much later that Steven's tears develop magical powers, but rather than the power to heal wounds, his tears have the power to resurrect the dead. Improperly aided by the Crystal Gems, Steven is often surprised by his newfound abilities, sometimes leading to embarrassing situations, like when he accidentally traps himself and Connie in an impenetrable bubble, or situations that shape his understanding of his identity, like when he fuses with Connie into a nonbinary person named Stevonnie. Similar to the developing queer youth, Steven's hybrid body changes in ways that are surprising and often different than what is expected. The story follows Steven as he comes to terms with how the changes to his body, and his understanding of his family's history, shape his identity as a Crystal Gem.

*Steven Universe* has an active fandom of children, teens, and adults alike. The series has been adapted into companion books, comics, video games, and toys. Critics have praised the show's beautiful art style and direct approach to topics of gender and sexuality. As Steven continues to grow into a Crystal Gem, viewers of all kinds can join him on his continuing magical adventures.

*Christopher J. Owen*

See also: Lilo and Stitch; Masters of the Universe.

## FURTHER READING

Dunn, Eli. "*Steven Universe*, Fusion Magic, and the Queer Cartoon Carnivalesque." *Gender Forum*, no. 56, 2016, pp. 44–57.

## Strugatsky, Arkady and Boris

The body of work by Arkady Strugatsky (1925–1991) and Boris Strugatsky (1933–2012) includes 28 novels, six short-story collections, and one play. Their early work is modeled after the science fiction of writers such as Stanislaw Lem and features stories of humanity exploring space and settling the galaxy through scientific achievement and courageous actions. Writing in Soviet-era Russia, the brothers wanted to bring some human scale to the monumental vision provided by communist writers and to instill a tangibility into their fictionalized futures through the scientific methods, theories, and endeavors of the present. However, in their later works the Strugatskys shift to a more socially conscious mode of science fiction. They question the dogmatic utopian ideals of their earlier works and begin exploring themes of humanity standing in its own way. Instead of mankind spreading outward, these stories are introspections on humanity's value within the cosmos, and the Strugatskys' aliens shift from shadows of our past to reflections of the distant and uncaring universe that surrounds us.

The novels and stories that comprise the Strugatskys' "Noon Universe" nicely illustrate the idealistic utopian vision of their early work. In this world, communism and technological advancements have all but eradicated hunger, poverty, and crime, resulting in an Earth with a surplus of resources and little need for manual labor. As such, humans have turned their eyes to the sky for expansion, and the development of near-instantaneous interstellar travel affords them a near-limitless reach. Throughout the universe, some humans work as "progressors" who infiltrate less-advanced civilizations to accelerate their development. These alien civilizations are, of course, humanoid and are typically indistinguishable from Earth-born humans, aside from some minor genetic differences. Thus, these aliens function as shades of humanity's possible pasts that must be saved by the technologically and culturally advanced Earthlings.

*Hard to Be a God* (1964), for instance, tells the story of an Earthling Progressor during an undercover mission to advance a race of humanoids that is stuck in the Middle Ages. The ruling class of this alien civilization blames the educated and artistic for the ills of society and so persecutes scientists, poets, artists, and doctors as enemies of the state. The story's core themes of religion's power to oppress and the often brutal violence that shapes human history are, of course, filtered through the eyes of the Earthling protagonist. These lessons, while illustrated through a distant civilization, are recognizable and relatable—or very un-alien—to our own existence.

While the aliens of the Noon Universe are simply extensions of humanity that allow the human characters and readers alike to ruminate on mankind's past and possible futures, the aliens of *Roadside Picnic* (1972), the Strugatskys' most famous novel and the basis for Andrei Tarkovsky's film *Stalker*, are notable for their absence and leave us wondering about humanity's worth on a cosmic scale by asking the question: what if aliens barely noticed us at all?

The novel begins more than a decade after an event deemed a visitation. Not much is known about the visitors; the only traces left behind are the six sites of their landings, called Zones, that display unearthly physical properties and the similarly bizarre objects scattered throughout them. These enigmatic alien artifacts play a central role in the novel as entities that entice humanity into a desire for transcendence yet fail to provide it. The only contact with the aliens is indirect, through what they have left behind. While the Zone and the various dangers within provide the story with a backdrop of danger, the objects demand the most attention. They bring space down to the terrestrial plane and render its infiniteness and emptiness tangible. They demand to be understood without providing the means to do so and, consequently, produce feelings of frustration, resentment, and ennui. In *Roadside Picnic*, humanity has taken to resolving this dilemma in familiar ways: scientists research the objects to find utilitarian functions, others transform them into earthly commodities to be bought and sold, and some even regard them as sacrilegious relics to be destroyed.

The character Dr. Valentine Pillman acknowledges this discrepancy and bristles at the definition of intelligence as an unrelenting thirst for knowledge. He argues that, if given the choice, humanity would rather subscribe to a religious dogma that "allows you to have an unparalleled understanding of absolutely everything while knowing absolutely nothing." To Pillman, the notion of intelligent alien beings with a psychology analogous to humans is further proof of that flaw.

Pillman uses the analogy of the novel's title to describe the nature of the visitation. Rather than by the result of a grand scheme, he posits that the visitation occurred by coincidence, negating any self-aggrandizing significance that humanity has grafted onto it. He likens it to a recently deserted picnic site where the indigenous fauna investigate the strange new features of their once-familiar landscape: tire tracks, puddles of automotive oil, and paper trash. Pillman proposes that the aliens were no more concerned with humanity than the picnickers were with the critters. The theory suggests adopting an ambivalent attitude toward that which may always remain incomprehensible. Ultimately, any effort to decipher meaning is in vain. Transcendence, then, be it utopian or otherwise, is found in the acceptance that there is no grand plan for the universe and that no one's out there to save us but ourselves.

*Ryan House*

See also: Dick, Philip K.; Lem, Stanislaw; *Solaris*.

**FURTHER READING**

Cederlöf, Henriette. *Alien Places in Late Soviet Science Fiction: The "Unexpected Encounters" of Arkady and Boris Strugatsky as Novels and Films.* University of Stockholm, 2014.

Csicsery-Ronay Jr., Istvan. "Towards the Last Fairy Tale: On the Fairy-Tale Paradigm in the Strugatskys' Science Fiction, 1963–1972." *Science Fiction Studies*, vol. 13, no. 1, 1986, pp. 1–41.

Lem, Stanislaw. "About the Strugatskys' Roadside Picnic." *Science-Fiction Studies*, vol. 10, no. 3, 1983, pp. 317–32. Reprinted in *Microworlds* by Stanislaw Lem, Harcourt, 1984, pp. 243–78.

# Sun Ra

Depending on one's definition of "birth," Le Sony'r Ra (his legal name after 1952) was born either as Herman Poole "Sonny" Blount in Birmingham, Alabama, in 1914 (died 1993), or as Sun Ra sometime between the mid-1930s and early 1950s, following a conversation with cosmic beings on Saturn. Much about Sun Ra's life remains obscure; until John Szwed's groundbreaking biography, Ra's birthdate could not even be established with certainty. This is, in part, because the artist went to great lengths to obscure it—even leading off one interview by saying, "I think of myself as a complete mystery. To myself." But his reticence about his own past must be balanced against the boundless communication he carried out through music. Whatever the nature of the alien message he received on Saturn, his devotion to its continued transmission was lifelong and absolute.

The exact date is the only persistent inconsistency of this encounter. Ra was otherwise very clear about the details of his voyage: aliens with little antennae over their ears and eyes teleported him across the solar system to inform him that he would serve as their messenger, speaking to the people of Earth through music.

Whether or not this visitation predates the great post–World War II UFO craze, Ra's experience transcends the flying-saucer narrative of the sort circulated by Raymond A. Palmer and analyzed by C. G. Jung, as evidenced by the profound life changes and abundant creativity that followed. For Sun Ra, there was nothing remotely metaphorical about the alien message he received; he had been told to serve as a conduit channeling the cosmic beings' "space music," so channel he would. By the time he changed his name, Ra—already a talented and ferociously dedicated jazz musician, with several successful ensembles under his belt—had left Birmingham for Chicago in order to assemble The Arkestra, the ever-changing, ever-touring performance troupe he would lead until his death in 1993. Over those four decades, Ra and his Arkestra would record over 1,000 songs across more than 100 albums, all the while playing concerts everywhere from Montreux to Tokyo to Egypt.

Throughout that time, the musical styles and personnel of the Arkestra remained in flux, but Sun Ra consistently drew on the iconography of science fiction and cosmic voyages for inspiration, whether in the bebop-inflected swing of *Sun Ra and His Solar Arkestra Visits Planet Earth* (1956), the electronic experimentation of *The Nubians of Plutonia* (1959), the stripped-down acoustics of *The Futuristic Sounds of Sun Ra* (1961), the outer limits–free improvisation of *The Heliocentric Worlds of Sun Ra* (1965), the polyrhythms and synthesizer blasts of *Space Is the Place* (1973), or the reconfigured songbook standards of *Sunrise in Different Dimensions* (1980). Ra embraced technological innovations not only in the studio, where he was among the first to make extensive use of tape delay and various electronic keyboards such as the Minimoog, but also in live concert. In particular, throughout the late 1970s and 1980s he incorporated the Outer Space Visual Communicator, a wholly visual instrument that took kaleidoscopic images drawn by the machine's inventor, Bill Sebastian, ran them through hundreds of sequencers, and projected the results in real time on a large screen behind the performers.

Although the music often verged on chaos, it was borne out of the strict discipline Ra imposed as bandleader. For a while, the Arkestra lived in a communal space in New York City, where Ra could and did command practices around the clock. He pushed musicians far outside their comfortable ranges of performance, requiring every Arkestra member to train as a percussionist, providing cryptic guidance during and after sessions, and occasionally abandoning members who he felt no longer made the grade. But this sternness was shot through with levity, especially in the form of the pseudo-Egyptian costumes worn by the group, partly as an immediately identifiable trademark among the crowded field of big-band jazz, partly as a reminder that avant-gardists ought not take themselves too seriously.

But the costumes and pageantry pointed as well to the idiosyncratic philosophy Sun Ra developed over decades of reading and public discourse. It was perhaps best presented in a series of lectures delivered in Berkeley in 1971, when Ra was artist-in-residence at the University of California, teaching a course on "The Black Man in the Cosmos." The reading list for the course, preserved by the university, included psi-fi favorites such as Madame Blavatsky, P. D. Ouspensky, and the Book of Oahspe, in addition to an array of black poets and Afrocentric scholarship. Ra's lecturing style proved to be as free-associative as his music, darting between numerology, African and American history, multilingual puns, and scriptural exegesis, in particular the King James Bible and the Book of the Dead. His synthesis of these elements owed much to the Freemasonry he first encountered in Birmingham, except infused with black nationalism and a cautious space-age optimism—a potent brew that, despite Ra's appeals to the wisdom of the past, would come to be known (somewhat anachronistically, given Ra's steady appeals to the wisdom of the past) as "Afrofuturism."

The ideas developed in these lectures and various interviews were given dramatic form in the 1974 film *Space Is the Place*, in which Sun Ra and the Arkestra touch down on another planet and decide it's ripe for colonization by black people, who will benefit from the lack of vibrational disturbances caused by whites. Ra seeks to teleport willing colonists via music, but to spread his message he must overcome white, racist NASA scientists, as well as the internalized racism of the black community, personified as the super-cool and stylish Overseer. Eventually Ra overcomes both, taking with him to the new planet all willing black folks (including, in at least one case, the "black parts" of one media mogul, leaving the capitalist "white parts" behind) and likely destroying Earth in the process. Though the core of the movie is Arkestral concert footage, and many of the plotted segments are played for laughs, nonetheless the message comes through that black humans on Earth must consider themselves aliens on a planet not their own; while cultural forms like jazz may offer respite or even escape, even those are subject to cooption by forces within the community that are complicit with the racist power structure.

*Andrew Ferguson*

See also: Bowie, David; Heaven's Gate; Okorafor, Nnedi.

## FURTHER READING

Ra, Sun. *The Wisdom of Sun Ra: Sun Ra's Polemical Broadsheets and Streetcorner Leaflets*, edited by Anthony Elms and John Corbett, University of Chicago Press, 2006.
Szwed, John F. *Space Is the Place: The Lives and Times of Sun Ra.* Pantheon, 1997.
Youngquist, Paul. *A Pure Solar World: Sun Ra and the Birth of Afrofuturism.* University of Texas Press, 2016.

## Superman

Created by Jerry Siegel and Joel Schuster, Superman, as he would become known, first appeared in *Action Comics* #1, June 1938. Since then, the hero has been the star of comic strips, comic books, radio shows, live-action television shows, television cartoons, video games, films (both live-action and animated), pop songs, and a Broadway musical.

Being heavily influenced by the fantastic pulp stories of the time, Siegel and Shuster placed Superman's origin on a distant, fictional planet, Krypton. At the zenith of its scientific advancement, the planet is dying, and its top scientist Jor-L (who would later become Jor-El) builds a rocket to launch his infant son, Kal-L (Kal-El), to Earth.

Kal-L is adopted on Earth by farmers Jonathan and Martha Kent, who name him Clark. As Clark grows older, he demonstrates various superpowers, such as significantly enhanced strength, speed, intelligence, and endurance. He is bulletproof, and his body can resist extreme heat and cold. Additionally, his eyes can see through any material (except lead) with x-ray vision, and they can project beams of intense heat. His lungs have immense capacity and strength, enabling him to expel tornado-force gusts of wind so cold that they can freeze objects.

Raised on the Kent farm in the fictional town of Smallville, Clark is taught traditional American values, such as the benefits of hard work, the necessity of morality, and the importance of justice. As a child in Smallville, Clark struggles to be himself, identify with humanity, and conceal his alien origin. The 2015 film

*Man of Steel* (dir. Zack Snyder) shows him as an elementary schoolboy running out of a classroom hysterically as his new powers begin to emerge. The television show *Smallville* recounts Clark's complicated life as a teenager, where his adopted father, Jonathan, forbids him from doing normal activities such as playing football for fear that Clark could accidentally hurt someone. A similar scene occurs in *Superman* (dir: Richard Donner, 1978) where a high-school Clark is the football team's towel person, bullied by the players on the team. Even as an adult, Clark struggles with the duality of being alien and human.

When he moves to Metropolis as a young adult and starts working as a reporter at *The Daily Planet*, Clark meets fellow reporter Lois Lane and instantly develops a crush on her. Lois, however, becomes infatuated with Clark's alter ego Superman, who openly reveals his alien origin, and treats Clark as a friend. For over half a century of publication, Clark hides his Superman identity from Lois for various reasons, depending on the storytellers. Following *The Death of Superman* (DC Comics, 1992) showcasing Superman's death and eventual resurrection, Lois and Clark get married in *Superman: The Wedding Album* (DC Comics, 1996) to coincide with the plot of the television series *Lois and Clark: The New Adventures of Superman* (1993–1997).

Cover of the comic book *Superman* #326, August 1978. (Wisconsinart/Dreamstime.com)

DC Comics ended its timeline with an incident called "Flashpoint" (2011) and began all its titles again at #1. The pre-"Flashpoint" Superman is one of the few who survived, because his city had been preserved outside of time and space for one year by the sentient computer Brainiac. During this year, Lois and Clark have a son, Jonathan Samuel Kent. After arriving in the post-Flashpoint timeline—also called the "New 52" timeline, which ran from 2011–2016—Clark and Lois change their last name to "White" and live as a normal couple. In essence, Clark has fulfilled his dream: to live a human existence with a loving family like the one in which he was raised. Although he secretly prevents incidents in this new timeline that caused tragedy in his own timeline, he remains in the shadows, hiding his Superman identity. He no longer has alien threats such as Mongul, Brainiac,

Mister Mxyzptlk, or General Zod bringing attention to his otherworldly origin. Instead, he can blend in with humans and take on the guise of a normal family man without worrying anyone will expose him.

Meanwhile, the New 52 timeline has its own Superman, one who is younger and not as powerful as Clark White. The New 52 Superman seems much more at peace with his alien nature. In fact, most of his story lines at this time focus almost entirely on Superman as a superpowered alien and not on Clark Kent, the masquerading space man. After fighting and subsequently being transformed into a New 52 version of Doomsday (the creature that killed Superman in the pre-Flashpoint *Death of Superman*), the New 52 Superman meets other versions of himself. One is a man who insists he is the real Clark Kent/Superman but has "solar flare" powers, and the other is Clark White, the Superman from pre-Flashpoint. The solar-flare Clark Kent shows that he is a threat to both Clark White's and the New 52 Superman's family and friends, so they join together to fight the solar-flare Superman. After the battle ends, Clark White is the only Superman to survive. Seeing that Earth needs a Superman, Clark White reprises his role as the Man of Steel and ushers in DC Comics' next phase: *Rebirth* (2016), where he has a clearer balance between his alien origin and his human life.

Since his first appearance in June 1938, Superman has undergone many changes: he has learned to fly, become vulnerable to kryptonite and magic, lost his powers, and gained new powers. The one thing that remains consistent with every incarnation of Superman is his alien origin and his attempt to reconcile it with his human identity.

*Brett Butler*

*See also*: Green Lantern; Martian Manhunter; Mekon, the; *Nemesis the Warlock*.

## FURTHER READING

Daniels, Lee. *The Complete History of Superman: The Life and Times of the Man of Steel*. Chronicle Books, 1998.
Eco, Umberto. "The Myth of Superman." *Diacritics*, vol. 2, no. 1, 1972, pp. 14–22.
Tye, Larry. *Superman: The High-Flying History of America's Most Enduring Hero*. Random House, 2012.

# T

## *Teletubbies*

*Teletubbies* (1997–2001) is a television program primarily aimed at preschool children. Created by Anne Wood and Andrew Davenport and developed by Ragdoll Productions, it was the first television program that specifically targeted children as young as 12 months old. Each episode follows a predictable pattern: the Teletubbies participate in a group activity, receive a video message via the television on their stomachs, watch said message, which always involves young human children involved in some activity, and then end with a group dance. Each activity is repeated, with the exception of the final group dance. All of the Teletubbies participate in the group activity and final group dance; however, only one Teletubby is selected to play the message in each episode. *Teletubbies* was also a major cultural phenomenon with live performances and memorabilia pushing the program and its characters to worldwide popularity. However, this worldwide popularity also opened up the program for criticism, particularly from religious conservatives, such as Reverend Jerry Falwell.

The stars of the program, the Teletubbies themselves, are the key aliens in the work. They live on a small, idyllic green world, guided by a singular animated sun with a baby's face in the center. Each Teletubby has its own signature color, head antenna, and personal object. Tinky Winky, the leader and largest of the group, is purple and male, with an upside-down, triangle-shaped antenna. His item of choice is a red bag, which, to some viewers, resembles a purse. The other male Teletubby is Dipsy, a neon green humanoid with a unicornesque horn for an antenna. He is the second-largest Teletubby, aloof and cool in demeanor, whose item of choice is a Dalmatian-patterned hat. The third Teletubby is the yellow female Laa-Laa. Her antenna is a set of asymmetrical and connected horns, with one side half the size of the other. She loves to sing and dance, and her item of choice is a large orange ball. The final Teletubby and second female of the group is Po. Her fur is a deep bright red, and her antenna is circular in shape. She is the smallest and most immature of the group and has chosen an orange scooter as her preferred item.

*Teletubbies*' intended purpose is to showcase a childlike wonder unencumbered by direct adult supervision and to, hopefully, replicate that sense of wonder in the children that watch the program, attend the live performances, or play with the toys and memorabilia. This goal replicates the ideas that other worlds and other creatures are ripe for discovery, as seen in television programs such as *Star Trek* and *Martian Successor Nadesico*. *Teletubbies* introduces that sense of discovery to a younger audience and creates a sense of exchange between the childlike aliens and human children. The Teletubbies themselves, with each video they watch of

The BBC children's series *Teletubbies* (1997–), featuring main characters (from left) Po, Laa-Laa, Dipsy, and Tinky-Winky. (PBS/Photofest)

human children on a supposed Earth, a video that is a physical part of their body, are enchanted by the regular lives of the unfamiliar children, as they cook with their parents, clean the family cars, or make crafts. At the same time, the audience—assumed to be children of similar age and maturity—experience a sense of discovery in watching the Teletubbies go about their daily routine. In this way, the otherness of the alien is diminished; instead, the Teletubbies and their child viewers become mutual virtual playmates who are partners on the journey of discovery that is growing up and maturing. As Jonathan Bignell argues in his article "Familiar Aliens: *Teletubbies* and Postmodern Childhood," "*Teletubbies* casts childhood as both familiar and alien—just as the Teletubbies themselves are—and poses television as a mediator of the uncertain boundaries between adulthood and childhood, familiar and alien, human and inhuman" (374). As the Teletubbies showcase a childlike wonder and evoke a similar wonder in their audience, they create a sense that childhood is an alien time of discovery, alien to the experience, maturity, and normality supposed in adulthood.

However, the "controversial" nature of the program—in particular the "gender performance" of Tinky Winky, a purple creature, somewhat maternal, whose item of choice is a "bag"—opens up problematic readings of gender and sexuality when examining nonhuman humanoids. Reverend Jerry Falwell, an outspoken social and religious conservative, marked these traits as "gay" and noted that this behavior would then teach young boys to be "gay." The problem that both Falwell and other readers of gendered behavior have when analyzing the Teletubbies

(Hendershot; Powell and Abels) is transposing human gender stereotypes onto nonhuman humanoid aliens. In these cases, Judith Butler's theory of performativity is not applicable. These critics apply Western gender norms to creatures not even of our planet; rather, viewers should look to the Teletubbies as examples not only of self-discovery but also as examples of freedom from human constraints of gender. Tinky Winky serves as a prime example of what masculinity can look like, offering a view of a world free of the limitations of ascribed gender performance. Though they can be seen as "uncannily monstrous and inhuman" (Bignell 380), the Teletubbies offer a view of intelligent life that makes the alien familiar and the familiar alien, and, by doing so, frees both their audience and themselves from human constraints so as to discover identities free from said constraints.

*Nathaniel Fuller*

See also: *Clangers, The*; *Dr. Xargle*; *Steven Universe*.

## FURTHER READING

Bignell, Jonathan. "Familiar Aliens: *Teletubbies* and Postmodern Childhood." *Screen*, vol. 46, no. 3, Autumn 2005, pp. 373–87.

Hendershot, Heather. "Teletubby Trouble." *Television Quarterly*, vol. 31, no. 1, Spring 2000, pp. 18–25.

Powell, Kimberly A. and Lori Abels. "Sex-Role Stereotypes in TV Programs Aimed at the Preschool Audience: An Analysis of *Teletubbies* and *Barney & Friends*." *Women and Language*, vol. 25, no. 2, Spring 2002, pp. 14–22.

## *Tenchi Muyo!*

The *Tenchi Muyo!* franchise began in 1992 with the first Original Video Animation (OVA) series, directed by Hiroki Hayashi, and was followed by a second OVA series, helmed by Kenichi Yatani in 1993–1994. The manga series *No Need for Tenchi!* (1994–2000), which was a spin-off from the anime, has had as lasting an effect on the anime and manga genre as its animated counterpart, especially for Western audiences. The franchise has several incarnations, but the original OVA series is the best known and was among the first anime titles readily available on mainstream broadcasting outside of Japan.

The series follows the titular character, Tenchi Masaki, an average 17-year-old boy on Earth who finds himself at the center of a galactic conflict. In the first episode, Tenchi unwittingly releases the powerful "demon" Ryoko, who is actually a space pirate wanted for the destruction she wrought on planet Jurai. Royal emissaries from planet Jurai, Princess Ayeka and her younger sister, Sasami, soon arrive, seeking vengeance. However, their ship is damaged in the pursuit, and the sisters end up stranded on Earth, where they are taken in by Tenchi and his family. Shortly thereafter, a galactic police agent, Mihoshi, bumbles her way to Earth in pursuit of Ryoko, crash-lands, and joins Tenchi and the others in what becomes a cornerstone in the "harem" anime genre.

In anime and manga, a harem series features a prominent male protagonist surrounded by a supporting cast of women, most of whom have some romantic or sexual interest in him. The male protagonist may show varying degrees of interest in each or all of the women, but the running question of the series is often "Which one will he choose?" Tenchi's harem involves alien women who all strive for his affection in various ways. These female characters—Ryoko, Ayeka, Sasami, and Mihoshi—are all humanoid without any distinct "alien" characteristics beyond pointy ears and the ability to pilot giant spaceships. However, despite appearing human, their "alienness" remains a staple of the series, as they must learn to cope with Earth customs, especially with regard to love. It is significant, then, that Tenchi's "harem" is composed of exclusively alien characters, as they become objects of desire—though specifically not for Tenchi.

The show's drama is the fierce competition for Tenchi's affection, especially between Ryoko and Ayeka. These female characters are beautiful, and frequent attention is paid to their bodies. Ryoko is often unabashedly naked and teases Ayeka for her smaller breasts; Ayeka makes repeated jabs at Ryoko's age by calling her skin or breasts "saggy"; Sasami will someday grow up into the lovely Tsunami (a personification of her living spaceship), though until then she is an adorable little-sister character; and Mihoshi's dark skin and platinum-blond hair makes her appear more exotic and alluring, complete with a Playboy-style bunny tail on her police uniform. In addition to individual body types, each woman has a distinct, even stereotypical, attitude. Ryoko is tomboyish, aggressive, and short-tempered. Conversely, Ayeka is haughty, refined, and easily embarrassed about sex, unlike Ryoko. Ayeka's younger sister, Sasami, is in every way a happy and bubbly child, acting more like a little sister than a romantic rival—though she is still seen as competition by Ryoko and Ayeka. Mihoshi is an almost painfully stereotypical "dumb blonde" who constantly causes trouble with her absentmindedness and ditzy demeanor. This alien harem, then, is peopled with different and distinct options, each one playing to a certain romantic trope (the aggressor/tomboy, the chaste girl, the little sister, the ditz). What is significant, though, is that in the original OVA series, Tenchi never shows any special interest in any of the girls. At best, Tenchi views and loves each of them as members of his family; at worst they annoy him. In this way, the series is less concerned with whom Tenchi will choose, but rather whom the (male) viewer chooses.

Many "fan-service" scenes, where the women are naked in hot springs or end up in sexual positions, happen without Tenchi even being present. Or when he is, he quickly flees the scene. Thus, the women (and their bodies) are not displayed so much for his benefit as for the male audience. Moreover, Tenchi shows no particular interest in their various appearances, and yet the series puts the girls in various scenarios that would test their womanly aptitude along with their unique personality and alien otherness. For example, in the seventh episode, "The Night Before the Carnival," the girls decide to do research on Earth's love customs by reading cheesy romance manga ("a handbook on how to win the love of someone you love—Earth style") and try out various techniques on Tenchi to win him over. Of course, their methods are tired tropes that are only compounded by the girls' lack of familiarity with them. Ryoko, in one attempt, "bumps" into Tenchi—but actually sends him flying—and coyly apologizes and introduces herself, which just leaves Tenchi bruised and confused. While Tenchi may be bewildered by the girls' actions, male viewers would recognize the tropes, which play into overblown fantasies of "meeting the one." In this way, the male viewer would connect with whichever character's attempt resonated most with him and spoke to his personal fantasy, making these women members of his harem rather than Tenchi's.

Indeed, there is "no need for Tenchi," as the original manga title would suggest, as these alien women are presented as not objects of desire for him but for the male audience. Considered one of the most famous harem titles, *Tenchi Muyo!* reveals a troubling and persistent trope of depicting women as objects of male desire, which is here compounded by their alien otherness—a sentiment that continues to echo throughout the anime and manga artform, even decades later.

*Charles Yow*

See also: *Animorphs*; *Masters of the Universe*; *Steven Universe*.

## FURTHER READING

Anime. "Tenchi Mayo!" *TV Tropes*. https://tvtropes.org/pmwiki/pmwiki.php/Anime/TenchiMuyo.

Martin, Theron. "The Complete Guide to 25 Years of *Tenchi Mayo!*" *Anime News Network*, May 2017. https://www.animenewsnetwork.com/feature/2017-05-24/the-complete-guide-to-25-years-of-tenchi-muyo/.116203.

## Tepper, Sheri S.

One of the most common images of aliens in popular culture is a cartoon of an alien demanding that an inappropriate person or object should "Take me to your leader." As far as I can discover, only Sheri Tepper (1929–2016) developed that into a novel: *The Fresco* (2000). The inappropriate person is a middle-aged Hispanic woman from California, and the two aliens appear to her like giant bugs. Only gradually does it emerge that some of the alien species were rather more interested in depositing their eggs inside large human males or in hunting humans for food than in helping Earth. *The Fresco* is more out-and-out satirical than most of Tepper's books; the aliens are much more comprehensible than most of Tepper's aliens, which tend to be mysterious, or dangerous, or both.

Most of Tepper's aliens can be divided into invisible slaves or giant planetary beings. Invisible slaves appear in different guises, and not all of them are alien: in two novels, however—*Raising the Stones* (1990) and *Six Moon Dance* (1998)—the invisible slaves are aliens and play a significant role in the narrative.

The Gharm of *Raising the Stones* are small, elf-like aliens whom the brutal Voorstoders (misogynist followers of a patriarchal religion) have brought with them to the planet Ahabar. The much more humane government on Ahabar asks the multiplanet Authority whether this slavery is actually legal. In a typical piece of Tepper irony, the question gets lost among the nitpicking legalists. Authority refers the question to the Religion Advisory, who refers it to the Theological Panel, which says that maybe slavery and cruelty are an integral part of religion. In the end, however, it is the brutal treatment of the Gharm that arouses the hostility of the rest of humanity to the Voorstoders and brings about their downfall.

The Timmys of *Six Moon Dance* are the invisible slaves who do not wholly fit into this pattern, in that their subservience and their labors on behalf of humans do seem to be in large part voluntary: if they wish, they could disappear at any time through the hidden passages in the walls of the houses, and, indeed, by the time the Questioner appears on Newholme to enquire after any possible infringements of Haraldson's Edicts (such as settling a planet that has an indigenous population, as the Timmys seem to be), they have already disappeared. They turn out to be merely individualized parts of Kaorugi, the vast being who fills the planet, but otherwise they fit the pattern. After a certain age, children are taught that the Timmys do not exist; they do not see them and never talk about them.

Kaorugi is just one of several planetary beings, or world-spirits, that we meet in Tepper's works. Kaorugi, in *Six Moon Dance*, is changed by its encounter with a Quaggi, a huge star-roving being with wings that act as solar sails. Tepper's ideas on world-spirits are probably influenced by Lovelock's ideas about Gaia: indeed, she mentions Earth's world-spirit in *Singer from the Sea*, which culminates in the revelation that Haven's world-spirit has produced humans with gills, who can live in Haven's seas.

The Marjorie Morningstar trilogy—*Grass* (1989), *Raising the Stones* (1990), and *Sideshow* (1992)—might better be called the Arbai trilogy, since Marjorie is mostly off-stage in the second and third books. The Arbai are Tepper's version of the Old Ones who frequently occur in science-fictional treatments of the human settlement of the Galaxy: they seem to be extinct but have left extensive ruins and some surviving technology. In *Grass*, Marjorie and her husband are sent to investigate why the planet Grass is, alone, free of the plague that is threatening human colonies. They are sent because they are expert horse riders. But the Hippae are not horses: they are huge, ferociously armored beasts who control their human riders; the hounds are as large as Earth's horses; and the foxen are far closer to dragons than to foxes. It takes Marjorie much of the book to unravel the complex connections between these alien species. The Hippae hunt the foxen because the foxen eat the peepers, which transform into hounds; some of the hounds transform into Hippae; and a few of the Hippae eventually transform into foxen. The foxen eat the peepers to attempt to control the population of the rabid Hippae, but they long to find a way out of this vicious genetic cycle. The highly intelligent foxen are at the evolutionary apex of life on Grass, and they know one secret about the Hippae. In their uncontrollable desire to dominate and destroy, the Hippae have used the planet-linking transporter machines of the Arbai to spread the plague that eventually wiped out the Arbai themselves.

At the end of *Grass*, Marjorie and one of the foxen enter an Arbai transporter. In *Raising the Stones* we learn that the prophetess arrived on the planet Thyker 1,000 years earlier, riding a dragon. "'My name is Morgori Oestrydingh,' she had said" (ch. 3). In *Sideshow* she is on the planet Elsewhere, calling herself Jory the Traveler; she travels with an old man called Asner. Elsewhere is the last planet in the human galaxy that has not been taken over—"enslaved"—by the Hobbs Land Gods, the last and most interesting of Tepper's aliens that we will look at.

Hobbs Land (settled by Hobbs Transystem Foods) had an indigenous people, the Owlbrit. The last of them died out not long after the human settlement began, but they left behind some of their language and their gods. *Raising the Stones* begins with the death of one of those gods. We see much of this through the eyes of Sam, Samasnier Girat, one of the most sympathetic of Tepper's humans. They bury the god, and they build a temple, eerily knowing exactly what to do. From the god's body a fungus spreads, and the fibers of that underground mycelium are used to spread the dominion of the gods. Hobbs Land becomes "enslaved" by the gods. Sam shows us what this "alien enslavement" consists of: a growth of empathy among individuals and a tendency for communities to settle their problems peacefully. By *Sideshow*, Jory and her friend Asner (the older Samasnier Girat) know that the Hobbs Land gods are not gods, or aliens, but merely a creation, the Arbai Device, left behind by the Arbai as a means for species to solve the problems of living together. Tepper is always trying to blur the distinction between human and alien; here, she suggests that this blurring is human destiny.

*Edward James*

See also: Butler, Octavia E.; Le Guin, Ursula K.; Russell, Mary Doria; Tiptree Jr., James.

**FURTHER READING**

Beswick, Norman. "Ideology and Dogman in the 'Ferocious' SF Novels of Sheri S. Tepper." *Foundation*, no. 71, Autumn 1997, pp. 32–45.
Jones, Gwyneth, "Sheri S. Tepper: Avenging Angels and Worlds of Wonder." *Imagination/Space: Essays and Talks on Fiction, Feminism, Technology, and Politics*, edited by Gwyneth Jones, Aqueduct Press, 2009, pp. 73–79.
Kelso, Sylvia. *A Glance from Nowhere: Sheri S. Tepper's Fantasy and SF*. Nimrod Publications, 1997.

## They Live

Director John Carpenter's *They Live* (1988) is both an important intervention in the alien-invasion sub-genre and a film that presents a glaring indictment of American society under the eight-year presidency of Ronald Reagan. Based on Ray Nelson's short story "Eight O'Clock in the Morning" (1963), it is a poignant satire that draws attention to concerning issues surrounding growing commercialism and the vacuity of consumer capitalism; failing American national identity and ideology under the auspices of so-called Reaganomics; fractured working classes and the victimization of the American working poor; surveillance culture; and the characterization of general media culture (specifically television) as a cultural pacifier.

The film follows everyman John Nada (Roddy Piper), characterized as a victim of the postindustrial climate of the late 1980s and a man who has nothing, as his name would suggest, but the clothes on his back. Finding his way to Los Angeles, and specifically a shantytown named Chesterfield, Nada meets Frank (Keith David), a fellow member of the working poor who is cynical about the conditions of everyday life under consumer capitalism ("He who has the gold makes the rules"). This is in contrast to Nada's own hopeful, optimistic, and perhaps naive views: "I believe in America. I follow the rules." The film, then, is a scathing satire of those who make the rules and those who blindly follow that ideology. As the film progresses, we see Nada transform "from mild-mannered, lower-class, conformist American patriot to volatile, classless, individualistic American anarchist."

As Nada begins to integrate into the community of Chesterfield, he witnesses a television broadcast interrupted by a mysterious signal that is a marked and significant disruption to the otherwise banal images on the television screen. As the images of product advertisements fade, a bearded man is heard articulating alternative propaganda through the set that is suggestive not of an invasion per se but a rather insidious hostile takeover from beings that are already among us: "We are living in an artificially induced state of consciousness that resembles sleep. . . . They have created a repressive society, and we are their unwitting accomplices. Their intention to rule rests with the annihilation of consciousness." This is the moment in the film where it becomes apparent that there is a resistance movement poised to counter the problematic ideals of those in control (a clearly alien presence) and the artifice of the film's narrative world (which has been installed by these otherworldly invaders).

The alien population (referred to as "creatures") are positioned as other to the working poor, and their true appearance, when revealed, is akin to a corrupted version of humanity itself. These creatures take the shape of seemingly ordinary members of society, albeit those that belong to the American upper classes, occupying a position of authority and high cultural esteem (namely police officers, politicians, and celebrities). Although the aliens appear normal on the surface, it is the manufacturing of special sunglasses that allows the resistance to see beyond the veil. The audience first see the ruling alien class through the eyes of Nada as he dons these "ideology sunglasses." The extraterrestrials appear as corroded skeletal humanoids with bulbous eyes and protruding jawlines (the aliens are rather aptly described by Nada as "real fucking ugly!"). Whereas the alien creature in *The Thing* is driven by the desire to attain complete human assimilation, and therefore eradication, the alien creatures in *They Live* are driven by the desire to enslave and master the culture that is beneath them.

The cityscape is also shown to be an artificial construct formed by the creatures, populated by diverse advertisement billboards and commercial retail outlets. Through the sunglasses, these landmarks are rendered in stark monochrome with advertisements revealed to be subliminal pronouncements, commanding the human race to "OBEY," "MARRY AND REPRODUCE," have "NO INDEPENDENT THOUGHT," and "CONSUME," "SLEEP," and "SUBMIT." The American dollar bill is replaced by sheets of blank paper adorned with a bold slogan: "THIS IS YOUR GOD." It is later revealed that ordinary members of society are effectively being recruited by the aliens and, if they are deemed useful, joining the elite invaders. The film's resistance leader Gilbert (Peter Jason) states that "the creatures are trading wealth, power" and that "most of us just sell-out right away . . . we'll do anything to be rich."

This is played out near the climax of the film as a spokesperson for the alien creatures refers to the masses gathered at a formal dining event aboard an alien craft as "the human power-elite" and explains that they have been instrumental in the "ongoing quest for multidimensional expansion." Carpenter's critique of consumerism and passivity in the face of mass culture is therefore manifested initially through the subliminal proclamations issued by those in control and the revelation of their class/capital agenda. The creatures are thus characterized as free enterprisers that "[exploit] America like a Third World country." Here, aliens function as a metaphor for "Reagan-era yuppies and the success ethic of the decade."

The legacy of the film is evinced by its lasting cult potential and in the many forms of popular culture that have borrowed and appropriated its imagery, ranging from the popularity of Sheppard Farley's "OBEY" alternative clothing label to the more recent *Consume* series of artworks produced by Hal Hefner. These works depict contemporary cultural figures such as Donald Trump, Hillary Clinton, Miley Cyrus, and Kim Kardashian in the same fashion as the film's skeletal alien humanoids. Slogans such as "Obey the Internet of False Idols" and "Trust My Image so that I may Prey Upon You" are indications that the sentiments initiated by Carpenter in 1988 were indeed prophetic and still find resonance in a cultural landscape where the 45th president of the United States is a former reality television star with a background in multi-billion-dollar real-estate development.

*Thomas Joseph Watson*

See also: *Close Encounters of the Third Kind*; Dick, Philip K.; *Thing, The*; V.

## FURTHER READING

Decker, Mark. "The Mysteries of Los Angeles; or *They Live*, 'Eight O'Clock in the Morning,' City Mysteries, and the Apotheosis of the Mechanic Hero." *Extrapolation*, vol. 55, no. 21, 2014, pp. 173–97.

Donovan, Barna William. *Conspiracy Films: A Tour of Dark Places in the American Conscious*. McFarland, 2011.

Wilson, D. Harlan. *They Live (Cultographies)*. Wallflower Press, 2015.

## *The Thing*

Comparable to the intangible dread that defines the tales written by revered horror writer H. P. Lovecraft and Jack Finney's *The Body Snatchers* (1955), John W. Campbell's pulp novella "Who Goes There?"—first published in the August 1938 edition of *Astounding Science Fiction* magazine—is often regarded as his most significant contribution to science fiction and one of the first major works from the genre's "Golden Age" (1938–1946). Described by Campbell himself as "mood-concept" science fiction, the paranoia-inducing story focuses on an isolated group of Antarctica-based scientists who recover an extraterrestrial that crash-landed and remained frozen for millennia. Thawing the alien revives it, and it is soon revealed to be a predatory creature that assumes the shape, memories, and personality of any living organism it assimilates. In the years since its publication, Campbell's novella has been used as the inspiration for three films: the Howard Hawks/Christian Nyby Cold War–era "flying saucer" classic, *The Thing from Another*

*World* (1951); John Carpenter's equally esteemed body-horror extravaganza, *The Thing* (1982); and its considerably less celebrated prequel, Matthijs van Heijningen Jr.'s *The Thing* (2011).

Belonging to the highly prominent slew of 1950s SF films—alongside *The Day the Earth Stood Still* (1951), *Invaders from Mars* (1953), *It Came from Outer Space* (1953), and so on—Hawks's/Nyby's film is the loosest adaption of Campbell's novel and differs from its source material in several key areas. Certainly the most distinct change comes with the depiction of the alien creature; while Campbell's novella describes it as possessing "[t]hree mad, hate-filled eyes" and "a face ringed with a writhing, loathsome nest of worms," the Hawks/Nyby "thing" (James Arness beneath the makeup) is a much simpler humanoid creature, strongly evoking Frankenstein's monster from Universal's original cycle (1931–1939). Furthermore, the creature in the film lacks the imitating capabilities of its novella counterpart, instead being a plant-based organism that reproduces asexually by depositing seedlings. Remorselessly attacking anything that inhibits its reproduction, this extraterrestrial is also presented as a tangible threat to our world. That the "thing" is also clearly distinguishable from the American scientists and military personnel—as opposed to imitating them—facilitates its being figured as a personification of the Cold War–threat that almost unanimously informed all 1950s flying saucer films.

Scripted by Bill Lancaster, Carpenter's film directly aims to invoke the acute paranoia and apocalyptic dread of Campbell's novella by returning the story to immense Antarctic isolation and reinstating the organism's imitation survival instinct, brought spectacularly to life by Rob Bottin's epochal practical special effects. Again, the titular "thing" embodies a particularly pessimistic view of extraterrestrial life and greatly contributes to what is an uncompromisingly bleak film. Indeed, regarding *The Thing*'s initial box office and critical failure due to its being released in the wake of Steven Spielberg's immeasurably more positive speculation of alien life, *E.T. the Extraterrestrial* (1982), Anne Billson writes that "[*The Thing*] couldn't have been released as a less opportune time." The character's official introduction to the organism arrives when the "sled dog imitation" that breached the camp reveals its true form in a gruesome effluvia of tentacles, viscera, and slime as it attempts to absorb the real dogs. From then on, Carpenter's film shapeshifts into a white-knuckle chamber piece interspersed with scenes of spectacular bodily insurrection as the team attempt to delineate the "imposters" among them and prevent the organism from taking over the planet.

Alongside Philip Kaufman's *Invasion of the Body Snatchers*, Tobe Hooper's *Invaders from Mars* (1986), David Cronenberg's *The Fly* (1986), and Chuck Russell's *The Blob* (1988), Carpenter's film is a remake of a discernibly McCarthy-era/Cold War–informed science-fiction film that reappropriates the subtext for its own cultural moment. The deadly cellular predator in *The Thing* can be equated to the unseen threat prevalent in the inception of the AIDS epidemic. Eerily corresponding with the treatment of AIDS, infected characters in the film are detected via a blood test.

Following the significantly increased stature of Carpenter's film since its disastrous original release, a direct prequel depicting the events of the doomed

The title creature from *The Thing*, a parasitic extraterrestrial that assimilates and then imitates other organisms (1982), directed by John Carpenter. (Pictorial Press Ltd./Alamy Stock Photo)

Norwegian camp—of which the 1982 film detailed only the aftermath—arrived in 2011. Though ably portraying the discovery of the alien spacecraft and providing seamless cohesion for motifs and ideas established in its predecessors, van Heijningen Jr.'s film arguably contravenes the 1982 film's status as a touchstone for practical effects; during postproduction, impalpable CGI was layered over what were originally practical creations supplied by Amalgamated Dynamics. However, just as Carpenter's film successfully allowed for a reappropriation of the cultural significance of "Who Goes There?," the 21st century has provided new contexts within which the central extraterrestrial can be explicated. Following 9/11 and other calculated attacks that have proliferated since, the notion of terrorist insurgents clandestinely existing in our midst is now a legitimate anxiety—one that strongly coincides with the themes of distrust and suspicion that define the film.

Much as in the numerous iterations of the *Body Snatcher* films (1956–2007), the amorphousness—and varying depictions—of Campbell's shapeshifting lifeform afford it an uncanny capacity to reflect the predominant cultural concerns across different eras. In addition to the films that have been explored here, "Who Goes There?" has inspired a variety of works outside of cinema, predominantly linked to Carpenter's film: between 1991 and 2011, Dark Horse Comics released five spin-off stories; in 2001, the *Outpost #31* fan site was launched, boasting all manner of trivia, FAQs, and information regarding the film; and Computer Artworks released the successful video-game sequel, *The Thing* (2002).

*Liam Hathaway*

See also: *Invasion of the Body Snatchers*; Polar Aliens; *They Live*; "Who Goes There?"

## FURTHER READING

Billson, Anne. *BFI Classics: The Thing*. British Film Institute, 1997.
Prince, Stephen. "Dread, Taboo and *The Thing*: Toward a Social Theory of the Horror Film." *The Horror Film*, edited by Stephen Prince, Rutgers University Press, 2004, pp. 118–30.
Trushell, John. "*The Thing*: Of 'Monsters, Madmen, and Murderers'—A Morality Play on Ice." *Foundation*, no. 76, Summer 1999, pp. 76–89.

## *Third Rock from the Sun*

*Third Rock from the Sun* (1996–2001) is part of a long tradition of "aliens on Earth" TV sitcoms. Created by Bonnie Turner and Terry Turner, its premise is that a party of alien explorers have been sent to Earth to act as anthropologists. At least in the early series, each episode consists of a confrontation with an absurd assumption made by the inhabitants of Earth and how the aliens negotiate with it.

The principal characters are Dick Solomon, the high commander, who acts as the paterfamilias; Sally Solomon, the head of security and "sister" of Dick; Tommy Solomon, information officer and the oldest member of the crew, as Dick's "son," and Harry, whose main function is to communicate with their alien boss and who is presented as functionally less intelligent than both the crew and their Earth neighbors. Naming the characters "Solomon" seems to be a deliberate coding of them as outsiders, and their presumed Jewishness is alluded to more than once in the early series.

The show had six seasons, but as is not uncommon with this kind of premise, the longer the aliens were on earth, the less alien they became and the more they were assimilated into the world around them. Although continual shifts of broadcast time probably did affect the show's ratings, this assimilation process is more likely the cause of its decline. The show attracted awards and nominations during its first three years, in the period 1997 to 1999.

In the first season the show was quintessentially Cartesian, its premise relying in part on emphasizing a body-mind split in which much of the humor comes from the contrast between the body and gendered or aged persona a character is expected to perform and the gendered and aged identity that they retain as their alien selves. Only three of the main cast fully enter into this. Harry, the transmitter, is at first exempt, although eventually their landlady's attempts to seduce him become overtly and mutually sexual. But even the remaining three characters are developed in ways that reflect as much the writers' assumptions as they do the discomfort of the characters with Earth (and American) norms.

Dick's role as masculine professor of physics and "provider" is relatively congruent with his role as high commander. His major discomforts are around how to negotiate humor, what happens when he becomes attracted to his office mate Mary Albright, and how he negotiates human dating patterns, including some very funny episodes where Dick has to deal with his own body. One of the funniest is "Moby Dick" (season 3), in which Dick goes on a diet, but it is funny in the end precisely because Dick realizes that he is in a privileged body and does not need to diet: he can simply buy larger trousers. Similarly, although Mary introduces him to feminism as a challenge to the gendered expectations he sees, she too often concedes to such expectations and makes many of the allowances for "Dick" that feminists are expected to make in their own personal life. Mary educates but fails to change Dick. In part this is because much of the time, if Dick is gendered it is less as male than as "math professor" in much the same way as Sheldon in *The Big Bang Theory* is gendered "geek" and thus allowed to behave very badly.

Tommy is cast as an adolescent boy. His negotiation with his body is funny, but it is a form of humor based on the notion that boys' bodies are uncontrollable, and their response to girls (there is no homosexuality in this series) is a function of the temptation of girls' bodies. Although Tommy is schooled by his girlfriend, too often the impression is left of a gendered world in which natural boyhood is tamed by women. In "Dick Behaving Badly" (season 2), for example, there are jokes that if Tommy wishes to be manly, he needs to get his girlfriend's permission first. Problematic perhaps is that the episode concludes with Tommy performing manliness and August, at least ironically, succumbing.

The greater weight of the performativity falls to Sally. At its best this is excoriating. In "I Enjoy Being Dick" (season 1), Sally takes a job as a waitress and rapidly comes to the conclusion that this role is entirely congruent with the definition of woman: "men are always bossing you around, no one ever says thank you, and you're expected to clean up after everyone." In "Dick, Smoker" (season 1), Sally is less than impressed by a car mechanic who talks past her to Dick, tries to overcharge her, and demonstrates the power of a lever in the right place.

As the show moved into season 3, it increasingly emphasized relationships and the performativity became more acquiescent. Sally, in particular, settled into a relationship with policeman Don Orville. This relationship is based on an overexaggeration of gendered roles in which Don's masculinity is undercut by his weight but restored by the 1930s rom-com tropes that the two perform.

By the third and fourth seasons, the more subversive aspects of the show are increasingly contained. Sally is increasingly locked into the domestic. Mary is increasingly pandering to Dick's ego while simultaneously expressing exasperation. The sense of alien estrangement weakens, and the show begins to feel more like *The Addams Family* in shape. In part, as already noted, this is due to the unavoidable assimilation of the family into American life, but it is also because physically gendered essentialism is early signaled as more important than social performativity. Sally, for example, has the "urge" to nurture in "Post Nasal Dick" (season 1), and Dick wants to slug a neighbor when he gets angry in "Angry Dick" (season 1). But it is also because, like *I Love Lucy* and later episodes of *The Simpsons*, too much of the humor humiliates Sally and femaleness, particularly female bodies—which are often presented as repulsive (they bleed, have hair under the arms, etc.). While the show does maintain the sense of outsiderness, increasingly the aliens perform not as critics but as overeager cultural migrants seeking to hide their origins.

*Farah Mendlesohn*

See also: *Futurama*; *Galaxy Quest*; *Hitchhiker's Guide to the Galaxy, The*; *Mork & Mindy*.

**FURTHER READING**

Feasey, Rebecca. *Masculinity and Popular Television.* Edinburgh University Press, 2008.

Gregori-Signes, Carmen. "'Apparently, Women Don't Know How to Operate Doors': A Corpus-based Analysis of Women Stereotypes in the TV Series *Third Rock from the Sun.*" *International Journal of English Studies*, vol. 17, no. 2, 2017, pp. 21–43.

Matthews, Nicole and Farah Mendlesohn. "The Cartesian Novum of *Third Rock from the Sun*: Gendering Human Bodies and Alien Minds." *Fantasy Girls: Gender in the New Universe of Science Fiction and Fantasy Television*, edited by Elyce Rae Helford, Rowman & Littlefield, 2000, pp. 41–59.

## Thompson, Tade

A writer of novels and short stories, Tade Thompson (1970–) has a wildly fecund imagination and a broad range of interests. As a result, he tends not to return to the same subject twice, although certain themes recur. Not the least of these is that much of his work is set in Africa, and in Nigeria in particular. Thompson's writing is uncompromisingly direct in its handling of government corruption, military brutality, and the conditions of everyday life. Thompson's first novel, *Making Wolf*, was an extremely gritty thriller, set mainly in West Africa, but his second novel, *Rosewater* (2016), and the related short story "Bicycle Girl" (2013) are much more overtly science-fictional.

Rosewater, the eponymous town in which much of the novel is set, is more accurately known as "the Donut," given that it is a circular shantytown that has grown up around a mysterious structure, a so-called biodome, that has sprung from the earth not far from Lagos. It is expanding, not unlike a mushroom, but no one has any idea where it has come from and what its purpose might be. What is known, however, is that once a year there is an event called the Opening, when a hole appears in the dome, and it expels spores that seem to have the property of healing. Thus, people have begun to gather annually, and Rosewater has come into being in order to service their needs (the actual name is "Flower Water," an acerbic reference to the fact that the town, which has little in the way of infrastructure, stinks).

While many people regard Utopicity, as the dome is eventually christened, as Lourdes and the Fountain of Youth all rolled into one, it is known also that the spores are undiscriminating in their effect and thus are just as likely to reanimate the recently dead as to heal the living, and they also reconstruct the human body in unexpected ways. This suggests that the spores themselves are without purpose and intent. That people nonetheless are willing to take the risk for the chance of healing is indicative of the constraints under which many of them live.

Karoo, the novel's protagonist, is the only person to have made contact with the inhabitants of the biodome. He is a "sensitive," able to read the minds of others, and a "finder." When the biodome erupted, it was hoped that he might be able to determine what it wanted, but he has consistently refused to discuss the experience. It is only when he learns that sensitives such as himself are starting to die of an unknown illness that he is forced to engage once more with the nature of the dome.

What is most striking about *Rosewater* is the way in which Thompson plays with ideas of the alien. The novel's very setting is a challenge to Euro-American readers, who are accustomed to very different living standards. Thompson addresses this in what might be called the "biography" of Rosewater, charting its development as a town in relation to the biodome's expansion and its response to the arrival of more visitors, placing their needs above those of the people actually living in the town. The biodome itself might seem benign in that it appears to offer healing and in a rudimentary fashion to provide services, such as electricity. It is only belatedly that one realizes that the biodome is in effect a gigantic honey trap, created by the aliens to attract visitors who will in turn become infected with xenospores, fulfilling the broader purpose of the aliens within the dome, which is to gradually kill Earth's inhabitants and take over the planet.

The duration of their scheme is another marker of the extremely alien nature of the dome's inhabitants, as is its remarkably elaborate structure, the gradual takeover and elimination of one group after another, and the multigenerational reconstruction of other groups into a form that is much more useful to the aliens. Its slow, organic, and stealthy evolution is very much at odds with the immediate transformations so characteristic of much contemporary genre SF. In fact, the appearance of the biodome does not mark the beginning of the takeover so much as merely denote its latest stage. Very few people have any idea how long the invasion has actually been underway. There is a nod, perhaps, to Wells's *War of the Worlds* and the Martians' terraforming of the Thames Valley to accommodate their own needs, but this vegetable empire is very different in both its nature and the speed at which it works. Rather than Earth microbes killing off the aliens, they instead exploit Earth's vegetation.

Of interest too is the way in which different alien factions respond to the ongoing transformation of humanity and engage with it, with some groups more willing to change their plans than others. Striking too is the way in which people have adapted the effects of the dome's presence, exploiting sensitives, for example, as a human firewall against undeclared, rogue talents, trying to steal bank passwords. In the end, humanity is, if not saved, then at least preserved for a while by the intervention of Oyin Da, the Bicycle Girl, who has discovered the research of a man called Roger Conrad. During Nigeria's colonial period, he built a machine capable of creating wormholes; Oyin Da found that machine and his papers and managed to make the machine work. Since then she has become a scientist and activist, hiding from the authorities in a parallel universe. Her formidable intellect quickly recognizes the potential for engaging with the inhabitants of the biodome directly, which her knowledge allows her to do, enabling her to propose a new relationship with humans that will potentially be more beneficial to both groups.

*Rosewater* in effect asks us to reconsider the presence of the alien in the world. Rather than modeling alien behavior on our own preferred methods for colonization (invasion and settlement), Thompson proposes an approach drawn from nature—an approach of gradual infiltration, stealthy overwhelming, and eventual transformation.

*Maureen Kincaid Speller*

See also: Okorafor, Nnedi; *War of the Worlds, The*.

## FURTHER READING

Coleman, Christian A. "Interview with Tade Thompson." *Light Speed*, Issue 89, 2017. http://www.lightspeedmagazine.com/nonfiction/interview-tade-thompson/.
Ryman, Geoff. "Tade Thompson." *Strange Horizons*. http://strangehorizons.com/non-fiction/100african/tade-thompson/.
Wood, Nick. "Interview with Tade Thompson." Short *Story Day Africa*, 2017. http://shortstorydayafrica.org/news/idont-like-linearity-i-find-it-boring-an-interview-with-tade-thompson.

## Tiptree Jr., James

James Tiptree Jr. (1915–1987) is an important figure in feminist science fiction not only for the stories that she wrote but also for the ways in which her mysterious identity challenged gendered assumptions about science-fiction writers. Born Alice Sheldon, she wrote under several pen names, including Tiptree, not only to protect her identity but also because of the criticism often faced by women writing science fiction. Tiptree was a prolific writer, and her works include a considerable number of short stories (collected together into several volumes), two novels, one book of poetry, and several posthumously published collections. Following her death, the James Tiptree Jr. Literary Award was established to celebrate works of science fiction or fantasy that explore and challenge notions of gender.

Originally published in 1990 and updated in 2004, *Her Smoke Rose Up Forever* collects Tiptree's most popular and critically acclaimed short fiction, presents Tiptree's exploration of gender roles through representations of the Other, and illustrates her most essential depictions of the alien.

Tiptree provides a number of different perspectives as to what aliens might look like, including beings that are depicted as bright lights, animals, plants, and sea creatures, as well as what might result from alien contact, including human extinction, interspecies breeding, and colonization. "The Screwfly Solution" (1977) is largely told through a series of letters and newspaper articles that focus on the spread of a plague and events of femicide that result from men being infected by the disease. The aliens are only briefly depicted in the story, and though they are initially described as angelic, it becomes clear that they are indifferent to the extinction of humanity. This indifference is also reflected in the title story, "Her Smoke Rose Up Forever" (1974), which features aliens described as mechanical skeletons who force the narrator to relive the events of his life and death over and over for their entertainment. While these narratives reinforce the idea that Earth could potentially become a vacation destination for aliens, other stories focus on humanity's desire for aliens and sexuality as a resource. "The Women Men Don't See" (1973) depicts two women who seek to escape from the oppressive sexism of Earth and who plead with alien explorers to take them away. In "And I Awoke and Found Me Here on the Cold Hill's Side" (1972), humans and aliens have been in contact with aliens from various worlds, sharing space ports. While the aliens remain largely indifferent to humanity, many humans have become sexually obsessed with aliens, regardless of their sexual compatibility. This desire for aliens has caused a cult-like worship that often ruins lives or results in self-sacrifice as a result of their uncontrollable desires. In spite of their indifference, it is clear from the tone of the story that humanity is in danger of becoming colonized by the aliens they worship or extinct from their lack of interest in other humans.

A more threatening depiction of the misappropriation of human sexuality can be found in "A Momentary Taste of Being" (1975), where overpopulation has forced humans to seek out new planets to inhabit. The colony ship discovers an inhabitable planet and sends out a group of explorers to learn more about the planet and its inhabitants, but only one member of the group returns, along with a plant-like alien who emits a mesmerizing light that seduces all those aboard the ship. This story explores interspecies breeding as it becomes clear that the humans are to be used as gametes for the reproduction of the alien species.

In contrast to narratives that depict the aliens as indifferent and destructive, other stories explore telepathic bonds between humans and aliens. While "On the Last Afternoon" (1972) represents one of the few alien-attack narratives in the collection, it also disrupts the traditional trope of human versus alien by exploring the telepathic bond between the protagonist and an alien creature. In this story, the lobster-like aliens who threaten the castaway human civilization are largely unaware of the human presence in their mating grounds, which continues Tiptree's depiction of aliens being indifferent, as the destruction of the human colony is the result of instinctual breeding rather than intentional attack. In the face of the attack, the human protagonist must join in a telepathic bond with a spore-like alien species to prevent the destruction of the human colonists. The theme of telepathic links between aliens and humans is further explored in "With Delicate Mad Hands" (1981), where a monstrously deformed human is drawn to an alien planet by a voice in her head. Upon arriving on the planet, she discovers that it is too radioactive to support human life, but she takes comfort in the arms of the alien creature who has been telepathically reaching out to her. In spite of the image of the united lovers, the story still reinforces the threat of the alien, as it is revealed that this planet learns of other cultures by luring them here and probing their dead brains. Finally, Tiptree's collection also offers a different perspective of the alien-human first encounter that reinforces the potential threat that humanity could pose to aliens. "We Who Stole the Dream" (1978) is told from the perspective of the Joilani as the mythology surrounding their emancipation, and it presents the humans as an invading alien species who has colonized their people.

Collectively, Tiptree's depictions of aliens refute the idea that aliens are inherently motivated by a desire to destroy humanity, instead often reflecting humanity's own indifference to the world around it. These stories reflect a continued feminist exploration of sexual desire, transcendence, and death that echoes throughout all of Tiptree's works.

*Amber Strother*

See also: Butler, Octavia E.; Le Guin, Ursula K.; Tepper, Sheri S.

## FURTHER READING

Pearson, Wendy. "(Re)reading James Tiptree Jr.'s 'And I Awoke and Found Me Here on the Cold Hill Side'." *Daughters of Earth: Feminist Science Fiction in the*

Twentieth Century, edited by Justine Larbalestier, Wesleyan University Press, 2006, pp. 168–89.

Phillips, Julie. *James Tiptree, Jr.: The Double Life of Alice B Sheldon.* St. Martin's Press, 2006.

Van Der Spek, Inez. *Alien Plots: Female Subjectivity and the Divine in the Light of James Tiptree's "A Momentary Taste of Being."* Liverpool University Press, 2000.

## Torchwood

The alien in the BBC's *Torchwood* series (2006–2011) is not an object—it is a state of existence facilitated by time and under the vagaries of the *deus ex machina* of the series: the Rift, a breach in the time and space continuum, situated over Cardiff, Wales. Created by Russell T. Davies, this *Doctor Who* spin-off details the activities of a small team of people who guard Cardiff—and the world—from the aliens, the alien technology, or the time-displaced who fall through this Rift. Set in the already established "*Doctor Who*-niverse," the Torchwood Institute (Torchwood is an anagram of Doctor Who) originates in the second season of *Doctor Who*, in "Tooth and Claw" (Russell T. Davies, 2006), when Queen Victoria founds it to guard the Earth against all supernatural and alien entities.

The overarching alien of the series, Torchwood's leader, Captain Jack Harkness, is first encountered in season 1 of *Doctor Who*, in the episode "The Empty Child" (2005) and gains immortality at the end of the first season of *Doctor Who* in "The Parting of the Ways" (2005). From the future, his temporal fluidity, along with his immortality, echoes his moral fluidity, reinforcing his alien qualities—yet his gender fluidity adds to his humanity rather than accentuates his alienness. All the members of the Torchwood team are alienated: divorced from their society by their histories, their work, and their knowledge. The character Gwen, recruited in the opening episode of the series, is their link to a normal life. The other members (Suzie, Toshiko Sato, Dr. Owen Harper, and Ianto Jones) are all at various times corrupted by the alien technology they encounter.

Whereas the first two seasons of *Torchwood* are a series of loosely linked episodes dealing with the stream of entities and items falling into the Rift, season 3, "The Children of Earth," is devoted to just one alien—the 4-5-6, an alien from a past that involved both the U.K. government and Jack Harkness. This season brings into focus the intersection of human and alien, the measure of and the attempt to define both. Season 4 is separate, with most of the action taking place in the United States, and the alien *du jour* a peculiar sense that the Earth itself can be alien to all of us simply because of our existence and interaction with it.

The alien encounters predominantly involve life-threatening entities in the first two seasons, such as the weevils: humanoid, predatory aliens that live mainly in the sewers, or the gaseous alien intent on taking orgasmic hits from the human lives she takes. The mind-reading alien who murdered her way through a couple of centuries before seducing Toshiko is political and desperate, but no more so than Suzie, so totally corrupted by alien technology she murders without compunction. Aliens such as the entity named "Adam," existing on the memories of others, reveal the loneliness of individual team members.

4-5-6, named for the particular wavelength on which it communicates, is a global existential threat, ready and able to destroy the fabric of global civilization for the sake of a drug high produced by a chemical reaction it receives from human children. This season insists that aliens make us alien to ourselves. It is a horrific exploration of utilitarianism and the sudden awareness of humanity's powerlessness in the face of the universe. The aliens encountered in the earlier seasons were human-sized, frequently taking human form, whereas 4-5-6 is massive, unclearly defined, and with an incomprehensible manner. It cannot be individually confronted. Its final defeat, engineered by Jack, costs him everything, but his decisions, both in the past and in engineering the defeat of this alien, call into question Jack's own humanity—perhaps his immortality has come at a cost—to make him the most pernicious alien of them all.

Unlike *Doctor Who*, *Torchwood* paints a darker picture of humanity through the alien other. While human kindness and goodness are part of the series, they exist alongside humanity's cruelty, corruption, and violence. *Torchwood* unflinchingly comments on the things that make our world the brilliant and messy place it is. Two powerful examples of the way the series uses the alien other to comment on human nature come from the episodes "Sleeper" and "Meat," both in season 2.

In "Sleeper" a young couple has been burgled. When the police arrive, the husband is unconscious, and the wife, Beth (Nikki Amuka-Bird), is unharmed, but the would-be burglars are dead. The police have no explanation. Later, when she is interrogated by Torchwood, Beth's duplicitous, alien nature is revealed, both physical (her alien/cyborg implants) and mental (she speaks in an alien language). Jack explains that she is "a sleeper agent. . . . They infiltrate planets, adapting their bodies, gathering intelligence . . . until they are ready to take over." No matter how hard Beth tries to hold onto her humanity, her alien and advanced technological body will not be controlled. Although she helps Torchwood stop the alien invasion, she accidentally killed her husband when she lost control of her cybernetic weapons as they embraced. She represents the West's love/hate relationship with technology as well as cultural anxieties regarding how technological and medical advances will change what it means to be human. Beth's inability to control her advanced body suggests that while these advances may improve our bodies and our quality of life, the human propensity for violence and aggression will remain intact and may also be enhanced.

The plot of "Meat" is simple enough, but the connotations are disturbing and attest to humanity's cruelty and ability to treat the other as far less then sentient. The hauling company that Gwen's fiancé works for is caught hauling tainted meat. The source, when revealed, is an alien life-form resembling a whale, only referred to in the episode as the cash cow. Jack postulates that when it was much smaller it came through the Cardiff rift in space and time and was beached there. The meat producers keep it alive, though heavily sedated, and repeatedly harvest its regenerating flesh. Although one of the men realizes their captive is in ever-increasing pain, the others see it as nothing more than meat. The Torchwood team discovers that the cash cow is sentient, and Jack tries to convince the butchers to stop exploiting the creature. The leader of the group simply responds, "It's just meat. That's all . . . . I'm making money here. This is my business."

During the Torchwood assault, the beast starts to work its way free and becomes a threat to the team trying to save it. When team member Dr. Owen Harper (Burn Gorman) realizes this, he makes a decision that is devastating, and euthanizes the beast with the sedatives he has prepared. As the creature dies, Owen looks into its eye and says, "I'm so sorry, I'm so sorry," and the beast sings something like a whale song before its eyes close for the last time. Jack asks Owen, "What have you done?" to which Owen simply replies, "Mercy killing."

Like all media texts, this one has many meanings. It is about the exploitation and oppression that are a part of capitalist systems. It displays human brutality and insensitivity and the ability of the oppressor, no matter how oppressed she or he is, to oppress others with the same or greater fervor. It shows the ugly side of humanity and its relationship with the other as well as the troubled and complicated relationship between animals and humanity—animals that are sometimes companions, sometimes beasts of burden, and sometimes food.

*Torchwood* effectively and powerfully uses the conventions of science fiction, especially the alien other, to comment on cultural anxieties and our concerns about our humanity in the 21st century.

*Susan A. George and Keira McKenzie*

See also: Doctor Who; Quatermass (Series); They Live; X-Files, The.

## FURTHER READING

Beattie, Melissa. "'My' Hero or Epic Fail? *Torchwood* as Transnational Telefantasy." *Palabra Clave*, vol. 20, no. 3, 2017, pp. 722–62.
Berger, Richard. "Screwing Aliens and Screwing with Aliens: *Torchwood* Slashes the Doctor." *Illuminating Torchwood: Essays on Narrative, Character and Sexuality in the BBC Series*, edited by Andrew Ireland, McFarland, 2010, pp. 66–75.
George, Susan A. "Remembering *Torchwood*: Investigating the Postmodern Memory Crisis on the Small Screen." *Practicing Science Fiction: Critical Essays on Writing, Reading, and Teaching the Genre*, edited by Karen Hellekson, Craig B. Jacobsen, Patrick B. Sharp, and Lisa Yaszek, McFarland Press, 2010, pp. 104–16.
Williams, Rebecca, editor. *Torchwood Declassified: Investigating Mainstream Cult Television*. I. B. Tauris, 2013.

## *Transformers*

*Transformers* is a franchise that was originally developed as a collaboration between American toy company Hasbro and Japanese toy company Takara Tomy. As with many toy franchises of the 1980s, *Transformers* was developed as both a toy line and an animated series, in hopes that the latter would serve as an advertisement for and bolster the sales of the former. The series and films both follow two conflicting factions of an alien robot race, the Autobots (the protagonists) and the Decepticons (the antagonists), as they fight for control of their home planet Cybertron, the Creation Matrix (the central control and reproductive power source of their race), and Energon, their main energy source. These robots have the power to change form—"transform"—between two main forms, usually a vehicle and something more humanoid, though the former varies between vehicles, weapons, radios, and even dinosaurs. The Autobots are "good" machines, cars, trucks, and the like, in bright colors, while the Decepticons are machines associated with violence and manipulation, fighter jets, tanks, and guns, in dark colors. Depending on the version of their backstory, the dueling factions find their way to Earth because of the destruction of their home world, the need to find a new source of Energon, or the war between the two factions that involves individual members of the faction near Earth's location. The series colloquially known as Generation One (1984-1993: the first three seasons of the animated series and the first animated film), which is the best-known representation of the franchise, centralizes the robot characters; both the animated series and film introduce a few token named human characters, with the largely unnamed civilians (usually American) serving as something for the Autobots to protect. The live-action franchise switches this focus, making a male human teenager the main protagonist. Earth acts as a stage for the faction conflict, revolving around the AllSpark. The primary victories and losses, unlike the animated series and film, are attributed to the humans and less so to the alien robots.

The animated series' plot maintains the status quo, with the protagonists—the Autobots—remaining the victors. The animated film, however, eliminates the status quo. Unicron, a world-eating machine planet with his own transformative powers, appears to attack Cybertron. During the film, Megatron successfully kills Optimus Prime, forcing new leadership for the Autobots. After a coup among the Decepticons, Megatron and his loyalists are jettisoned from the faction and rebirthed by Unicron. The remainder of the film is a space adventure, in which the Autobots travel to different planets in search of their separated allies while trying to determine who the new "Prime" should be. Eventually they confront Unicron and his Decepticon allies, defeat them, and have one of their members reborn as the new Prime.

The live-action films—five, between 2007 and 2017, all directed by Michael Bay—focus on the fight for the AllSpark, the central life force of Cybertron. It has been sent to Earth, where it is discovered by a human explorer. Sometime later, his descendant, Sam, rediscovers it and the fight is brought to Earth. The U.S. military becomes involved after encounters with the Decepticons in the Middle East. While the two factions battle, the Autobots align with the humans, and Sam succeeds in killing Megatron. In the second film, the Autobots and humans have formed a treaty to pursue the Decepticons. Megatron reanimates, meets with his master, and goes to kill Sam. One Decepticon, in the form of a human girl, attempts to kill Sam but is killed herself. The two forces again battle, and Sam and Optimus are both killed. Through outside alien forces, both are revived, and they kill Megatron's master and force a Decepticon retreat. In the third film, the Autobots are firmly ensconced in the U.S. military, fighting Decepticon threats, as the robot and human sides battle traitors in their midst. The Decepticons gain control, have the Autobots deported and seemingly killed. However, in the final battle, they destroy the Decepticon leadership and fully integrate themselves into Earth and the American community.

*Transformers* (2007), directed by Michael Bay and starring Shia LaBeouf, Tyrese Gibson, Megan Fox, and (shown here) Optimus Prime (voice: Peter Cullen). (Paramount Pictures/Photofest)

The franchise represents the struggle between male authority and villainous femininity, or acts as a metaphor for cultural integration. Simon Bacon argues that the battles in the live-action films are a battle between the sexes, with the Autobots acting as masculine patriarchs with the Decepticons the wicked women concerned with procreation and seduction. He positions the Decepticons as analogous to the xenomorphs of the *Alien* series, sinuous seductive creatures (others) that procreate at the cost of other, predominantly, human life. The final film of the trilogy is Megatron's gambit to create more Decepticons, giving Bacon's argument some merit. However, the original franchise positions the entire Transformer race as masculine, with only a single token female Autobot. Furthermore, their non-human forms, even the female one, are attached to typical symbols of masculinity: the military, construction, and automobiles. Their humanoid forms are also symbolically representative of the idealized masculine body: broad shoulders and "muscular" chests. Another reading is to look at the Transformers as a way of integrating the alien into the dominant culture. The arc of the live-action films is one which positions the Autobots and Decepticons as dueling archetypes of immigrants. The former act as the "model minority" and do everything they can to present a positive image. They follow the rule of law, they work with the government, and they excise the negative element of their culture—the Decepticons. The Decepticons are the illegal immigrant archetype taken to its most hyperbolic negative form. They seduce, manipulate, kill, undermine, and invade. They influence "good" members of the community to take their side and commit criminal acts. The good immigrant, then, to secure their place on Earth—America—removes the negative element and, as a reward, is given full citizenship as an (American)

Earthling. In both, however, the familiar is made alien and familiar again, as the theme song states, "robots in disguise."

*Nathaniel Fuller*

See also: *District 9*; *Pacific Rim*; *V*.

**FURTHER READING**

Bacon, Simon. "(S)Mothering Reproduction: Procreation, Gender and Control in the *Transformers* Films by Michael Bay." *Femspec*, vol. 12, no. 2, 2012, pp. 47–65.

Geraghty, Lincoln. "Repackaging Generation One: Genre, Fandom, and *The Transformers* as Adult/Children's Television." *The Shifting Definitions of Genre: Essays on Labeling Films, Television Shows and Media*, edited by Lincoln Geraghty and Mark Jancovich, McFarland, 2008, pp. 181–200.

Shook, John R. "First Contact." *Transformers and Philosophy: More Than Meets the Mind*, edited by John R. Shook and Liz S. Swan, Open Court, 2009, pp. 18–27.

## *2000 AD*

*2000 AD* (1977–) is a weekly comic, published in Britain since 1977, originally published by IPC, then by Fleetway from 1987 and Rebellion from 2000. Past editors include Pat Mills, Richard Burton, and Matt Smith. The comic has been home to writers such as Neil Gaiman, Alan Moore, and Dan Abnett. Notable artists have included Carlos Ezquerra, Kevin O'Neill, and Mike McMahon. The editor has always been presented as the alien Tharg.

Created by Pat Mills, Tharg (aka Tharg the Mighty, the Mighty One, or the Mighty Tharg) is a godlike alien from Quaxxan, the sixth planet in the system orbiting the massive star Betelgeuse—the second-brightest star in the constellation Orion. Tharg possesses striking green skin and white hair and is of imposing physical stature. His eye color varies based on what he is looking at. Since emigrating to Earth from Quaxxan (due to his home planet's high cost of living), Tharg's purpose in life has been to provide "thrill power" to humans (or Earthlets, as he prefers to call them). He is an immensely powerful alien who is capable of flight, can exist in space without a ship, and possesses the ability to open dimension warp, facilitating interdimensional travel. He has a subspace communicator, the Rosette of Sirius, integrated into his forehead. Tharg's glitzy style and trendy appearance, coupled with his sharp sense of humor, bullying of editorial droids and PVC-eating, as well as his fervent denial that he is a front for a host of human editors, make him an entertaining parody of a certain type of high-powered media mogul. That he really is a front for a host of human editors is testimony to the self-reflexive capacity of *2000 AD* and its creators.

*2000 AD* has always been a subversive and rebellious comic. The replacement for the comic *Action*, which was set in the present day, antiauthoritarian satire has been at the heart of *2000 AD*'s penetrating storytelling. Pat Mills created the "Invasion" strip for the first issue, which saw the Volgans' execution of a Thatcher-like female British prime minster. The Volgans were based on the Russians, and the British armed services were depicted as an ineffective middle-class bureaucracy, mimicking much traditional World War II and Cold War fiction. Later episodes of the story depicted the antiauthoritarian working-class hero Bill Savage achieving victory for the Brits using his proletarian common-sense intellect.

Although the longest-running of *2000 AD*'s strips, *Judge Dredd*, set in the future police state Mega City One, contains very few aliens, they have always been a core feature of the comic's politico-satirical content. Some of the strips featuring aliens ("aliens" here primarily designating "extraterrestrial life" and not including "interdimensional beings") in *2000 AD* to date are: *Dan Dare* (1977–1979), *The V.C.s* (1979–2006), *Nemesis the Warlock* (1980–1999), *D.R. & Quinch* (1983–1987), *Skizz* (1983–1995), *Bad Company* (1986 to date), *Tyranny Rex* (1988–2004), and *Judge Dredd vs. Aliens* (2003). Even though the Treens of *Dan Dare*, the Geeks of *The V.C.s*, *Nemesis the Warlock*, the Krool of *Bad Company*, and Ridley Scott's Aliens in *Judge Dredd* were all enemies of humanity, aliens in *2000 AD* are not always simply a force for evil. In *Nemesis the Warlock*, the antihero protagonist is a fire-breathing alien demon who fights the evil dictator of the human Terran Empire, Torquemada. Torquemada has sworn to obliterate all alien life. Unlike the rebel alien Nemesis, Torquemada has no redeeming qualities, even though he is homo sapiens.

*2000 AD*'s *Bad Company* highlights the darker aspects of the human psyche. The strip flips the subject-object position of human vs. alien to expose the bizarre nature of the human unconscious. The Krool of Bad Company are complex. While they are clearly viciously malevolent, sadistic creatures, hell-bent on causing as much abject suffering to humanity as possible en route to an infinite empire, their scientism and social organization can be read as a critique of humanity's darker political moments. The Krool are technologically sophisticated; they have developed the ability to create War Zombies to fight for them, hybrids of different alien species, and devices to cut out a human's soul. The heroes of Bad Company are Krool-human hybrids, thus blurring the boundary between humans and aliens throughout the strip. The leader of Bad Company, Kano, was originally a human but had half a Krool brain implanted by the Krool. Kano looks like Frankenstein's monster. He loses his mind due to sharing consciousness with the Krool and goes on murderous rampages.

The strips *D.R. & Quinch*, *Skizz*, and *Tyranny Rex* all have alien protagonists. *D.R. & Quinch* and *Skizz* were written by Alan Moore. D.R. & Quinch are two alien teenagers who drop out of school and decided to wreak havoc upon Earth's history. Skizz is a send-up of Thatcher's Britain. After the extraterrestrial hero Skizz crash-lands on Earth, he is hunted and eventually killed by the lunatic government operative Mr. Van Owen, who presumes Skizz to be a scout for an alien invasion. Tyranny Rex, as a strong alien female lead (a green lizard-like Sauron with a big tail), steals the genes of celebrities to sell to the super-rich.

*Michael O'Brien*

See also: Mekon, the; Mœbius; *Nemesis the Warlock*.

## FURTHER READING

Bishop, David. *Thrill-Power Overload. 2000 AD: The First Forty Years*. Rebellion, 2017.
Milligan, Peter and Brett Ewins. *The Complete Bad Company*. Rebellion, 2011.
Mills, Pat, Kevin O'Neill, and Jesus Redondo. *The Complete Nemesis the Warlock: Book 1*. Rebellion, 2006.

# V

*V* first appeared on NBC as a two-part miniseries in 1983, starring Mark Singer and Jane Badler. Due to the miniseries' overwhelming popularity, it was quickly followed by an additional miniseries, *V: The Final Battle* (1984), and a weekly television show, *V: The Series* (1984–1985). The original miniseries was written and directed by Kenneth Johnson, who had previously worked on science-fiction shows such as *The Six Million Dollar Man* (1974–1978), *The Bionic Woman* (1976–1978), and *The Incredible Hulk* (1978–1982). Johnson initially planned to create a miniseries of Sinclair Lewis's classic antifascist novel *It Can't Happen Here* (1935); however, producers at NBC worried that the material would be too controversial for television audiences, insisting that Johnson replace the story's fascists with duplicitous aliens.

*V* is a somewhat familiar alien-invasion narrative that borrows many of the tropes of 1950s Hollywood B-movies, such as *The Day the Earth Stood Still* (1951) and *Invaders from Mars* (1953). At the start of *V*, alien spaceships suddenly appear in the skies of major cities around the world. Although their presence is an implied threat, the aliens, who look entirely human aside from their odd voices and their need to wear sunglasses, claim to come in peace. They explain that they have come to Earth because their home planet is experiencing environmental problems and that they require chemicals and minerals found only on Earth. In return for these resources, the aliens (called the Visitors) promise to share their advanced knowledge of science and technology with the people of Earth.

The Visitors quickly gain enormous influence over the Earth's leaders and secretly control their minds through a process called "conversion." They also take over the media. Scientists who are suspicious of the aliens are widely criticized by the media and slowly begin to disappear, sometimes returning completely in agreement with the aliens' plans. Other scientists find themselves distrusted, persecuted, and forced to go underground, turned into scapegoats by the masses, who have been influenced by the Visitors. Working in coordination with the military, the Visitors declare martial law, arrest the scientists involved in the conspiracy, and send them to camps. What emerges from the narrative is a powerful allegory for Nazi Germany, with the persecuted scientists serving the role of the Jews. The Visitors' costumes and actions clearly parallel those of the Nazis in World War II, and the narrative also features a story line involving Holocaust survivor Abraham (Leonardo Cimino), who notes the connection between the Visitors' treatment of scientists and his experiences in Nazi Germany.

*V*'s themes of totalitarianism, social oppression, and "conversion" reflect America's ongoing cultural paranoia around communist threats. Emerging near the end of the Cold War, when America was negotiating peace treaties with communist countries, *V* demonstrates cultural suspicion around the possibilities of harmony between nations. Like many Cold War films of the 1950s, such as *Invasion of the Body Snatchers* (1956), *V* uses an aliens-in-disguise narrative to demonstrate ongoing fears of threat. Despite their outward human appearance, the Visitors are actually humanoid reptilian creatures who wear synthetic skins and prosthetic eyes that conceal their real identity. Their true purpose is not to collect minerals for their home planet but to harvest the planet's water supplies and to kidnap humans, some who they plan to turn into food, and others who they will use as soldiers in the aliens' ongoing conquest of other planets. Though the Visitors are not presented in much detail, *V* creates an exaggerated contrast between the humans and the aliens that is meant to highlight the difference between communist and "American" values. The Visitors are portrayed as almost entirely uniform and conformist, wearing identical outfits and sunglasses, which contrasts with the humans' diversity and individual spirit. There are, however, several aliens who resist their "Supreme Leader," and *V: The Series* does explore the possibilities of the coexistence of humans and aliens (Johnson left during the production of *V: The Final Battle* over creative differences). The last half of the miniseries focuses on the humans as they build an underground resistance against the Visitors. In fact, the title of the series comes from the large red "V" (meaning "Victory") spray-painted over the Visitors' billboards to remind individuals of the need to resist. At the miniseries' conclusion, the humans are just barely able to stave off the Visitors' threats, and it ends with them just beginning their fight against the aliens. In a conclusion that is obviously meant to speak directly to audiences at home, the humans urge one another to continue the fight against oppression and to protect their fundamental values.

In 2009, *V* was remade as a short-lived weekly television show that adapted the original material to address post–9/11 anxieties. Like the original miniseries, the reimagined *V* (2009–2011) traces the Visitors' arrival on Earth in need of the planet's minerals. However, as the show gradually unfolds, it is revealed that some Visitors have already been living on Earth for decades in "sleeper cells." These aliens have lived ordinary existences, working jobs in the government, military, and religion, all while secretly sabotaging those organizations from within to gradually undermine American society. In contrast to the original series' portrait of the Visitors as uniform and conformist, in the reimagined *V* the threat could be anywhere or anyone, even a close friend or romantic partner. As the series goes on, episodes focus on the interrelationship between the Visitors' arrival and the growth of terrorist attacks happening around the country. By shifting the alien threat from an external invading force as in the Cold War context of the original miniseries to an internal threat already living within society, the reimagined *V* reflects the heightened sense of paranoia and anxiety that characterized post–9/11 American society around the fear of infiltration and terrorism.

*Zak Bronson*

See also: *Invasion of the Body Snatchers*; *District 9*; *Men in Black*.

**FURTHER READING**

Browning, John E. "Holocaust-as-Horror, Science Fiction and the 'Look' of the 'Real/Reel' in *V* (1983)." *The Fantastic in Holocaust Literature and Film: Critical Perspectives*, edited by Judith B. Kerman and John E. Browning, McFarland, 2014, pp. 163–73.

Copp, Dan. *Fascist Lizards from Outer Space: The Politics, Literary Influences and Cultural History of Kenneth Johnson's* V. McFarland, 2017.

Koistinen, Aino-Kaisa. "Passing for Human in Science Fiction: Comparing the TV Series *Battlestar Galactica* and *V*." *NORA: Nordic Journal of Women's Studies*, vol. 19, no. 4, 2011, pp. 249–63.

## Vinge, Vernor

Vernor Vinge (1944–) is well known for dramatizing, across his body of work, the social impact of runaway progress in information technologies. His aliens, who remain largely confined to his three "Zones of Thought" novels, are less often remarked upon, and yet they too represent a facet of Vinge's thematic focus.

In this setting, the galaxy is divided into four Zones, each characterized by physical laws that place a cap on the maximum speed of information transfers—and therefore on communication, propulsion, thinking power, and societal complexity. The first Zone is the Unthinking Depths; there, physical laws are so restrictive that even the most primitive forms of civilization are hard to achieve. Within the second Zone of Thought, the Slow Zone, starfaring civilizations and sophisticated forms of automation do exist, although neither higher forms of AI nor FTL are possible.

The inhabitants of the Slow Zone and the Depths are unaware of these physical laws. They learn otherwise only if they blunder into the Beyond, the third Zone, where the speed of information transactions increases exponentially until, once we break through the Beyond and into the Fourth Zone, the Transcend, there are no more limits: the speed of data is such that information itself becomes alive, no longer shackled to physical substrates. In the Transcend, bodiless gods rule the depths of intergalactic space, and the inhabitants of the Beyond call them Powers. The Powers constitute the topmost tier of Vinge's alien taxonomy, and in *A Fire Upon the Deep* (1992) we meet two—the Lovecraftian-named Old One and the Blight, a Power turned destructive and parasitic. The Powers don't have a physical shape, but they can borrow the forms of slaved machinery and flesh sentients. Their intelligence and processing speeds are unmatchable, and the only safety from them, ironically, is in the Slow Zone.

For humans living in the Beyond, Earth is a myth, lost in the Slow Zone out of which they emerged long ago. The Beyond teems with life of all sorts, and the novels describe only a very few of its implied thousands of species. *A Fire Upon the Deep* and *Children of the Sky*, both set partly in the Beyond and partly in the Slow Zone, feature a smattering of humanoid civilizations of minor dramatic impact (the Dirokimes, the Aprahanti, and the Kalir) and two nonhumanoid civilizations of crucial import. The first of these are the Skroders/Skroderiders, a cybernetic construct made up of the fusion between the Skroders, a sentient plant species whose fronds are used for communication, and the riders themselves, motor and short-term memory units with which a long-ago benefactor had equipped the Skroders. The Skroderiders' story is a tragic one: their benefactor, it turns out, was the Blight itself, who wanted a ready-made command-and-control system it could hijack at will. The riders are designed to subvert the Skroders' nervous system, giving it over to the Blight and turning the entire species into its mindless weapon.

The other alien civilization of crucial relevance, protagonist of both *Fire* and *The Children of the Sky* (2011), are the Tines, a canid species whose sentience is based on the idea of distributed-node consciousness. A Tine individual is actually the conglomerate of four to eight singleton members. Each of these singleton members links himself/herself to the others in the conglomerate through ultrasonic waves emitted by a membrane on his/her head. The aggregate of all the signals forms a hive mind, a consensual thought-unit existing somewhere within this compound waveform. For a Tine, self-awareness and individuality vanish only if its entire pack is killed; otherwise, they evolve gradually with the replacement of individual members over a period of many decades, so that a Tine can, in effect, survive as a continuous consciousness for centuries.

The only other alien species featured in the "Zones" novels appears in *A Deepness in the Sky* (1999), set in the Slow Zone about 30,000 years before the events in *Fire*. The Spiders reside on a planet orbiting a star littered with scraps of highly advanced tech. Now at an early-20th-century level of equivalent technological development, they become unwittingly embroiled in the squabbles between two humanoid civilizations, each attracted to their system by the lure of technological and commercial advancement. The Spiders' struggle toward a free industrial society, parsed by the actions of a small group of liberal thinkers under the leadership of an Edison-like genius figure, tracks the same struggle among the humans. In the end, the progressive forces on both sides win through a commercial, military, and information-gathering alliance that manages to defeat the regressive forces pitted against them.

Between them, the "Zones of Thought" novels constitute an exploration of the use of information technologies in the service of—or against—the advancement of a free civilization, and the alien species directly involved in this exploration are designed to further it. Unlike the rest of Vinge's humanoid aliens, the Skroderiders, the Tines, and the Spiders look and think in ways strange enough to force the human characters to communicate with them carefully and inventively—that is to say, we humans have to really *think* about information delivery if we want to meaningfully engage with them. Also, each civilization embodies one or more facets of Vinge's preoccupation with information processes as a function of identity, individual and collective freedom, and social control. The Powers are information made self-aware, Great Old Ones whose presence in the galaxy of the far future spells out the promise and the danger of truly transcendent AI in our own world, today. The Skroderiders are precisely an illustration of that danger, cyborgs enslaved to a cruel command-and-control setting. The Tines, for their part, embody the signal-to-noise perspective on individual consciousness and social order, while the Spiders are us. As alien as they look to human eyes, their society's path to advancement recaps 20th-century humanity's faithfully enough that to look at them is to see our faces, distorted and changed but, in the end, still our own.

*Simone Caroti*

*See also*: Liu, Cixin; Reynolds, Alastair; Sterling, Bruce; Watts, Peter; Wilson, Robert Charles.

**FURTHER READING**

Vinge, Vernor. "The Coming Technological Singularity: How to Survive the Posthuman Era," 1993. edoras.sdsu.edu/~vinge/misc/singularity.html.

Walton, Jo. "*A Deepness in the Sky*: The Tragical History of Pham Nuwen." *What Makes This Book So Great*, Tor, 2014, pp. 21–23.

# W

## The War of the Worlds

H. G. Wells is considered a foundational figure in science fiction, pioneering many of the tropes that would come to define the genre. As a committed socialist, much of his later writing takes on a strongly didactic tone. Even in the scientific romances of the 1890s and 1900s, however, Wells utilized the idea of the alien to encourage critical reflection from his readership. His most culturally enduring aliens are surely the ruthless and technologically superior Martians of *The War of the Worlds* (serialized in 1897, published as a book in 1898).

Wells understood that time, as well as space, could be alien—even when that alien is ourselves. In an 1893 paper entitled "Man of the Year Million," Wells uses current trends to speculate on the likely form of humanity a million years hence, and the result—bald, bulbous heads, vestigial mouths and no ears, oversized hands at the end of long, slender limbs—set the template for popular depictions of aliens, including his own Martians in *War of the Worlds* and the so-called gray alien of UFO lore. In this and other work Wells wished to displace the anthropocentric notion that humanity was special by pointing out that it was subject to the same kind of biological changes, evolutionary pressures, and possibility of extinction as any other species on Earth.

Self-reflection is also behind the most famous of Wells's alien creations, the Martian invaders of *The War of the Worlds*. Physically described as giant heads wreathed by tentacles and possessed of "intellects vast and cool and unsympathetic," their form, psyches, and vastly superior technology are a result of the great age of Martian civilization, vastly outstripping humanity's tenure on Earth. Yet, because Mars is such an old planet, the Martians turn to Earth for the resources their own planet now lacks, and their great superiority means that they look upon the native human population as lower life-forms—little more than pests to be exterminated (just as, Wells makes clear, English settlers treated the Tasmanians). Thanks to illustrations and adaptations in visual media, the apparatus of this invasion has become as iconic in popular culture as the aliens themselves: the towering Martian tripods, the disintegrating heat rays mounted on metal tentacles, and the red weed that conquers the English ecosystem as easily as the Martians do humanity. Indeed, *The War of the Worlds* is not a novel of heroism or resistance, but of survival amid conquest. The novel's nameless narrator can do little more than scurry, hide, and record his observations as the Martians overcome humanity's futile attempts at military resistance and run rampant over the English countryside and in London. In the end, nothing human proves equal to the Martian

Actor, director, and producer Orson Welles (right) with British author H. G. Wells, following Welles's infamous radio dramatization of Wells's book *The War of the Worlds* in 1938. (Hulton Archive/Getty Images)

threat; instead, the invaders are brought low by terrestrial bacteria against which they possess no immunity, and the Martians, their machines, and their plants die off.

Immediate critical and popular success for the novel led to many new printings, some illustrated and some (like the first American serializations) already adapting the narrative by changing the location of the invasion to one more familiar to their audience. By far the most famous (or infamous) of such adaptations was Orson Welles's radio drama on Halloween night, 1938, which the actor tailored to the medium by presenting the narrative as a series of radio broadcasts, occurring that very day in New Jersey (rather than Victorian England). Afterward, the broadcast was blamed for inciting panic across the United States as unknowing radio listeners took the drama for genuine radio reporting and believed the nation was under attack. Recently, scholars have debated the extent to which this panic actually occurred and how much of it was manufactured in the media afterward; while it seems unlikely, as sources reported later, that a million radio listeners succumbed to the illusion of invasion, the belief in the hysteria has become just as much part of the popular narrative about *War of the Worlds* as the novel itself. Welles himself initially played down the panic and disclaimed responsibility amid legal threats in the immediate aftermath, only to embrace his persona as the man who frightened America in subsequent decades, freely embellishing the incident with often fictive anecdotes. Reportedly, some of the accidental listeners did not realize Welles's invaders were aliens, fearing instead that they were German. Indeed, the broadcast played to contemporary fears of invasion by foreign powers as the threat of World War II loomed. However, changes to the narrative and context meant that this adaptation lacked the self-critique of Wells's original text.

*The War of the Worlds* has since been adapted into many popular forms of media like graphic novels, television series, and even a musical album—*Jeff Wayne's Musical Version of The War of the Worlds*, in 1978. The highest-profile adaptations since Welles are the two big-budget Hollywood-made movies based on the novel; the first directed by George Pal in 1953 and the second directed by Steven Spielberg in 2005. The 1953 film is a loose adaptation, changing the setting to 1950s California and adding many characters, a romantic subplot for the lead (no longer mere observer but a scientist actively fighting the invasion), and heavy religious messaging. The film replaced the Martian tripods (then difficult to recreate on film) with hovering vessels shaped like manta rays; these have become nearly as iconic a depiction of the alien as the original tripods. The use of atomic weaponry by the American military in the film taps into the film's depiction of Cold War anxiety, the fear of foreign invasion with apocalyptic consequences for the whole planet.

The 2005 Spielberg film comes closest to recapturing the original sense of the novel. While this film never names its aliens as Martians (contemporary audiences are, by now, too familiar with Mars as a dead world), it replicates the tripods and heat rays with the latest special-effects technology. Although the specifics of the plot are considerably altered, like the original novel it mediates the audience's perspective through a single character, a lackluster father trying to keep his children safe during the invasion; this restricted perspective echoes the chaos and helplessness of Wells's narrative. The film's depiction of a sudden alien attack in New Jersey was explicitly meant to evoke post–9/11 fears of sudden violence in a country that had once considered itself safe within its borders. But the film is less about warfare and more about the refugee experience suffered by the family at the forefront of the film, anonymous members of the fleeing masses. In this way, it asks its American audience to put itself in the position of the many displaced peoples whom they had only ever seen on television news reports; by this act of empathetic imagination, it comes closest to Wells's original critique of smug imperialist superiority nestled within a popular narrative of alien invasion.

*Steve Asselin*

See also: *Invasion of the Body Snatchers*; *Close Encounters of the Third Kind*.

## FURTHER READING

Cantrill, Hadley. *The Invasion from Mars: A Study in the Psychology of Panic*. Princeton University Press, 1940.
Markley, Robert. *Dying Planet: Mars in Science and the Imagination*. Duke University Press, 2005.
Parrinder, Patrick. *Shadows of the Future: H. G. Wells, Science Fiction, and Prophecy*. Liverpool University Press, 1995.

## *Warhammer 40,000: Dawn of War III*

*Warhammer* began in 1983 as a fantasy-related tabletop war game developed by the English firm Games Workshop. In 1987 they released a science-fiction version, *Warhammer 40,000*, set in the 41st millennium, which did not do much to hide its fantasy origins: two of the alien races, the Eldar and the Orks, are closely related to Tolkien's elves and orcs. There are related comics and a large number of books set in this universe.

The video-game version, *Warhammer 40,000: Dawn of War*, was released in 2004, and after three expansion packs there was a sequel in 2011. Number 3 arrived in April 2017. It was developed by Relic Entertainment and Feral Interactive and published by SEGA and Feral Interactive in the United States. In this iteration of the game, *Warhammer* began to address the complaints and suggestions regarding the campaign mode of the two previous games, specifically the inability of the player to have a story in which the aliens were not simply regarded as the enemy (or a circumstantial ally at best) and thus included a more varied background for the motivations of the other two factions.

In *Dawn of War 3*, the three factions that compete for the Spear of Khaine—a mysterious item that would greatly increase the power of those who possess it—are separated by races, similar to what happens in almost every game in the *Warhammer* franchise. The first are the humans (including both the Imperial Guard—soldiers of the Imperium—and the Space Marines, a metahuman faction consecrated to the will of the Emperor), the Orks (green-skinned humanoids that make their weaker and smaller cousins, the Gretchins, work for them), and the Eldar, an ancient race of humanoids with elven traits.

While the campaign of the first game of the *Dawn of War* series was entirely anthropocentric, *DoW3* offers the perspective of the three factions, and thus provides more insight on their motives and purposes. For instance, the Eldar seek the Spear of Khaine because of a religious prophecy, while the Orks see the potential of such a weapon and aim to use it to conquer the universe. The playing faction of humans, however, seeks the destruction of the spear.

The Eldar, the Imperium, and the Orks are also depicted as having different technological levels: while the former seems to use technologies that almost move from science fiction to magic (the bonesingers, some sort of psychic engineers, are the backbone of such technology), the Imperium's technology seems to be not too far from the one that can be found in 2017 (with the exception of everything related to space traveling). Orks, finally, are presented as cunning tribal clans that use everything they find to adapt it to their needs. One of the best examples of this would be the Killa Kan, a crude copy of the Space Marines' Dreadnought.

Every game from the *Dawn of War* series starts with the player, as the commander of the Blood Ravens chapter of Space Marines, immersed *in media res* in a battle against the Orks that invariably ends with a green-skins massacre. This suggests a reading in which (at least non–pink-skin) aliens are regarded as the enemy and are weaker than humans or, at least, lack tactical development.

The Orks are shown as the opposite of the Eldars. The Eldars are solemn and deep, as the opening cutscene of the campaign vouches for, using sentences such as "Fiery skies shall light the way, and blood shall spill over the Wandering World" (2017). Their tone is prophetic, serious, and direct, without a hint of doubt or humor. On the other hand, Orks are irreverent, both in form and in content. Orks' subtitles are a phonetic corruption of English: "We're in, boiz" (2017). Moreover, interactions with Orks and Gretchins are humorous. In mission 2, in which the player has to protect an enormous cannon that the Ork leader will later use to attack the Eldars, one of the Gretchin engineers shows off the defensive mechanisms of the cannon, should it be under attack. One of them is a speaker that aims to demoralize the enemy so they feel bad and retreat, and the other are popguns and fireworks. Both the overseriousness and the joking tone of both alien races suggests disconnection with humanity, which is depicted as sharing part of the qualities of the Eldars and Orks, presenting missions that are not as serious as the former's but not as funny as the latter's either. This is further reinforced by the recommended gameplay of each race: while Orks' potential relies mainly on early game and Eldars rely on late game, the Space Marines have enough good early units and enough technological development to face both factions without (too much) trouble.

*Warhammer 40.000: Dawn of War III* presents a relationship with the alien in which, whatever the perspective, the other is invariably the enemy, although they sometimes cooperate against a major threat. This is motivated by a constant state of war between races that crystallizes in radically different views of the same events. Although there are villains in every faction and there are sometimes battles within each faction (especially Orks), the frequency of those in comparison to battles between races is minimal. War is always eventually waged against the other.

*Jaime Oliveros*

See also: *FTL*; *Mass Effect* (Trilogy).

## FURTHER READING

Carter, Marcus, Mitchell Harrop, and Martin Gibbs. "Drafting an Army: The Playful Pastime of Warhammer 40,000." *Games and Culture*, vol. 9, no. 2, 2014, pp. 122–47.

Carter, Marcus, Mitchell Harrop, and Martin Gibbs. "The Roll of Dice in Warhammer 40,000." *9th Game Research Lab Spring Seminar*, 2013, Tampere, Finland.

Park, David J., Sameer Deshpande, Bernard Cova, and Stefano Pace. "Seeking Community Through Battle: Understanding the Meaning of Consumption Processes for *Warhammer* Gamers' Communities Across Borders." *Consumer Tribes*, edited by Bernard Cova, Robin Kozinets, and Avi Shankar, Elsevier, 2007, pp. 212–24.

## Watts, Peter

Canadian science-fiction writer Peter Watts' (1958–) PhD in marine science means this scientist-writer's works are based on solid science, so much so that Watts has made a habit of including pages of reference material at the end of each novel. In addition to his fiction having a sound basis in science, Watts also leverages the power of multimedia with the rifters.com website, which includes novel-related material. This material is presented as coming from other genres, such as a pharmaceutical company presentation about gene therapy used to produce vampire characteristics in humans or a fictional report to the pope on the threat posed by a cult that rewires members' temporal lobes in order to make scientific discoveries by communing with the Divine.

Watts's primary alien story is *Blindsight* (2006), a Hugo Award–nominated hard-science-fiction novel that draws upon classic alien-encounter tropes while presenting the reader with philosophical questions based on sound scientific principles. (The sequel was *Echopraxia*, 2014.) *Blindsight* begins as a classic alien-encounter story when aliens send probes or "Fireflies" to earth. This "Firefall" arrives undetected and scatters across the surface of the earth in a precise grid before emitting a radio signal and disintegrating. The fact that aliens seem to have surveyed (or taken a picture of) the Earth generates global anxiety and a frenzied effort to deploy a ship and crew to the location of the signal.

But the crew of the *Theseus*, sent to investigate the source of a signal being broadcast by a passing comet and assumed to be directed toward the alien homeworld, is anything but typical. The story is told through Siri Keeton, a man with only half a brain as a result of a radical childhood hemispherectomy conducted to cure epileptic seizures, and a Synthesist who interprets complex information and distils it for others to understand. The crew is led by Sarasti, a vampire resurrected by modern science, and also includes Susan James, a linguist whose brain has been surgically altered to generate multiple personalities so as to increase mental processing by dividing the labor; Isaac Szpindel, who has been so altered by implants that he can barely feel his own flesh; and Amanda Bates, the military officer wired into her weapons. The crew are posthuman modifications of the baseline, making them alien in their own right, but given the utter strangeness of the aliens, they are perfectly suited for first contact.

Unlike the stereotypical "take me to your leader" first communication with the aliens, the first exchange in *Blindsight* is a warning from the aliens not to approach. The humans continue conversation and interact with what seems to be an intelligent species that easily converses with them. Unfortunately, as the linguist in the group learns, what appears to be intelligent conversation is nothing more than a Chinese room—in other words, they are conversing with a species that has no self-awareness. This is also what Siri is, in a way, making him more like the aliens than any other crew member, and his alienation and inability to interpret the communication made by his own crew suggest that humanity's much-celebrated use of language as a distinguishing feature from animals may be overrated.

In constructing his aliens, Watts follows the architectural principle "form follows function." In that principle, the way that people use a space matches the physicality of the space. In other words, people inhabit people-sized and -shaped spaces, and the aliens who inhabit the alien vessel that calls itself *Rorschach* look like the ship they inhabit.

They dub the aliens they meet "scramblers," plastic-skinned, multi-limbed, radially symmetrical creatures as big as humans that are fast enough to move only during the saccades of human eyes so that they seem near invisible to the crew. At the same time, they consist mostly of motor and sensory neurons without processing, leading the crew to compare them to a blood cell with waldos. The crew witnesses the scramblers devouring one of their own, thinking it is some kind of internecine warfare.

It turns out the scramblers aren't the aliens—*Rorschach*, their vessel, is—and the scramblers that the crew catches to study are actually spies that allowed themselves to be captured so that they can then return, be torn apart by their counterparts, and share what they have learned. This is how the aliens share information. While human beings use language, to *Rorschach* language is a signal with no usable intelligence. All it does is consume resources like a virus. Firefall is a reconnaissance to find out about the enemy and *Theseus*'s travels to *Rorschach*'s location are an invasion of that enemy.

This is the primary cognitive challenge that Watts presents in the book: how does a species like humans, with our heavy reliance on language to communicate, make contact with an alien species for whom language appears to be a weapon?

The problem of communication that arises in the novella *The Island* poses a similar question: how to communicate with a being 100 million kilometers wide with the brainpower of 20 billion human brains that photosynthesizes off a red dwarf star and communicates via light signals.

For Watts, the answer to the question of how to communicate with an alien species whose experience and evolution is so different from our own is that you don't. This failure to communicate suggests that the alien acts as a mirror in which we are shown how limited our capacity for communication would be when dealing with any being that doesn't resemble us. Siri Keeton, the brain-damaged interpreter who is almost as alien as the actual aliens, may be human, but ultimately, the novel demonstrates through Siri and the aliens that failure to communicate with another being whose experience is different from one's own is inevitable. The conclusion may be a nihilistic one, but it's based in some pretty sound science extrapolated into a first-contact story.

*Michelle Braun*

See also: *Arrival*; Liu, Cixin; Reynolds, Alastair; Vinge, Vernor.

## FURTHER READING

Glaz, Adam. "*Rorschach*, We Have a Problem! The Linguistics of First Contact in Watts's *Blindsight* and Lem's *His Master's Voice*." *Science Fiction Studies*, vol. 41, no. 2, 2014, pp. 364–91.

Kowalewski, Hubert. "In Space No One Can Hear You Speak: Embodied Language in Stanislaw Lem's *Solaris* and Peter Watts' *Blindsight*." *Extrapolation*, vol. 56, no. 3, 2015, pp. 353–76.

Whitmarsh, Patrick. "'Imagine You're a Machine': Narrative Systems in Peter Watts's *Blindsight* and *Echopraxia*." *Science Fiction Studies*, vol. 43, no. 2, 2016, pp. 237–59.

## *The Way of Thorn and Thunder: The Kynship Chronicles* by Daniel Heath Justice

The relationship between James Cameron's film *Avatar* (2009) and Ursula K. Le Guin's *The Word for World Is Forest* (1976) is sufficiently well established to have a Wikipedia entry in addition to academic commentary (Barnwell). What is less well-known is the film's resemblance, intentional or otherwise, to Cherokee scholar and novelist Daniel Heath Justice's trilogy, *The Way of Thorn and Thunder*. While most reviewers have read Justice's trilogy as "high fantasy," the novel can also be read as a science-fictional investigation of the clash between two planetary cultures imagined in relationship to the historical experiences of colonization by Native Americans, in general, and the Cherokee, in particular. While there is no rational explanation given for the Melding that occurs between the Eld Green and the world of Humans, the trilogy's affinity with both *The Word for World Is Forest* and *Avatar* make it worth considering within the broad definition of science fiction, although it is clearly—and aptly—on the borderlines.

Daniel Heath Justice (1975–) describes himself as "a Colorado-born Canadian citizen of the Cherokee Nation." As of 2017, he holds a Canada Research Chair in Indigenous Literature and Expressive Culture at the University of British Columbia and is the author of *Our Fire Survives the Storm: A Cherokee Literary History* (2006) and coeditor of *Sovereign Erotics: A Collection of Two-Spirit Literature* (with Qwo-Li Driskill, Deborah Miranda, and Lisa Tatonetti; 2011). His most recent book is *Badger*, a 2015 entry in the Reaktion Books' Animal series. Justice lives with his husband, Kent, "in the traditional territories of the shíshálh people" on the west coast of British Columbia. Along with his work on indigenous literature, Justice has contributed work to indigenous queer studies focusing on kinship, masculinity, and Two-Spirit people.

*Thorn and Thunder* narrates the conflict between the Folk of Eld Green and the human colonizers who arrived in their land following the Melding between their worlds. Following First Nations' traditions of regarding all living things as relations, the Folk include multiple peoples who make up the Seven Sister nations; some of these are humanoid and some animal. The two predominant humanoid species are the Kyn Nation, who live in relationship to the *wyr*, the elemental life source that is embodied in the Eternity Tree, and the Tetawi Nation of short brown-skinned people who live in matrilineal clans. The Melding took place 1005 years before the story begins, at a time when Humans have deeply penetrated the Everland; the Folk remain in the wild places or live with Humans in various degrees of assimilation and/or servitude. However, this is not enough for the ambitions of some humans, particularly the Dreydmaster (High Priest of the Dreyd religion), Lojar Vald, who sees the extinction of the Folk not only in terms of colonial Human right, but also as a means to his ascension to godhood. Vald's ambition, combined with Human greed for land and wealth, leads to the expulsion of the Folk, who are driven westward to an inhospitable land far from the lush green world of the Old Everland. *Thorn and Thunder* thus narrates a largely irresolvable conflict between Humans and aliens (called "Unhumans" by the colonizers) that roughly reiterates the narratives of both *Word* and *Avatar* but is resolutely told from the perspective of the alien/indigenous. In this way, Justice both utilizes and inverts the trope of the alien as other; the Folk are indeed other to the Humans, but, as obvious stand-ins for First Nations people, they are both the moral and narrative center of the trilogy. To put it at its simplest, settlers (generally Europeans) are other to the Cherokee.

This central trope of otherness that valorizes indigenous perspectives is very much in line with Justice's academic focus on indigenous literature that works to empower and decolonize. While the destruction of the Hometree in *Avatar* echoes that of the Eternity Tree in *Thorn and Thunder*, Justice entirely avoids the White (Human) Savior trope that drives the former. While there are some good Humans, notably the Reachwarden Qualla'am Kaer, whose sense of justice compels him to abandon the colonial politics of the Reach, the central battle is fought (and won) by representatives of the Folk, notably the She-Kyn warrior Tarsa'deshae, her female and male lovers, Jitani and Daladir, the He-Tetawa Tobhi, and the She-Tetawa Quill. The divisive results of colonization are represented by the Celestials, Kyn who have converted to Human religion and rejected the *wyr* and the Way of Deep Green. The Celestial leader, Neranda, is also instrumental in the Folks' victory over Vald when she realizes that her assimilationist approach has failed the Folk and is contributing to their destruction instead of their survival.

In defeating Vald, the Folk free themselves to establish a new green world in their place of exile, reestablishing the *wyr* through the rebirth of the Eternity Tree, now known as the Forevergreen Tree (*Avatar* again partially echoes this through the role of the Tree of Souls in the victory of Jake and the Na'vi). The decolonizing hopefulness of the novel is evident in the reestablishment of indigenous culture, albeit in a damaged and diminished new homeland. Furthermore, Justice takes pains to echo Cherokee historical experience in his depiction of the Darkening Trail of the Expulsion—an obvious reference to the Cherokee Trail of Tears (1839–1850), in the centrality of women as warriors, and in the existence of a third gender, the Zhe-Kyn, who are healers. The destruction of indigenous gender systems was one of the most insidious effects of colonization; Brian Joseph Gilley claims in "Two-Spirit Men's Sexual Survivance against the Inequality of Desire" that Two-Spirit Cherokee see themselves as "having the responsibility to restore and maintain *duyuktv* [balance, truth, justice] through practicing Cherokee lifeways and ending gender oppressions" (Gilley, 125). Justice himself takes up that responsibility by imagining Humans/Europeans as aliens in an indigenous world.

*Wendy Gay Pearson*

*See also*: *Avatar*; Gwyneth Jones's Aleutians; Le Guin, Ursula K.; Russell, Mary Doria.

## FURTHER READING

Amberstone, Celu. "Interview with First Nations Fantasy Author Daniel Heath Justice." *SF Canada*, Spring 2008, www.sfcanada.ca/.

Barnhill, David. "Spirituality and Resistance: Ursula K. Le Guin's *The Word for World Is Forest* and the Film *Avatar*." *Journal for the Study of Religion, Nature and Culture*, vol. 4, no. 4, 2010, pp. 478–98.

Gilley, Brian Joseph. "Two-Spirit Men's Sexual Survivance against the Inequality of Desire." *Queer Indigenous Studies: Critical Interventions in Theory, Politics, and Literature*, edited by Qwo-Li Driskill, Chris Finley, Brian Joseph Gilley, and Scott Lauria Morgensen, University of Arizona Press, 2011, pp. 123–31.

## Weinbaum, Stanley G.

Stanley G. Weinbaum (1902–1935) began writing science fiction professionally in 1930, unfortunately dying of lung cancer just five years later. He published numerous SF short stories during his lifetime, with longer SF works appearing posthumously, including *The New Adam* (1939) and *The Dark Other* (1950). Weinbaum is best known for "A Martian Odyssey" (1934). This highly influential first-contact story initially appeared in *Wonder Stories* and later saw dozens of reprints. "A Martian Odyssey" and its lesser-known sequel, "Valley of Dreams" (1934), are two of the nine stories that constitute his Planetary Series. All set in the same universe, the series introduced a host of fascinating aliens, the most famous of which was Tweel, half plant, half animal, who vaguely resembles an ostrich, from "A Martian Odyssey" and "Valley of Dreams."

"A Martian Odyssey" centers on the adventures of space cowboy Dick Jarvis and the alien Tweel. The spaceship *Ares* makes the first landing on Mars, and Jarvis embarks on an extended exploration of the planet. The engine of his small ship fails, causing him to crash-land hundreds of miles from the *Ares*. Jarvis soon witnesses two creatures locked in combat, the friendly Tweel and one with tentacles. Noticing Tweel carries a bag, Jarvis determines he must come from an advanced civilization, and so Jarvis saves him from the tentacle creature. The tentacle creature is later revealed to be a deadly "Dream Beast," capable of luring its prey with hallucinations. The Dream Beast is indicative of Weinbaum's dangerous aliens; it does not appear to have advanced intelligence, is not capable of direct communication with humans, seems to have nothing in common with human interests, and seems to lack clearly defined motivation.

Conversely, Weinbaum's friendly aliens complicate human exceptionality. While initially seeing Tweel as "the creature," Jarvis soon discovers that while he cannot understand any of Tweel's language, Tweel quickly picks up some of his, leading Jarvis to question his conceptions of human superiority. Toward the end of the story, when talking of Tweel's "race," Jarvis states Tweel is from "a civilization and culture equal to ours and maybe more than equal." This sentiment sounds insane to Jarvis's human companions, who hear this story from Jarvis after the fact. But for Jarvis, his encounter with Tweel leads to more than understanding; it results in mutual respect and friendship. Later, Jarvis and Tweel encounter a race of barrel-shaped creatures whose actions they fail to understand. The creatures seem to share one central mind and spend their time gathering rocks and vegetation before crushing themselves under a giant wheel. Despite being able to repeat words to Jarvis, the individual creatures appear as mindless cogs, perhaps symbolic of anxieties surrounding communism. When Jarvis steals their healing crystal from them, an action he seems to deem acceptable due to the barrel creatures' lack of intelligence and individuality, the aliens turn on him, and he barely escapes before the *Ares* can rescue him. Despite being able to escape on his own, Tweel stays with Jarvis until he knows he is safe, leading Jarvis to muse that Tweel behaved far better toward him than most of his fellow humans would.

In "Valley of Dreams," Jarvis and one of his companions from the *Ares*, Leroy, discover an ancient and mostly deserted city built by Tweel's people, the Thoth. They learn Tweel's people had visited Egypt, giving rise to the Egyptian god Thoth. As a parting gift, Jarvis gives Tweel the atomic blaster from one of their rockets, much to the dismay of the other humans, who automatically assume Tweel's people might be their enemies one day, a notion Jarvis finds both absurd and selfish.

Weinbaum gave his aliens their own purposes, many of which are opaque to the human characters, and aliens such as the Thoth and the Lotus Eaters from the story of the same name (1935) question and challenge the superiority of the human mind in an alien location. His friendly aliens offer humans opportunities for growth, suggesting a certain amount of intelligence is what makes certain beings worth of respect, while aliens who possess pure otherness are something to be feared or exploited.

*Skye Cervone*

*See also*: Burroughs, Edgar Rice; Heinlein, Robert A.; Moore, C. L.; Smith, E. E. "Doc."

## FURTHER READING

Huntington, John. "A Martian Odyssey." *Rationalizing Genius: Ideological Strategies in the Classic American Science Fiction Short Story*, edited by John Huntington, Rutgers University Press, 1989, pp. 119–25.
Schweitzer, Darrell. "Why Stanley G. Weinbaum Still Matters." *New York Review of Science Fiction*, vol. 22, no. 3, issue 255, November 2009, pp. 16–20. Reprinted in *The Threshold of Forever: Essays and Reviews*, edited by Darrell Schweitzer, Wildside Press, 2017, pp. 57–67.
Suvin, Darko. "Stanley Weinbaum: We've Met the Aliens and They Are Us." *Extrapolation*, vol. 52, no. 2, 2011, pp. 227–45.

## The Wess'Har Series by Karen Traviss

The Wess'Har sequence (2006–2010) consists of six books: *City of Pearl, Crossing the Line, The World Before, Matriarch, Ally,* and *Judge.* The books begin when Environmental Hazard Officer Shan Frankland is approached by a government minister to join a mission to Cavanagh's Star to find out what happened to a lost colony. She accepts a Suppressed Briefing and sets out, a little puzzled as to why she has agreed but with a curious sense of mission and a feeling it will serve as an atonement.

Frankland is a police officer who has worked the beat in Reading (a small city in the south of England) and who has seen the consequences of human action. She is unimpressed. Frankland is also a neo-pagan, a vegan, and has a suppressed history of supporting ecoterrorism. All this is crucial because it constructs an outsider status that, combined with Franklin's veganism, means she is inclined to see humans as *just another animal*—and one perhaps less worthy of respect than others.

When Frankland and the crew of Marines and Scientists land on Constantine 2, they find not only a small but thriving Christian pacifist vegan colony but three alien groups: the Bezeri, intelligent cephalopods who are indigenous to the planet but recovering from a near-extinction event; the Wess'har, mostly noninterventionist vegans who believe in keeping the harmony of all living things; and the diplomats, the Ussissi, who shuttle between the Wess'har and the Insenj. The Wess'har arrived at the request of the Bezeri to wipe out the Insenj, invaders from a neighboring planet in search of living space to resolve their own overcrowding. Not only were the Insenj profligate, but on Constantine 2 they were infected by a bacteria called C'naatat, which renders its host infinitely adaptable and, as a side-effect, near indestructible and immortal.

The key to these books is who and what are "people." The Wess'har regard every living thing as "people." Shan Frankland thinks she does but begins to realize that this is a belief grafted on, and as the Christians of Constantine are tested by subsequent events, it becomes clear that it is only a surface belief for them also. The scientists on the mission do not grasp the concept, and when one dissects a Bezeri infant found (apparently) dead on the shore, things begin to spiral downward. The discovery of C'naatat and the recognition by the intelligence agent Rayat and the commander of the ship, Lindsay Neville, of its threat and, at the same time, their refusal to accept fully the Bezeri as people leads to a misguided attack on the island that harbors the parasite. The cobalt bombs poison the water and kill off the Bezeri.

The events that unfold lead to one nation of the spider-like Issenj accepting Wess'har help to reduce their population and reconstruct their planet through a deliberate program of military action and biowarfare: the eviction of the Christians and the Wess'har decision to call in their older cousins, the Eqbas Vorhi, who are, as someone describes them in the final book, "militarized vegans" (*Judge*) who have no truck with nonintervention if people are at risk. On the basis of what they have learned about Earth's politics and climate change, both the Wess'har and the Eqbas Vorhi conclude that the people of Earth are in danger. Neither of them are talking about the humans. The series concludes with a mission to Earth and a pact with the Pacific Rim countries, which is eventually rolled out across most of the Earth governments, involving drastic population reduction through war, famine, and probably, but not confirmed, biowarfare. Even vegans aren't safe, as the Eqbas Vorhi also seek to roll back agribusiness for the sake of the planet and its other peoples and are utterly opposed to a humanocentric definition of terraforming or anything that looks like it.

Two interspecies romances also run throughout the books: a sexual romance between Shan Frankland, the Wess'har Aras, and Ade Bennett, sergeant of marines, made possible and necessary by the consequences of C'naatat; and also between Eddie Marchallat and the juvenile Wess'har Giyadas, with whom he falls in love in the role of an uncle and for whom he relinquishes the Earth. Both romances function to emphasize the peopleness of people and to force a rethink of who and what "people" are and what the basis of individual identity is.

The trajectory of the books is to render the alien species as ever more *people* and the humans as ever more alien. The Wess'har do not lie, they are open about information, they share without thinking about it, and they do not believe in motive. The only thing that matters to them is the action taken and the consequence of that action. But arguments about morality shift constantly in these books: just as the utter smugness of the Wess'har becomes perhaps too much to bear in Book Three, *The World Before*, it comes under pressure from the challenges in *Matriarch* and *Ally*. Although Shan Frankland is constitutionally inclined to agree with them, by the end of the novel they are taking on some of her point of view. The Bezeri begin the book as victims of genocide twice over, gentle, artistic, culturally attractive. When given a second chance through being infected with C'naatat, which allows them to walk on land, they turn out to be voracious predators, held back only because they had already hunted all their large competitors to extinction. Individuals of the Issenj, who at first glance seem the most unchangeable, hive-like, least individualistic, and most swayed by crowd dynamics, turn out to be willing to take the biggest chances and to fully accept what needs to be done. Humans, on the other hand, look more and more illogical, swayed by fantasy, and resistant as the series goes on: the least civilized. Their right to exist on their planet becomes ever more conditional, the things that need to be done to restore it ever more palatable.

*Farah Mendlesohn*

*See also*: Cherryh, C. J.; Gwyneth Jones's Aleutians; Miéville, China.

## FURTHER READING

Pak, Chris. *Terraforming: Ecopolitical Transformations and Environmentalism in Science Fiction*. Liverpool University Press, 2016.

Sullivan, Heather I. "Unbalanced Nature, Unbounded Bodies, and Unlimited Technology: Ecocriticism and Karen Traviss's Wess'har Series." *Bulletin of Science, Technology & Society*, vol. 30, no. 4, 2010, pp. 274–84.

Vint, Sherryl. "Existing for Their Own Reasons: Animal Aliens." *Animal Alterity: Science Fiction and the Question of the Animal*, edited by Sherryl Vint, Liverpool University Press, 2010, pp. 135–56.

## White, James

From 1953 to 2000, in the United Kingdom, United States, and in translation, James White (1928–1999) created many memorable alien individuals and species. White is best known for the "Sector General" series set around a multi-environment, multispecies hospital floating in intergalactic space, but other works also feature aliens.

White's stories are presented as puzzles and problems to be solved, often alongside moral or spiritual dilemmas for the viewpoint characters. They typically seek ways to avoid or mitigate the threat, actuality, or outcome of interspecies conflict. Interspecies relationships, and interpersonal relationships between species, are major concerns. Solutions emerge from understanding the motivation, character, and physiology of the alien, and communication is key. Viewpoint characters of different species view individuals of all species as worthy of respect and consideration. Aliens are shown as allies, collaborators, colleagues, friends, and life mates; as well as patients and combatants, puzzles to be solved; and sometimes, temporarily, as enemies. Initially, Earth human males predominate as actors and authority figures, while female and nonhuman individuals are undercharacterized. Later books feature a variety of viewpoints and characters of different sexes and species and include aliens in conversation, while not entirely escaping the earlier focus on human male authority and concerns.

The Sector General stories and novels were published between 1957 and 1999. These typically involve a medical emergency presenting a practical or moral problem, often both at once, which must be solved to save an alien patient's life, or, sometimes, to keep or restore peace. Alien physiology and environments are described, and each species is given a four-character classification that summarizes these (e.g., "an AUGL patient—one of the 40-foot, armored, fish-like natives of Chalderescol II"). These classifications are a memorable feature of the stories, although White confessed to having no system for assigning them. "Alien physiology tapes" also feature: these store memories of medical experts and can be impressed upon the mind of another individual of any species. Characters—both human and alien—generally refer to themselves and others as "it," which aids the reader in aligning Earth humans with their alien peers and allows White to have fun in episodes featuring gender or sexuality. Later stories retain these features while developing the complexity of character and situation.

The series features viewpoint characters of several different species. Surgeon Dr. Conway and Psychologist O'Mara, both Earth Human (DBDG) males, appear throughout, developing relationships with colleagues and patients of many species and solving puzzles presented by their illnesses, injuries, and behaviors. O'Mara first appears in "O'Mara's Orphan" (1960) as "a good rule-of-thumb psychologist with plenty of common sense who was not afraid to take calculated risks" (3). As chief psychologist through many books, O'Mara is charged with keeping interspecies relationships in the hospital harmonious, until its ultimate retirement in *Mind Changer* (1998). Likewise, the Cinrusskin (GLNO), Dr. Prilicla—"six-legged, exoskeletal and insect-like, with the empathic faculty"—appears for the first time in "Visitor at Large" (1959); develops its career throughout the series; and is a major viewpoint character as the ranking medical officer in *Double Contact* (1999), working with military colleagues to renegotiate a botched first contact. The multilimbed, two-stomached Sommaradvan (DCNF) Trainee Cha Thrat's many misadventures in *Code Blue Emergency* (1987) form the basis of its subsequent career at Sector General. *The Genocidal Healer* (1991) features the huge, multi-armed Tarlan (BRLH) Surgeon-Captain Lioren coming to terms with having inadvertently decimated an entire planetary population.

White depicted a very wide range of alien physiologies among the staff and patients of Sector General. The elephantine Tralthan (FGLI) Thornnastor, with its delicate symbiote OTSB, appears in "Sector General" (1957) as an intern surgeon and becomes a senior diagnostician capable of retaining impressions of up to 10 minds of different species simultaneously. Caterpillar-like Kelgians (DBLF), crab-like Melfians (ELNT) and chlorine-breathing Illensans (PVSJ) jostle along the hospital corridors. "Trouble With Emily" (1958) (6) features the "pint-sized" Dr. Arretapec (VUXG), who lives in a jar and looks like a prune floating in syrup, as well as the potentially sentient Brontosaurus-like creature who is its "patient." The stories in *Major Operation* (1971) culminate in Dr. Conway's successful treatment of a "strata creature" (no classification given) who is the size of a small continent.

White's other works also feature aliens, most notably *All Judgement Fled* (1963). An alien ship arriving in the solar system attracts a human expedition to make first contact. The emphasis is on the humans grappling with the communications and practical difficulties presented by the alien ship and on convincing an alien civilization that human beings are friends rather than enemies. The alien creatures themselves are viewed only through human eyes. In *Open Prison* (aka *The Escape Orbit*) (1965), a human interstellar empire is at war with the empire of the alien Bugs because "to the ordinary beings of both species their physical aspect was mutually loathsome" (7). There may be hope for survival and future reconciliation. The aliens barely feature and are viewed only through human eyes.

In *The Watch Below* (1966), a small group of humans struggle to survive in the bowels of a wrecked tanker, while the refugee fleet of the water-breathing Unthans approaches Earth. Shared experience ultimately allows humans and aliens to come to an accommodation, while in *Federation World* (1988) two Earth Human applicants for citizenship in the Galactic Federation are involved with alien species while they train as potential First Contacts.

*Caroline J. Mullan*

See also: Brin, David; Cherryh, C. J.; Simak, Clifford D.

**FURTHER READING**

Langford, David. "*Hospital Station* by James White (1962)." *The Greenwood Encyclopedia of Science Fiction and Fantasy: Themes, Works, and Wonders*, edited by Gary Westfahl, Greenwood Press, 2005, pp. 1084–86.
Westfahl, Gary. "Doctors' Ordeals: The Sector General Stories of James White." *No Cure for the Future: Disease and Medicine in Science Fiction and Fantasy*, edited by Gary Westfahl and George Slusser, Greenwood Press, 2002, 111–18.
White, James. *The White Papers*. NESFA Press 1996.

## Whitlatch, Terryl

Terryl Whitlatch (1961–) is an American artist, creature designer, and animal anatomist—she calls herself an "artistic scientist"—with over a quarter century of experience working in the film and media industries, where she has become an industry favorite, populating imagined versions of earth, alien planets, and fantasy worlds with unique yet biologically possible beings. The daughter of an illustrator and biology teacher, Whitlatch studied vertebrate zoology and anatomy at Sonoma State University, hoping to become a paleontological reconstructionist, before completing her education in art and illustration at California College of Arts and Academy of Art University.

As an artist, Whitlatch's practice begins from anatomically rigorous studies of living organisms and proceeds through extrapolation of what is (or might be) strictly possible for extinct, extant, and imagined life-forms, given particular biological and ecological conditions. As a result, her work traverses science fiction, fantasy, and realist genres of creature design and rendering. Like the literary practitioners of "hard SF," who value scientific realism in their fiction, Whitlatch has been lauded for her realistic accuracy and expressive range in the design of unreal yet plausible organisms. Whitlatch has contributed creature art and conceptual designs to dozens of projects, working as a client for natural-history museums and zoological organizations, such as the San Diego Zoo and World Wildlife Fun, and for media companies, especially on animated films, television shows, video games, and source- or artbooks for Lucasfilm and its subsidiaries, Pixar, Disney, EA, Chronicle Books, and many others from the 1980s onward. Her non-alien art and design work contributed significantly to the creature concept design of films such as *Jumanji* (1995), *The Indian in the Cupboard* (1995), *Dragonheart* (1996), *Brother Bear* (2003), *The Polar Express* (2004), *Curious George* (2006), *Alvin and the Chipmunks* (2007), *Beowulf* (2007), *Brave* (2012), and *Jumanji: Welcome to the Jungle* (2017), among others.

But Whitlatch is perhaps best known among SF aficionados for her role in shaping the alien ecology of the *Star Wars* franchise in the late 1990s and early 2000s—and to a certain segment of the fan population, most unfamiliar with her role and name, she is infamous. Whitlatch first worked for George Lucas, director of *Star Wars Episode IV: A New Hope* (1977), during the production of the 1997 Special Edition of the original *Star Wars* trilogy. These edits of the original films are notorious among traditionalist fans for digitally adding, altering, and editing scenes, largely in an effort to flatten overperceived inconsistencies in the original films. Many of the digital additions to the Special Editions are alien creatures added to bring "life" to what was, originally, a rather biologically sparse visual universe. Whitlatch created the alien creatures that inhabit Lucas's edits, such as the mobile design for the dewbacks (a kind of desert lizard) used by Imperial stormtroopers in the Special Edition of *A New Hope* (originally the dewbacks were stiff, stationary props). Whitlatch also did the digital design of Jabba the Hutt, which was retroactively added into *A New Hope* to create continuity with his look in the original cut of *Star Wars Episode VI: Return of the Jedi* (1983) (in 1977 he was a rather boring human). Her design for Jabba the Hutt was recycled in *Star Wars Episode I: The Phantom Menace* (1999), where he appeared as a young crime lord on the then rather populous desert world of Tatooine. Whitlatch was key to making *The Phantom Menace* an extravaganza of alien species and creatures. She contributed designs for all of the alien species who compete in the Boonta Eve podrace that eventually unites Anakin Skywalker with his destiny, as well as the alien creature designs for the inhabitants of the planets Tatooine and Naboo. This included the fan-hated and first all-digital movie character Jar Jar Binks, as well as Anakin's podracing nemesis Sebulba. Whitlatch also designed aliens for *Men in Black* (1997) and *John Carter* (2012), the Disney adaptation of Edgar Rice Burroughs' *A Princess of Mars* (1912).

Whitlatch's contributions to the visual presence of aliens in American culture, as well as her prowess as an alien and creature design artist, are cataloged in several books. *The Wildlife of Star Wars: A Field Guide* (Chronicle Books, 2001) showcases the many creatures she created for Lucas while also expanding on the designs of earlier *Star Wars* aliens—down to the anatomical level. Her picture book *The Katurran Odyssey* (Simon & Schuster, 2004) launched a fantasy trilogy written with David Michael Wieger, based on her world-building art, about mythoreligious conflict on a planet of sentient lemurs; the trilogy has yet to be completed. Whitlatch's significance as an industry leader in alien and fantastic creature design is further attested in a series of three books about creature design. Her importance to the field of SF and fantasy art has been recognized multiple times by *Spectrum*, a book series that operates as the key adjudicator of excellence in the fantastic arts; she has been regularly featured as a guest artist of the Spectrum Fantastic Art Live exhibitions since 2013; and she was a judge for *Spectrum 23* (Flesk Publications, 2016).

Between projects, Whitlatch is an educator. She was previously an instructor of Creature Design and Construction/Anatomy at the Academy of Art University, creator of a series of Gnomon Workshops online courses in creature design and anatomy, and international speaker for the art-education program Schoolism. Whitlatch is a prolific international guest lecturer and workshop leader and is currently a resident artist at Imagination International Inc. Studios, where she runs the Creatures of Amalthea creature design curriculum.

*Sean Guynes-Vishniac*

*See also*: Burroughs, Edgar Rice; Mœbius; *Men in Black*; *Star Wars*.

**FURTHER READING**

Whitlatch, Terryl. *Animals Real and Imagined: Fantasy of What Is and What Might Be.* Design Studio Press, 2010.

Whitlatch, Terryl. *Principles of Creature Design: Creating Imaginary Animals.* Design Studio Press, 2015.

Whitlatch, Terryl. *Science of Creature Design: Understanding Animal Anatomy.* Design Studio Press, 2015.

## "Who Goes There?"

John W. Campbell (1910–1971) is arguably the most influential editor of science fiction in the first half of the 20th century. As editor of *Astounding Science Fiction* from 1937 until his death in 1971, Campbell is generally credited with shaping Golden Age science fiction. A prolific writer of space adventure stories, Campbell published under multiple pseudonyms. The most pertinent is Don A. Stuart (transparently derived from the name of his wife, Dona Stuart, which has led to speculation about her possible role in the writing). His novella "Who Goes There?" was published under this pen name (in *Astounding Science Fiction*, August 1938) and has been filmed on three different occasions: *The Thing from Another World* (1951), John Carpenter's *The Thing* (1982), and *The Thing* (2011). While Campbell's science fiction published under his own name had been heavily focused on space adventure and space opera, the stories written under the Stuart name concentrate on social commentary and values. The stories written under Campbell's own name offer little reason for analysis and feature archetypal characters who are poorly developed, stock penny-dreadful plots, and aliens who are either extremely benevolent or malevolent with no shading of gray.

The plot of "Who Goes There?" (1938) revolves around a scientific mission to Antarctica. Nearing the end of an Antarctic winter, the researchers find a frozen spaceship (from 20 million years previous) and attempt to thaw it out using thermite. The charge ignites the ship's magnesium hull, but the crew members save the ship's pilot, a seeming mass of vegetable matter who had frozen just feet from the ship while, the crew speculates, searching for warmth. The crew proceeds to thaw the alien, which revives it, and the alien proves to be able to replicate the image, memories, and personality of anything it devours so long as the alien has enough mass to do so.

The alien (presented solely as the thing) immediately replicates and replaces a member of the crew and is found out when it uses what remains of its own mass to attempt to replicate a sled dog. The crew witness the dog transformation and interrupt it, which leads them to begin to distrust one another concerning their status as human or alien. After using science to deduce the "state" of each being within the base, they find that nearly all the animals and 14 of the crew members have become aliens. Each is killed and its body burned, which leads to paranoia among the remaining crew members.

One member of the crew, Blair, the pathologist who had pushed for the thawing of the thing, goes insane with guilt and is locked in a remote cabin for a week while the majority of the scientific testing and events take place. Upon arriving at Blair's cabin, the remaining members of the crew determine that Blair has been taken over by the alien and is working on an atomic-powered antigravity device that would have allowed it to traverse the Drake Passage in one leap—resulting in the destruction of humanity. Humanity saved, the story ends with the "grace of God and half an hour" in the final paragraph.

One of the most interesting concepts regarding the thing as alien comes from Campbell's use of the Stuart pseudonym, which freed him from the very constraints he imposed on authors as editor of *Astounding Science Fiction* (later *Analog*). In the story, the thing is presented as being both more powerful (telepathy and shapeshifting) and more advanced technologically (spaceship and atomic power) than the men at the station. As an editor, Campbell seemingly wouldn't have accepted a story where the aliens were smarter or better than humans (specifically men); when writing under the Stuart pseudonym he didn't feel constrained by these same rules. The alien creates atomic power in a small shack—"a neat little thing for doing what men have been trying to do with 100-ton cyclotrons" (15 paragraphs from the end of the text) and creates a "shimmery sphere" made of "pure force" that works as an "atomic generator" (13 paragraphs from the end of the text) that is far beyond any human technology of its time. Given this creation and the magnesium-hulled spacecraft, coupled with telepathic abilities, the thing would appear to be from a more advanced civilization than the humans included in the story. While the humans are still able to "save the world" in the end (due to their ability to experiment and the weapon they have available, namely a blowtorch), it provides an interesting examination into the freedom Campbell found in writing the "Stuart" stories.

While presenting the thing as a sentient being with its own anatomy, thoughts, and abilities, Campbell never examines the alien as anything beyond the malevolent "other." The thing is presented without motivation for its deeds. It is referred to only as a "thing" (often prefaced by the adjective foul or evil) or "it" throughout the text and is presented merely as an element to dispose of within the text. While Campbell's alien may be working as a stand-in for communist anxieties within the story, the alien is so underdeveloped that it lacks any clear referent. Like many of the characters (human and alien) within Campbell's major works as an author, there is not enough development to speculate with any certainty about its meaning.

Peter Watts' "The Things" attempts to engage some of these deficiencies in Campbell's original story by presenting the same events of Campbell's "Who

Goes There?" from the perspective of the alien. Throughout this Hugo Award–nominated and Shirley Jackson Award–winning story, the things are depicted as sentient explorers who are attempting to raise the level of beings on Earth, having done so for many other planets, only to find themselves attacked for attempting to help. This treatment shows the remarkable change in the engagement of the other over the span of 70 years in science fiction and is strongly suggested for additional reading.

*Daniel Creed*

See also: Polar Aliens; *Thing, The*; Watts, Peter.

## FURTHER READING

Berger, Albert I. *The Magic That Works: John W. Campbell and the American Response to Technology.* Borgo Press, 1993.

Glasberg, Elena. "Who Goes There? Science, Fiction and Belonging in Antarctica." *Journal of Historical Geography*, vol. 34, no. 4, 2008, pp. 639–57.

Leane, Elizabeth. "Locating the Thing: The Antarctic as Alien Space in John W. Campbell's 'Who Goes There?'" *Science Fiction Studies*, vol. 32, no. 2, 2005, pp. 225–39.

# Wilson, Robert Charles

Robert Charles Wilson (1953–) is one of the most successful science-fiction authors working in Canada in recent decades, as evidenced by his Hugo Award–winning novel *Spin* (2005) and his other awards and nominations. Aliens are prominent in only a handful of his novels, but what emerges are ancient-alien species governed by complex programming traveling amid a cold universe infinitely more complex than anyone realizes.

In the Hypotheticals sequence—*Spin*, *Axis* (2007), and *Vortex* (2011)—a membrane called the Spin surrounds Earth and slows down time to a fraction of its passage in outer space. An Arch is also gradually assembled that forms an interstellar network that enables transit from Earth to other inhabitable planets. The Hypotheticals remain unknowable even after Turk Findley and Isaac Dvali, both of whom had been absorbed by the alien Hypotheticals in *Axis,* return 10,000 years later at the start of *Vortex* to seemingly herald a long-awaited first contact with the mysterious aliens. It isn't until the end of *Vortex* that the radically transformed Dvali learns the ancient race of Hypotheticals is long extinct. The only testimony to their existence is the self-replicating machinery that floats through space and archives all the resources and life-forms of thriving ecosystems. All that is left of the Hypotheticals is the complex programming of autonomic machinery merely fulfilling the goals of a long-dead species lost to the void of space.

This is a consistent narrative pattern. In *Darwinia* (1998), Guilford Law learns all existence is a stored recording on a universal Archive constructed eons ago by ancient races to cache all the wondrous examples of sentience in the universe. The Miracle—that is, the moment an immense section of Europe was replaced with an alien ecosphere dubbed Darwinia—is the result of psilife corrupting the Archive, a virus merely following the edicts of life: expand and reproduce. In *Burning Paradise* (2013), Cassie, her younger brother Thomas, and a handful of other characters keep the secret that the radiosphere, a mysterious layer surrounding Earth, is part of a living network dubbed the hypercolony that intervenes in Earth's history and, where relevant, eliminates potential threats via human-looking agents called sims. The sims are modeled after the "philosophical zombie," which is a being that possesses the external traits of a human but itself lacks any sentience or conscious experience. The sims are therefore nothing more than empty vessels for the hypercolony to interact with the human world, but Cassie learns that the hypercolony has already left Earth. What remains of the radiosphere is the dying hive that has been infected by alternate entities who follow the hypercolony across the galaxy as part of its own life cycle. The humans on Earth are merely useful resources and/or collateral damage in an alien conflict over "life" that moves from planet to planet indiscriminately. Finally, *Blind Lake* (2003) depicts a handful of characters trapped when Blind Lake, a research facility tasked with observing the Subject, an alien on a planet circling 47 Ursa Majoris, is mysteriously quarantined. Marguerite Hauser struggles with truly understanding this alien being, all the while juggling her domestic complications: her ex-husband Ray, a narcissistic and emotionally abusive bully; her burgeoning relationship with the guilt-laden Chris; and her socially awkward daughter, Tessa, who is again talking to Mirror Girl, a spectral presence only she sees in reflective surfaces. Thanks to a visitation effected by Mirror Girl, Marguerite learns that not only is the Subject following a biological programming imbued in its species' genetics, but the complex Cities on the alien planet are part of a longer history of star-faring races that remain, again, unknowable even to Earth's brightest minds. In the end, these novels make no attempt to anthropomorphize their aliens; instead, the aliens remain truly *alien*, strange and unfathomable, while the novels focus on the intimacies of their characters' daily lives amid these alien enigmas.

Wilson's earlier work contains many of the seeds fleshed out in his later work, but such novels as *The Harvest* (1992) and *Bios* (1999) use alien encounters to address issues of transcendence and radical posthumanism. In *The Harvest*, an alien artifact orbiting Earth eventually leads to an offer of immortality for humanity, but the novel follows two groups of people who have refused the offer and must rethink their understanding of *humanity* when the majority of people will apparently live forever as data archived and downloaded into resculpted bodies. There is a subtle nostalgia in *The Harvest* for an abandoned humanity that will not achieve a posthuman transcendence that itself is suspect, particularly when it comes to questions of identity and the cost of immortality. Zoe Fisher, the protagonist of *Bios*, has been engineered for service on Isis, a distant planet that will function as part of humanity's slow crawl into outer space. *Bios* depicts members of the crew fascinated by Isis's indigenous beings whose actions defy human intelligibility; however, even the planet's microbiology makes the planet inhospitable. The two planetary bases and the Isis Orbital Station begin to degrade, and connections with Earth are lost, thereby stranding the crew in this futuristic research facility and eventually dooming everyone to at-times-horrific deaths. Zoe spends her remaining hours amid the aliens and learns from them that every organism, every blade of grass, every cell contributes to a larger living consciousness, a "world soul" that binds all life. At the moment when death has claimed all the characters, *Bios* ends with a hopeful affirmation of life, a transcendent complexity that attests to the novel's final line: "We have a lot to learn."

*Graham J. Murphy*

*See also*: Liu, Cixin; Reynolds, Alastair; Vinge, Vernor; Watts, Peter.

## FURTHER READING

Murphy, Graham J. "Higher Verisimilitude and the Weirdness of the Universe: An Interview with Robert Charles Wilson." *Journal of the Fantastic in the Arts*, vol. 20, no. 2, 2009, pp. 210–220.

# X

## X-COM, XCOM

The origins of the *X-COM* game series (created by Mythos Games/MicroProse // Fireaxis Games/2K Games, 1994–2001, 2012–present) lie with the 1994 game titled *UFO: Enemy Unknown*, whose success spawned a rebranding into *X-COM: UFO Defense* and the launch of five further game titles under the same brand, until changes in the ownership of the franchise stopped its development in 2001. After a hiatus, the franchise was bought by 2K Games, to be rebooted and reimagined in 2012 as *XCOM: Enemy Unknown*, so far spawning two more games and additional download contents. The main entries in the series are round-based strategy games in which players move tactical units over conflict maps in order to fulfill strategic objectives.

The main premise of the franchise is an alien invasion of Earth that needs to be countered by a multinational military coalition called XCOM. Players take the position of the Commander, the leading military officer, and are tasked with coordinating the anti-alien forces and developing a world strategy against the invasion. In keeping with a military setup, the aliens encountered in the games' missions are separated into the ranks and units of an invasion army, with several different species working together under the command of an alien race called the Ethereals or Elders. The main body of the army consists of a wide variety of units. Sectoids are reminiscent of the Grays of popular culture, small wiry creatures with gray skin, large heads, and dark eyes that communicate via "psionics." Thin Men are infiltration units that pass as pale humans but are revealed to be snake creatures in human skins. Mutons are brutish humanoids in combat armor with little intelligence but enormous strength. Chryssalids are chitinous insect creatures that implant corpses with their eggs and reanimate them as zombies. In addition to these different alien species, the invaders seem capable of both biological and cybernetic experimentation, creating augmented units such as Floaters, flying cyborgs that were engineered from Muton DNA, or a variety of human-alien hybrids that can be found in *XCOM 2*, an alternate-timeline sequel portraying XCOM as the resistance movement after the invasion was successful.

The original game series provides limited information on the motivation of the aliens, but in the reboot it is revealed that the Ethereals, several-thousand-year-old humanoids with four arms and little physical strength but overwhelming telepathic abilities, have used their powers to conquer other species, experimented on them, and then transformed them into their army. The main motivation of the invasions (not just of Earth) is disclosed to be the transcendence of the Elder minds from their ancient Ethereal bodies, to migrate their "selfs" into new and more physically durable host bodies. In humanity, the Elders seem to have finally found a species that is capable of providing both genetic and psionic merging, culminating in the Avatar species as a human-alien hybrid into which the Elder minds can be downloaded.

In keeping with the military orientation, the invasion forces are depicted within a "set of simple binary oppositions—above all, human versus inhuman, us versus them" in which the aliens feature as clear-cut threat to humanity: "an enemy to be feared, hated, and destroyed" (Badmington 3). The game mechanics and the limited background in the old *X-COM* series certainly strengthen this reading in that there is no option in any of the games other than to escalate the conflict or understand it as a threat. In this, the series gestures back toward invasion narratives of the 1950s and their simple projection of these binaries onto the Cold War. But to say that the newer series *XCOM* also celebrates this simplicity is to ignore, as Istvan Csicsery-Ronay Jr. has pointed out, that aliens also function as humanity's double, especially in regard to our technoscientific progress: "Aliens are necessary because the human species is alone. The lack that creates them is an Other to whom we can compare ourselves. . . . The alien is the fictive event horizon parallel singularity from which we may derive what we are" (5). As such, the Ethereals' advanced and superior technology not only shapes their colonizing tactics (abduction, experimentation, subjugation) but also their ontological status—they are representative of a scientifically driven transhumanism in that they see their technological progress as a means to transcend biological limitations. Similar to what thinkers such as Nick Bostrom or Hans Moravec have articulated, the Ethereal's plan is to "liberate" themselves from their failing bodies, shedding "our biological traits [,which are] out of step with the inventions of our minds" (Moravec 4). Other "lesser" species are just a means to that end, but it is the human that brings success in this endeavor.

It is interesting to note that the Ethereals' motivation of transcendence is an addition to the series in 2012. With progress in biogenetic and information technology (such as the Human Genome Project or artificial intelligences), transhumanist thought has gained prominence, and mainstream media more strongly reflect this change (see Schmeink 5–6, 37) than in 1994. The function of the alien endeavor is two-fold, though, and does not just reflect humanity's striving for transcendence. The Ethereals are portrayed by the game in the context of a religious paradigm, the ship is referred to as a temple, the Ethereals are visually marked as priests, the rhetoric is that of "uplift" and "ascendency." Clearly, the ancient aliens are representations of an old theistic world order, one that humanity has left behind. In contrast, the will to resist the alien overlords and the scientific method of reverse-engineering their technology allow for the humans to create transcendence themselves. Science, as epitome of humanist thinking, allows humanity to become transhumanity and successfully resist the alien invasion by evolving into a human-psionic hybrid. In the end, it is this paradigmatic connection of the human with technological transcendence and an evolution away from biological limitations that remains as a message from the *XCOM* games. Whereas the alien is representative of an old and restrictive world order, humanity's embrace of science will lead to its eventual next step in evolution.

*Lars Schmeink*

*See also*: *FTL*; *Metroid*; *StarCraft*.

**FURTHER READING**

Badmington, Neil. *Alien Chic: Posthumanism and the Other Within*. Routledge, 2004.
Csicsery-Ronay Jr., Istvan. "Some Things We Know About Aliens." *The Yearbook of English Studies*, vol. 37, no. 2, 2007, pp. 1–23.
Moravec, Hans. *Mind Children: The Future of Robot and Human Intelligence*. Harvard University Press, 1988.
Schmeink, Lars. *Biopunk Dystopias: Genetic Engineering, Society, and Science Fiction*. Liverpool University Press, 2016.

## *The X-Files*

Created by Chris Carter, *The X-Files* (1993 to 2002, 2008, 2016–present) is a genre-crossing television program that aired on the Fox network from September 19, 1993, to May 19, 2002. It concluded after nine seasons, 202 episodes, and a 1998 film of the same name. A second film, *The X-Files: I Want to Believe*, followed in 2008, and in 2016, a six-episode event season aired on Fox between January 24 and February 22. Despite being advertised as a limited series, this season 10 revival ended on a cliffhanger, and soon after its conclusion, Fox and Carter announced an 11th season to follow in 2017 and 2018. Although the series began in a Friday-night time slot, a day with traditionally low television ratings, *The X-Files* slowly became more popular with viewers, eventually shifting to a Sunday-night spot and achieving cult and event-television status.

The popularity of *The X-Files* resulted in two spin-off series: *Millennium* (1996 to 1999) and *The Lone Gunmen* (2001). During both spin-offs' runs, the protagonists of all three shows made appearances in each other's series. All three shows also have comic and book series based on them, and *The X-Files* itself is the topic of hundreds of nonfiction books, both fan-focused and scholarly. There have been numerous *X-Files* games and toys, including a card game, several video games, and a variety of action figures. Additionally, during the course of its airing, *The X-Files* received critical acclaim, appearing on many best-of television lists and earning multiple Peabody, Golden Globe, and Emmy Awards, including best actress and best actor for Gillian Anderson and David Duchovny. The show's catch phrases "The Truth Is Out There" and "Trust No One" are permanent additions to the North American pop-culture lexicon.

The show itself centers on Fox Mulder (Duchovny) and Dana Scully (Anderson), two FBI agents who investigate a classification of cases that are considered unsolvable or unimportant, designated "X-Files." Mulder, a disgraced agent and believer in the unknown, is driven to investigate the strange and supernatural by the childhood abduction of his sister, Samantha. Scully, a doctor and far more skeptical agent, is assigned to the X-Files with the express purpose of watching Mulder and reporting on his activities to her superiors. It is not long, however, before Scully and Mulder begin trusting each other and working against the people monitoring them. Throughout the series, they investigate both "Monster of the Week" and "Mytharc" cases, the former focusing on stand-alone supernatural stories (e.g., "Squeeze," "Clyde Bruckman's Final Repose," and "Bad Blood"), and the latter focusing on the overall alien-conspiracy story arc. In conceiving the

A scene from the episode "Rush" from season eight of the *The X-Files* (1993–2002, 2016–), starring Gillian Anderson as Agent Dana Scully and David Duchovny as Agent Fox Mulder. (Fox Broadcasting/Photofest)

show, Carter consciously reversed gender stereotypes by making Scully the more rational of the two, although he complicates this stance later by also exploring Scully's Catholicism within the framework of the extraterrestrial unknown.

The alien threat within *The X-Files* appears, on the surface, to come almost entirely from external sources. Certainly, Mulder's overarching, series-spanning concern is with the abduction of his sister, Samantha, which carries all the hallmarks of a gray-alien close encounter of the fourth kind: a sudden cessation of natural sounds, large-scale vibration, a blindingly bright light, and levitation of objects and people. Both the monster and mythology episodes provide a plethora of extraterrestrials, including grays, parasitic ice worms, long-clawed aliens, gender-shifting Anabaptists, super-soldiers, faceless aliens, Martian entities, bounty hunters, and sentient black oil. While some of *The X-Files*' aliens are stand-alone creations, most fit directly into the main conspiracy narrative that runs through the series concerning the "colonists." The colonists, or grays, have a long-term plan to take over the earth and eradicate humanity through the use of their black oil form, also known as "Purity." The faceless aliens, on the other hand, oppose this colonization and actively work against the grays. The various types of extraterrestrials that appear in the mythological arc have their own motivations and complex relationships with each other, although almost all present a level of external danger to humans.

As the show progresses, however, the extraterrestrial threat becomes far more insidious as its true nature becomes clear. The colonists are working together with the Syndicate, a global group of powerful, high-placed individuals who are conspiring with the grays to create alien-human hybrids who will be able to survive alien conquest. In order to further this goal, the Syndicate gives members of their own family to the grays and facilitates the abduction of humans for testing purposes. This plotline, the conquest of the earth by alien *and* human forces, presents the largest threat to the characters individually and the world as a whole. It is the alien within, a deeper danger, and far more difficult to defeat than a wholly external menace.

Yet it is not just the presence of human collaborators that infuses this subplot with dread; the alien threat also comes from within human bodies. The alien bounty hunters, who carry out the more murderous orders of the grays, appear to be fully human. They are, in fact, shape-shifters who are infected with the black oil. Further, the black oil takes over specific named characters, bending those individuals to their will. Most notably, amoral antagonist Alex Krycek (Nicholas Lee) is infected in "Piper Maru" and is completely under the oil's control until it leaves him trapped in a silo with a UFO ("Apocrypha"). Both Scully and Mulder are themselves subject to abduction, tests, and fragmented memories over the course of the narrative ("Ascension" and "Requiem"). For *The X-Files*, our own bodies are a battleground between the familiar and the alien.

Thematically, *The X-Files* grapples with the alien as both a recognizable external threat and a nearly invisible internal one. Even Mulder's and Scully's bodies are subject to invasion, yet their bond—first platonic, then romantic—exists to help them find the balance between believer and skeptic. Although the series presses them to trust no one, the truth is that there is humanity to be found in each other, even while surrounded by the alien other.

*Eden Lee Lackner*

*See also*: Fort and Forteanism; Grays; Roswell (Place); Roswell (TV); *Torchwood*.

## FURTHER READING

Delasara, Jan. *PopLit, PopCult and The X-Files: A Critical Exploration*. McFarland, 2000.
Mooney, Darren. *Opening The X-Files: A Critical History of the Original Series*. McFarland, 2017.
Shearman, Robert. *Wanting to Believe: A Critical Guide to The X-Files, Millennium and The Lone Gunmen*. Mad Norwegian Press, 2009.

# About the Editors and Contributors

MICHAEL M. LEVY was author of a book on Natalie Babbitt and coauthor of the award-winning *Children's Fantasy Literature: An Introduction*. He died in 2017 after beginning work on this book. It is completed in his honor by his friends and colleagues from around the world.

FARAH MENDLESOHN is coeditor of the Hugo Award–winning *Cambridge Companion to Science Fiction* and author of *The Inter-Galactic Playground: Science Fiction for Children and Teens* and *The Pleasant Profession of Robert A. Heinlein*.

TIMOTHY J. ANDERSON, MFA, teaches communication studies at MacEwan University in Edmonton, Alberta.

STEVE ASSELIN obtained his doctorate from Queen's University and currently teaches literature at the University of Alberta's Augustana Campus. His research interests include eco-criticism, travel literature, speculative fiction, and utopianism. Previous research projects have involved polar fiction in the 19th century and ecological catastrophism at the fin-de-siècle; he is currently pursuing a project on political economy in 19th-century climate-change fiction.

SARA AUSTIN is a PhD candidate at the University of Connecticut. Her work focuses on identity and bodies in children's and popular culture.

CASSANDRA BAUSMAN is an assistant professor at Trine University, where she teaches courses in contemporary and genre literature and popular culture. She was the IAFA's Emerging Scholar recipient at her first-ever ICFA and received her PhD from the University of Iowa.

GREGORY BENFORD is a professor of physics at the University of California, Irvine. He is a Woodrow Wilson Fellow, was Visiting Fellow at Cambridge University, and in 1995 received the Lord Prize for contributions to science. In 2007, he won the Asimov Award for science writing. His fiction has won many awards, including the Nebula Award for his novel *Timescape*. He has published 42 books, mostly novels.

MEAGAN BLACK won the 2015 Lillian I. Found Awards for lyric poetry and is currently completing her master of fine arts degree at the University of British Columbia. Outside of school, her interests include used-book sales, working for *Arc Poetry Magazine*, and never finishing the edits on her first YA novel.

MARK BOULD is a reader in film and literature at UWE, Bristol. Founding editor of the journal *Science Fiction Film and Television*, he now coedits the monograph series *Studies in Global Science Fiction*. His most recent books are *M. John Harrison: Critical Essays* (2018), *Solaris* (2014), *SF Now* (2014), and *Africa SF* (2013).

MICHELLE BRAUN holds a PhD in English from Northeastern University with a dissertation on representations of posthumanism and biotechnologies in 21st-century literature. She is currently preparing a book chapter on Peter Watts for *Bridging the Solitudes: Essays on Canadian Science Fiction, Fantasy & Horror*.

ZAK BRONSON is a PhD candidate in media studies at the University of Western Ontario, where he studies ecology and contemporary science-fiction film.

SUSANA BROWER received her MA in English at the University of California, Riverside, the home of the world-famous Eaton Collection. Her master's project compared Christopher Columbus's and *Battlestar Galactica*'s treatment of the "alien other," and she has previously published on the intersections of Welsh mythology and popular culture. She currently works as the assistant coordinator of UC Riverside's undergraduate peer-tutoring program.

KAREN BURNHAM is the author of the critical study *Greg Egan*. She is a critic and reviewer for venues such as *Locus* magazine and *Strange Horizons*.

ANDREW M. BUTLER is the author of *Solar Flares: Science Fiction in the Seventies* (Liverpool University Press) and *Eternal Sunshine of the Spotless Mind* (BFI/Palgrave). He is currently working on SF romcoms.

BRETT BUTLER is an assistant professor at Morgan State University, focusing on male and masculine studies, comic books and graphic novels, and popular culture.

ROSE BUTLER is an associate lecturer and doctoral candidate in film studies at Sheffield Hallam University, where she is completing a thesis on masked killers in horror cinema. Her broader research interests include the cultural study of genre film and contemporary television, with a particular emphasis on crime and horror.

RITCH CALVIN is an associate professor of women's, gender, and sexuality studies at SUNY Stony Brook. He is a past president of the Science Fiction Research

Association, published a monograph on feminist epistemology and science fiction, and edited a book on Judith Merril's nonfiction.

ALEXANDER CAMPBELL is a London-based journalist and editor with a keen interest in both science fiction and history, in particular polar history.

SIMONE CAROTI is course director of fantasy and SF at Full Sail University in Winter Park, Florida. He has published two books, one on the generation starship and the other on Iain M. Banks's Culture series, and is currently under contract for a third.

SKYE CERVONE is a PhD candidate in comparative studies at Florida Atlantic University, where her dissertation project looks at capitalism's relationship to animals in science fiction. She serves as the public information officer for the International Association for the Fantastic in the Arts and is an editor for the *Eaton Journal of Archival Research in Science Fiction*.

BODHISATTVA CHATTOPADHYAY is researcher at the Department of Culture Studies and Oriental Languages, University of Oslo, and editor-in-chief of *Fafnir: Nordic Journal of Science Fiction and Fantasy Research*.

CAIT COKER is a genre historian specializing in science-fiction fandom and women's writing. Her essays have appeared in *The Journal of Fandom Studies* and *The Journal of Transformative Works and Cultures*, among others.

THOMAS CONNOLLY has a PhD from Maynooth University, Ireland. His research examines the history of the "human" in Anglo-American SF, using posthumanist theories. He was the recipient of the 2012 John and Pat Hume Doctoral Scholarship and has published articles on Wells and Clarke.

DANIEL CREED is a PhD candidate at Florida Atlantic University whose dissertation project examines the creation of memory and the experience of fantasy literature. He is the current Fantasy division head for the International Association for the Fantastic in the Arts and an editor with the Eaton Journal of Archival Research in Science Fiction.

IAN DERK is a PhD student in communication at Arizona State University. His main research interests include digital rhetoric, social media, gaming, and public memory.

AMANDA DILLON received her PhD in literature, drama, and creative writing from the University of East Anglia in 2012 and works on critical theory, science fiction, historiography, and world building. She currently teaches history at UEA and manages the journal *European History Quarterly*.

NADER ELHEFNAWY is the author of several books, including the novel *The Shadows of Olympus* and *Cyberpunk, Steampunk and Wizardry*, a history of the science-fiction genre. He can be found online at his blog, Raritania.

ANDREW FERGUSON is an assistant editor of *Foundation: the International Review of Science Fiction* and a visiting assistant professor of English at Washington & Lee University. His biography of R. A. Lafferty is forthcoming from University of Illinois Press.

PAWEŁ FRELIK is an associate professor in the American Studies Center, University of Warsaw. His research interests include science fiction, video games, fantastic visualities, digital media, and transmedia storytelling. He has published widely in these fields, serves on the advisory boards of *Science Fiction Studies*, *Extrapolation*, and *Journal of Gaming and Virtual Worlds*, and is the coeditor of the New Dimensions in Science Fiction book series at the University of Wales Press.

NATHANIEL FULLER is a PhD student and lecturer at Morgan State University. His publications include book reviews and interviews in *The Fourth River* (2007, 2009); short fiction "Welcome to Anteaterland" in *Queer Fish* Volume 1 (2011) and "Aster" in the *Oak Orchard Review* (2012); and poetry in the anthologies *Happy Holidays* (2016) and *Storm Cycles* (2016). His current research project examines intersectionality and whiteness in contemporary queer multicultural young-adult novels.

SUSAN A. GEORGE, PhD, an independent scholar and rural librarian, is the author of *Gendering Science Fiction Films: Invaders from Suburbs* and coeditor, with Regina Hansen, of *Supernatural, Humanity, and the Soul: On the Highway to Hell and Back*. Her work focuses on the construction of gender and the effect of technology on the body in fantastic media.

JONNA GJEVRE is a PhD in British literature from the University of Wisconsin, Madison. Formerly a professor at the University of Wisconsin, Stout, she has taught courses in science fiction, creative writing, and film. She has presented papers on genre fiction at several conferences and has published short stories and a novel.

JOAN GORDON is an editor of *Science Fiction Studies* and has won the Science Fiction Research Association's Pilgrim Award for lifetime achievement in SF scholarship.

REBECCA STONE GORDON is an MA student in biological anthropology at American University. She studies depictions of anthropology and archaeology in popular culture, the history of anatomy and the body, and science fiction and horror. She also holds an MS in audio technology and communication studies.

SEAN GUYNES-VISHNIAC is a PhD in English at Michigan State University. He is coeditor of *Star Wars and the History of Transmedia Storytelling* (Amsterdam UP, 2017) and *Unstable Masks: Whiteness and American Superhero Comics* (forthcoming), former editorial assistant to *The Journal of Popular Culture*, and current book reviews editor of *Foundation: the International Review of Science Fiction*.

STEFAN HALL is an associate professor of communication at High Point University, where he teaches courses primarily in game and interactive media design. In addition to his teaching, he also is cochair of the Department of Communication at the Nido R. Qubein School of Communication. His research interests include video games, film, comic book and sequential art, and science-fiction studies.

JENNIFER HARWOOD-SMITH completed her PhD at Trinity College Dublin and has published on subjects ranging from worldbuilding in *The Hitchhiker's Guide to the Galaxy* to identity theory in *Battlestar Galactica*. She has contributed to *The Routledge Companion to Imaginary Worlds* and has enjoyed discussing aliens since she could first talk.

LIAM HATHAWAY is a doctoral candidate at De Montfort University, where he is completing a thesis on the "killer bug" film, charting its development from the 1950s to the present. He is broadly interested in the cultural implications of genre cinema, including horror, science fiction, and the thriller.

RACHEL HILL is currently studying for an MA in cultural studies at Goldsmiths University and preparing a dissertation on the treatment of astrobiology and ethics through science fiction. Her academic interests include science-and-technology studies, science fiction, and continental philosophy.

MICHAEL J. HOLLOWS is a PhD student at Liverpool John Moores University, studying writing science fiction, with a particular focus on war and science fiction and the alien as other.

RYAN HOUSE earned a master's degree in English from Washington State University in 2015 and is currently applying to PhD programs in media, film, and digital studies. His research interests include ecocriticism and narrative in video games, electronic literature, and film.

KEVIN HOWLEY is professor of media studies at DePauw University. His research and teaching interests include media sociology, cultural politics, and community communication. His work has appeared in *MediaTropes*, *Television & New Media*, and *Sociology Compass*. He is author, most recently, of *Drones: Media Discourse & the Public Imagination*.

MEGAN ISAAC is an associate professor of English at Elon University. She has published in fields ranging from writing to Shakespeare to young-adult literature to the gothic novel.

EDWARD JAMES was editor of *Foundation: the International Review of Science Fiction* for over a decade, is author of *Science Fiction in the Twentieth Century*, and is coeditor of the Hugo Award–winning *The Cambridge Companion to Science Fiction*.

MICHAEL JOHNSTONE is a lecturer in the Department of English at the University of Toronto, teaching courses in science fiction, fantasy and horror, Romanticism, and Jane Austen. He has presented several times at the Academic Conference on Canadian Science Fiction and Fantasy. He has also published short fiction in *On Spec* and *Compostela: Tesseracts Twenty*.

CATHARINE KANE is a PhD student at Illinois State University. She is interested in how social unrest between the 1970s and 2000s affected middle-grade science fiction and fantasy.

KELLY KANE is a social psychology PhD candidate at Iowa State University. She studies narrative persuasion theory.

JENNIFER KAVETSKY received her PhD in English from the University of California, Riverside. Her dissertation drew on UCR's extensive SF archives, and her scholarly work focuses on the Golden Age science-fiction community. She currently oversees UCR's Undergraduate Writing Center.

ANTHONY KEEN is coeditor of the website FA—The Comiczine (http://comiczine-fa.com/) and contributes to The Slings and Arrows Graphic Novel Guide (http://theslingsandarrows.com/). He has written widely on science fiction and fantasy.

PAUL KINCAID is the author of *Iain M. Banks* (Illinois University Press) and two collections of essays, *What It Is We Do When We Read Science Fiction?* and *Call and Response*. He has received the Clareson Award from the Science Fiction Research Association and the British Science Fiction Association's Non-Fiction Award.

EDEN LEE LACKNER received her PhD in English literature from Victoria University of Wellington, New Zealand. Her dissertation concerned Edward Gorey's play with genre across his oeuvre. She holds an MA in Victorian literature from the University of Calgary, and she is a member of the Horror Writers Association.

DAVID LENANDER was an undergraduate when the local Mythopoeic Society discussion group started with graduate students Michael Levy, P. C. Hodgell, and Ruth Berman at the University of Minnesota.

BARBARA LUCAS holds a master's degree from Case Western Reserve University. Her work has been published in *Fan Fiction and Fan Communities in the Age of the Internet* and *Women in Science Fiction: An Encyclopedia*. She is a member of the Science Fiction and Fantasy Writers of America and the Horror Writers Association.

JONATHAN MACK is a lecturer and researcher in film and media, primarily focusing on the relationships between medial forms. His work on intermediality in film has been published in *Adaptation* and *Cinema Journal*, and he recently contributed to the edited collection *The 100 Greatest Videogame Characters*.

LAUREN MAGUIRE is a master's student at the University of British Columbia, studying children's and young-adult literature. Her research focus is posthumanism.

CRAIG IAN MANN is associate lecturer in film studies at Sheffield Hallam University, where he was awarded his doctorate in 2016. He is currently preparing his thesis, a cultural history of the werewolf film, for publication. His wider specialization is in the cultural analysis of horror and science-fiction cinema.

MELANIE A. MAROTTA is a lecturer in the Department of English and Language Arts at Morgan State University. She is an editor for the Museum of Science Fiction's *Journal of Science Fiction* and has been a member of the Science Fiction Research Association since 2012. Her research focuses on SF, the American West, contemporary American literature (in particular African American), young-adult literature, and ecocriticism. She is currently working on a collection about the SF Western.

KEIRA MCKENZIE holds a PhD in creative writing from Edith Cowan University, Western Australia, focused on the sublime and grotesque in Lovecraft to introduce the grotesque sublime. Publications include short stories, academic essays, poetry, and artwork.

SHELLIE MCMURDO is a visiting lecturer in film studies at Roehampton University. Her current research examines found-footage horror in relation to events such as 9/11, the expansion of social media, and the renaissance in documentary filmmaking. Her research interests are the horror genre, new media, and true crime.

EMILY MIDKIFF earned her doctorate in children's literature and literacy from the University of Minnesota in 2017. Her research interests include picture books, comic books, graphic novels, speculative fiction, and mythology. Uniting several of these interests, her current project focuses on young children's science-fiction literature.

ELIZABETH MILLER holds an MLIS from the University of Washington and currently works as technical services librarian at the Culinary Institute of America.

T. S. MILLER teaches medieval literature and science fiction at Sarah Lawrence College.

CAROLINE J. MULLAN has been engaged with science fiction as a reader and convention organizer for over 40 years. Her essays about science fiction and the community of SF fandom have appeared in Hugo Award–winning fanzines *Banana Wings* and *Journey Planet* and in the publications of the British Science Fiction Association.

GRAHAM J. MURPHY is professor with the School of English and Liberal Studies (Faculty of Business), Seneca College, where he regularly teaches science fiction–related and/or utopia-related courses. His latest book is *Cyberpunk and Visual Culture*, coedited with Lars Schmeink.

TANJA NATHANAEL is an ABD pursuing an English Literature doctorate at the University of Southern Mississippi. Her essay "Rose Is England: Nationhood, British Invasion Anxiety, and Why the Doctor Will (Almost) Always Rescue His Companions" appears in *Who Travels with the Doctor? Essays on the Companions of Doctor Who*.

VAL NOLAN is a lecturer in creative writing at Aberystwyth University. His work has appeared in *Review of Contemporary Fiction*, *Irish Studies Review*, and *Journal of Comic Books and Graphic Novels* and is forthcoming in *Science Fiction Studies*. His own fiction has appeared in *Interzone*, the "Futures" page of *Nature*, and *The Year's Best Science Fiction*, while his story 'The Irish Astronaut' was shortlisted for the Theodore Sturgeon Award.

MICHAEL O'BRIEN is a PhD candidate at the University of Glasgow, where he is writing a thesis entitled *Mythological Cognition in Contemporary Religious Science Fiction and Fantasy*, examining Maya Kaathryn Bohnhoff, Philip K. Dick and Philip José Farmer's use of conceptual blending to blend science and religion in their fiction.

EDWARD O'HARE is a PhD candidate at Trinity College Dublin studying representations of Antarctica in Gothic literature. His areas of research interest include British and American science fiction and horror literature, and he has published on Robert Paltock's *The Life and Adventures of Peter Wilkins, a Cornish Man*.

JAIME OLIVEROS is a student at the University of Huelva, English teacher at the University of the People, associate professor at Alfonso X the Wise University, and president of the Spanish Association ALEPH for Young Hispanic Researchers. His main research is in fantasy and identity in *The Kingkiller Chronicle*'s storyworld.

CHRISTOPHER J. OWEN is a PhD candidate in English literature at Anglia Ruskin University, Cambridge. His research investigates the representation and narratological function of intersectional systemic oppression in the fictional worlds of contemporary children's fantastika literature. He is an editorial assistant for *The Year's Best Weird Fiction.*

MICHAEL R. PAGE teaches science fiction at the University of Nebraska-Lincoln. He is the author of *The Literary Imagination from Erasmus Darwin to H.G. Wells, Frederik Pohl,* and *Saving the World through Science Fiction: James Gunn, Writer, Teacher and Scholar.* His most recent project is an annotated edition of James Gunn's 1951 master's thesis on modern science fiction.

WENDY GAY PEARSON is an associate professor at University of Western Ontario and coeditor of *Queer Universes: Sexualities in Science Fiction,* among other things.

FIONA PICKLES has been actively involved in media fandom since the late 1970s; she is an inveterate viewer, reader, writer, illustrator, publisher, editor, and convention organizer.

LÚCIO REIS-FILHO is a PhD candidate in film and media studies at University Anhembi Morumbi | Laureate International Universities (São Paulo, Brazil), historian, and author specializing in the relations between cinema, history, and literature.

MIKE RENNIE is a senior lecturer with special responsibilities at the Royal Military Academy, Sandhurst. He is a chartered psychologist and holds a PhD in psychology from York University. His research interests include the psychology of persuasion and influence. He is also a long-time fan of science fiction and fantasy.

IAN SALES is an award-winning science-fiction author and has reviewed books for *Interzone* and *Vector.* He curates the *SF Mistressworks* website.

ANDY SAWYER is the librarian of the Science Fiction Foundation Collection at the University of Liverpool Library. He was the director (2002–2012) of the MA in science-fiction studies for the School of English, University of Liverpool. He has published numerous essays and reviews on SF/fantasy, contributed to many reference books, and edited collections.

LARS SCHMEINK is professor of media studies at the Institut für Kultur- und Medienmanagement Hamburg and the president of the Gesellschaft für Fantastikforschung. He is the author of *Biopunk Dystopias: Genetic Engineering, Society, and Science Fiction* and coeditor of *Cyberpunk and Visual Culture* and *the Routledge Companion to Cyberpunk Culture.*

KAREN SCHRIER is an associate professor and director of the Games & Emerging Media Program at Marist College. She is also author of *Knowledge Games: How Playing Games Can Solve Problems, Create Insight, and Make Change* and editor of the *Learning, Education & Games* series.

ALISON SCOTT is a long-time SF fan, an editor of the Hugo Award–winning fanzine *Plokta*, and a keen foodie and observer of popular culture.

JONATHON SIDE is a fan of science fiction and fantasy who, having played *Oddworld* and *StarCraft*, is happy to contribute what he knows about them.

MEREDITH SNYDER is a PhD student at the University of Alberta.

PATRYCJA SOKOŁOWSKA is a PhD student at the Institute of English Cultures and Literatures at the University of Silesia in Poland. Her current research is focused on the literature of the weird, both in its early period and the New Weird, and H. P. Lovecraft's influence on the genre.

MAUREEN KINCAID SPELLER is senior reviews editor at *Strange Horizons*, assistant editor with *Foundation: the International Review of Science Fiction*, a critic, reviewer, consulting editor, and proofreader.

KEITH A. SPENCER is a PhD student in literature at the University of California, Santa Cruz. He is a science and technology editor at Salon.com and has written about aliens, sci-fi, and pop culture for *Jacobin*, *Dissent*, and *Salon*, among other publications. He is the author of the book *A People's History of Silicon Valley*.

AMBER STROTHER recently received a PhD in English from Washington State University with specializations in contemporary American literature, gender and sexuality studies, and speculative fiction. She is currently the Blackburn Fellow at Washington State University.

THOMAS JOSEPH WATSON lectures in media theory and film at Northumbria and Teesside Universities. His academic publications concern areas of pornography and horror cinema. Thomas is the coeditor of *Snuff: Real Death and Screen Media* (Bloomsbury, 2016).

PAUL WILLIAMS received his MA in English from Idaho State University in spring 2018. He learned to read when he discovered K. A. Applegate's *Animorphs* series and has remained with genre fiction ever since. A former high-school English teacher, his interests include narrative theory, neo-nineteenth-century fiction, religion, and any other topic he can fit under the umbrella of fantasy literature. He is now pursuing his PhD at ISU, where he serves as assistant editor for the *Journal of the Fantastic in the Arts*.

CARL WILSON is film editor and writer for PopMatters.com. Carl's work has appeared in fifteen edited collections, including three volumes of *World Film Locations*, five volumes of the *Directory of World Cinema* series, and PopMatters' books on Doctor Who and Joss Whedon.

# About the Editors and Contributors

DENNIS WILSON WISE is a lecturer at the University of Arizona after having received his doctorate from Middle Tennessee State University in 2017. He specializes in the intersections between political theory—especially modern political liberalism—and fantasy literature, particularly in Tolkien. Wise's academic work has appeared in journals such as *Tolkien Studies*, *Mythlore*, and others, and he currently serves as reviews editor for *Fafnir: Nordic Journal of Science Fiction and Fantasy Research*.

CHARLES YOW is a PhD student at the University of Southern Mississippi. He is studying gender and motherhood in Victorian literature and has additional interests and scholarship in various forms of animation, including Japanese animation and Disney.

# Index

Page numbers in **bold** indicate main entries in the volume.

Abrams, J. J.: *Cloverfield*, 86–88; *Star Trek* reboot, 242
*Abyss, The*, **27–29**; characters and plot, 27–28; as Cold War narrative, 27–28; NTIs (nonterrestrial intelligences), 27–28; themes, 28
Adamski, George, 84
*Alien* (series), **29–31**; *Alien*, 29–31, 207–208; alien's reproductive method, 31; *Alien: Covenant*, 29, 208; *Alien: Resurrection*, 29; *Aliens*, 29, 31; *Alien3*, 29, 31; design of alien, 30–31; and horror genre, 29–30; and motherhood, 31; *Prometheus*, 29, 207–209
*Alien Autopsy (Fact or Fiction?)*, **32–33**; cultural relevance, 33; debunked by *The World's Greatest Hoaxes and Secrets Revealed!*, 32; satirized by *The X-Files*, 32
Alien child: alien-as-child category, 13–14, 16; child-as-alien category, 13–16; and *Close Encounters of the Third Kind*, 15; and crossover stories (young and old audiences), 14; definition of, 13; and *Ender's Game* (Card), 14; fear of and eerie child as alien, 15–16; figuratively alien children, 15; and *Futurama*, 14; human-alien hybrid child, 16; and *Moon Girl and Devil Dinosaur* series, 14; and *Star Trek: Voyager*, 16; stories intended for children, 13–14; and sympathy with aliens, 14; and *2001: A Space Odyssey*, 15; and *The X-Files*, 16
Alien invasion. *See* Invasion narratives
*Alien Nation*, **33–36**; *Alien Nation: The Udara Legacy* (television movie), 34; and American melting-pot mythos, 35; buddy-cop dynamic, 33–34; cancellation, 35; cultural relevance, 34–35; exploration of racism, 35; television movies, 34
*Alien Nation* (film), 33, 173
Alien spaceship design, **36–38**; in *Alien*, 37; in *Babylon 5*, 37; in *Battlestar Galactica*, 36; in blended science fiction and horror films, 37; challenges of, 36; in *Close Encounters of the Third Kind*, 36; cultural commentary, 37–38; in *Dark City*, 36–37; in *E.T. the Extra-Terrestrial*, 36; in *Farscape*, 37; in *Independence Day*, 36; in *Lifeforce*, 37; and sentience, 37; in *Star Trek* franchise, 36
*Alien vs. Predator*, 20, 21, 23, 206
Alienism, 7
Aliens did not build the pyramids, **38–39**; and Egyptology, 39; and Egyptomania, 39; and pseudoarchaeology, 38–39
*Aliens Love Underpants*, **40–42**; *Aliens in Underpants Save the World*, 40, 41; *Aliens Love Dinopants*, 40; *Aliens Love Panta Claus*, 40; BBC CBeebies *Bed Time Story* presentation, 40; as invasion story, 41; stage production, 40
Allen, Irwin: *Voyage to the Bottom of the Sea*, 28
Almond, David, **42–44**; *Clay*, 42, 43; *Heaven Eyes*, 42–43; influences on, 42–43; *Skellig*, 42, 43
*Amazing Stories*, 6, 232
Anaximander, 4
Ancient aliens, 38–39, 168, 214, 309
*Ancient Aliens* (History Channel program), 38

*Animorphs*, **44–46**; and alien as child, 14; and cultural collision, 46; storyline, 44–45; themes, 45–46
Anthropy, Anna, 162–163
Apartheid, 103–104
Applegate, K. A.: *Animorophs*, 14, 44–46; *Everworld*, 44; and mature themes, 44; *Remnants*, 44. See also *Animorphs*
*Area 51*, 19–20
Aristotle, 4
Arnason, Eleanor, 12, **46–48**; *Daughter of the Bear King*, 47; *Hidden Folk*, 47; Hwarhath stories, 47, 48; Lydia Duluth stories, 47; *Mammoths of the Great Plains*, 47; *Ring of Swords*, 10, 12, 47–48; *The Sword Smith*, 46–47; *Tomb of the Father*, 47; *To the Resurrection Station*, 47; *A Woman of the Iron People*, 47
*Arrival*, 28, **48–50**; basis of, 48, 49; characters and plot, 48–49; themes, 49–50; U.S.-centric worldview of, 49–50
*Asteroids*, 19
Attebery, Brian, 47
*Avatar*, **51–53**; and alien-invasion trope, 52; characters and plot, 51; inspiration for, 52; themes, 52–53; "white savior" motif, 52–53

*Babylon 5*, **54–56**; portrayals of aliens, 54–55; spaceship design, 37; storyline, 55–56; themes, 55–56
Baker, Graham, 33, 173
Banks, Iain M., **56–58**; and ambiguous utopia; *Consider Phlebas*, 57; Culture series, 56–58; *Excession*, 57; *The Hydrogen Sonata*, 57; *Look to Windward*, 57, 58; *Matter*, 57; *The State of the Art*, 56; *Surface Detail*, 57; *The Wasp Factory*, 56
*Battlestar Galactica*, 36, 180, 216
*Battlezone*, 19
Bermuda Triangle, 85
Blake, William, 42
*Blake Stone: Aliens of Gold*, 20
Blomkamp, Neill, 103, 104
*Body Snatchers, The*, **58–60**; *Body Snatchers* (Ferrara), 59, 157; Bugs Bunny short, 60; *The Invasion* (Hirschbiegel), 59, 157; *Invasion of the Body Snatchers* (Siegel), 17, 59, 155–157, 283; *Invasion of the Body Snatchers* (Kaufman), 59, 157, 267; *Los nuevos extraterrestres* (*The New Extraterrestrials,* Simón), 60; novel by Jack Finney, 10, 45, 58–59, 155–156, 266; *Pod* (Keating), 60; and pod people, 59–60, 155–157
Booker, M. Keith, 28
Bowie, David, **60–62**; *Aladdin Sane*, 61; "Ashes to Ashes," 60, 62; *Blackstar*, 62; *Diamond Dogs*, 61; *Earthling*, 62; *Low*, 62; in *The Man who Fell to Earth*, 61, 171–173; *The Rise and Fall of Ziggy Stardust and the Spiders from Mars*, 61; *Scary Monsters*, 62; "Space Oddity," 60; *Station to Station*, 61–62; *Ziggy Stardust and the Spiders from Mars* (documentary), 61
Brin, David, **62–64**; *Brightness Reef*, 64; *Startide Rising*, 63; *Sundiver*, 63; *Uplift Storm* trilogy, 64; Uplift universe, 62–64; *The Uplift War*, 63
*Brother from Another Planet, The*, **64–66**; and intersectionality, 65; trope of alien mixers, 65; trope of messianic figure, 65–66; trope of sublime encounter, 65
Burk, Bryan, 86
Burroughs, Edgar Rice, 6, **66–69**, 125; *Beyond the Farthest Star*, 67; *The Moon Maid*, 67; Mars series, 66–68; Moon series, 67–68; and "noble" aliens, 68; *Pirates of Venus*, 67; *A Princess of Mars*, 6, 67, 302; themes, 68–69; "Under the Moons of Mars," 66–67, 232; Venus series, 67–68
Butler, Judith, 260
Butler, Octavia E., **69–71**; *Adulthood Rites*, 70; "Amnesty," 70; "Bloodchild," 69; *Dawn*, 69–70; first science-fiction writer to receive MacArthur Foundation "Genius" Grant, 69; *Imago*, 70; themes, 69; Xenogenesis series, 10, 11, 69–70
Butterworth, Nick: *Q Pootle 5*, 13

Cameron, James: *The Abyss*, 27–28; *Aliens*, 28, 29–31, 115; *Avatar*, 28, 51–53, 68, 293; *The Terminator*, 28. See also *Aliens* (series); *Avatar*
Campbell, John W., 7; editor of *Astounding Science Fiction*, 80, 82; editor of *Unknown*, 127; "Who Goes There?" 9–10, 59, 80, 206, 266–268, 303–305. See also "Who Goes There?"

# Index

Canavan, Gerry, 11, 167
Card, Orson Scott, **72–73**; and alien-as-child motif, 14; *Children of the Mind*, 73; *Earth Unaware*, 73; *Ender's Game*, 10, 11, 14; Ender Saga, 72–73; *Ender's Shadow*, 72; Formic War novels, 73; and genocide theme, 73; *Speaker for the Dead*, 72–73; *Xenocide*, 73
Carter, Paul A., 7
Cavendish, Margaret, 4, **74–76**; *The Description of a New World, Called the Blazing-World*, 4, 74; and "Infinite Nature," 75; *Observations upon Experimental Philosophy*, 74
*Chariots of the Gods?* (von Däniken), 38, 84–85
Cherryh, C. J., **76–78**; Chanur series, 77; *Cuckoo's Egg*, 76–77; "Foreigner" series, 76; *Forty Thousand in Gehenna*, 77; *Hestia*, 77; *Hunter of Worlds*, 77; *The Pride of Chanur*, 76; representations of radical otherness by, 77; *Serpent's Reach*, 77; Union/Alliance Universe, 76; *Voyager in Night* 77; *Wave without a Shore*, 77
Chiang, Ted: "Story of Your Life," 48–49. See also *Arrival*
*Clangers, The*, **78–80**; characters, 78–79; production history, 78–79; referenced in "The Sea Devils" episode of *Doctor Who*, 79; soundtrack album, 79; themes and storylines, 79
Clarke, Arthur C., **80–82**; and child as alien, 15–16, 81–82; *Childhood's End*, 15–16, 81–82; *The City and the Stars*, 82; "History Lesson," 80–81; and humanist bias, 80–82; influence of, 80, 240; influences on, 80; "Loophole," 80; "A Meeting with Medusa," 80, 214; *Rendezvous with Rama*, 81, 215; "Rescue Party," 80; "Second Dawn," 80; *The Songs of Distant Earth*, 80; *2001: A Space Odyssey*, 81–82; and universal detente, 229
Clement, Hal, **82–84**; *Cycle of Fire*, 84; and hard science fiction, 82; *Iceworld*, 82, 83; *Mission of Gravity*, 82, 83; *Needle*, 82–83; *Star Light*, 83
*Close Encounters of the Third Kind*, 28, 65, **84–86**, 116; alien spaceship design, 36; alien technology, 86; characters and plot, 85; and child as alien, 15; production history, 85–86

Clover, Joshua, 103
*Cloverfield*, **86–88**; and found footage, 87; as giant monster film, 87–88; *10 Cloverfield Lane*, 88
Cohen, David X., 129. See also *Futurama*
Cold War narratives and themes: *The Abyss*, 27–28; *The Body Snatchers* (Finney), 10; *A Colder War*, 207; *The Day the Earth Stood Still* (Wise), 28; and Dick, Philip K., 101; *Dr. Strangelove*, 207; *E.T. the Extra-Terrestrial*, 117; and Heinlein, Robert A., 148; and Le Guin, Ursula K., 159; "The Liberation of Earth," 10; and Liu, Cixin, 166; *The Man Who Fell to Earth*, 171; science-fiction films of the 1950s, 84; *Solaris*, 235; *Star Trek* ("Errand of Mercy"), 240; *The Thing from Another World*, 266–267; *V*, 283; *War of the Worlds*, 289; *X-COM*, 309; xenophobia, 10
Colonial-imperialist themes and stories, 6; and alien child, 13; *Aliens Love Underpants*, 40, 41; aliens built the pyramids, 39; *Animorphs*, 44; *Arrival*, 50; *Avatar*, 103; *The Body Snatchers*, 59; and Burroughs, Edgar Rice, 68–69; colonial invasion, 9; *District 9*, 103; Dr. Xargle books, 111; *Embassytown*, 185–186; genetic imperialism, 108–109; and Heinlein, Robert A., 148; and Le Guin, Ursula K., 158–159; "The Liberation of Earth," 10; and Liu, Cixin, 167; *Pacific Rim*, 204; and Russell, Mary Doria, 222; and Smith, E. E. "Doc," 232; *Speaker for the Dead*, 73; Uplift universe, 63–64; *War of the Worlds*, 5, 289; *The Way of Thorn and Thunder*, 294–295; Xenogenesis series, 11. See also Genocide
*Computer Space*, 18, 19
Condon, Peter, 88–90, 89
Condon Report, The, **88–89**; commission and preparation of, 88–89; and Project Blue Book, 89; purpose of, 89; *Scientific Study of Unidentified Flying Objects* (full name), 88–89
*Contact*, **90–93**; *Contact: A Novel* (Carl Sagan), 90, 92; film by Robert Zemeckis, 90; plot, 90–91; themes, 92
Cort, Ben, 40
Cosmic pluralism, 3–4

*Cowboys and Aliens*, **93–94**; basis and inspiration for, 93–94; characters and plot, 93; invasion story, 93; themes, 94
Crichton, Michael: *Sphere*, 28
*Critters*, **94–96**; *Critters*, 95–96; *Critters 2: The Main Course*, 95–96; *Critters 3*, 95–96; *Critters 4*, 95–96; *Critters: Bounty Hunter* (fan film), 96
Curie, Marie, 14
Cusick, Raymond, 105

*Dances with Wolves*, 52
*Dark Crystal, The*, **97–98**; alien design, 98; characters and plot, 97; production history, 97; puppetry, 97, 98; themes, 98
Darnell, Mike, 32
Darwinism, 5, 167; Social Darwinism, 159
Deacon, Alexis: *Beegu*, 13
*Dead Space*, **99–101**; characters and storyline, 99; and Fermi Paradox, 100; humans in, 100; and third-person shooter games, 100
*Defender*, 19
Del Toro, Guillermo, 88, 203–205
Denzler, Brenda, 32
*Destroy all Humans!*, 22–23
Dick, Philip K., **101–102**; "Beyond Lies the Wub," 101; *Clans of the Alphane Moon*, 101; *Galactic Pot-Healer*, 102; *Nick and the Glimmung*, 101; "Not by Its Cover," 101; *Now Wait for Last Year*, 101; *Our Friends from Frolix 8*, 101–102; and patriarchal characters, 101–102; themes of, 101; *The Three Stigmata of Palmer Eldritch*, 101; (posthumously published as *Radio Free Albemuth*), 102; "We Can Remember It For You Wholesale," 101; *The World Jones Made*, 102
Dick, Thomas, 5
Disney, 81, 301: *John Carter* (adaptation of *A Princess of Mars*), 302; *Lilo and Stitch*, 13, 164–165; *20,000 Leagues under the Sea* (Disney), 28. See also *Lilo and Stitch*
*District 9*, **103–104**; as apartheid allegory, 104; characters and plot, 103–104; depiction of racism, 104; themes, 103–104; white savior motif, 103
*Doctor Who*, 78, **104–107**, 180, 211, 224; and anxieties toward indigenous peoples and refugees, 106; and change, 105; "Closing Time," 106; Daleks in, 105, 107, 180; "The Empty Child," 16; invasion narrative, 105–107; monsters in, 105; production history, 104–105; "The Sea Devils," 79; themes, 104–107. See also *Torchwood*
Donaldson, Stephen R., **107–109**; *The Chronicles of Thomas Covenant the Unbeliever*, 108; *Gap* cycle, 107–108; *Thomas Covenant the Unbeliever* trilogies, 107, 108; and existentialism, 107–109; *The Future of Human Nature*, 109; *Our Posthuman Future*, 109
Dr. Xargle, **109–111**; American editions, 110; animatronic television show, 109; book series, 109–111; *Dr. Xargle's Book of Earth Mobiles*, 110; *Dr. Xargle's Book of Earth Tiggers*, 109–111; *Dr. Xargle's Book of Earthlets*, 109, 110
Duke Nukem 3D, 20, 23
Dyallhis, Nictzin, 6

Ellison, Harlan, **112–114**; "A Boy and his Dog," 112; *Dangerous Visions* (editor), 112; "I Have No Mouth and I Must Scream," 112, 113; "I'm Looking for Kadak," 112; Kyben war stories, 112; "'Repent, Harlequin!' Said the Ticktockman," 112; television writing, 112–113; "A View from the Gallery" (*Babylon 5* episode), 112–113; "The Wind beyond the Mountains," 112
Emshwiller, Carol: *The Mount*, 10, 11–12
*Enemy Mine*, **114–116**; characters and plot, 114; influence of, 115; novella by Barry B. Longyear, 114; themes, 114–115
Epicurus, 4
*E.T. the Extra-Terrestrial*, 65, 85, **116–118**, 267; and alien as child, 14; alien spacecraft design, 36; characters and plot, 116; and child as alien, 13; concept for, 116; themes, 117–118
*E.T. The Extra-Terrestrial* (video game), 21
Existentialism, 107–109

*Farscape*, **119–121**; alien spaceship design, 37; characters and storyline, 119; "Crackers Don't Matter," 120; "I, E.T.," 119; "Jeremiah Crichton," 119; "John Quixote," 119; "Kansas," 119; themes, 120; treatment of the alien in, 119–120; "Unreal Reality," 120

Favreau, Jon, 93, 94
Fearing, Mark: *Earthling!*, 14
Fincher, David, 29
Finney, Jack: *The Body Snatchers*, 10, 45, 58–59, 155–156, 266
*Firefly/Serenity*, **121–123**; "Bushwhacked," 121; characters and storyline, 121; "Objects in Space," 121; "Safe," 121; science-fiction Western, 121; and terraforming, 123; the Verse, 121–123
Firmin, Peter, 78–79
First-contact themes and stories: and invasion, 11; *Arrival*, 50; and Bowie, David, 61; *The Brother from Another Planet*, 65; and Card, Orson Scott, 72; *Close Encounters of a Third Kind*, 85; and Lem, Stanislaw, 160; *Men in Black*, 182; and Russell, Mary Doria, 221; and Sawyer, Robert J., 226–227; and Watts, Peter, 292–293; and Weinbaum, Stanley G., 295; and White, James, 300; and Wilson, Robert Charles, 305; *White Queen*, 139; *A Woman of the Iron People*, 47
Fischer, Dennis, 117
Flammarion, Camille, 5, **123–125**; *La Fin Du Monde* (The End of the World), 124; *La pluralité des mondes inhabités* (The Plurality of Inhabited Worlds), 123; legacy of, 125; *Les mondes imaginaires et les mondes réels* (Imaginary Worlds and Real Worlds), 123; *Lumen*, 123; *Uranie*, 123
Flint, Homer Eon, 6
Fort and forteanism, **125–127**; *The Books of Charles Fort*, 126; *Lo!*, 126; *New Lands*, 126; *The Outcast Manufacturers*, 125; unpublished works, 125; *Wild Talents*, 126; *X*, 125–126; *Y*, 126; *Z* (renamed *The Book of the Damned*), 126–127
Frakes, Jonathan, 32
*Frankenstein; Or, The Modern Prometheus* (Shelley), 43, 205–206, 208, 209, 211, 267, 281
Frazier, Kendrick, 33
Freedman, Claire, 40
Fritze, Ronald, 38–39
Froud, Brian, 97–98
*FTL: Faster Than Light*, **127–129**; gameplay, 128; rougelike strategy game with narrative elements, 127–128; and view of aliens, 129

*Futurama*, 14, **129–132**; centralization of aliens, 131; characters and storyline, 130–131; feature-length films, 129; production history, 129

*Galaga*, 19
*Galaxian*, 19
*Galaxy Quest*, **133–135**; concept of, 133; themes, 134
Genocide, 9–12, 50, 72–73, 159, 177, 184, 195, 227, 249, 298; and *Celestis* (Park), 10, 11; definition of, 9; and *Ender's Game*, 11; and insect-like invaders, 11–12; and "The Liberation of Earth," 10, 11; and *The Mount*, 11–12; and *Ring of Swords*, 12; and *The Sparrow* and *Children of God*, 10, 11; and *Starship Troopers*, 11; and *War of the Worlds*, 9, 12; and "Who Goes There?" 9–10; and Xenogenesis series, 11
Gernsback, Hugo, 6, 232
Giger, H. R., 30–31
Godwin, Francis, 4
Golden Age of American science fiction, 3, 7–8, 80, 127, 232, 266, 303
Golden Age of arcade games, 19–20
Grays, **135–137**; abduction accounts, 135–136; descriptions of, 135, 136; in literature, 135; in Western mythology, 136–137
Great Moon Hoax, 4, 5
Green Lantern, **137–139**; first appearance of, 137; history of, 137–138; in Silver Age of comics, 137–138; and social justice, 138
Groening, Matt, 129. See also *Futurama*
Gwyneth Jones's Aleutians, **139–140**; *North Wind*, 139–140; *Phoenix Café*, 139–140; *White Queen*, 139–140

Haldeman, Joe W.: *The Forever War*, 11
*Half-Life 2*, **141–143**; alien invasion, 141–142; characters and events, 141; *Half-Life*, 141; and history of aliens in video games, 20; themes, 141–142
*Halo: Combat Evolved*, 20, **143–144**; first-person shooter game, 143; *Halo*, 20, 22, 23; *Halo 4*, 144; themes, 143–144
Hamilton, Edmond, 6, 232
Hard science fiction, 82, 198, 224, 291
Heaven's Gate, **144–147**; and Applewhite, Marshall, 145–157; belief system, 145;

events of, 144–145, 147; founders, 145; and Nettles, Bonnie, 145–147; "walk-ins," 146–147
Hecht, Ben, 126
Heinlein, Robert A., **147–149**; *Double Star*, 147, 148; *Have Space Suit—Will Travel*, 147–148; influence of, 147; *The Moon Is a Harsh Mistress*, 147; *The Puppet Masters*, 59, 148; *Red Planet*, 148–149; *Rocket Ship Galileo*, 147; *Space Cadet*, 147; *The Star Beast*, 147; *Starship Troopers*, 11, 141, 147, 148; *Stranger in a Strange Land*, 147, 148–149; *Tunnel in the Sky*, 147
Henson, Jim, 97, 98
Herbert, Frank: *Dune*, 15, 142
Herschel, John, 4, 5
*Hidden, The*, **149–151**; characters and plot, 149; cultural relevance of, 150; *The Hidden 2*, 151; themes, 150
*Hitchhiker's Guide to the Galaxy, The*, **151–154**; cinematic adaptation, 153–154; novels by Douglas Adams, 151; presentation of the alien in, 151; radio plays, 151; television series, 151; themes 152–154
Home console and computer games, history of, 20–23
Hynek, J. Allen, 85, 90

Ignatieff, Michael, 9, 10
Imperialism. *See* Colonial-imperialist themes and stories
*In Search of Ancient Astronauts*, 38
*In Search of . . .* (series), 38
*Invader Zim*, 14
*Invaders from Mars*, 145, 174, 267, 282
Invasion narratives, 9–12; and alien child, 14, 17; *Aliens Love Underpants*, 41; *Animorphs*, 44–45; *Avatar*, 52–54; *The Blazing-World*, 75; *The Body Snatchers*, 58–60; *Close Encounters of the Third Kind*, 84; *The Condon Report*, 88; *Contact*, 92; *Cowboys and Aliens*, 93; *Critters*, 95; and Dick, Philip K., 102; *Dr. Who*, 105–107; Dr. Xargle stories, 111; and Ellison, Harlan, 112; and *E.T.*, 117; *Half-Life*, 141–143; and Heinlein, Robert A., 148; *The Hidden*, 151; *Invaders from Mars*, 145, 174, 267, 282; *Invasion of the Body Snatchers*, 155–157; *The Last and First Men*, 239; *Lilo and Stitch*, 165; and Lovecraft, H. P., 168, 169; *Mass Effect* trilogy, 175; *Pacific Rim*, 203; *Quatermass* series, 210–211; *Rosewater*, 272; *Space Invaders*, 236–238; *They Live*, 264–265; *Three Body Problem* trilogy, 166; *Torchwood*, 276; *2000 AD*, 280–281; *V*, 282–283; in video games, 18–20, 22–23; *The War of the Worlds*, 287–289; *X-COM*, 308–309; *The X-Files*, 312
*Invasion of the Body Snatchers*, **155–157**; characters and plot, 155; and McCarthyism, 155–156; themes, 155–157. *See also Body Snatchers, The*
*Iron Giant, The* (film), 15

Jeunet, Jean-Pierre, 29
Johnson, Kenneth, 33, 282–283
Johnson, Mark, 133
Jones, Gwyneth. *See* Gwyneth Jones's Aleutians
Jones, Jim, 145, 146

Key, Alexander: *Escape to Witch Mountain*, 13
Keyhoe, Donald, 90
Kipling, Rudyard: *The Jungle Book*, 17
Kneale, Nigel, 210
Kopkind, Andrew, 64–65

*Labyrinth*, 97
Le Guin, Ursula K., **158–160**; and *Avatar*, 293; *City of Illusions*, 158; *The Dispossessed*, 158; Hainish novels, 158; *The Left Hand of Darkness*, 158–159; *Planet of Exile*, 158; on *Ring of Swords* (Arnason), 48; *Rocannon's World*, 158; *The Telling*, 158; "Vaster than Empires and More Slow," 159; *The Word for the World Is Forest*, 159; themes, 159
Lehner, Mark, 39
Lem, Stanislaw, **160–162**; *Eden*, 160; *Fiasco*, 160, 161; *His Master's Voice*, 160, 161; *The Invincible*, 161; *Solaris*, 160–161; themes, 160–161
*Lesbian Spider Queens of Mars*, **162–164**; browser-based game, 163; *Lesbian Spider Queens of Mars 2: Tarantula's Turn*, 162; and power, 162–163; and sexuality, 162–164
*Lifeforce* (film), 37, 95

*Lilo and Stitch*, **164–166**; and alien child, 13; characters and plot, 164; themes, 164–165; treatment of the other in, 165

Liu, Cixin, **166–168**; *Remembrance of Earth's Past*, 166; themes, 166–167; *Three Body Problem* trilogy, 166

Lovecraft, H. P., **168–170**; "The Call of Cthulhu," 168–169; "The Colour Out of Space," 169; as controversial figure, 168, 170; "Deep Ones," 169; "The Dunwich Horror," 169; and haunted house trope, 168; "The Shadow out of Time," 169; "The Shadow over Innsmouth," 169

Lucian of Samosata, 3

*Man Who Fell to Earth, The*, **171–173**; and Bowie, David, 61, 171–173; film, 171–172; and sexuality, 171; television film, 172–173

Martian Manhunter, **173–175**; first appearance, 173; origin story, 173–174

*Mass Effect* (Trilogy), **175–177**; and history of aliens in video games, 20, 22; *Mass Effect: Andromeda*, 175; *Mass Effect 2*, 176; *Mass Effect 3*, 175; storyline of, 175; success of, 175; themes, 176–177

*Masters of the Universe*, **177–179**; aliens in, 178; characters and storyline, 177–178; *He-Man*, 177; *She-Ra*, 177; techno-fantasy in, 177; themes, 178–179

McCarthyism, 59, 156, 267

Mekon, The, **179–181**; backstory, 179–180; characters and plot, 179–180; flagship serial of the *Eagle*, 179; themes, 180–181

*Men in Black*, **181–183**; aliens in, 182–183; basis of, 181; characters and plot, 181; as inversion of space opera, 181; themes, 181–183

*Metroid*, **183–185**; game series of exploration platformers, 183; gameplay, 183–184; and history of aliens in video games, 20, 21; and xenocide, 184

Miéville, China, **185–187**; and cultural relevance, 187; *Embassytown*, 185–187

Mithen, Steven, 30–31

Mœbius, **188–190**; *After the Incal*, 189; *The Airtight Garage*, 188–189; *The Incal*, 189; influence of, 189–190; "Le bandard fou" ("The Horny Goof: The Devilishly Clever Story of a Syldanian Wild Pecker"), 188; *Le Monde d'Edena* (The Gardens of Aedena), 189

*Moon Girl and Devil Dinosaur*, 14

Moore, C. L., **190–192**; "Black Thirst," 190–191; "The Bright Illusion," 191; collaboration with Henry Kuttner, 191; "Dust of Gods," 191; *Ilar*, 192; *Judgment Night*, 191–192; "Shambleau," 190–191; "Vintage Season," 192; "Yvala," 191

*Mork & Mindy*, **192–194**; characters and storyline, 192–194; influence of, 194; production history, 192

Nama, Adilifu, 104

Nation, Terry, 105

*Nemesis the Warlock*, **195–196**; characters and plot, 195–196; end of comic strip, 196; as parable of racial intolerance and genocide, 195; world and themes of, 195

Newman, Sydney, 104–105, 211

Nishikado, Tomohiro, 18, 236–237

Niven, Larry, **196–198**; *Ringworld* series, 196–197; *Ringworld*'s characters and plot, 197; Tales of Known Space series, 197

O'Bannon, Dan, 29, 31, 189

O'Bannon, Rockne S., 37, 119

*Oddworld*, **199–201**; *Abe's Oddysee*, 199; *Munch's Oddysee*, 199

Okorafor, Nnedi, **201–202**; *Binti* series, 201–202; *The Book of the Phoenix*, 201; *Lagoon*, 201, 202; *Zahrah the Windseeker*, 201

Orientalism, 6–7, 180

Oz, Frank, 97, 244

*Pacific Rim*, **203–205**; characters and plot, 203; critical backlash against, 204; and familiar tropes, 203–204

Padgett, Lewis: "Mimsy Were the Borogoves," 16

Palmer, Christopher, 102

Park, Paul: *Celestis*, 10, 11

Petersen, Wolfgang: *Enemy Mine*, 28, 114–116

Plato, 4

Poe, Edgar Allan: *The Narrative of Arthur Gordon Pym*, 206; "The Unparalleled Adventure of One Hans Pfaall," 5

Polar aliens, **205–207**; and "At the Mountains of Madness" (Lovecraft), 206; conspiracy theories, 207; and *Dr. Strangelove*, 207; and *Frankenstein* (Shelley), 205–206; and *The Narrative of Arthur Gordon Pym* (Poe), 206; and Symmes, John Cleves, 206
Postgate, Dan, 79
Postgate, Oliver, 78–79
*Prometheus*, 29, **207–209**; and *Aliens* franchise, 207–208; characters and plot, 208–209; themes, 209
Pseudoarchaeology, 38–39
Pseudoscience, 38–39, 59

*Quake*, 20, 141
*Quatermass* (Series), **210–212**; characters and storyline, 210–211; production history, 210; *Quatermass II*, 210–211; *The Quatermass Conclusion*, 211; *The Quatermass Experiment*, 210;

Reagan, Ronald, 86, 95, 115, 117, 150, 172, 264, 266
*Redshirt*, 22
Reeves, Matt, 86
Reinl, Harald, 38
*Repo Man*, **213–214**
Retro revival (video games), 23
Reynolds, Alastair, **214–216**; *Absolution Gap*, 215; *Chasm City*, 215; "Galactic North," 215; *House of Suns*, 215; Merlin novellas, 216; Poseidon's Children trilogy, 215–216; *The Prefect*, 215; *Pushing Ice*, 215; *Redemption Ark*, 215; *Revelation Space*, 215; Revelation Space novels and stories, 214
Rosenberg, Scott Mitchell, 93
Rosny, J.-H., 5, 125
Ross, Tony, 109. *See also* Dr. Xargle
Roswell (place), **216–219**; events, 216–217; Roswell aliens in popular culture, 217–218; and victim alien narrative, 217
*Roswell* (TV), **219–221**; basis of, 219; characters and plot, 219; and human-hybrid concept, 220–221; success of, 219–220; themes, 220
Ruppersburg, Hugh, 86
Russell, Mary Doria, **221–223**; *Children of God*, 10, 221–223; *The Sparrow*, 10, 221–223

*Saga*, **224–225**; alien in, 225; characters and storyline, 224; space opera comic-book series, 224; themes, 225
Sagan, Carl: *Contact: A Novel*, 90–92
*Saints Row IV*, 23
Santilli, Ray, 32–33
Sawyer, Robert J., **226–227**; *Calculating God*, 226; *End of an Era*, 226, 227; *Factoring Humanity*, 226; *Foreigner*, 226; *Hominids*, 226; *Illegal Alien*, 226; Quintaglio Ascension trilogy, 226; *Rollback*, 226–227; *Starplex*, 226; *Wake*, 226
Sayles, John, 65–66, 116
*Scientific Study of Unidentified Flying Objects. See* Condon Report, The
Scott, Ridley, 29, 37, 281; *Alien*, 30, 211; *Prometheus*, 207–209
Scott, Robert Falcoln, 206
Sendak, Maurice: *Where the Wild Things Are*, 17
*Serious Sam: The First Encounter*, 23
Shakespeare, William: *Romeo and Juliet*, 224; *The Tempest*, 42
Shelley, Mary, 43, 205–206, 208, 211
Shoefield, Gary, 32
Sholder, Jack, 149. See also *The Hidden*
Siegel, Don, 59, 155–156. See also *Invasion of the Body Snatchers*
Siegel, Jerry, 255. See also *Superman*
Simak, Clifford D., **228–229**; *All Flesh Is Grass*, 228–229; "The Big Front Yard," 228–229; *City*, 228; *Cosmic Engineers*, 228; "Desertion," 228; *Destiny Doll*, 228; *The Goblin Reservation*, 228; *Mastadonia*, 228; *They Walked Like Men*, 229; *Time Is the Simplest Thing*, 228; *The Visitors*, 228; *Way Station*, 228–229; *The Werewolf Principle*, 228
Smash Martians, **229–231**; *Campaign*'s "ad of the century," 229; Martians' antecedents, 230; role of the alien, 230; unintended consequences of ad, 231
Smith, Adam Brampton, 40
Smith, E. E. "Doc," 6, 80, 138, **232–234**; *Lensman* series, 233–234; *Skylark DuQuesne*, 232; *The Skylark of Space*, 232; *Skylark of Valeron*, 232; *Skylark* series, 232–234; *Skylark Three*, 232;
Smith, Eric D., 103
Smith, Joseph, 206
Smith, Toby, 33

*Solaris*, **234–236**; alien in, 234–235; concept of, 234; modern relevance of, 235; novel by Stanislaw Lem, 234

*Space Invaders*, **236–238**; conceit of, 236; and history of aliens in video games, 18–19, 20, 23; origins of, 236–237; success of, 237

Speyrer, David, 141. See also *Half-Life 2*

Spielberg, Steven: *Close Encounters of the Third Kind*, 15, 28, 36, 65, 84–86, 116; *E.T. the Extra-terrestrial*, 65, 85–86, 116–118, 267; *Hook*, 85; *Jaws*, 85, 87; *Jurassic Park* trilogy, 87; *Men in Black* (producer), 181; *War of the Worlds*, 288–289. See also *Close Encounters of the Third Kind*; *E.T. the Extra-terrestrial*

Stapledon, Olaf, 7, **238–240**; *The Flames*, 238; influence of, 240; *Last and First Men*, 238, 239; *Last Men in London*, 238; *A Modern Theory of Ethics*, 238; *Odd John*, 238, 240; *Philosophy and Living*, 238; *Sirius*, 238; *Star Maker*, 238, 239

*Star Trek*, **240–242**; Abrams's reboot of, 242; Borg in, 241–242; concept of, 240; *Deep Space Nine*, 242; *Enterprise*, 242; *Star Trek: The Next Generation*, 241; *Star Trek VI: The Undiscovered Country*, 241; *Voyager*, 242

*Star Wars*, **243–245**; and alien language, 244; history of, 243; planets and interplanetary travel, 243; representation of aliens in, 243–245; and sound design, 244–245

*StarCraft*, **245–247**; depiction of alien species, 245–246; real-time strategy game, 245; storyline, 245–247

Sterling, Bruce, **247–249**; *Crystal Express*, 248; *Involution Ocean*, 247; "Man Made Self," 247; *Mirrorshades: The Cyberpunk Anthology* (editor), 247; Schismatrix, 247–248; "Swarm," 248–249

*Steven Universe*, **249–251**; aliens in, 249; characters and storyline of, 249; first animated series created solely by a woman, 249; themes, 250–251

Straczynski, J. Michael, 37, 54. See also *Babylon 5*

Strugatsky, Arkady and Boris, **251–253**; *Hard to Be a God*, 252; Noon Universe, 251–252; *Roadside Picnic*, 252–253

Sturrock, Peter, 90

Sun Ra, **253–255**; early history of, 253; *The Futuristic Sounds of Sun Ra*, 254; *The Heliocentric Worlds of Sun Ra*, 254; *The Nubians of Plutonia*, 254; *Space Is the Place*, 254–255; *Sun Ra and His Solar Arkestra Visits Planet Earth*, 254; *Sunrise in Different Dimensions*, 254

Superman, **255–257**; first appearance of, 25; New 52 timeline Superman, 256–257; origin story, 255–256; pre-Flashpoint and post-Flashpoint Superman, 256

Swift, Jonathan, 4; "A Modest Proposal," 222

Tatchell, Terri, 103

*Teletubbies*, **258–260**; controversial nature of, 259–260; first television program for children as young as twelve months old, 258; intended purpose of, 258–259

*Tenchi Muyo!*, **260–262**; characters and storyline, 260–261; "fan-service" scenes in, 261; history of, 260; themes, 261

Tenn, William: "The Liberation of Earth," 10, 11

Tepper, Sheri S., **262–264**; *The Fresco*, 262; *Grass*, 263; Marjorie Morningstar trilogy, 263; *Moon Dance*, 262; *Raising the Stones*, 262, 263; *Sideshow*, 263–264; *Singer from the Sea*, 263; *Six Moon Dance*, 263

Tevis, Walter: *The Man Who Fell to Earth*, 61, 171

*They Live*, **264–266**; basis of, 264; character and plot, 264–265; depiction of aliens in, 265; legacy of, 266; themes, 265–266

*Thing, The*, **266–269**; and Finney's novel *The Body Snatchers*, 266; initial critical and box office reception, 267; recent increased stature of, 267–268

*Third Rock from the Sun*, **269–271**; characters, seasons, and storyline, 269–271; and gender, 270

Thompson, Craig: *Space Dumplins*, 14

Thompson, Tade, **271–273**; "Bicycle Girl," 271; "Flower Water," 271; *Making Wolf*, 271; *Rosewater*, 271–272

Tiptree Jr., James, 12, **273–275**; "And I Awoke and Found Me Here on the Cold Hill's Side," 273; and feminism, 273–274; *Her Smoke Rose Up Forever*,

273; "A Momentary Taste of Being," 274; "On the Last Afternoon," 274; "The Screwfly Solution," 273; "We Who Stole the Dream," 274; "With Delicate Maid Hands," 274; "The Women Men Don't See," 273
*ToeJam & Earl*, 21–22
*ToeJam and Earl: Panic on Funkotron*, 21–22
*ToeJam & Earl III: Mission to Earth*, 22
Torchwood, **275–277**; alien in, 275; characters and plot, 275; "Meal," 276–277; production history, 275; "Sleeper," 276
Transformers, **277–280**; animated film, 278; concept of, 277; history of, 277; live-action films, 278; themes, 279–280
*True History* (Lucian of Samosata), 3
*20,000 Leagues under the Sea* (Disney), 28
*2000 AD*, **280–281**; and alien child, 13; *Bad Company*, 281; concept of, 280; strips that include aliens, 281
Tyson, Neil deGrasse, 14

*Unknown* (magazine), 127
*Unreal*, 20

*V*, **282–284**; alien-invasion narrative, 282–284; concept of, 282; themes, 282–283; two-part miniseries, 282; *V: The Final Battle*, 282, 283; *V: The Series*, 282, 283
Van Vogt, A. E.
Victorianism, 5
Video games, aliens in: alien-invader games, 18–21; aliens as protagonists, 21; arcade games, 18–20; *Alien vs. Predator*, 20, 21, 23, 206; *Area 51*, 19–20; artistic influences on, 19, 21–23; *Asteroids*, 19; *Battlezone*, 19; *Computer Space*, 18, 19; cultural influences on, 18, 21–23; *Defender*, 19; *Destroy all Humans!*, 22–23; *Duke Nukem 3D*, 20, 23; economic influences on, 18, 19, 23; *E.T. The Extra-Terrestrial*, 21; *Galaga*, 19; *Galaxian*, 19; Golden Age of arcade games, 19–20; *Half-Life*, 20, 141; *Halo*, 20, 22, 23; home console and computer games, 20–23; *Mass Effect*, 20, 22; *Metroid*, 20, 21, 183–185; and narrative structure, 19–20; parodies of classic alien-invasion concept, 22; *Redshirt*, 22; retro revival, 23; *Saints Row IV*, 23; *Serious Sam: The First Encounter*, 23; *Space Invaders*, 18–19, 20, 23, 236–238; technological influences on, 18–21, 23; third-person shooter games, 100; *ToeJam & Earl*, 21–22; *ToeJam and Earl: Panic on Funkotron*, 21–22; *ToeJam & Earl III: Mission to Earth*, 22; winnable games, 19–20; *XCOM: Enemy Unknown*, 23, 308; *XCOM: UFO Defense*, 23; *Xevious*, 19. See also *Half-Life 2*; *Mass Effect* (trilogy); *Metroid*; *Space Invaders*
Vietnam War, 28, 84
Villeneuve, Denis: *Arrival*, 28, 48–50; *Enemy*, 49
Vinge, Vernor, **284–286**; *Children of the Sky*, 284–285; *A Fire Upon the Deep*, 284–285; Zones of Thought novels, 284–286
Von Däniken, Erich, 38, 84–85

*War of the Worlds*, 9, 17, 45, 105, 135, 142, 145, 236, 239, 272, **287–289**; adaptations of, 288; description of aliens, 287; and history of aliens in science fiction, 5–6; radio broadcasts, 288; themes, 287–288
*Warhammer 40,000: Dawn of War III*, **289–291**; gameplay, 290; tabletop war game, 289; video games, 289–290
Warren, Eugene, 101
Warrick, Patricia S., 101
Watts, Peter, **291–293**; *Blindsight*, 291–293
*Way of Thorn and Thunder: The Kynship Chronicles* by Daniel Heath Justice, **293–295**; and *Avatar*, 293; narrative of, 294; themes, 294–295, trope of otherness in, 294–295
Webber, C. E., 211
Weinbaum, Stanley G., 7, **295–297**; *The Dark Other*, 295; "A Martian Odyssey," 84, 295–296; *The New Adam*, 295; "Valley of Dreams," 295–296
*Weird Tales*, 7, 190–191
Wells, H. G., 80, 125; *The First Men in the Moon*, 232; "The Man of the Year Million," 125, 180; "The Star," 5; *The War of the Worlds*, 5–6, 9, 17, 45, 105, 135, 142, 145, 236, 239, 272, 287–289. See also *War of the Worlds, The*

Wess'Har Series by Karen Traviss, **297–299**; *Ally*, 297, 298; *City of Pearl*, 297; *Crossing the Line*, 297; *Judge*, 297; *Matriarch*, 297, 298; *The World Before*, 297, 298

Whedon, Joss, 119, 121. See also *Firefly/Serenity*

White, Armond, 104

White, James, **299–301**; *All Judgement Fled*, 300; and alien psychologies, 300; *Code Blue Emergency*, 300; *Double Contact*, 300; *Federation World*, 301; *The Genocidal Healer*, 300; *Major Operation*, 300; *Mind Changer*, 300; Sector General series, 299–300; stories as puzzles or problems, 299; *The Watch Below*, 301

Whitlatch, Terryl, **301–303**; creature concept designs, 301–302; influence and success of 302–303; and *Star Wars* franchise, 302

"Who Goes There?" **303–305**; awards for, 305; concept and plot, 303–304; film versions, 303, 304–305; pseudonym used by, 303, 304

Wilkins, Chris, 229–230

Wilkins, John, 4

Willis, Jeanne, 109. *See also* Dr. Xargle

Wilson, Donald, 211

Wilson, Robert Charles, **305–307**; *Axis*, 305; *Bios*, 306–307; *Blind Lake*, 306; *Darwinia*, 305–306; *The Harvest*, 306; Hypotheticals sequence, 305; *Spin*, 305; *Vortex*, 305

Wise, Robert: *The Day the Earth Stood Still*, 28, 66, 171

Wood, Robin, 85–86

Wyndham, John: *Chocky*, 16; *The Kraken Wakes*, 207; *The Midwich Cuckoos*, 16

*X-COM, XCOM*, **308–310**; gameplay, 308; history of, 308; *XCOM: Enemy Unknown*, 23, 308; *XCOM: UFO Defense*, 23

*Xevious*, 19

*X-Files, The*, **310–312**; alien threat in, 311–312; characters and storyline, 310–311; production history, 310; spin-off series, 310; themes, 312

Yaccarino, Dan: *Blast Off Boy and Blorp* series, 13–14